# THE ROUND TABLE MOVEMENT AND IMPERIAL UNION

JOHN E. KENDLE

# The Round Table Movement and Imperial Union

UNIVERSITY OF TORONTO PRESS
TORONTO AND BUFFALO

© University of Toronto Press 1975
Toronto and Buffalo
Printed in Canada

**Library of Congress Cataloging in Publication Data**

Kendle, John Edward.
  The Round Table movement and imperial union.

  Bibliography: p.
  Includes index.
  1. Imperial federation. 2. Africa, South — Politics and
government — 1836-1909. 3. Great Britain — Colonies —
Administration. 4. Milner, Alfred Milner, 1st Viscount,
1854-1925. I. Title.
  JN276.K456    325'.31'06341    73-81758
  ISBN 0-8020-5292-4

ILLUSTRATION CREDITS

p. 5    From Vladimir Halperin, *Lord Milner and the Empire*
        (London, Hamlyn Group 1952), frontispiece
p. 19   From J.E. Wrench, *Geoffrey Dawson and Our Times*
        (London, Hutchison Publishing Group, 1955)
p. 49   From L.S. Amery, *My Political Life*, II: *War and Peace 1914-1929*
        (London, Hutchison Publishing Group), opposite p. 368
p. 76   From *The Round Table*, No. 182, March 1956, opposite p. 103
p. 118  From *Punch*, 17 July 1912, p. 43
p. 134  From *Punch*, 26 October 1910, p. 291
p. 148  From *Punch*, 13 May 1914, p. 363
p. 246  From *Punch*, 25 June 1919, p. 495
p. 280  From Lord Altrincham, *Kenya's Opportunity: Memoirs, Hopes and Ideas*
        (London, Faber and Faber, 1955), opposite p. 32

For Judy

# Contents

Preface  ix
Introduction  xiii

1
Milner and the kindergarten  3
2
The kindergarten and South African union  22
3
The movement is formed  46
4
The prophet's first mission  73
5
Imperial defence and foreign policy  107
6
Home Rule all round  130
7
On the eve of war  156
8
'The Problem of the Commonwealth'  181
9
Study or propaganda  206
10
India  224

11
The peace and after 248
12
The twilight years 274

Conclusion 301
Bibliography 307
Index 319

ILLUSTRATIONS

Lord Milner 5
The Milner kindergarten 19
Leo Amery 49
Lionel Curtis 76
The Knight of the Maple-Leaf 118
The New John Bull 134
The Swashbucklers 148
A Redress Rehearsal 246
Sir Edward Grigg 280

# Preface

The Round Table movement was an organization devoted to the study of imperial problems and to the promotion of imperial unity. Founded in 1909 by a group of young men who had served under Milner in South Africa, it played an important role in British and imperial affairs for well over a decade. The ideas of the Round Table members and many of their individual efforts have been known to students of British and empire-commonwealth history for many years but so far only an occasional chapter, article, or passing paragraph has been written about the movement. Even Dr Walter Nimocks's perceptive monograph, *Milner's Young Men: The 'Kindergarten' in Edwardian Imperial Affairs,* is concerned more with its origins than with its activities.[1] This book is an attempt to provide a long-needed study of the Round Table movement, particularly of the London group. Fortunately, the sources are fairly extensive and the discovery or release of additional material will probably not alter the story in any fundamental way. It should be emphasized that the book is essentially a study of the movement's interest in imperial union and not of the activities of individual members. Consequently I have not examined in depth such topics as Philip Kerr's years as Lloyd George's secretary, Lionel Curtis's involvement with Ireland, or the part played by many of the London members in the foreign policy discussions of the 1930s. Furthermore, I have not attempted a rounded study of

---

1 Dr Nimocks's book is a revision of his Vanderbilt PHD thesis (1965): 'Lord Milner's Kindergarten" and the Origins of the Round Table Movement.' Readers should note that a full citation of the author-short title footnote entries can be found in the Bibliography.

each issue that attracted the movement's attention. Detailed and balanced studies of such subjects as imperial defence, the imperial war cabinets, and the peace conference are already available. I have approached such problems from the vantage point of the movement and have merely attempted to evaluate the degree, the nature, and the success of the Round Table's involvement and to assess the effect of each experience on the movement itself.

I first became interested in this subject in 1960-1 when the late A.L. Burt was a visiting professor at the University of Manitoba in Winnipeg. Professor Burt had been a member of the Edmonton group during World War I and he regretted that the Round Table movement and its ideas had not attracted more attention from historians. He believed a study of the organization would be a salutary exercise for a young Manitoba student. Despite this baptism it was some years before I could devote much time to a study of the Round Table but whenever possible I gathered material in Great Britain and Canada. The receipt of a Canada Council grant enabled me to visit Australia and New Zealand in 1967-8. Xerox and microfilm removed the need for a trip to South Africa.

In writing a book of this nature one becomes indebted to people in many countries. With special thanks to Muriel Ellis, formerly of the Manuscript Division of the Public Archives of Canada, and to Ian Wilson of Queen's University Archives, I am grateful to the librarians and staff of New College, and the Bodleian Library, Oxford; the Scottish Record Office, Edinburgh; the British Museum, the Commonwealth Relations Office, the Round Table Offices, the Royal Commonwealth Society, and the Institute of Commonwealth Studies, all in London; the Public Archives of Canada, Ottawa; Queen's University Archives, Kingston; the University of Toronto Library; the University of Manitoba Library, St John's College Library, the Manitoba Provincial Library, all in Winnipeg; the National Archives of Australia, the National Library of Australia, the Australian National University Library, all in Canberra; the University of Melbourne Archives, Melbourne; the Mitchell Library, Sydney; the Alexander Turnbull Library and the General Assembly Library, Wellington; the University of Auckland Library; and the University of Cape Town Library.

My thanks also to the late Sir Keith Steel-Maitland of Stirling, Sir John Ilott of Wellington, Dr Jean Laby of Melbourne, and Professor George Glazebrook of Toronto, who allowed me to look at material in their possession. Dermot Morrah, a former editor of *The Round Table*; the late John A. Stevenson, an early Canadian contributor to the journal; Sir Keith Hancock, Sir Leslie Melville, and the late Sir Kenneth Bailey, members in Australia in the twenties and thirties. Professor George Glazebrook, long

Many anomalies existed in anglo-dominion affairs before World War I. By 1909, when the movement was formed, the lack of dominion representatives on any body determining foreign policy, the ineffectiveness of the imperial conference system, the methods of conducting Colonial Office business, and the insignificant role of the dominion representatives in Great Britain seemed no longer suited to the growing importance and self-consciousness of the dominions. Changes obviously needed to be made. One of the movement's major goals in its early years was to help bring about these changes in imperial organization. It advocated the creation of a secretariat free from Colonial Office dictation, the separation of dominion from crown colony affairs, and the appointment of a secretary of state for imperial affairs. It suggested that the high commissioners and the agents-general be given greater political responsibilities with perhaps the right to attend important Foreign Office or Committee of Imperial Defence meetings. A Dominions House, or at the very least a Dominions Department, was also recommended; and the dominions themselves were advised to appoint cabinet ministers responsible for imperial affairs. The movement succeeded in having all these ideas heard at the 1911 Conference, but without result. This failure ended its efforts to alter the imperial structure from within. Thereafter the members concentrated on improving the dominions' position in matters of defence and foreign policy and in studying the Curtis memoranda on imperial problems. They hoped time and the proper education of the public would allow them to put their case in more favourable circumstances. By the 1930s most of the changes they had suggested in 1910-11 had been implemented.

The story of the Round Table movement begins with the kindergarten's arrival in the Transvaal to serve under Milner. There the young men from Oxford who later founded the Round Table organisation learned their first imperial lessons and committed themselves to the imperial mission.

this argument in Australia and New Zealand. Moreover, it was by no means clear how the empire or anglo-dominion relations would evolve. There were some indications that the dominions wanted a considerable measure of independence but other signs that they desired to maintain a close relationship with Great Britain. Very few thought that the relationship would be as loose as it became in the 1920s and 1930s and many thought, even hoped, that it would be tighter and more closely-knit.

The Round Table movement was most active in the years 1909-1920. During that time it made two significant contributions to the evolution of the empire-commonwealth. Perhaps the major one was its contention that India should be given self-government. One of the primary motivating factors of all advocates of imperial union was a wish to maintain the unity of the race. For many it was simply a desire to offset the political, military, and commercial advances of the foreign powers who were challenging British supremacy in all fields. But for others it was based on a belief in the political wisdom of the British and in their system of government. Many believed the British had a duty and a moral responsibility to educate 'the backward peoples' of the world to an understanding of the British system. This could only be done effectively if the British race remained united. By preaching the arts of self-government a united commonwealth would be able to make a major contribution, perhaps the most significant ever made by one state or empire, to the stability of the world and the advance of its 'subject races.' The members of the Round Table movement believed strongly in this aspect of the imperial mission, but they went even further. Since all men were capable of governing themselves provided they were given time to learn the necessary skills, they came to advocate self-government for India. Even before the outbreak of the first war Lionel Curtis and Philip Kerr had given voice to this revolutionary idea. It was not always so. They arrived in South Africa believing like many others of their time that 'the backward people' were inherently inferior intellectually, incapable of emerging from the most elementary of tribal systems. Their years in South Africa, intensive discussions with men of Indian experience, and concentrated study of the British parliamentary system changed their minds. They came to believe in the 'principle of the commonwealth,' the extension of self-government to all men capable of exercising it. They advocated its transfer to India and envisaged its eventual grant to a number of black dominions. Their continued affirmation of this principle set them apart from the majority of their contemporaries.

The second important contribution of the movement was the publicity and stimulus it gave to a critical examination of anglo-dominion relations.

associated with the Canadian branch, granted valuable interviews. Harold Hodson, a former editor of *The Round Table,* and Sir Alfred Stirling, former Australian ambassador to Italy, kindly wrote lengthy letters recounting their association with the movement. My thanks also to Professors Gerald Graham, W.L. Morton, Leslie Upton, Donald Denoon, and DeWitt Ellinwood who either discussed the movement with me or rendered advice and support at crucial moments. Professor John La Nauze of the Australian National University and Professor Keith Sinclair of the University of Auckland made me welcome during my sojourn in their departments. A special thanks to Rosemary Shipton for her editorial advice and to May Richardson of the Australian National University and Brenda Hammond of London, England, for typing my drafts. Finally, I am grateful to the Canada Council for the grant which allowed me to extend my research and to my wife who came to like the life of an itinerant.

This book is now published with the help of grants from the Social Science Research Council of Canada, using funds provided by the Canada Council, and from the Andrew W. Mellon Foundation to the University of Toronto Press.

JK
Winnipeg
7 March 1974

# Introduction

The Round Table movement was founded by a group of young men who believed in the inherent superiority of British civilization and in the Englishman's duty to carry the fruits of that civilization to humanity. They believed this duty could best be discharged if the British commonwealth were politically united in one world state. They were not abashed by their fervent pananglo-saxonism; in fact they gave it little thought. Their beliefs were commonly held and generally accepted in the England of their day, and they rarely had need to question them. For them the British race was a definable entity with an important mission to perform; the only questions worth considering were how and when this could best be done.

Earlier efforts to achieve an imperial union had failed to excite much enthusiasm and support. When the debate over the relationship of Great Britain to her overseas possessions had begun in earnest in the late nineteenth century many of those concerned specifically with the self-governing colonies had favoured some form of union, and in 1884 the Imperial Federation League had been formed to channel their energies and stimulate activity. A number had believed their goal could be achieved by the establishment of a *kriegsverein* for defensive purposes while others, such as Joseph Chamberlain, had faith in a system of imperial preference. Few of these men seem to have contemplated a looser relationship, and they appear to have had little knowledge or understanding of the sense of pride and accomplishment which pervaded the self-governing colonies. Not surprisingly all the early efforts to achieve closer union met with little success. The Imperial Federation League collapsed in 1893 and its off-shoots the Imperial Federation (Defence) Committee and the British Empire League never amounted to much. Joseph Chamberlain's tariff reform campaign split the Unionist party and was ultimately given a lukewarm reception both at home and abroad. As for defence, Australia and Canada opted for their own navies in 1909, a decision symbolic of the suspicion awaiting any scheme of union. Despite this apparently hostile atmosphere the founders of the Round Table movement were convinced that imperial union was still attainable and they launched a highly sophisticated campaign to bring it about. What made them so optimistic was Great Britain's attitude toward the dominions in the field of foreign affairs.

Before 1914 the settlement colonies were no more than dependencies in this crucial area of government policy. Despite representation on the Committee of Imperial Defence and visits to London by their premiers, the dominions had no influence on foreign policy and defence decisions or upon the ultimate issue of peace or war. And as long as they refused to contribute substantially to the British coffers the British government was unlikely to alter the *status quo*. The movement contended that this anomalous situation could only be resolved by imperial union – by the establishment of an imperial parliament responsible for defence and foreign affairs in which all the dominions and Great Britain would be represented and to which they would all contribute a tax. By agreeing to union the dominions would not be endangering their self-government but would be underlining their right to be regarded as equals in matters of mutual concern.

The movement made its appeal when there was considerable uncertainty in the dominions about the imperial relationship. A great deal has been written about colonial and dominion nationalism and its assertiveness before 1914, much of it exaggerated. Colonial feeling was not readily definable as either nationalism or imperialism. Admittedly there was a greater self-consciousness after the Boer War but this often dove-tailed into a wider commitment, and many of those who thought at all about such matters still retained a strong strain of loyalty to the empire, to Great Britain, to 'home,' to the race.[1] The Round Table movement appealed to this strain in dominion feelings. It was not difficult to convince a number of Canadians, Australians, and New Zealanders that the fate of the world might well lie with a unified empire; that it alone could provide the stabilising element in a world of increasing tension, turmoil, and international friction. Geopolitical considerations, an acute sense of isolation, and a vulnerable shoreline reinforced

1 For recent studies and discussion of these issues see Penny, 'Australia's Reaction to the Boer War' and 'The Australian Debate on the Boer War'; Berger, *The Sense of Power*; Page, 'Carl Berger' and 'The Canadian Response'; Cole, 'Canada's Nationalistic Imperialists,' 'The crimson thread of kinship,' and 'The Problem of "Nationalism" and "Imperialism."'

THE ROUND TABLE MOVEMENT AND IMPERIAL UNION

# 1
# Milner and the kindergarten

The Transvaal had been a worry to British governments for some decades. Settled in the 1830s by trekking Dutch farmers (known either as Boers or Afrikaners), who had been antagonized by British rule, the Transvaal had been granted its independence in the 1850s. Independence had lasted until 1877 when efforts to unify the four South African colonies of Natal, Cape Colony, the Orange Free State, and the Transvaal had resulted in the annexation of the republic. This unfortunate action led to an uprising by the Afrikaners and to the defeat of the British at Majuba Hill in 1881. Self-government had been restored to the republic in 1884 subject to the suzereignty of Great Britain over the Transvaal's foreign affairs, but the whole episode had engendered great bitterness and the Boers never forgave the British their rash action.

In the mid-eighties the Transvaal was a poor backward pastoral state rapidly running out of good land and losing many of its young men to other centres, but with the discovery of gold the whole balance of power in South Africa was quickly altered. After 1886 immigrants poured into the Transvaal. Overnight Johannesburg became a boom city and British and colonial capitalists moved in. By the mid 1890s there were some 44,000 foreigners ('uitlanders') in the republic, most of them miners and labourers of British origin. This activity on the Rand coincided with the emergence of German interest in overseas colonies. The German annexation of South-West Africa in 1884 was an ominous development, and in following years the British feared that the Transvaal might link up with the Germans and block the British missionary route to the north as well as endanger the strategic function of the Cape. Paul Kruger, the president of the Transvaal, was quick to seize the advantage provided by the international rivalry and the scramble for gold. He saw a chance to challenge British paramountcy and to assert Transvaal independence.

The tense relations between Great Britain and the Transvaal were exacerbated by the Afrikaner attitude to the 'uitlanders.' Although they paid very high taxes and often had to do military service, the 'uitlanders' were granted no political rights and had to establish fourteen years residence before qualifying for citizenship. Kruger's reasons were entirely logical. The 'uitlanders' made up the majority of European males. If they were granted a vote Kruger feared that the Afrikaners would have their authority in the Volksraad challenged and would lose their chance of gaining independence. Matters came to a head in 1895 when Cecil Rhodes, mining magnate, founder of Rhodesia and premier of the Cape, agreed to support a rising of 'uitlanders' in Johannesburg. The plan called for Dr Starr Jameson, the administrator of the British South Africa Company in Rhodesia, to lead a force into the Transvaal to support the local uprising. Although the Johannesburg *coup* was called off at the last moment, Jameson rode into the Transvaal at the head of a small force on 29 December 1895. Four days later he surrendered to Afrikaner troops. After the raid the atmosphere became electric, and Kruger began to prepare for a full-scale conflict with the British.

It was in this tense situation, in February 1897, that Joseph Chamberlain, the British colonial secretary, appointed Sir Alfred Milner governor of Cape Colony and high commissioner of South Africa. It was not an obvious choice. Milner's reputation had been built on his brilliance as a financial expert in Egypt and his highly proficient chairmanship of the Board of Inland Revenue. He had never served in the self-governing colonies, and he had no experience of South Africa and its problems or the responsibilities of a colonial governorship. Furthermore, he had a natural disinclination for politicians and the political art of compromise. A man who favoured clean-cut decisions, Milner referred scathingly to political pragmatism as 'drift.' He had an orderly mind and once he had determined his objective he preferred to move, not necessarily hastily, but nevertheless inexorably toward it.[1] Milner hardly seemed the sort of man required as high commissioner in a South Africa still seething fifteen months after the Jameson Raid. But he had other qualities of which Chamberlain was fully aware. Like Chamberlain, he was dedicated to the maintenance and, if possible, the consolidation of the empire. For him the empire was a substitute religion; he had an unqualified faith in its power for good and its civilizing mission and, like Chamberlain, he believed there was a danger to the empire inherent in the South African

1 For an incisive analysis of Milner's ideas and character see Stokes, 'Milnerism.'

Lord Milner in 1914

situation. If the Transvaal were permitted to go its own way the possibility of a united South Africa and a united empire would rapidly recede. His task was to keep the Transvaal within the empire by negotiation and compromise if possible, and by other means if necessary.

Milner served in South Africa for eight years until his retirement in May 1905. After negotiations failed and war broke out in October 1899 he devoted his energies to preparing for the restoration of a civil administration in the Boer republics. His powers were strengthened in 1900 when in addition to his responsibilities as high commissioner he was made governor of the Orange River Colony and the Transvaal.[2] With a vast reconstruction programme in mind he began to recruit young men to his staff. Some of them worked more closely with him than others and were dubbed Milner's 'kindergarten.' In time they became the nucleus of the Round Table movement.

Milner was born in Germany in 1854 of English parents and spent many of his first fifteen years in that country. On the death of his mother he returned to England in 1869 where he soon gained great academic distinction, initially at King's College, London, and then at Jowett's Balliol. Oxford made an enormous impression on him and it was there that he first became interested in the British empire. The early 1870s was a time of incessant debate over Britain's relationship to the rest of the world and to her colonies, and a strong movement for imperial union was developing. In 1873, during his first year as an undergraduate, Milner heard a speech at the Oxford Union by a Canadian, George Parkin,[3] on the subject of imperial federation and the imperial mission. Fascinated, he arranged a meeting with Parkin and from that day his commitment to the empire and to imperial union never wavered.[4]

After leaving Oxford Milner tried law but soon deserted to journalism and the *Pall Mall Gazette* edited by John Morley,[5] a Liberal Little Eng-

---

2 He gave up the governorship of the Cape in 1901. The Orange Free State Republic was annexed by Britain in May 1900 as the Orange River Colony. The Orange River Colony entered the Union of South Africa in 1910 as the Orange Free State province.

3 George Robert Parkin (1846-1922); author and lecturer on imperial federation; principal of Upper Canada College 1895-1902; organising representative of Rhodes Trust Scholarship Trust 1902-22; KCMG 1920

4 Years later, on the eve of taking up his appointment in South Africa, Milner wrote to Parkin, now a close friend: 'My life has been greatly influenced by your ideas and in my new post I shall feel more than ever the need of your enthusiasm and broad hopeful view of the Imperial future ...' Milner to Parkin, 28 April 1897, Headlam, *The Milner Papers*, I, 42

5 John Morley, 1st Viscount Morley of Blackburn (1838-1923); editor *Fortnightly Review* 1867-82; editor *Pall Mall Gazette* 1880-3; MP (L) 1883-95, 1896-1908; chief secretary for Ireland 1886 and 1892-5; secretary of state for India 1905-10; lord president of the Council 1910-14

lander. On Morley's retirement in 1883, W.T. Stead,[6] an ardent imperialist, assumed the editor's chair, and Milner became his assistant for a few months. Stead rapidly changed the *Gazette* from a rather staid publication into a thrusting example of the new journalism, and with Milner's help gave considerable space to the empire and liberal imperialism. It is doubtful if Milner's experience at the *Gazette* deepened his commitment to the empire, certainly it did not widen his experience of it. This did not come until 1889 when on the advice of George Goschen,[7] the chancellor of the Exchequer, whom he had once served as a private secretary, he was appointed director-general of accounts in Egypt. He quickly demonstrated his abilities and was promoted to under-secretary for finance in 1890. Milner remained in Egypt for three years. While there he fell partly under Cromer's spell and developed a theory of empire which emphasised Britain's civilizing mission. In his book *England in Egypt* published in 1892 Milner argued that only the British race and British civilization could properly guide dependencies such as Egypt toward civilized independence. Only by continuing her guardianship and acting upon 'the simplest ideas of honesty, humanity and justice' would England ensure the progress and welfare of the Egyptian people.[8] Despite its high-flown phrases it was a book – and a theory of empire – that emphasised sound administration rather than political evolution.

On his return from Egypt in 1892 Milner was selected by Goschen as chairman of the Board of Inland Revenue. During the next five years he had no direct connection with the empire or imperial affairs, and when appointed high commissioner of South Africa in 1897 was strangely without experience for so important and arduous a post. He was not, however, without conviction about his duty and his purposes in South Africa.

Late in life Lord Milner wrote down his 'Credo,' what he considered to be the 'Key to my position.' Although written in the evening of his public career, it is a valid statement of Milner's position in the 1890s. His ideas concerning the state and the empire changed very little after his Oxford days. He was, he claimed,

a Nationalist and not a cosmopolitan ... A Nationalist is not a man who necessarily thinks his nation better than others, or is unwilling to learn from others. He does

6 William Thomas Stead (1849-1912); editor *Northern Echo* 1871-80; assistant editor *Pall Mall Gazette* 1880-3; editor 1883-9; founded *Review of Reviews* 1890; *American Review of Reviews* 1891; *Australasian Review of Reviews* 1894
7 George Joachim Goschen, 1st Viscount created 1900 (1831-1907); MP (L) 1863-85; (U) 1887-1900; first lord of the Admiralty 1871-4; a founder of the Unionist party 1886; chancellor of the Exchequer 1887-92; first lord of the Admiralty 1895-1900
8 See Milner, *England in Egypt*, 331 and 354.

think his duty is to his nation, and its development. He believes that this is the law of human progress, that the competition between nations, each seeking its maximum development, is the Divine Order of the world, the law of Life and Progress.

I am a British (indeed primarily an English) Nationalist. If I am also an Imperialist, it is because the destiny of the English race ... has been to strike fresh roots in distant parts ... My patriotism knows no geographical but only racial limits. I am an Imperialist and not a Little Englander, because I am a British Race Patriot ... It is not the soil of England, dear as it is to me, which is essential to arouse my patriotism, but the speech, the tradition, the spiritual heritage, the principles, the aspirations of the British race ...

The wider patriotism is no mere exalted sentiment. It is a practical necessity ... England, nay more, Great Britain, nay more, the United Kingdom is no longer a power in the world which it once was ... But the British Dominions as a whole are not only self supporting. They are more nearly self-sufficient than any other political entity ... if they can be kept an entity ...

This brings us to our first great principle – follow the race. The British State must follow the race, must comprehend it wherever it settles in appreciable numbers as an independent community. If the swarms constantly being thrown off by the parent hive are lost to the State, the State is irreparably weakened. We cannot afford to part with so much of our best blood. We have already parted with much of it, to form the millions of another separate but fortunately friendly state. We cannot suffer a repetition of the process.[9]

Milner left for South Africa convinced that he would have to prevent at all cost a further disruption of empire. As he explained to Parkin, '... S.A. is just now the weakest link in the Imperial chain, and I am conscious of the tremendous responsibility which rests upon the man who is called upon to try and preserve it from snapping. Any elation I might otherwise have felt at being elected for so big a post is quite swallowed up in my solemn sense of the great national interests at stake.'[10] Milner at no time really despaired of the maintenance of British supremacy in South Africa, but he realized the difficulties involved. Once it became apparent to him that the Boers were not prepared to accept Great Britain's arguments on the status of the 'uitlanders,' he decided that there was no alternative to war and the establishment of British supremacy by force. He believed the war would be brief and that he could then bolster the economy, attract immigrants, and make South Africa, particularly the Transvaal, truly British. Not to act decisively might mean the dissolution of the empire into its separate parts.

9 *The Times*, 27 July 1925. See also Hancock, 'Boers and Britons.'
10 Milner to Parkin, 28 April 1897, Headlam, *The Milner Papers*, I, 42

Throughout his eight years in South Africa Milner returned repeatedly to the theme of imperial union and the place of a British South Africa within that union. He realized that Britain's relative economic and military position in the world was declining and recognized the need for imperial unity if the civilizing mission of the British race was to be backed by adequate power. The ideal he had in mind was a united South Africa as one of a group of sister nations spread throughout the world, each independent in its own concerns, but allied for a common purpose.[11] He often spoke of the establishment of an imperial council and hoped that a British Transvaal would be the first step toward a British South Africa which in turn would be the first step in the consolidation of the British empire.[12] Until his experiences in the first world war forced him to reappraise his position, he continued to believe in the need for an organic union in the hope that all the self-governing colonies could play their part in deciding the great questions of defence and foreign policy

By this stage in his career Milner also held strong views on two other important matters – the party system and the native question. He had been severely critical of the party system, democracy, and parliamentary government for some years. He had nothing but distaste for party politics and the shifts and compromises to which politicians were driven, and he was convinced that colonial and imperial policies should not be a party subject. His distrust of democracy was shared by many of his contemporaries among the ruling elite, but not his loathing for the British constitution. They would have viewed with some trepidation the appearance on the national stage of Milner's desired 'great *Charlatan* – political scallywag, buffoon, liar, stump orator ... who is nevertheless a *statesman*.'[13]

As for the native question, Milner's ideas were a combination of social darwinism and the christian ethic. He believed that the white man had to rule in South Africa because he was 'elevated by many, many steps above the black man'; steps which it would take the latter centuries to climb, and which the vast bulk of the black population might never be able to climb at all. But white rule could only be justified if the white man used his superior civilization for the benefit of the subject race. Milner thought that much more should be done for the education of the natives than had yet been attempted in South Africa. He did not mean that they should be educated like Europeans. Their 'different' requirements and capacities made that impossible,

11 Speech in Durban, 21 Oct. 1901, in Milner, *The Nation and the Empire*, 47-8
12 Speeches in Johannesburg, 8 Jan. 1902 and 28 May 1904, ibid., 55 and 67. Also Milner to Lord Brassey, 25 Feb. 1901, Headlam, *The Milner Papers*, II, 159-60
13 See Milner to Lady Edward Cecil, 25 March, 24 April, and 16 May 1903, Headlam, *The Milner Papers*, II, 446-8.

but they should be trained to develop their natural aptitudes for their own good and that of the community. The British government had a duty to raise the black man in the scale of civilization; and when individual black men did progress far enough they should be treated appropriately. He adopted Rhodes's maxim in these matters: 'equal rights for every civilized man.' This was a deceptive phrase. It appeared to be high-minded and progressive, but in reality it was based on a deep-seated belief in white supremacy. The white man would always decide who was or was not civilized.[14]

Milner's ideas about imperial union, the political system, and the British civilizing mission, with all their inherent idealism, prejudices, and contradictions, were not unusual for the time but his fervour and passion were quite distinct. The kindergarten were to drink deeply at Milner's ideological well, and for the rest of their lives their basic ideas and ideals owed much to Milner's beliefs and convictions.

Once the war had begun Milner saw his task as that of the creator of a unified South Africa with a British majority. He also realized that any changes he wished to bring about would have to be done quickly before representative government, or even self-government, were established in the Boer republics.[15] After he was appointed governor of the Transvaal and the Orange River Colony Milner concentrated his efforts on restoring stability and introducing efficient administration to the two northern colonies. To im-

14 For Milner's views on this issue see Milner to Asquith, 18 Nov. 1897, Headlam, I, 177-80; Milner to Chamberlain, 6 Dec. 1901, ibid., II, 307-13; speech in Johannesburg, 18 May 1903, ibid., 466-70; and Milner to H. Ramsey Collins, 7 Sept. 1904, ibid., 511-12; also speech in Cape Town, 28 June 1900, Milner, *The Nation and the Empire*, 22-6.
15 The following excerpt from a letter to Sir Percy Fitzpatrick sums up Milner's attitude a few weeks after the outbreak of war: 'One thing is quite evident. The *ultimate* end is a self-governing white Community, supported by *well-treated* and justly governed black labour from Cape Town to Zambesi. There must be one flag, the Union Jack, but under it equality of races and languages. Given equality all round, English must prevail, though I do not think, and do not wish, that Dutch should altogether die out. I think, though all South Africa should be one Dominion with a common government dealing with Customs, Railways, and Defence, perhaps also with Native Policy, a considerable amount of freedom should be left to the several States. But though this is the ultimate end, it would be madness to attempt it at once. There must be an interval, to allow the British population of the Transvaal to return and increase, and the mess to be cleared up, before we can apply the principle of self-government to the Transvaal ... How long the period of unrepresentative government may last, I cannot say. I, for one, would be for shortening it as much as possible, but not before a loyal majority is assured.' Milner to Sir Percy Fitzpatrick, 28 Nov. 1899, very confidential, Headlam, *The Milner Papers*, II, 35-6; see also Milner to Major Hanbury Williams, 27 Dec. 1900, confidential, ibid., 242-4.

plement his vast reconstruction programme he needed a large number of administrators at all levels, and the majority of these were eventually drawn from Cape Colony, though many also came from Great Britain. His problem was the dearth of suitable men with the right sort of experience who were sufficiently flexible in approach and unafraid of hard work. English civil servants tended to be too set in their ways, and many men who might have been suitable found it more lucrative to work for the mining companies. Milner demanded ability, education, energy, an open mind, initiative, and willingness to work for a small salary. Although youth was not a necessity, neither was it an obstacle. He believed in youth and trusted it, consequently many young men rose rapidly to positions of some authority under him.[16]

Among these young men were the few who were to become the kindergarten. They were not a large number but they were quickly singled out by critics of Milner's administration and dubbed the 'kindergarten,' or the 'finest flower of Varsity scholarship.'[17] The term came to have wider uses of abuse, but it really meant those young men who worked and lived in close contact with Milner and who were all graduates of Oxford, mainly of New College. Many young men of that day were anxious to work in South Africa under Milner, for he seemed to represent all that was most attractive in the imperial mission. Rather aloof and austere to many, he often inspired those close to him, particularly the young. Robert Brand later recalled that Milner could 'inspire all those who worked with him with admiration and affection' and that he treated young men as if their assistance was needed and appreciated,[18] while Leo Amery wrote of the 'kindness and understanding which he showed to all young men.'[19]

The kindergarten was not recruited in a planned or formal way. In fact, recruitment was extremely haphazard, relying for the most part on personal friendships, contacts in the Colonial Office, and Oxford associations. It was only when the various individuals were drawn together in South Africa to work under Milner that a group cohesiveness and close friendships developed.[20] The first to arrive was J.F. (Peter) Perry, a recent graduate of New

16  See Denoon, *A Grand Illusion*, 43-58.
17  The term 'Kindergarten' originated in a sarcastic remark made by Sir William Marriot. For Smuts's scathing comments see Hancock and Van Der Poel, *Smuts Papers*, II, 151.
18  *The Listener*, 15 Oct. 1953, 631
19  Amery, *My Political Life*, I, 100
20  In preparing the following section on the recruitment of the Kindergarten I am heavily indebted to Nimocks, *Milner's Young Men*, 17-44. Two other sources of great value were Denoon, *A Grand Illusion*, and Ellinwood, 'Lord Milner's "Kindergarten."' Also Curtis, *With Milner in South Africa; The Round Table, Who's Who*, and Amery, '*The Times' History of the War in South Africa*

College, a fellow of All Souls, and for some years a junior official in the Colonial Office. In August 1900 he became the imperial secretary to the high commisioner with the specific responsibilities of supervising the administration of the native reserves of Basutoland, Swaziland, and Bechuanaland, and of acting as the liaison between the imperial government and Southern Rhodesia. Two months later Lionel Curtis arrived with a letter of introduction from Lord Welby, vice-chairman of the London County Council, under whom he had served briefly after leaving New College. Earlier in the war he had spent some months in South Africa as a bicycle messenger in the City Imperial Volunteers, but had returned to England in the first months of 1900. Curtis was appointed to Milner's personal staff as one of many private secretaries, among whom was Basil Williams, the historian, who eventually became an associate of the kindergarten. Shortly after Curtis's arrival, Milner decided to move his headquarters north to Johannesburg from where he could better supervise the reconstruction programme. In the spring of 1901 he moved into 'Sunnyside,' a splendid house with an extensive park located on the north side of the city, and for the remainder of his stay in South Africa 'Sunnyside' was the administrative centre of the British government. Perry and Curtis took a small house three miles from 'Sunnyside,' the first of many such dwellings that the members of the kindergarten and the Round Table were to share in common.[21] Just as the move north was made Patrick Duncan arrived (mid-March 1901). A Balliol man, he had joined the staff of the Board of Inland Revenue in 1894 where he had served as Milner's private secretary. Milner offered him the post of colonial treasurer in the newly formed Crown Colony government of the Transvaal. Although thirty-one when he arrived and thus a few years older than the others, Duncan formed a close friendship with Perry and Curtis.

In May Milner took a brief home leave, and while in England offered Leo Amery a post as his personal secretary. Amery, also a Balliol man, was then engaged in writing *The Times History of the War* and had to refuse the offer, but he suggested John Buchan as a substitute. Milner accepted and Buchan reached South Africa in late 1901. Buchan was never considered to be a member of the kindergarten, although he remained friendly with its members and their interests after he left South Africa in 1903.[22] Two others also arrived in late 1901: Hugh Wyndham, a graduate of New College, was a

---

21 For Curtis's South African experiences to 1902 see Curtis, *With Milner in South Africa*.
22 Amery, *My Political Life*, I, 150ff. Also Smith, *John Buchan* and Buchan, *Memory Hold-the-Door*

young cousin of Milner's close friend George Wyndham, the chief secretary for Ireland 1900-5; Geoffrey Robinson had been the Colonial Office clerk responsible for sorting the numerous applications for South African administrative service. A longtime friend of Perry, Robinson had been most anxious to serve with Milner; and it was probably due to Perry's influence that Robinson was appointed as the high commissioner's secretary for municipal affairs. By mid-November Robinson was settled in Johannesburg. Thus by the end of 1901 five members of the kindergarten — Perry, Curtis, Duncan, Wyndham, and Robinson — were already at work gaining administrative experience, attempting to direct a planned society, and coming to grips for the first time with the problems of South African disunity.

In Milner's overall reconstruction programme the city of Johannesburg occupied a critical position, and he hastened to extend his control over it. He established a Commission for the Constitution of Johannesburg with authority to examine local government conditions and to recommend improvements. On 20 March 1901 Curtis was appointed secretary of the commission. Curtis's experience in these matters was limited to a few months as private secretary to Lord Welby; but he was enthusiastic, and the commission soon recommended the establishment of an appointed town council and the appointment of a town clerk with broad powers to establish progressive municipal government. These recommendations met with Milner's approval, and on 13 April 1901 Curtis was appointed temporary town clerk, the appointment becoming permanent in January 1902. Basil Williams became Curtis's assistant while Robinson, as a private secretary, was responsible for municipal affairs in the Transvaal and worked closely with Curtis. Concerned by the complexity of financial matters, Curtis asked for the assistance of Lionel Hichens, a New College friend and former fellow messenger in South Africa, who had been serving in the Egyptian Ministry of Finance for nine months. Hichens accepted and held the position for two years.

Early in 1902, while on a brief visit to England, Curtis was instructed to find another assistant with legal training who could advise the Johannesburg Council on questions of law. Curtis recommended a mutual friend of himself and Hichens, Richard Feetham, another New College man. When Feetham arrived in mid-1902 he so quickly proved his worth that Milner was able to send Curtis to Pretoria as assistant colonial secretary responsible for the reform of municipal government in the Transvaal. Feetham was then chosen town clerk of Johannesburg, a post he held till Milner's retirement in 1905. By early 1903 Feetham was in need of assistance. Basil Williams had left to establish a new educational system in the Transvaal and Hichens had been promoted to colonial treasurer of the Transvaal, replacing Patrick Duncan who had become colonial secretary. On the advice of Sir William Anson, the warden of All Souls, John Dove, a New College man and a friend of Curtis, Feetham, and Hichens, was appointed. Before the year was out two other members of the kindergarten were given positions of greater responsiblility. In April 1903 Geoffrey Robinson became Milner's personal private secretary, and worked closely with him until his departure in 1905. This arrangement resulted in a close and friendly relationship unlike that formed by others of the kindergarten who always tended to treat Milner with a respect bordering on awe. A few months later Patrick Duncan was made acting lieutenant-governor of the Transvaal government.

Also vital to Milner's reconstruction programme was sufficient labour for the mining industry whose prosperity was essential if settlers, especially British settlers, were to be attracted and the economy of the country revitalized. If a British South Africa was to materialise and reconstruction was to succeed, labour had to be found; therefore on 10 February 1904 the Transvaal Legislative Council passed an ordinance permitting the importation of Chinese labour. Peter Perry, who had resigned from Milner's staff late in 1903 to become chairman of the Rand Native Labor Association, became responsible for recruitment and travelled to the China coast to direct operations. Although Chinese labour helped restore the prosperity of the mines, Milner knew that neither this prosperity nor a flood of British settlers would be sufficient to unify South Africa. If his dream of union was to materialise, the colonies would have to recognise that they had joint problems which demanded joint consideration. From mid-1902 he attempted to concentrate colonial attention on such matters of mutual concern as police and railways.

Money was obtained from the British government to finance these joint operations, and in May 1903 an Intercolonial Council was created composed of official and non-official representatives from the Transvaal and the Orange River Colony. Milner hoped that the council, apart from relieving him of many administrative tasks, would stimulate colonial leaders to think in common terms. Milner was president of the council and he chose as secretary a close friend of Perry's, Robert Brand, another New College man and a fellow of All Souls. Brand arrived late in 1902 while plans for the council were still in the developmental stage, and he remained until 1909 when union was assured. He was one of the most able members of the kindergarten, and quickly became a leading figure in that small band. He and Duncan, more than any of the others, were to have a direct effect on the nature of South African union in their capacities as advisers to Smuts and the Transvaal government. To help with financial matters, Lionel Hichens, in addition to his other tasks, was named treasurer of the council.

Brand's duties were onerous and he soon asked for assistance. On his advice, Milner appointed Philip Kerr, also a former student at New College, who had been known to Brand at Oxford. Kerr was already in South Africa, having arrived early in 1905 to join the staff of Sir Arthur Lawley, the lieutenant-governor of the Transvaal. The transfer to the Intercolonial Council was effected in April. Although Kerr quickly enjoyed the company of the kindergarten and was unquestionably a member of the group, he had virtually no contact with Milner in South Africa. One week after Kerr joined Brand's staff Milner left the country. Dougie Malcolm, the last member of the kindergarten to arrive and a close friend of Perry and Robinson, was in the same position. Ever since 1903, when as a young Colonial Office official he had acted as Milner's private secretary for a few weeks on one of the high commissioner's visits to England, he had nursed a desire to serve with Milner. But no position had been available for him and he was finally appointed private secretary to Milner's successor Lord Selborne. Like Kerr, Malcolm was quickly accepted by the more established members of the kindergarten.

With the arrival of Malcolm the kindergarten was complete. Curtis named nine members: Curtis, Malcolm, Feetham, Dove, Brand, Kerr, Hichens, Duncan, and Robinson.[23] Buchan had left South Africa before the kindergarten had begun to think of themselves as a group with coherent ideas and purposes, even though they were considered a group by outsiders. But it seems unfair of Curtis to exclude Perry and Wyndham who were closely associated until they became absorbed in tasks outside Johannesburg. Amery was definitely not a member, although he shared their views and was closely attached to Milner, and had even served briefly as a secretary while in South Africa on other business.

The kindergarten were aptly named. The oldest were Duncan and Dove at thirty-one; the others were mainly in their late twenties, although Brand at twenty-four and Kerr at twenty-three were the youngest on arrival. Though youthful and inexperienced they were obviously a talented group, a fact they were sometimes too eager to demonstrate. Many of their critics and some of their associates found them 'viewy,' too eager to expound at length and with arrogant assurance on any subject. Not all were like this, certainly not Duncan who at this early stage in his career was the most mature. Hichens, Brand, and Malcolm also had steadying qualities which enabled them to handle their tasks quietly yet with shrewdness and firmness. Throughout

23 Curtis, *With Milner in South Africa*, 344-5

their years in South Africa the kindergarten considered Duncan their leader. His natural dignity made him an excellent chairman, and he presided over their discussions with wisdom and authority leavened by a caustic wit. Geoffrey Robinson was similarly blessed with a good deal of plain common sense and solidity of character. His judgment was generally sane and Milner relied heavily upon him. Robert Brand was very young when he arrived and his ideas and suggestions doubtless seemed impertinent to his superiors on the inter-colonial council. But, as they soon learned, Brand was a man of considerable ability. With a self-deprecating manner and a gentle voice he guided the council through the difficult aftermath of the Boer War. No one was higher in his praise of Brand than Smuts who had first-hand experience of his qualities in 1908-9 when the two men endeavoured to hammer out a South African constitution.

Despite the kindergarten's varied abilities two of its members stand out: Lionel Curtis and Philip Kerr. More than any of their colleagues, Curtis and Kerr were to leave their mark on South Africa and the empire. Both were idealists, deeply committed throughout their lives to noble causes, and both could be 'airy and viewy'; Curtis more so than Kerr. Philip Kerr was a very charming and strikingly handsome young man with a quick, perceptive, and analytic mind, capable of extremely hard work. He had an equable temperament and though he held strongly to his views he rarely lost his temper when discussing them. Born a Catholic, religion was the mainspring of his being, but he was already torn by inner doubts and fears not to be stilled until he embraced Christian Science in 1914. Like Kerr, Lionel Curtis was deeply preoccupied with the ways of men, the ideals they lived on, and the goal to which they were bound. Even at this time he possessed a burning zeal for causes which he thought worthy and threw himself into them with complete self-abandonment, pressing into service all those around him regardless of their pleas. The kindergarten soon dubbed him 'The Prophet.' Curtis made many mistakes in South Africa and in his later ventures, but there was no doubting his sincerity, his passionate idealism, and his strange hypnotic power for making others work for his ends. His major weakness, and the one on which many of his later efforts were to founder, was his single-mindedness. He lacked perspective and often refused to recognize contingencies or, at times, fundamental truths. His kindergarten colleagues often disagreed with him, but they all respected him and were stimulated by his exuberance. In time they learned how to modify his zeal or to deflect it, but there were moments when even they failed.

With few exceptions the kindergarten came from the nobility, the gentry, and the clergy, those classes which had provided leadership in British public life for centuries. Wyndham and Kerr both inherited titles; Brand, the younger son of Viscount Hampden, was created a Baron in his own right in 1946; Malcom's mother was a daughter of Lord Charles Wellesley; Robinson's family were Yorkshire squires and he came into an inheritance in 1917; and the fathers of Curtis and Feetham were both Anglican clerymen. In addition, Brand's father had been governor of New South Wales in the years 1895-99 and was a Liberal MP before succeeding to the title. With these backgrounds it is clear that many of the kindergarten would quite naturally have been motivated by a sense of duty and the importance of public service, attitudes reinforced at the public schools where the majority of them went. Malcolm and Robinson went to Eton; Brand and Feetham to Marlborough; Hichens to Winchester; Dove to Rugby, and Curtis to Haileybury. As a Catholic Kerr attended Oratory school at Edgbaston while Duncan received schooling in Scotland. By the time the kindergarten arrived at Oxford in the 1880s and 90s New College was a rising and increasingly prominent college while Balliol, although still vigorous, was no longer the intellectual heart of the university. The majority of the kindergarten went to New College; the only exceptions were Duncan of Balliol and Robinson of Magdalen. Academically the kindergarten did well and four of them, Duncan, Robinson, Malcolm, and Kerr, gained firsts; but Curtis, who was to devote so much of his life to research and writing, was not outstanding as a student.

The kindergarten as a group shared many of the ideas and attitudes prevalent in late Victorian England or, to be more specific, late Victorian Oxford. The unity of the body politic, the Burkean concept of organic unity, social darwinism, and the relationship of the races were all being discussed at that time. The belief in the superiority of European and especially English civilization was often combined with an almost religious sense of responsibility toward non-Europeans. The kindergarten were exposed to these ideas and concepts throughout their school and university days and in their early careers, and like so many others of their time they came to believe implicitly in the imperial mission and in a positive solution to imperial problems.

The kindergarten were at Oxford when the reaction against *laissez-faire* liberalism and commitment to the 'new imperialism' were strong. The ideas of Dicey and Freeman were influential, particularly Freeman's view of the linear development of self-government from the Anglo-Saxon moot through the English parliamentary system. Of equal, if not greater, importance for the future founders of the Round Table movement was the in-

fluence of the ideas of T.H. Green and his school. Although philosophic idealism was not as influential among undergraduates as it had been in Milner's
day, it made an enormous impression on the kindergarten, particularly on
Curtis and Kerr. Green's philosophy suggested two ideas of great significance for them: the view of the state as a positive, moral good; and the idea
that social improvement or reform was a moral duty. The positive concept of
the state was always a consistent element in the thinking of the kindergarten
and the movement.[24] The ideas of Arnold Toynbee, the man who had so affected Milner, were highly regarded at Oxford, and once again Curtis seems
to have been most influenced. While at the university he belonged to a group
which studied labour and social problems. When he left Oxford in 1895 he
was active at the Haileybury school mission in Stepney, a London slum area,
and took part in the Oxford University Settlement in Bethnal Green, as did
Duncan and Feetham. Curtis was so interested in the life of the poor that he
twice posed as a tramp in order to experience all the ramifications of the life.
For a brief period in the nineties he was also associated with Octavia Hill, the
pioneer in housing reform and the development of urban open spaces.

The kindergarten's tutors were primarily classical scholars, which helps
explain the group's deep respect for the growth of western civilization. Curtis, especially, tended to identify British culture with that of Greece. The Oxford system also emphasized British and European history and Kerr's tutor
was H.A.L. Fisher, the famous historian of Europe whose instruction was
reflected in his early articles in *The Round Table*. Imperial and colonial history was not yet an integral part of the Oxford syllabus, and after graduation
few of the kindergarten showed much immediate concern for imperial problems. The majority involved themselves in domestic affairs. Dove, Curtis,
Feetham, and Duncan studied law, although Curtis never really practised it
and Feetham was the only one to devote himself to it in later life; and six of
them chose civil service careers. Thus most of the kindergarten probably
went to South Africa with a more open mind than Milner. They were less
committed at this stage and more concerned for the full development of the
country. Their broader views led them to work unceasingly for South African union after 1905, at a time when Milner had become disillusioned and
bitter.

Under Milner the kindergarten were put in positions of real administrative responsibility which demanded and developed some of their best tal-
ents. Almost all of them were involved with the Transvaal, the colony most
important for the development of South Africa. They were in touch with

24  Ellinwood, 'Lord Milner's "Kindergarten,"' 69-70

The Milner kindergarten
Standing (left to right): Robert Brand, Herbert Bauer, Lionel Hichens
Middle row: Hugh Wyndham, Richard Feetham, Lionel Curtis, Patrick Duncan,
J.F. Perry, Dougal Malcolm
Front row: John Dove, Philip Kerr, Geoffrey Robinson

both Boers and Britons and were in a position to see the need for a unified South Africa. Although only Duncan ever held really high office under Milner, others of the small band were in positions of influence, particularly Curtis, Feetham, Brand, Hichens, and, later, Kerr. The kindergarten was only a very small element within the government but it was conspicuous, and to the general public it appeared coterminous with the government. They were subjected to a great deal of criticism both as a group and individually. One visitor pronounced them 'hard-working, intelligent, well-meaning and tactless,'[25] while another commentator described the government as a 'small band of fledglings; most of them trained in the public schools and universities of England' and complained that 'youth was accompanied by a display of superiority and assertiveness foreign to the customs of colonial life.'[26] Even Basil Williams remarked that 'the young men of the administration are too much to themselves ... live out together in the country, don't see Johbergers [sic] much and if they do are rather superior.'[27]

The individual who was criticized more than any other member of the kindergarten was Lionel Curtis. His enthusiasm and inexperience caused him to make mistakes, and his natural air of authority could become annoying. Basil Williams, Curtis's deputy, commented in rather prophetic terms in 1902: 'Curtis has certainly run the business very well ... run the whole show, imposed his will on the nominated council ... He is rather tiresome with it all.'[28] In his capacity as assistant colonial secretary for local government Curtis was unquestionably well-meaning but he was guilty of a number of errors which required some haste to correct.[29]

During their years in South Africa a strong camaraderie developed among the kindergarten, a natural consequence of years of close association in various administrative tasks, their common living quarters, and shared social life.[30] At this time all of them, with the exception of Perry, were bach-

25 Fletcher-Vane, *Pax Britannica*, 277
26 Goldman, *A South African Remembers*, 132
27 Basil William's diary for January 1902, Williams Papers; quoted in Denoon, *A Grand Illusion*, 175
28 Ibid., 164-5
29 See F.B. Smith (director of agriculture) to Williams, 22 Aug. and 4 Dec. 1904, Williams Papers, ibid., 203-4. Leo Amery was more generous. He argued that Milner's 'belief in youth, energy and adaptability combined with first-class brains was abundantly justified by the result. The "Kindergarten" often made mistakes. Their ideas about money were sometimes over-generous. Their manner occasionally too cocksure. But by sheer enthusiasm, ability, devotion to duty and passionate loyalty to their chief they achieved a gigantic task.' Amery, *My Political Life*, I, 177; see also LeMay, *British Supremacy*, 82.
30 For the information in the following paragraph see Nimocks, *Milner's Young Men*, 45-53.

elors. When Perry married in August 1901, Curtis lived alone for a time but by October had moved into the Perry household. After his arrival in late 1901, Geoffrey Robinson also shared the Perrys' hospitality at various intervals. Others of the kindergarten lived in a house near 'Sunnyside' rented by Hugh Wyndham. This lasted until Milner's retirement and Wyndham's decision to leave Johannesburg and take up farming. By then plans were being made for the establishment of a house which could serve as a dwelling place for most of the kindergarten. In April 1905 Feetham decided to turn Johannesburg municipal government over to John Dove and to practise law in the city. He acquired land not far from 'Sunnyside' and commissioned Herbert Baker, the architect and a friend of the kindergarten, to build a house. It was completed in July 1906 and from that time 'Moot House' became the home of Feetham, Brand, Dove, Kerr, and George Craik.[31] For three years after its completion Moot House served as the centre of activities for the kindergarten and their South African and English friends and as a meeting place for those interested in South African union. All of the kindergarten were extremely busy with little time for leisure, but recreation when it was taken tended to be shared and of two kinds: either vigorous early morning rides and lengthy hunting trips and treks in the bush, or quiet and relaxed lawn parties and dinners at 'Sunnyside.' This sharing of living quarters, leisure, duties, and interests helps account for the close friendships and spirit of camaraderie which developed. Their common experience of Oxford, especially of New College and of All Souls, was an added tie.[32]

The most important tie, of course, was Milner. If it had not been for him the kindergarten would not have existed. In those days he was the centre of their world; the man who provided firm leadership but yet enabled them to act for themselves. For five years the kindergarten only had to persuade one strong ruler of the correctness of their views and analyses. This was indeed heady power and its impact, aided by youth and inexperience, was considerable. It helped persuade them all that problems could be resolved and ends achieved by persuasion and decree. Some of the kindergarten later found this early conviction hard to abandon.

31 Craik was not a member of the kindergarten but was a close New College friend who had originally come to South Africa in the same unit as Curtis and Hichens. After serving from 1903-9 as legal adviser to the Transvaal Chamber of Mines he eventually returned to London to become chief constable of the metropolitan police and an intimate of the Round Table movement.

32 Four of the kindergarten, Brand, Perry, Robinson and Malcolm, were Fellows of All Souls, as was their associate Amery, and as Curtis and Reginald Coupland were to be in later years.

# 2
# The kindergarten and South African union

The draft constitution of the Union of South Africa was approved by the four South African colonies in June 1909. In August the Imperial Parliament passed the South Africa Act and on 31 May 1910 the Union of South Africa finally came into being. During the three years before the approval of the draft constitution Milner's kindergarten were intimately involved in the cause of closer union. They were the propagandists of union. They extolled the merits of colonial integration and attempted to acquaint Boer and Briton with the intricacies and blessings of a single state. They drafted the Selborne Memorandum, organised the closer union societies, and published and edited *The State,* the only magazine which attempted to bridge the ethnic and language barriers in the quest for a united South Africa.

Despite their considerable achievements the role of the kindergarten should not be overemphasized. They did not create the interest in union nor did their efforts provide the initiative or stimulus. South African union had been a matter of debate and concern for some years before 1906, particularly among the Boer politicians, and until the Boers decided that union was in their interests nothing the kindergarten attempted would have had much effect. Smuts[1] and J.X. Merriman[2] are the key figures in the closer union story;

---

1 Jan Christian Smuts (1870-1950); state attorney, South African Republic 1897; prominent Boer leader during the Boer War 1899-1902; colonial secretary, Transvaal 1907-10; member of the South African cabinet 1910-19; prime minister 1919-24 and 1939-48; member of the Imperial War Cabinet 1917 and 1918; South African representative at the Paris peace conference
2 John Xavier Merriman (1841-1926); South African statesman; commissioner of crown

without their initiative and ideas, and of men like them, all the kindergarten's efforts would have been in vain. But given those men and the interest of the Boers, the kindergarten were able to exercise some influence. When the kindergarten first turned their energies to unification both the Boer and British communities were reluctant to force the pace, the latter because they realised that more British settlers would be needed to ensure a British union and the former because they feared that a union arranged before the grant of responsible government to the republics would be union on British terms. The Boers were well aware that time was on their side and though individual politicians, and on one occasion a party (the Bond), expressed interest there seemed little reason to rush the matter. Once Boer electoral victories had been achieved in the Transvaal, the Orange River Colony, and the Cape, as they were between February 1907 and February 1908, then the Boer leaders were prepared to move toward union no longer in fear of a British majority, and the kindergarten's efforts were finally justified.

In the summer of 1906 the majority of the kindergarten, with the exception of Geoffrey Robinson who was by then editing *The Star*, were still attached in one way or another to the government of the Transvaal, to the municipality of Johannesburg, or to the Inter-Colonial Council, positions which they had held at the time of Milner's departure. Although they continued to have a great respect for their former chief and still shared many of his views on South Africa, they were by now beginning to form different impressions about the paths and methods to be pursued owing to their closer acquaintance with ever-changing South African conditions and their greater awareness of the new political forces emerging in the colonies. The British decision in December 1906 to introduce responsible government in the two Boer colonies did not depress the kindergarten who were convinced that Milner's dream of a British South Africa might still be realised if the four colonies could be united into one state. They believed unification would bring a necessary stability to South African affairs which in turn would attract investment as well as large numbers of British immigrants. As Sir Percy Fitzpatrick put it: 'both races hope for prosperity, prosperity means expansion, expansion means immigration, immigration means British!'[3] It was, of course, a forlorn hope, but in 1906 it seemed possible.

lands, Cape Colony 1875-8 and 1881-4; treasurer-general, Cape Colony 1890-3 and 1898-1900; prime minister and colonial treasurer, Cape Colony 1908-10; member of the National Convention 1908-10

3 Quoted by Wallis in *Fitz*, 137. Sir James Percy Fitzpatrick (1862-1931); South African statesman and author; member of the Reform Committee; arrested after Jameson Raid;

It is difficult to know why the kindergarten pledged themselves to union exactly when they did. Lionel Curtis was later to give credit to the chance reading of Frederick Scott Oliver's biography of *Alexander Hamilton*.[4] Ostensibly a study of Hamilton's role in the achievement of American union, the book was actually an impassioned plea for the closer integration of the British empire. Admirably and lucidly written by a man with high ideals and a strongly developed sense of mission, it was well suited to appeal to 'young men who see visions.' The kindergarten had probably decided to work for South African union before Oliver's book reached Johannesburg. Nevertheless it seemed vitally relevant to the South African situation, and had a profound and lasting effect on the group, particularly Curtis and Kerr, bolstering their confidence and affirming them in their goal.[5] Certainly by mid-1906 the kindergarten were intimately acquainted with the difficulties confronting South Africa. The four colonies were bitterly divided over railway and native policy, and customs tariffs were a continual source of friction. All this suggested potential chaos unless something could be done to draw the colonies closer together. At the end of July Curtis informed Milner of the kindergarten's decision and outlined the plans agreed upon after a number of preliminary meetings. It is an interesting proposal and foreshadowed the methods that the Round Table movement later adopted.[6]

The kindergarten decided that Curtis would draft a memorandum containing both an analysis of the situation in South Africa and a plea for unification. In order to prepare himself for his task he would travel extensively throughout the country gathering information. Each stage of his mem-

---

found guilty of high treason; fined £2000; stalwart of the Unionist party; member of the Transvaal parliament pre-1910 and Union parliament post-1910

4 Oliver, *Alexander Hamilton*. Frederick Scott Oliver (1864-1934); businessman and publicist; partner in the firm of Debenham and Freebody; an ardent tariff reformer; favoured imperial union; close friend and confidant of many leading British politicians 1906-34; among his publications were *Ordeal by Battle* (1915) and *The Endless Adventure* (1930-5).

5 Milner began reading the book in late April 1906, shortly after its publication; on completing it he began reading the *Federalist Papers*. A copy was circulating among the kindergarten by September 1906. See diary entries 30 April, 13 and 16 June 1906 and 27 and 28 July 1907, vols. 269 and 270, Milner Papers, and Robinson's diary, 10 Sept. 1906, Dawson Papers, cited in Nimocks, *Milner's Young Men*, 78. See also [B.K. Long], 'The Month: Mr Oliver and South African Union,' *The State*, II, Aug. 1909, 121-40.

6 This letter has not been traced but it can be pieced together from two extensive letters written by Milner to Robinson, 21 Aug. and 21 Sept. 1906, Dawson Papers, précised by Nimocks. *Milner's Young Men*. 78f.

orandum would be reviewed by a sub-committee of the kindergarten. Once the draft had been completed Curtis would then visit Canada, Australia, and the United States in order to acquire overseas experience and perspective. On his return a final revision would be undertaken and this version, theoretically representative of the opinions of the whole kindergarten, would be given to Lord Selborne, Milner's successor as high commissioner, to be used in any manner he thought appropriate.

In this same letter Curtis appealed to Milner for assistance in obtaining funds from the Rhodes Trust to finance the venture. Although Milner was somewhat skeptical of his young follower's most recent enthusiasm, he did use his influence with his fellow trustees and by late September was able to inform the kindergarten that £1000 would be made available to them by the Rhodes Trust for a one-year period. In agreeing to make the money available the Rhodes Trust did not attempt to influence the findings of the kindergarten but they did make certain stipulations. They wanted Lionel Curtis, as 'Organising Secretary' of the venture, to resign from the Transvaal government and devote himself full-time to the preparation of the memorandum. Curtis's work, and that of the kindergarten as a whole, was to be supervised by Lord Selborne who was to be kept well-informed at every stage. Whether or not the completed memorandum should be exploited by Selborne was left undecided, although the trustees would have preferred to keep Selborne's part in its preparations hidden in order that the memorandum could be publicly debated without prejudice. The trustees were firm about one thing: they wanted the Rhodes Trust's connection with the project kept secret.[7]

While the kindergarten's plans were being discussed in London a number of meetings were held in South Africa during August, and on 1 September the scheme was taken to Selborne who quickly gave it his whole-hearted support.[8] Unlike Milner, Selborne believed that early unification of South Africa would be in the best interests of the country, of British South Africans, and the empire. Once Selborne's approval had been secured Curtis spent much of September and October touring the four South African colonies assessing the attitudes of the British and Afrikaner population toward union. On his return to Johannesburg in October he resigned his post as as-

---

7 The stipulations can be found ibid., 79-80, précising Milner to Robinson, 21 Sept. 1906, Dawson Papers.

8 See Robinson's diary, Aug. 1906 and 1 Sept. 1906, Dawson Papers, cited ibid., 80-1.

sistant colonial secretary in charge of municipal affairs and began to draft the memorandum on unification. During those weeks the other members of the kindergarten met repeatedly to discuss their plans and critically assess Curtis's findings. When necessary, individuals from outside the kindergarten attended these 'moots.' Discussion ranged widely over a variety of matters relevant both to unification and to South Africa's position in the imperial framework. The value and intensity of these discussions led to the formation early in October 1906 of the Fortnightly Club, an organisation for the more public discussion of current problems. For the next two years, particularly in the early period, the club served as an excellent place for the kindergarten to air their ideas and form their opinions. The presence of a number of men not normally a part of the inner committee added to the flexibility, flavour, and value of the discussion.

At the first meeting on 4 October 1906 Richard Feetham probed to the heart of the most immediate issue when he gave a paper on 'Some problems of South African Federation and reasons for facing them.' It was the first attempt by the kindergarten to define the problem facing the four colonies. Feetham argued that federation could no longer be left to after-dinner speeches. It was time to think out a concrete plan. He pointed out that economic problems and the presence within South Africa of a vast native population which outnumbered the European four to one underlined the need for prompt action. The longer they waited the greater the difficulties, 'because the greater the estrangement between the different colonies, the greater the growth of incompatible vested interests, the stronger the forces of Colonial as opposed to National sentiment.' Feetham believed that the current differences over railway rates would only be the first of many. And once the Transvaal and the Orange River Colony had been given responsible government intercolonial differences would probably take a more violent form. A central government was essential if economic stability was to be achieved and the native question dealt with uniformly.

It was also necessary that British interests and influence be preserved. If the current state of affairs continued, South Africa would be Dutch rather than British in sentiment and character because the quarrels between the colonies mainly affected the interests of the British commercial communities. The causes of conflict and disagreement could not be altogether removed by federation, but once representatives met in the same parliament, 'the influence of British communities ... will be able to make itself felt with new force throughout South Africa.' Feetham thought federation should be faced without delay, and he bitterly attacked 'the little Transvaaler' point of view. 'If Union is to be achieved, every Colony will no doubt have to make some concessions – the question of the concessions which it is worth while for the individual Colony to make, in order to secure the undoubted benefits of Union, is one which each Colony will have carefully to weigh, but for any Colony deliberately to postpone the attempt to secure federation, in the hope of first bringing the other Colonies to their knees, seems to me to be a counsel of despair, the acceptance of which is likely to make federation altogether impossible.'

Feetham chose federation as the form of government in the belief that the enormous area and expected population of the four colonies would make a unitary system impossible. Also, there seemed little reason for thinking that a unitary system would ever be practical politics. None of the existing units seemed prepared to merge themselves entirely and lose their identity in one South African state. It was obvious, however, that if circumstances permitted Feetham would prefer a unitary system. Although he advocated a tightly-knit form of federation with a strong central government, he pointed out that the colour question and the subsequent problem of the franchise might be an insuperable obstacle to federation.[9]

During these weeks Curtis was hard at work preparing a rough draft of the memorandum on unification and Philip Kerr wrote an article on the intricate question of railway rates, which was subsequently expanded under the critical eyes of Brand, Hichens, and Duncan and appended to the Selborne Memorandum. Kerr wrote to his family about the preparation of the Curtis 'Egg':

There is great secrecy about the whole thing. Everybody is so mysterious that it is bound to leak out. Curtis is really writing a great despatch, which is subjected to the

9 Feetham's paper plus many others read at Fortnightly Club meetings are in the Library of the University of Cape Town. I am grateful to the staff there for preparing copies for me. Kerr also elaborated at this time on the difference between unification and federation in South Africa: 'Federation is what will ultimately come. It is really only a matter of time. But I think it will come sooner than people imagine. Unification is practically speaking impossible. You could not now destroy the inter-colonial boundaries if you tried. Besides there are a number [of] departments of government which it would be impossible for a single central government to manage, as the problems are local, and particular in each different colony, and can only be satisfactorily settled by people intimately concerned with them, for instance the Mines Department, and at present Education, and a good deal of taxation as well. Railway Unification is a different thing and is equally attainable either under Unification or Federation. It simply means that the railways should be administered by a single authority instead of five different ones.' Undocumented letter from Kerr to his mother, cited in Butler, *Lothian*, 23

criticism of what is known as the Moot, which consists of Lord Milner's Kindergarten viz. Duncan, Hichens, Curtis, Feetham, Robinson, Malcolm, Brand, Rodwell and myself. When we have done mauling the thing it is to be submitted to Lord Selborne for approval. Then it is to be published to the startled gaze of South Africa. My paper is designed to prove that we can't get sound railway management in South Africa until they are unified ... It is proposed to 'launch' what we call the Federation Egg about New Year's Day ...[10]

By late October Curtis had completed the first portion of his memorandum, and on 28 October there assembled 'a great moot of the Federation Committee – Duncan, Hichens, Feetham, Curtis, Brand, Kerr and [Robinson] – and went solidly through Lionel Curtis's first [chapter of the] "egg."'[11] During the next few weeks the moot met continuously to examine succeeding sections of the memorandum which were distributed in proof form to facilitate discussion. As the memorandum neared completion Selborne played a more important role in the committee's activities, and it was primarily at his direction and under his guidance that all contentious material was removed and the memorandum shortened and reorganised. The result was a more readable and appealing document, unlikely to offend either the Boers or the British.[12] Inevitably, a certain degree of friction developed between Selborne, on the one hand, and Duncan, Hichens, and Curtis, on the other, when the high commissioner insisted on forwarding copies of the memorandum to London so that the Colonial Office could be kept abreast of developments. The moot, quite understandably, feared that publication of the memorandum might be jeopardised by Selborne's insistence on keeping the Colonial Office informed.

The problem of how Curtis's memorandum could be used to best effect had preoccupied the kindergarten for some weeks in the autumn of 1906. They knew that it would carry more weight if it appeared over Selborne's signature, but they also realised that simply to go ahead and publish it in that

10 Ibid., 22-3
11 Robinson's diary, 28 Oct. 1906, cited in Nimocks, *Milner's Young Men*, 83. The first public speech by a member of the kindergarten on the subject of unity was by Curtis on 27 Oct. 1906 on his retirement from the post of assistant colonial secretary. A copy of the speech is enclosed in Curtis to Jebb, 19 Nov. [1906], box 1, Jebb Papers. A week later Robinson was writing to Jebb 'the federation plot grows apace & L.C. is laying a gigantic egg.' Robinson to Jebb, 4 Nov. 1906, box 3, ibid.
12 Williams, ed., *The Selborne Memorandum*, xxi; and Thompson, *Unification of South Africa*, 67n. See also Robinson's diary 13 and 22 Dec. 1906, Dawson Papers, cited in Nimocks, *Milner's Young Men*, 83.

manner would smack of British interference and would offend the sensitive Boers. Finally, in November 1906 Curtis visited Jameson, the premier of Cape Colony, told him of the kindergarten's activities, and asked for his assistance. Jameson agreed to help and in late November formally requested Selborne, as high commissioner, to review the state of intercolonial friction.[13] Selborne immediately sent copies of this request to the governments of Natal, the Transvaal, the Orange River Colony, and Southern Rhodesia. When the response was favourable he forwarded copies of the memorandum, entitled 'A Review of the Present Mutual Relations of the British South African Colonies,' to the governments concerned early in January 1907. Later in the month Kerr's memorandum on 'South African Railway Unification and its effect on Railway Rates' was distributed to the five governments as a supplement to the major report.

The circulation of the 'Selborne Memorandum' having been satisfactorily arranged, it remained for the kindergarten to decide when and how it should be published. Selborne wanted to publish immediately in the hope that it would help stop the growth of 'the little Transvaaler' viewpoint,'[14] but he was dissuaded by the Natal government. After some deliberation the kindergarten agreed that if possible the memorandum should be published under the aegis of both white communities, and with this in mind they approached Francis S. Malan,[15] a young Afrikaner leader in Cape Town who was prominent in the Afrikaner Bond. Malan was also the editor of *Ons Land*, an important Boer newspaper, and for some time had openly supported union. Curtis, who had first met Malan the previous autumn, arranged a further meeting early in 1907 and forwarded a copy of the Selborne Memorandum to him for his consideration. After reading it Malan was convinced that it should be published, and he agreed to move for the tabling of the memorandum in the Cape Assembly. In consequence the Selborne Memorandum was tabled on 3 July, 1907 and released to the press the same day.

This memorandum was a powerful document in favour of closer union. It hammered home again and again that only union could provide the centralised control and direction necessary to resolve the colonies' most urgent needs. The opening section sketched briefly the background to current prob-

---

13  Jameson's letter is reprinted in Williams, ed., *The Selborne Memorandum*, 4-6.
14  Selborne to Duncan, 31 Dec. 1906, Duncan Papers, cited in Thompson, *Unification of South Africa*, 69
15  Francis S. Malan (1871-1941); South African statesman; practised law in Cape Town; editor of *Ons Land*, supported Afrikaner Bond; opposed Rhodes; member of the National Convention 1908-10; member of the Union cabinet

lems and attempted to underline the many mutual interests of the Boers and the British in South Africa. It clearly pointed out that South African affairs were more important than the affairs of an individual colony, and that only through integration could South Africans achieve the same independence in internal affairs as that enjoyed by Canadians and Australians. The next two sections, dealing respectively with railway and customs policies, were ruthless condemnations of the disunity and the intercolonial strife resulting from separate policies in matters crucial to the economic stability and viability of South Africa. Further sections pointed out that not only was union essential if South Africa's defence forces were to be effective but it was crucial for a solution of the native problem. Only a centralised government could properly handle the difficult native labour problem and introduce some coherent guidelines for the distribution of labour and the control of immigration. If South Africans wanted to fulfil their mission, then separate native policies would have to be abandoned. Moreover, only union would bring the political stability necessary to provide an attractive area for the investor and enable South Africa to deal with the vexed question of expansion.

Curtis concluded by pointing out that the situation was growing ever more urgent. It was useless to suggest postponing a decision to a more convenient time. There was no such thing as 'a more convenient season' for uniting a divided country. It was well known that 'Divisions left alone tend to emphasize and perpetuate themselves day by day until any really firm union becomes impossible.'[16]

It was a propagandist memorandum and a good one, much in the style of Oliver's *Hamilton*, and it served the purpose of stimulating an interest in union. It was not original and contained little political theory, relying mainly on arguments used many decades before in the American and Canadian contexts. One commentator has suggested that the kindergarten were naïve to assume that Boer and Briton could resolve the native problem together, and has pointed out that the memorandum was concerned almost entirely, 'apart from an occasional flourish,' with the problems of white South Africa.[17] Given the political realities of the South African problem at that time and the specific purpose of the memorandum, the kindergarten's approach was probably the only pragmatic one.

When the kindergarten had first planned to generate interest in closer union, the circulation of a memorandum and its possible publication had been con-

16 Williams, ed., *The Selborne Memorandum*, 160
17 Thompson, *Unification of South Africa*, 66

sidered as only a first step toward the establishment of a fairly active and wideflung organisation whose purpose would be to attract and maintain an interest in South African union among both politicians and the public.[18] Once the Selborne Memorandum had been circulated to the various governments in early January, the kindergarten decided to pursue this idea. Curtis wanted to try and use the occasion of an Inter-colonial Defence Conference in Johannesburg from 21-24 January 1907 to lay the basis of a national organisation to work for closer union. The kindergarten were well aware that any organisation founded on a national basis would have to be bipartisan in inspiration and composition if it were to have any hope of success. Knowing this, Curtis approached Jan Smuts early in January and, after a preliminary conversation at the Rand Club, wrote at length to the Boer leader outlining his ideas.[19] He thought that the presence in Johannesburg in late January of representatives from all the colonies 'offered an opportunity for a meeting between men from different parts of South Africa who share the belief in common that South African union is the only measure which will give self-government in its true form.' He revealed that Abe Bailey,[20] the mining magnate and self-styled successor to Rhodes' mantle, had offered to give a private dinner to enable Duncan to state the case for union 'not merely from the sentimental but from the official and technical point of view.' He asked Smuts:

Would it ... now be possible to establish a 'National Union' presided over by Chief Justice de Villiers and by Sir James Rose Innes, and perhaps also by the Chief Jus-

18 This aspect of their scheme had received the support of Richard Jebb, a student of imperial relations and the recent author of the much heralded *Studies in Colonial Nationalism*. While visiting South Africa in 1906 Jebb had met the kindergarten and had discussed South African union many times with Curtis. He had suggested that the kindergarten might profit from the study of the Canadian Club, a wideflung organisation for the discussion of contemporary problems which had recently been started in Canada. On returning to England Jebb took advantage of Mackenzie King's presence in London to ask him to send Curtis full particulars about the Canadian Club organisation. Mackenzie King immediately despatched a long and informative letter to Curtis which was circulated among the kindergarten in late December 1906. At the time Mackenzie King was deputy minister in the Canadian Department of Labour. See Jebb to Mackenzie King, 11 Oct. 1906; and Curtis to King, 30 Dec. [1906], King Papers.

19 Curtis to Smuts, 7 Jan. [1907], printed in full in Hancock and Van Der Poel, *Smuts Papers*, ii, 314-17

20 Sir Abe Bailey (1864-1940); South African mining magnate and legislator; member of the Reform Committee at the time of the Jameson Raid; imprisoned 1896 and fined £2000; succeeded Cecil Rhodes as member for Barkly West 1902-5; elected Transvaal parliament 1908; member for Krugersdorp 1910-24; staunch supporter of Unionist party; developed the South African Townships, Mining and Finance Corporation Ltd

tices of the Orange River Colony and Natal, in order to assure the non-political character of the organisation. The only qualification should be persons who believe in superseding the present system of divided government by a National Union extending from Tanganyika to the Cape of Good Hope. Given that common ground all shades of opinion inside that limit will be admissable, for the very purpose of the Union will be to thrash out the issue between these differences of opinion in such a way that the whole nation may take part in the discussion.[21]

In order to carry out this programme it would be necessary to have facts and figures. Therefore the first responsibility of a 'National Union' would be to collect, collate, and print such necessary facts as the duties, debts, and assets and the population and franchise figures of all four governments. Without this sort of information a constitutional conference would have to adjourn for six months until it could be assembled. The second duty of the 'Union' would be to prepare papers similar to the famous American *Federalist Papers*. These would be less concerned with federal government itself than with discussing the hard concrete problems which needed resolving in South Africa. The first paper might lay bare the issues between unification and federation, while the second might show what duties were proper for the central government and for local administration. These first two papers would probably raise a number of controversial points. If freely distributed in both tongues they might lead to the preparation of outside papers which the 'Union' could publish. Other papers could then be prepared by experts, so that definite proposals on all the major issues could be considered. Curtis reasoned that if the plan were accepted there would be need for an editor or an editorial board. A publication committee composed of, among others, Feetham and Smuts with Curtis as honorary secretary could take care of routine.

Curtis, however, did not believe that the 'Union' should rely exclusively on printed matter. Experience had shown that the mass of the people were never reached in this way. The 'Union' should also establish branches in every part of South Africa where lecturers could give the people a first-hand account of the problems facing the country and recruit support for the 'Na-

---

21 De Villiers, Lord, of Wynberg (1842-1914); chief justice, Cape Colony 1873-1910; chairman, National Convention 1908-10; chief justice of the Union 1910-14; arranged the 1899 meeting between Milner and Kruger – the final attempt to prevent the outbreak of war in South Africa; Sir James Rose-Innes (1855-1942); entered Cape parliament 1884 and became attorney-general in Rhodes's ministry in 1890; chief justice, Transvaal 1902-10; chief justice of the Union 1914-27

tional Union.' He suggested an annual subscription of 5s to cover membership and recommended that no more than a £50 annual contribution from any one person be accepted, so that from the outset the 'Union' would exist on a broad foundation. When its task had been accomplished the 'National Union,' like the Corn Law League, should be dissolved. Although Curtis assured Smuts that he had gone into detail only to make criticism easier, his plan of January 1907 became virtually the blueprint for the closer union societies. On 7 January, the day after Curtis wrote to Smuts, Duncan invited Louis Botha[22] to attend Bailey's dinner. In doing so he was frank about the purpose of the meeting. It was, he said, 'to consider whether a movement can be made at the present time in which men of all political parties can join to help forward the cause of union.'[23]

Despite these efforts the kindergarten's attempt to draw leaders of the Boer and British communities together to consider the formation of a national organisation for closer union activity proved a failure. Both Smuts and Botha were by this time most sympathetic to closer union ideas and not as suspicious of the kindergarten's motives as Merriman of the Cape, but they realised that it would be far wiser for the Boers if Boer governments were in power in the Orange River Colony, the Transvaal, and the Cape before serious efforts at union were made.

Disappointed by the refusal of the Boer leaders to co-operate, the kindergarten met with leaders from the British community on 20 January, a day before the scheduled dinner at Bailey's, to discuss their future actions.[24] It was agreed that plans for a National Union, as outlined by Curtis, could not be pursued without Afrikaner encouragement and support. Instead, the kindergarten agreed 'to form a small private committee in each colony to help Curtis in collecting materials and to postpone any public propaganda, the formation of a league etc. till he has done so.'[25] It was also decided to ask Lord Milner if the £1000 originally given by the Rhodes Trust to cover the expenses of preparing the Selborne Memorandum could be transferred to

22  Louis Botha (1862-1919); South African statesman and soldier; commandant-general of Transvaal forces 1900-3; founder of Het Volk; prime minister, Transvaal 1907-10; prime minister of South Africa 1910-19; represented South Africa at Paris peace conference
23  Duncan to Botha, 8 Jan. 1907, copy, Duncan Papers, cited in Thompson, *Unification of South Africa*, 69
24  Present besides the kindergarten were Sir George Farrar, a leader of the Progressive party in the Transvaal; C.P. Crew, a Unionist (Progressive) party leader from the Cape; and J.G. Maydon from Natal. See Curtis to Jebb, 2 Jan. 1907, box 1, Jebb Papers; and Robinson to Milner, 20 Jan. 1907, box 193, Milner Papers.
25  Robinson to Milner, 20 Jan. 1907, ibid.

cover Curtis's expenses. Apparently the kindergarten had succeeded in raising funds elsewhere, probably from Bailey, and the Rhodes Trust money had
not been required for that purpose.[26]

The Rhodes Trust subsequently complied with this request, but in the
meantime Bailey's dinner, although not the occasion the kindergarten had
originally planned, resulted in 'a large subscription on the spot to cover preliminary expenses' and removed for the time being kindergarten dependence
on Rhodes Trust money. As so often before Robinson was delegated to write
to Milner: as a result of the dinner 'they are all in favour (i.e. Duncan, Hichens, & Curtis himself) of asking you to take back the £1000 and not to think
they are ungrateful to you. Their fear is that some day hereafter the thing
might leak out and a capitalist job be suspected. They don't want to have
anything up their sleeve, that's all.'[27] Whether or not the money was taken
back is not clear although Bailey and Selborne certainly became the principal suppliers of kindergarten funds in the following months.[28] There is
some suggestion that later on the Rhodes Trust did help the kindergarten on
a £ to £ basis.

Informing Smuts about the decision to abandon a formal organisation
for the time being, Curtis made it clear that he was always willing to be
guided by Smuts's advice. Typically, Curtis put a dramatic caste to it: 'All I
want is leaders to serve as a Junior, in the legal sense, or perhaps I might say,
Counsel for whom I may work as a Solicitor.' He offered to see Smuts whenever possible and to tell him 'without reserve all I have done or am thinking
of doing.' He would consider any appointment with Smuts 'as prior to all
other.'[29] During the next two years Smuts remained in constant touch with
the kindergarten, particularly with Curtis, Brand, and Duncan.

Shortly after the kindergarten's failure to establish a bipartisan national
organisation the Transvaal election was held on 20 February 1907. Despite
all the efforts of the kindergarten on behalf of the Progressives, it resulted in
an overwhelming victory for Het Volk, the Afrikaner party. The emergence
of political parties in the Transvaal and the Orange River Colony was a fairly

---

26  In January 1907 the original £1000 was still 'banked in the joint names of Feetham, & [Rob-
inson] & still untouched,' ibid. In his letter to Milner, Robinson made it clear that though the
kindergarten would be grateful for a transfer of funds they wanted an understanding that if
the need arose the source could be made public. Curtis was 'beginning to feel a little nervous
about having any resources at his back which he is unable to disclose.' Ibid.
27  Robinson to Milner, 3 Feb. 1907, box 76, Milner Papers
28  L. Curtis, 'Essays in Construction,' undated and unpublished typed draft, Curtis Papers
29  Curtis to Smuts, 24 Jan. [1907]; printed in full in Hancock and Van Der Poel, *Smuts Papers*,
II, 319-20

recent development. During the war there had been no organised political activity in the two republics, and from the signing of the peace in May 1902 until the grant of responsible government in 1906 the affairs of the Transvaal and the Orange River Colony had been administered by British officials with the advice of appointed Executive and Legislative councils. By the time Milner left in 1905 political organisations had begun to be formed by both the British and the Boers, so that when responsible government was returned there existed mediums through which the white population could strive for power.

Afrikaner political organisation in the Transvaal had begun to take definite form in May 1904 when a meeting was held under the chairmanship of ex-Boer General Louis Botha to condemn the use of Chinese labour and other acts of the Milner administration. A further meeting in January 1905 resulted in the formation of a party, Het Volk (The People), to voice the grievances and define the position of the Transvaal Afrikaners. Botha became chairman and was assisted by a committee whose most influential member was Smuts. In 1906 a similar organisation was formed in the Orange River Colony. Led by former officials of the Orange Free State it was called Orangie Unie. No Afrikaner party was formed in Natal, but Het Volk and Orangie Unie in conjunction with the well-established Afrikaner Bond in the Cape became the spearheads of the new Afrikaner political involvement. The English political parties lacked the fervour and the intensity of their Afrikaner rivals. The Constitutional party was the sole organisation of the scattered British population in the Orange River Colony while in the Transvaal the British population was divided in its allegiance. One party, the Transvaal Responsible Government Association, later known as the Transvaal National Association, was supported primarily by English-speaking Johannesburgers. It favoured the grant of self-government and the reduction of colonial status. The second British party was the Transvaal Progressive Association organised and financed by the leading financiers and mining companies of Johannesburg, which favoured the retention of British authority and opposed the grant of responsible government in the immediate future.[30]

At this time, before they committed themselves more fully to the idea of responsible government in the two colonies, the kindergarten gave their support to the Progressives; one of their number, Hugh Wyndham, who had become a farmer on the Vaal River after Milner's retirement, stood as a

30 For a summary of the party organisation in South Africa see Thompson, *Unification of South Africa*, 20-9; also Davenport, *The Afrikaner Bond*.

Progressive candidate for the district and Geoffrey Robinson supported the party in the editorial columns of *The Star*. Despite the efforts of the kindergarten, Het Volk won an overwhelming victory, gaining a majority of five over all other parties and, in alliance with the Responsibles, controlled forty-three of the sixty-nine seats. Louis Botha quickly formed a government with Smuts as his first lieutenant. The Transvaal victory was only the first of three for the Boer political parties. In November 1907 the Orangie Unie won a sweeping victory in the Orange River Colony, gaining thirty of thirty-eight seats in the legislature, and in February 1908 the recently-created and Boer-dominated South Africa party under J.X. Merriman ousted Jameson and his Cape Colony Progressive (Unionist) government. Thus in one year, from February 1907 to February 1908, a major transformation occurred in the political life of South Africa and only one colony, Natal, could be said to have a government still sympathetic to Milner's policies.

The Boer victory in the Transvaal resulted in many changes for the kindergarten. Those who had held positions in the crown colony government before the election resigned immediately. Duncan turned over the office of lieutenant-governor to Smuts and returned to England to study law. After being admitted to the bar in 1908, he came back to the Transvaal where he soon became involved in the closer union movement as a legal adviser to the Transvaal delegation at the National Convention.[31] Hichens, who had been colonial treasurer of the Transvaal for four years, also resigned and returned to England in late March. In 1907-8 he served as a member of the Royal Commission on Decentralisation in India and in 1909 chaired a committee which visited South Africa to evaluate the Southern Rhodesian public service. Finally, in 1910 he became chairman of the shipbuilding firm of Cammell Laird & Co, a position he held till his untimely death in 1940. John Dove, the town clerk of Johannesburg, also resigned but unlike Duncan and Hichens he remained in South Africa becoming chairman of the Transvaal Settlement Board with headquarters in Pretoria. Dougie Malcolm remained on as Selborne's secretary, and Brand and Kerr, secretary and assistant secretary respectively of the Inter-Colonial Council, retained their positions until its dissolution in June 1908.

In the months following the February election Kerr devoted most of his time to his duties as secretary to the Indigency Commission of which both Curtis and Feetham, now a Johannesburg lawyer, were members. Kerr

31 Shortly before he left in March 1907 a 'kinderfest' was held in his honour and Milner's health was drunk. Robinson to Milner, 5 March 1907, box 45, Milner Papers. Present were Robinson, Malcolm, Dove, Kerr, Perry, A.E. Balfour, Curtis, Hichens, Brand, Craik, Feetham, and Duncan.

found the work and travelling involved particularly arduous and by the time he completed drafting the commission report in June 1908 he was showing the signs of strain which were to plague him for many years. In addition to their commission responsibilities, Curtis and Feetham were both appointed by Selborne to the Legislative Council, the upper house of the Transvaal legislature, where to some effect they combined forces to criticise government policies.[32] Of those who had resigned before the introduction of responsible government in the Transvaal, Fred Perry was working closely with the Chamber of Mines; Hugh Wyndham was a farmer, and, of course, Robinson was editor of the Johannesburg *Star*. Robinson's influence in South African and imperial matters and his opportunities to promote Milnerian ideals were vastly increased in 1906 when he was appointed South African correspondent for *The Times* – an event which marked the beginning of a long and influential relationship with England's most famous and powerful newspaper.

Those of the kindergarten who remained in South Africa after the Transvaal election were soon deeply involved in their closer union activities which had never really ceased to preoccupy them even during the election fervour. Although the kindergarten had spoken of founding small committees in all the colonies to assist Curtis in compiling and sifting information on union, they appear to have made no effort to do so, or at least no successful effort. The closest to a committee in the Transvaal, where the majority of the kindergarten lived, was the Fortnightly Club, which continued to discuss various aspects of union. In fact this was probably the forcing ground for many of the kindergarten's ideas, and perhaps the only opportunity for having anything approximating a public airing. Throughout these months Curtis, who by now was recognised as the dynamo of the kindergarten, continued to prepare material on the lines originally suggested to Smuts. He never ceased to think of his closer union mission, and as early as May 1907 had in mind 'starting a weekly paper here on the line of the Outlook or Spectator, whose special business it will be to promote federation, and to deal with the political questions of the day on a non-party basis.'[33]

By September 1907 the idea was taking more definite shape. Kerr wrote of it to his family:

You know the general objects of the paper – the promotion of Federation in every possible way. A combination of political circumstances ... make it important that

32 Robinson to Milner, 24 March 1907; and Fitzgerald to Milner, 25 March 1907, box 193, Milner Papers
33 Kerr to his parents, May 1907, undocumented reference in Butler, *Lothian*, 28

there should be no delay in getting the question thoroughly laid before the public and thoroughly explained. If it isn't there is a danger of the Federal constitution being engineered by the Dutch alone, without much, or indeed any, public discussion, in such a way as to leave the British or more advanced section of the population at a disadvantage, and so perpetuate the racial trouble. The only way in which Federation can be pushed on its merits at this moment is by a body of people not identified with either of the two great political parties, the Progressives and the Bond or Het Volk. That body of people is already partly in existence, and with a little more time and effort it can be made very considerable. The kernel however of the movement is the Kindergarten, i.e. Curtis, Duncan etc. and a certain number of other people who are keen on the subject. Perhaps the measure of most importance in connection with the preaching of Federation is a propagandist paper, which can rally the Federalists round it, and explain constantly to the public what's what and who's who. The general principles of the question have already been explained in Lord Selborne's Federation Memorandum but the facts and the details constantly change and require to be explained.

Kerr was prepared to assume the editorial responsibilities, providing the others, particularly Curtis and Duncan, acted as a consultative committee.[34]

The kindergarten's belief in South African union had once been fervently held by Milner, but by mid-September 1907 he was embittered. Since his return to England he had remained largely aloof from domestic party warfare, and had viewed with a jaundiced eye the electoral victory of the Liberals in January 1906 and their decision to grant responsible government to the Transvaal and Orange River Colony. To him this meant the end of the Milnerian dream of a united British South Africa loyal to the empire. He believed that the British community, for their own sake, should cease to feel a responsibility to the mother country, and should instead attempt to consolidate and defend its own position in South Africa. He did not intend to cease his own criticisms of the Liberal government and its policies, but he told his young followers, 'it is one thing to condemn that policy ... [and] quite another for you over there to *waste your strength* upon it. For [you] have better work to do in making the best of your own position under the altered circumstances.'[35] By this time Milner's pessimism did not have the effect on the kindergarten that it might have had five or even three years earlier. They not believe that the cause of a united South Africa, self-governing and loyal to the empire, was lost. Their mentor's bitter advice was ignored.

34  Kerr to his family, Sept. 1907, ibid.
35  Milner to Robinson, 14 Sept. 1907, Dawson Papers; quoted in Nimocks, *Milner's Young Men*, 72-3; partly published in Wrench, *Geoffrey Dawson*, 58-60

Although to some extent engrossed in the work of the Indigency Commission, Curtis devoted most of his time in late 1907 and early 1908 to compiling and analysing material on the four colonial governments. By February 1908 he had begun drafting a lengthy study of South African government assisted as before by an editorial committee composed primarily of Duncan, Kerr, Brand, and William Marris,[36] a member of the Indian Civil Service on loan to the Transvaal government. As Curtis completed the draft it was circulated for criticism, then revised, printed, and recirculated in instalments for further analysis.[37] While these preparations were underway B.K. Long,[38] an associate of the kindergarten, performed a valuable service for the group by completing an analysis and comparison of the federal constitutions of the United States, Canada, Australia, Germany, and Switzerland. This work, entitled *The Framework of Union: A Comparison of Some Union Constitutions*, was published early in 1908 at a time when the kindergarten still believed federation to be the only possible form of government for a united South Africa.[39]

Their belief in federation was reflected in the early pages of the first instalments of Curtis's massive study *The Government of South Africa*, but rapidly changing conditions in South Africa necessitated a different emphasis in later instalments. By June 1908 the kindergarten, particularly Curtis, had become firm advocates of a unitary form of government for South Africa. It is possible that the kindergarten, on investigating more closely the merits of federation and unification, had become convinced of the superior merits of the unitary system; certainly Lionel Curtis later argued that this had been the case.[40] It is more probable, however, that the increased interest in union among Afrikaners and their growing preoccupation with a unitary rather than a federal form of government was the real reason for the kindergarten redirecting their arguments. For them the achievement of union was

36 William Sinclair Marris (1873-1945); born in New Zealand; joined Indian Civil Service 1895; services lent to Transvaal 1906-10; magistrate and collector, Aligarh, United Provinces 1910-12; acting secretary to government of India, Home Department, 1913-16; joint secretary to government of India 1917-19; home secretary, government of India 1919-21; governor of Assam 1921-2; governor of United Provinces 1922-8; member Council of India 1928-9; vice-chancellor, Durham University, 1932-4.

37 Curtis, *The Government of South Africa*, I, ix; also Robinson's diary, 29 Feb. and 31 March 1908, Dawson Papers, cited in Nimocks, *Milner's Young Men*, 98

38 Basil Kellet Long (1878-1944); South African news editor and legislator; elected to Cape parliament 1908; law adviser to National Convention 1908-10; member Union parliament 1910-13; dominions' editor *The Times* 1913-21; editor *Cape Times* and chief South African correspondent *The Times* 1921-35; member Union parliament 1938-43

39 Long, *The Framework of Union*. Curtis revealed Long's authorship in the preface to his *Government of South Africa*, xi

40 Curtis, *The Government of South Africa*, x-xi

imperative, and if Afrikaner support for union was more likely to be achieved by the adoption of a unitary system then the kindergarten were prepared to play their part and provide the necessary information and arguments.

The factors which had brought about a Boer willingness to support immediate unification were the victories of the Orangie Unie party in the Orange River Colony in November 1907 and the triumph of Merriman and his South Africa party at the Cape. Thus, by early 1908 the Afrikaners were politically dominant in the Transvaal, the Orange River Colony, and the Cape, and no longer had any fears of a British directed or controlled union. The crucial government decision to form a united South Africa was taken on 4 May 1908 at a meeting of the intercolonial conference assembled to discuss rail and customs problems. On the initiative of Smuts and Merriman, the two principal architects of South African union, the conference, representative of all four self-governing colonies, adopted resolutions favouring closer union and an early meeting of a National Convention to thrash out a constitution. It was ultimately decided to hold the first meeting of the convention on 12 October in Durban.

Ever since January 1907 Curtis had remained in touch with Smuts who had always taken an interest in the activities of the kindergarten. The antipathy between the group and the Boer leader has been much exaggerated, although it would be equally wrong to over-emphasize the degree of influence of Curtis and his friends. Whatever the precise nature of the relationship the kindergarten kept in close contact, and by mid-March 1908 Curtis could write to a London friend that 'we find the Transvaal Government reaching out their hands for our results. We are helping them in every way and as our diagrams and tables are produced, copies of them are sent to Smuts.' He hoped that the conference in May would result, 'if things go right,' in the appointment of an Inter-Colonial Commission to enquire into the whole question of South African union. Curtis believed that 'the publication of our book with all the mass of data we have collected appended to it, will naturally give an impetus in that direction and therefore we are all straining every nerve to get the book ready for publication in some form or other in the course of May.'[41] By early June 1908 the kindergarten had managed to publish the first two instalments and the edition had been sold within a few days.[42] Three more instalments followed during the next three months and

41 Curtis to 'Rob' (R.M.H.), 16 March 1908, box 1, Jebb Papers
42 Curtis to Jebb, 13 June 1908, ibid. In order that the book might reach a wide reading public in South Africa as well as those in a position of power and influence it was decided to sell it at the very low price of 10s, a sum which barely covered the cost of printing and binding.

all were finally published in two volumes in early October. Shortly before the convention opened Curtis told his English friend Richard Jebb that 'the book is finished...and will be distributed amongst the delegates on Saturday night. They have had the provisional edition long ago of course...we resolved to start on this wild campaign just two years and a month ago...I scarcely dreamed that the movement could make so much progress in so little time. But the grass was very dry and the flames ran the moment the match was dropped into it...I am satisfied that our work has greatly advanced the movement. Without it the convention would simply have had to adjourn for want of information.'[43]

Curtis's assessment of kindergarten usefulness was somewhat overdone. The problem of union had long been a primary concern of Smuts and Merriman, and certainly enough work had been done by Smuts before the convention to have ensured that it would not have had to adjourn for lack of material. Nevertheless, the kindergarten's role was important. The information and raw material gathered by Curtis and others over the months proved most valuable to the delegates in general and to Smuts in particular; perhaps even more important than *The Government of South Africa* which contained a strongly argued case for closer union and, after the opening pages, for a unitary form of government. That book was not the objective compilation and analysis projected in January 1907, but then Lionel Curtis was incapable of abstracting his own ideas and convictions from his work. No doubt he believed the book to be objective, and was probably not aware of how obviously propagandist it was. *The Government of South Africa* was the second, *The Selborne Memorandum* being the first, of a number of supposedly objective studies written by Curtis which when finished were simply propagandist pieces; lucid, well-written, and strongly argued all of them, but nevertheless exhortive in tone and limited in argument and the use of evidence.

Another facet of kindergarten influence in late 1908 and early 1909 was the part played by Robert Brand and Patrick Duncan. From late August until the assembling of the convention in Durban, Brand was attached to Smuts as a personal assistant. During those six weeks the two men, aided by

This was made possible by taking up the old Rhodes Trust offer of £1000 which the kindergarten had rejected early in 1907. As Curtis explained to Milner late in October 1908: 'it would have been a tremendous drag on us if we had to raise the whole sum of the money required for the printing of 'The Government of South Africa' as [sic] a time when we wanted to appeal for fighting funds for the movement as a whole.' Curtis to Milner, 31 Oct. 1908, box 77, Milner Papers

43 Curtis to Jebb, 30 Sept. 1908, box 1, Jebb Papers

one or two others from outside the kindergarten, worked feverishly to prepare a draft constitution for consideration in Durban. The ideas and essential drafting were Smuts's but Brand was able to advise, criticise, and supply information. His influence is unquestioned and his kindergarten experience was of great help to him. It was probably through Brand that the kindergarten kept in touch with Smuts in following months. Patrick Duncan, recently returned from England, joined the Smuts's camp as a full-time legal adviser to the Transvaal delegation shortly before the convention and remained in that capacity until union was agreed upon in May 1909. Through them the kindergarten had a personal bridge to the inner councils and undoubtedly it was fully used.[44]

Throughout most of 1908 and early 1909 the kindergarten were instrumental in the organisation of closer union societies throughout the four colonies. The idea of forming public groups in all the colonies to disseminate information about union had first been broached by the kindergarten early in 1907, but at the time had been abandoned as unfeasible. With the drafting of *The Government of South Africa* well in hand and all the major Boer leaders committed to union by early 1908, it was decided to go ahead with the original scheme.[45] The first Closer Union Society was successfully founded in Cape Town in May 1908 and was followed within the month by the creation of one at Johannesburg. Curtis was pleased with the results and hoped that a strong national executive could soon be formed to co-ordinate activities throughout the colonies.[46] This did not materialize until October when representatives of the eleven existing groups met in Durban to elect a central executive. W.P. Schreiner[47] was elected president. In following months, with *The Government of South Africa* completed, Curtis travelled extensively in the four colonies in his capacity as honorary secretary of the Closer Union Societies, and when the first annual meeting was held in March 1909 there existed sixty groups throughout South Africa. Much of this success was due to the unrelenting hard work and sense of mission of Curtis, ably assisted by other members of the kindergarten. Only through their organisational skills and persistent persuasion were so many in South Africa awakened to the urgent need for discussion about closer union. Despite their controlling in-

44  For a detailed treatment of the influence of Brand and Duncan on Smuts and the convention see Thompson, *Unification of South Africa*, 157-80.
45  Curtis to 'Rob' (R.M.H.), 16 March 1908, box 1, Jebb Papers
46  Curtis to Jebb, 13 June 1908, ibid.
47  William Philip Schreiner (1857-1919) supported Rhodes before the Jameson Raid; after, he became a leader of the Afrikaner Bond; prime minister, Cape Colony 1898-1900; senator after Union; high commissioner to London 1914-19

fluence the kindergarten shunned the limelight and did their best to ensure that a broad cross-section of the South African public held positions of authority in the groups. At all times Curtis attempted to ensure that the Closer Union Societies would be bipartisan in composition and in this he and the kindergarten were generally successful. At the national level many Afrikaners were active in the executive while others were prominent in the local societies. Despite this attempt to secure an equality within the organisation, it is probably true that the Closer Union Societies had more impact on the British than on the Boer community. But the societies did stimulate a general awareness of the problems and issues involved and acquainted many throughout the four colonies with possible solutions. All in all their impact was considerable.

In conjunction with the formation of the Closer Union Societies the kindergarten also founded a periodical, thus implementing another idea mooted since early 1907. Stimulated by Curtis and under the editorship of Philip Kerr, *The State* made its first appearance just before Christmas 1908. It was devoted almost entirely to the movement for closer union, although it did carry a considerable number of articles on external matters as well as essays, short stories, and poetry. *The State*, a monthly publication, remained under Kerr's direction until June 1909 when for all intents and purposes the kindergarten's mission and that of *The State* were accomplished. Kerr then returned to England with Brand, sailing on 30 June with the delegates from the four colonies who were going to London to see the Union bill through parliament. *The State* was then edited by B.K. Long until publication ceased in 1912. Although it was described as 'rather stodgy,'[48] it attracted a considerable number of influential writers among them H.A.L. Fisher, Curzon, Selborne, and Herbert Baker,[49] and aroused much interest within South Africa. As Kerr pointed out to Milner on sending him a copy of the first number: 'It is a fair indication of the time ... to find Botha, Smuts and Farrar, Abraham Fischer and Moor, and Merriman, Malan and Jameson writing letters to a bilingual paper, edited by an Englishman, urging their own supporters to buy it ... It looks like the beginning of the end of racialism when Het Volk & the Bond allow an 'alien' newspaper to reach their followers.'[50]

48  L. Phillips to Jebb, 11 Jan. 1909, box 3, Jebb Papers
49  Herbert Baker (1862-1946); architect; arrived in South Africa 1892 and restored 'Groote Schuur'; designed Union Buildings in Pretoria; left South Africa 1913; designed the new city of Delhi and the new Bank of England building in London; later knighted
50  Kerr to Milner, 22 Dec. 1908, box 77, Milner Papers; see also Butler, *Lothian*, 32-3. Abraham Fischer (1850-1913); a founder and the first president of Orangie Unie; prime minister of the Orange River Colony 1907-10. Sir Frederick Robert Moor (1853-1927) was prime minister of Natal 1906-10.

*The State* was published in both English and Dutch and sold well in both languages at the low price of 6d a copy, made possible by the generosity of Bailey who contributed £3000 and of Lord Selborne who contributed £2000 originally made over to him by Lord Salisbury.[51] The ideas of the societies were also promoted in newspapers and pamphlets and, of course, in papers read at society meetings.

In February 1909 the National Convention ended with the publication of a draft constitution, and the kindergarten immediately published a 'Special Constitutional Number' of *The State* containing the complete text of the draft, an analysis of it by Patrick Duncan, and an article on proportional representation by Brand. The kindergarten generally favoured the draft constitution. In accordance with decisions made at the opening meeting of the Closer Union Societies the previous October, a general convention of the societies met in Johannesburg in early March 1909 to consider the draft constitution and to reach a decision on policy. Delegates from all fifty-three groups attended the session which was organized and closely supervised by the kindergarten. After three days of lively and often-times critical debate the convention unanimously endorsed the draft constitution and recommended its adoption by the four colonial governments. After some disagreement among the four colonies at the third National Convention in May and June, the amended draft constitution was finally approved by the legislatures of all the colonies. In August the Imperial Parliament gave its approval to the South Africa Act, and on 31 May 1910, on the eighth anniversary of the Treaty of Vereeniging, the Union of South Africa came into being.

When the Imperial Parliament passed the South Africa Act in 1909 it was only three years since Milner's kindergarten had decided to work for South African union and only two years since the publication of the Selborne Memorandum. When they had originally become involved the kindergarten had envisaged a fierce and difficult battle before their goal was won; but they soon discovered that there existed a strong belief in union among the leading Boer politicians. Very quickly the kindergarten realised that their role would be to provide information and to stimulate interest and awareness; to become, in effect, the public relations officers of union. The initiative, the stimulus, and the bone-wearying negotiations and drafting would be out of their hands.

In later years the kindergarten were inclined to over-emphasize their role in the closer union movement. This was not a malicious or self-justifying act on their part; undoubtedly they came to believe in the vital importance of their own work. But their memories were playing them false; for though it

51  Curtis, 'Essays in Construction'

would be difficult to imagine union being achieved in quite the same way without the kindergarten, it would unquestionably have been achieved. It is here that we perhaps have a clue to the later misfortunes of the Round Table movement. Their experiences in South Africa convinced the kindergarten that the same methods of organisation and the same propaganda techniques would be sufficient to bring about imperial union. They forgot, however, that no strong undercurrent of opinion in favour of union existed in the empire as it had in South Africa. The success of the closer union movement in South Africa blinded the kindergarten to some of the basic realities of that success. It had been too easy for them there; they were riding with the current in South Africa. On the imperial stage it was quite different; they were usually battling against the current rather than moving easily with it, and too often consulting men in the dominions who were not always the best reflectors of dominion attitudes toward the imperial relationship. Nevertheless, their years in South Africa were of crucial importance for the kindergarten. They had become fast friends drawn together in their work and their mission. They had benefitted enormously from their experiences and responsibilities and had gained confidence in themselves and in their ideas. They left South Africa dedicated to each other, believing that together they had made a valuable and positive contribution to the achievement of South African union. Together they thought they could achieve more significant results in the imperial sphere.

The imperial problem had begun to bulk large in many kindergarten minds long before their South African sojourn was over. Curtis, Kerr, and Robinson had all expressed ideas on the subject to Milner by late 1908, and early in 1909 meetings had been held in South Africa to consider founding an organisation to deal with the wider problem. The degree of attention paid to imperial defence in *The State* in 1909 reflected this new interest. The kindergarten thus left South Africa convinced of the merits of organized propaganda and behind-the-scenes discussion and of the need to work for the preservation of the unity of the empire and the clarification of imperial citizenship. For the rest of their lives the empire-commonwealth was to be a continuing concern for all of them.

# 3
# The movement is formed

In considering the founding of the Round Table movement developments and activities in both Britain and South Africa must be held in balance. In Great Britain Milner and Leo Amery pursued, quite independent of the kindergarten, the goal of closer union of the empire through such organisations as the Coefficients and the Compatriots and by means of speeches, personal persuasion, articles, and correspondence. In South Africa the kindergarten became increasingly preoccupied with the imperial implications of South African union and began discussing the formation of an organisation to achieve a wider integration. By late 1908 the two groups were in touch, and from then on worked closely together.

Although disillusioned when he returned to England in 1905 and rebuked by the Commons, Milner was soon involved in closer union activities. He became president of the Compatriots, a group formed late in 1904 by Leo Amery for the discussion of imperial affairs and the advocacy of imperial union. He immersed himself in the details of the Rhodes Trust of which he was an early trustee, and he was concerned in a financial and to some extent a political capacity with the Pollock Committee, a body devoted to making changes in imperial organisation. Throughout 1906 he dined often with the Coefficients, a group formed by Sydney and Beatrice Webb for the discussion of social and imperial problems, the Compatriots, and the Pollock Committee, and had numerous discussions with Amery and Jameson about the state of the empire. By early 1907, he was giving some consideration to starting imperial study groups in South Africa,[1] and was also instrumental, in conjunction with Earl Grey,[2] the governor general of Canada, in securing £1000 from Rhodes Trust funds to enable Stephen Leacock,[3] the Canadian political scientist and humorist, to travel extensively in Australasia, South Africa, and Canada 'as an Imperial missionary.'[4] Milner soon concentrated his energies on the approaching Colonial Conference, and shortly before the conference opened he published an article in *The National Review* entitled 'Some Reflections on the Coming Conference' in which he defined his attitude toward closer union.[5]

While the conference was in session Milner took every opportunity to meet the visiting premiers and invited two of them, Jameson and Deakin,[6] to dine with the Compatriots. He was particularly anxious to secure Deakin's presence and wrote at length to the Australian, explaining that the club comprised 'the most active and forward of the younger "Imperialists," the people who believe in a frank partnership of the several States of the Empire.' The object of the meeting would be an exchange of views and the establishment of personal relations which might make subsequent co-operation possible. 'For my own part I feel acutely the want of touch. So many things go wrong for lack of it, wh. might be prevented. It seems to me that there is a very much greater amount of agreement, both here & in "the Colonies," among thinking men, with reference to the better organisation of the Empire, than many people imagine. But for want of any proper means of regular communication & cooperation we are all helpless, & the worn-out-old machine creaks

1 J.P. Fitzpatrick to Milner, 11 Jan. 1907, box 45, Milner Papers
2 Albert Henry George Grey, 4th Earl (1851-1917); MP (L) 1880-6; administrator of Rhodesia 1896-7; director of the British South Africa Co 1898-1904; governor-general of Canada 1904-11; an original Rhodes trustee
3 Stephen Butler Leacock (1869-1944); on staff Upper Canada College 1891-9; on staff McGill University 1901-36; head of the Department of Economics 1908-36
4 Grey to Milner, 16 Feb. 1907, box 193, Milner Papers; Grey to Dr Peterson, 25 March 1907, box 173; Grey to Hawkesly, 9 April 1907, box 210; Grey to Leacock, 18 April 1907, copy, box 173; Grey to Lady Northcliffe, undated, vol. 24, Grey Papers. In addition he had a number of discussions about imperial organisation, attended two rather unsatisfactory meetings of the Pollock Committee in February, and dined twice with the Compatriots in February and March. Milner diary, 4, 14, and 22 Feb. and 22 March 1907, vol. 270, Milner Papers
5 Milner, 'Some Reflections on the Coming Conference', *The National Review*, April 1907, 193-206
6 Alfred Deakin (1856-1919); Australian statesman; represented Victoria at the Colonial Conference 1887; instrumental in achievement of Australian federation; attorney-general in first Australian government 1901-3; prime minister of Australia 1903-4; 1905-8; and 1909-10

along. We get the same old muddles every time – New Hebrides is only the latest instance – & finally the whole thing will go to pieces, *when nobody really wants it to*, for need of forethought and timely statesmanship.'[7]

Both Jameson and Deakin ultimately dined with the Compatriots on 26 April. About 120 members attended and Deakin and Patrick Duncan, home on leave from South Africa, were both seated at Milner's table.[8] Six days later Milner and Deakin had a long private conversation, but apart from these meetings there appears to have been no attempt on the part of Milner to influence Deakin's attitude and arguments at the Colonial Conference.[9]

The conference was a disappointment to Milner. The efforts of Deakin, Jameson, and Joseph Ward,[10] the New Zealand premier, to streamline the conference system by establishing a secretariat free from Colonial Office control met with limited success. Their fellow premiers, Laurier of Canada and Botha of the Transvaal, and the British government would only agree to the creation of a secretariat within the Colonial Office, manned by Colonial Office staff and under the aegis of the colonial secretary. Their efforts to separate dominion from crown colony business suffered a similar fate. The Colonial Office was simply divided into sub-departments; one, a dominions department, was placed under the supervision of an assistant under-secretary. The 1907 conference thus resulted in a change in form but not in substance, and as far as the dominions were concerned the Colonial Office remained the linchpin in the imperial structure. It was not a very satisfactory state of affairs, and in following years imperial organisation became the subject of a heated controversy in Great Britain and the dominions. Milner, Amery, and the Round Table movement were soon intimately involved.

Until this time Leo Amery had been preoccupied with *The Times History of the War*, but just before the conference he wrote a series of penetrating articles on the conference system for *The Times*. A few days after the sessions ended, and shortly before Deakin departed for home, he wrote an effusive letter to the Australian, claiming that the premier had given all imperialists a great moral lift and urged him to revisit England as soon as possible. He even suggested that Deakin might do the most good for the Unionist party, 'the imperial party,' by returning to England as its leader.[11] Two months later he

7  Milner to Deakin, 25 Feb. 1907, MSS 1540, Deakin Papers
8  Milner diary, 26 April 1907, vol. 270, Milner Papers
9  Milner diary, 2 May 1907, ibid.
10 Sir Joseph George Ward (1856-1930); New Zealand statesman; entered national politics 1890; member of Balance and Seddon cabinets 1891-1906; prime minister 1906-12 and 1928-30; deputy prime minister 1915-19
11 Amery to Deakin, 19 May 1907, MSS1540, Deakin Papers

Leo Amery in 1911

forwarded copies of the Selborne Memorandum to Deakin and Arthur Jose,[12] *The Times* correspondent in Australia, and to George Denison[13] and Earl Grey in Canada with the comment that 'It is really an extraordinarily good document and one which mutatis mutandis applies to no small extent to the Empire as a whole. I am sure the more we can induce people all over the Empire to read works bearing on Federal problems such as this memorandum and Oliver's Hamilton the greater our hopes of success at future Conferences.'[14]

By September Milner and Amery had arranged to work together in an effort to effect changes in imperial organisation. In return for £300 a quarter Amery agreed to involve himself in a general way in imperial affairs but specifically in preparations for the next imperial conference.[15] He hoped to do 'privately and personally what the Secretariat would have done officially and regularly'; to do what he could by correspondence and personal contact to achieve more positive results at the next conference. His first problem was to determine the best issues to promote. For instance, 'what is the right line to pursue towards the new organisation in the C.O. Should we go on pressing to get the 'Secretariat' enlarged & made more independent, or would it not now be better to concentrate on the "Dominion Deptmt" ... insist on getting a second permanent-under secretary, & not merely an assistant under-secretary like Lucas, as the head of it, & wait for a change of Govt, when the whole department could be lifted clear out of the C.O. & transferred to the Prime Minister. That would meet one set of our needs – the clear separation of the affairs of the constituent states from those of the dependencies. The other, the consultative, could be met by regular meetings between the High Commissioners, & (to begin with) the Colonial Sec, or Under-Sec but later I hope a special Minister attached to the Prime Minister (a sort of under Prime Minister) as Secretary for Imperial affairs, who would be to the P.M. what the High Commissioners are to their P.M.'s.'[16]

With these ideas whirling in his mind Amery left for South Africa, partly to recuperate from a serious operation, but primarily to establish Com-

12  Arthur Wilberforce Jose (1863-1934); historian and journalist; assistant professor of modern literature University of Sydney 1893-9; *The Times* correspondent in Australia 1904-15; editor of *The Australian Encyclopedia* 1919-27
13  George Taylor Denison (1839-1925); soldier and author; helped found 'Canada First' movement in 1868; senior police magistrate of Toronto 1877-1923; leading Canadian figure in the imperial federation movement
14  Amery to Jose, 15 July 1907, Jose Papers; Amery to Grey, 15 July 1907, box 173, Grey Papers. In a letter to George Denison, Amery said: 'It is interesting to see the influence of Oliver's book on the writer.' Amery to Denison, 15 July 1907, vol. 12, Denison Papers
15  Amery to Milner, 30 March 1908, box 193, Milner Papers
16  Amery to Deakin, 29 Aug. 1907, MSS 1540, Deakin Papers

patriot groups in that country in order to further discussion of imperial affairs.[17] His trip was inspired by Milner and paid for out of Rhodes Trust funds and was a great success. With the assistance of Jameson a flourishing Compatriots group was soon established in Johannesburg. Robert Brand became a member, and with Robinson kept Milner well informed of the group's activities. A few months later Amery urged Arthur Jose to found a similar group in Sydney.[18] By establishing overseas branches of the Compatriots, Amery hoped 'gradually to create a real brotherhood of those interested in Imperial unity all over the Empire. Such an organisation though very loose might yet prove immensely useful at every great crisis (especially if it enclosed all the most able people who can be got together) or during the time of a Conference when opinion required moulding.'[19]

Amery's principal concern on arriving back in England in March 1908 was to raise enough money to allow Halford Mackinder,[20] the eminent geographer, to go into politics and join in the imperial secretariat work. His efforts were soon successful, and that summer Mackinder joined Amery as virtually a full-time imperial missionary under the general direction of Milner.[21] Milner himself continued to meet often with Amery and others such as Fabian Ware,[22] Richard Jebb,[23] and E.B. Sargant[24] to discuss imperial questions,[25] and acquired the assistance of Arthur Steel-Maitland[26] as a political private secretary.[27] One of Steel-Maitland's first tasks was to make arrangements for Milner to tour Canada late in the year. With the assistance of Ar-

17  Amery to Grey, 22 Sept. 1907, box 173, Grey Papers
18  Amery to Jose, 27 March 1908, Jose Papers
19  Amery to Deakin, 12 Jan. 1908, MSS 1540, Deakin Papers
20  Halford Mackinder (1861-1947); geographer; director of the London School of Economics and Political Science 1903-8; MP (U) 1910-22; member of several government committees and royal commissions; knighted 1920
21  Amery to Milner, 4 April 1908, box 194, Milner Papers; H.J. Mackinder to Amery, 22 May 1908, box 193, ibid.
22  Fabian Ware (1869-1949); assistant director of education, Transvaal 1901; director of education, Transvaal 1903-5; editor of the *Morning Post* 1905-11; founder Imperial War Graves Commission, vice chairman 1917-48
23  Richard Jebb (1874-1953); publicist; a leading analyst of the empire-commonwealth; travelled in Egypt, North America, Australia, New Zealand, Japan, India 1897-1901; travelled in Canada, Australia, South Africa 1906, West Indies 1909; a tariff reformer; among his publications were *Studies in Colonial Nationalism* (1905); *The Imperial Conference* (1911).
24  E.B. Sargant had served in South Africa as an adviser to Milner on education matters.
25  Milner diary, 2 and 3 April; 6, 14, 22, 28, and 29 May 1908, vol. 271, Milner Papers
26  Arthur Steel-Maitland (1876-1935); MP (C) 1910-35; chairman of the Unionist party 1911; parliamentary under-secretary for the colonies 1915-17; minister of labour 1924-9; 1st baronet, created 1917
27  Milner diary, 27 May 1908, vol. 271, Milner Papers

thur Glazebrook,[28] a Toronto broker and an old friend of Milner's, an itinerary was quickly arranged and the sailing date fixed for the autumn.[29] Before leaving Milner had a number of meetings with Perry, Hichens, Kerr, and Robinson, all home on leave, and as always with Amery.[30] One such encounter with Amery resulted in the conviction that it would be essential for the next conference 'to make a really decided move on the constitutional question in the direction of exchanging colonial subordination for Imperial coordination.' The one feasible proposal Amery and Milner agreed upon was the definite removal of all the work dealing with the self-governing colonies from the Colonial Office and the establishment of a new imperial office to handle it. The new office would be responsible to all the self-governing states of the empire. Amery thought the scheme 'far reaching ... and at the same time simple':

If the new Imperial Office were really started in 1911, and run by the right sort of person, e.g. Milner, for three or four years, and a good class of high Commissioners over here, whose interviews with the Imperial Office would gradually develop into an informal weekly or fortnightly sub-Conference, things might be ripe by 1915 for the Imperial Conference to take over the control of the India Office, Crown Colonies and Foreign Office ... it might be possible by 1915 to develop a department which would effectively direct the general line of Imperial defensive policy, while leaving the actual administrative control of the various land and sea forces to the different states.[31]

These were heady ideas, and Milner left for Canada on 11 September still very much attracted by them and determined to do all he could to further them. He was in Canada until 6 November and during that time gave

28 Arthur James Glazebrook (1859-1940); publicist; born in London; educated at Haileybury; went to Canada 1873; with Bank of North America 1883-1900; exchange broker in Toronto 1900-34
29 In July Steel-Maitland wrote to Professor Hugh Egerton requesting information about books on 'The present position of Canada, both internally as determined by its historical and political development, and by existing racial and religious conditions, and externally, as determined by the neighbourhood of Canada to U.S.A., to Asiatic countries, and its relations to other foreign nations. The probable course of future development. That is to say the increase of power and population, its composition, industrial and agricultural, its geographical distribution, and lastly the racial development including that of the existing peoples and the type of future immigration.' The reason Milner wanted the information, said Steel-Maitland, 'is in its bearing on the Imperial question generally and especially on the question of political evolution, (Federation alternatives), Defence, and the fiscal question.' Steel-Maitland to Egerton, 29 July 1908, copy, Steel-Maitland Papers. See also Fabian Ware to Willison, 13 June 1908, Willison Papers.
30 Milner diary, 24, 27, 29, and 31 July and 5 and 6 Aug. 1908, vol. 271, Milner Papers
31 Amery to Deakin, 7 Aug. 1908, MSS 1540, Deakin Papers

speeches to the Canadian clubs in Vancouver, Winnipeg, Toronto, Ottawa, and Montreal and to the Board of Trade in Montreal.[32] All his speeches dealt with various aspects of imperial union and the benefits which could arise from it. Canadians had rarely heard such a detailed and passionate statement of the 'new imperialism.' Shortly after his arrival he explained that he did not wish to make numerous speeches or to give the impression that he had come to lecture the people of Canada. He had come 'to learn and not to preach.'[33] However, some of Milner's friends in Canada, particularly Glazebrook, believed that Milner should 'preach,' and to as many people as possible. Arrangements were therefore made with Sir Edmund Walker,[34] the president of the Canadian Bank of Commerce, to supply Milner and Steel-Maitland with letters of introduction to many of the bank's managers in Western Canada.[35] Naturally, Milner found this assistance invaluable for gathering information. But it did not give him access to the sort of opinion that he should have been tapping nor did it reach very deeply into the cross-sections of Canadian life. This was a continual failing of British imperialists, not least of the future Round Table movement. They were too inclined to talk with men who shared their own views and to listen only to what they wanted to hear. Many never appreciated the difference in assumptions and attitudes between Great Britain and the dominions.[36]

Glazebrook's reaction to Milner's tour was all too typical of what many Englishmen assumed to be the norm. Glazebrook, of course, had thought the trip 'an absolute success': 'What was so completely satisfactory to me was that he seemed to have left behind him in England all the slightly pessimistic vein, which would not have been popular or useful in this country, but at the same time he did not hesitate to say certain things of a more or less critical description ... in Toronto ... he struck a new note, the note of earnestness and simplicity and freedom from cant. His remark for instance that when he thought about the Empire he did not feel very much like waving the flag or singing "Rule Britannia" but rather that he would like to go off into a corner and pray, fairly lifted the house ...'[37]

---

32 For the texts of the speeches see Milner, *The Nation and the Empire*, 302-65.
33 Milner to Denison, 20 Sept. 1908, copy, box 169, Milner Papers
34 Sir Byron Edmund Walker (1848-1924); president, Canadian Bank of Commerce 1907-24; chairman, board of governors, University of Toronto 1910-23; elected Chancellor, University of Toronto 1923
35 Walker to H.V.F. Jones, 11 Nov. 1908, copy, Walker Papers
36 Beloff, *Imperial Sunset*, I, 39
37 Glazebrook to Jebb, 2 Nov. 1908, copy, box 2, Jebb Papers

In addition to speech-making two other matters preoccupied Milner's last days in Canada. The first was a discussion of imperial organisation with Governor General Earl Grey. Grey was much attracted to the idea of an imperial office or dominions house and he agreed to approach Laurier on the matter at an appropriate time in the future.[38] The second diversion was Milner's involvement in the formation of a small club in Toronto for the discussion of Canadian and imperial affairs. The organisers were Glazebrook and Ernest Du Vernet,[39] a prominent Toronto lawyer, and on their invitation Milner and Steel-Maitland met twice with future members, among whom were Professors Kylie[40] and Feiling[41] of the history department, University of Toronto, and John Willison, the editor of the Toronto *News*.[42]

Although Milner wrote to Glazebrook almost immediately after leaving Toronto offering advice about the club, it was Steel-Maitland who kept in touch in following months. Glazebrook was soon bubbling with ideas, and even Du Vernet, usually a man of lesser commitment, was 'really enthusiastically interested.'[43] Plans were also made to start a Montreal branch, but Glazebrook thought it wise to delay its organisation until it was seen how the Toronto experiment worked.[44] It was just as well, for the club's activities languished early in the New Year due to the illness of both Glazebrook and Du Vernet, and it was not until February that Glazebrook felt able to push matters once more.[45] Although a correspondence was opened between the club and Geoffrey Robinson in South Africa and a few meetings were held, the club failed to become the centre of discussion that both Milner and Glazebrook had envisaged.[46] But it was useful in that a number of men were

---

38 For an elaboration of this aspect of Milner's trip see Kendle, *Conferences*, chap. VII.
39 I have not been able to get any further information on Ernest Du Vernet.
40 Edward Joseph Kylie (1880-1916); historian; educated University of Toronto and Balliol College, Oxford; lecturer 1904-8 and assistant professor 1908-15 in history, University of Toronto; in 1915 appointed adjutant of the 147th Battalion, Canadian Expeditionary Force
41 Keith Feiling (1884-    ); knighted 1958; lecturer University of Toronto 1907-9; lecturer Christ Church, Oxford 1909; student and tutor 1911-46; Chichele Professor of Modern History, Oxford, 1946-50; emeritus professor 1950-
42 Milner diary, 24 and 26 Oct. 1908, vol. 271, Milner Papers. John Stephen Willison (1856-1927); journalist and author; knighted 1913; editor-in-chief Toronto *Globe* 1890-1902; editor of the Toronto *News* 1902-10; Canadian correspondent of *The Times* 1910-27; a Liberal to 1902, he then began supporting the Conservatives.
43 Glazebrook to Milner, 18 Nov. 1908, box 169, Milner Papers. Grey to Laurier, 31 Dec. 1908 and Laurier to Grey, 31 Dec. 1908, box 251, Grey Papers; also Grey to Steel-Maitland, 11 Jan. 1909, Steel-Maitland Papers
44 Glazebrook to Steel-Maitland,6 Jan. 1909, Steel-Maitland Papers
45 Glazebrook to Steel-Maitland, 26 Jan. 1909, ibid.
46 Steel-Maitland to Glazebrook, 20 Feb. 1909, ibid.

brought together by imperial concerns who later on were to be a convenient nucleus for the central Round Table group in Canada.

As for Milner, he summed up his experiences in the northern dominion in a way that indicated how little rather than how much he had learned. Instead of forcing him to reappraise his ideas his trip seemed to have had little affect.

As between the 3 possibilities of the future 1. Closer Imperial Union 2. Union with the U.S. and 3. Independence, I believe definitely that No. 2 is the real danger. I do not think the Canadians themselves are aware of it . . . they are wonderfully immature in political reflection on the big issues, and hardly realise how powerful the influences are . . . On the other hand, I see little danger to ultimate imperial unity in Canadian 'nationalism.' On the contrary I think the very same sentiments, wh. make a great many especially of the younger Canadians vigorously, and even bumptiously, assertive of their independence, proud and boastful of the greatness and future of their country, and so forth, would lend themselves, tactfully handled, to an enthusiastic acceptance of Imperial unity on the basis of 'partner-states.' This tendency is, therefore, in my opinion rather to be encouraged, not only as safeguard against 'Americanisation,' but as actually making, in the long run, for a Union of 'all the Britains.' It is obvious that Canada could play a far greater role, and have a more important and more distinctive proposition, in such a political structure, than she can ever have in a purely North American Union.[47]

Despite all their efforts in the previous three years Milner and Amery had not succeeded by late 1908 either in establishing a viable empire-wide organisation to suit their needs – although beginnings had been made in South Africa and Canada – or in influencing the reorganisation of the imperial structure. Part of the explanation was simply a lack of numbers. Stephen Leacock, Fabian Ware, Halford Mackinder, Arthur Jose, and Arthur Steel-Maitland had all been useful in their various ways, but were a poor substitute for a dedicated like-thinking group such as the kindergarten. But throughout these years the kindergarten had been preoccupied with South African affairs, and though contact between themselves and Milner and Amery had

---

47 Milner to J.S. Sanders, 2 Jan. 1909, copy, ibid. See also his remark to Curtis: 'I am more than ever impressed, after my visit to Canada, by the fact that the only real and permanent tie of Empire is race. I do not mean for a moment that we should try, or can expect, to make all the great self-governing States of the Empire "British", but without a strong and enduring British leaven, a large mass of the population to whom British traditions, British history, and the British language are dear, it is impossible permanently to retain any great white community in political connection with the mother country.' Milner to Curtis, 1 Dec. 1908, Curtis Papers

been continuous it had never been developed. This state of affairs soon changed.

On returning to England early in November Milner found a letter awaiting him from Lionel Curtis in which Curtis stated an interest in working towards a solution of 'the imperial problem.'[48] From then on the activities of Milner and Amery and those of the kindergarten in South Africa gradually merged as the young administrators became more concerned with imperial affairs.

Their interest in the wider question had been stimulated by the approach of union in South Africa. For the first time they had been forced to come to grips with the problem of South Africa's relationship to Great Britain. They had realised that owing to the lack of a national government South Africa had had to let Great Britain make decisions in the areas of defence and foreign policy that a nation should make for itself. Union would now make such action possible, and public men in South Africa were beginning to ask what policies would be best. The kindergarten did not believe that a proper solution to either the South African or the imperial problem would emerge unless all the dominion leaders had 'a definite conception of their future relations with the other constituent parts of the Empire.'[49]

As far as Curtis was concerned it was becoming increasingly apparent that Great Britain and the dominion 'must come to some definite business arrangement for the support and control of Imperial defence and foreign policy or the Empire must break up ...' It had to be brought home to the dominions that the mother country could not continue to bear the brunt of defence expenditure, and Great Britain would have to be persuaded that any financial support toward imperial defence worth having from the dominions would have to be accompanied by a corresponding measure of control over defence and foreign policy. Although wearied by his exertions of the past two years, Curtis was prepared to throw what strength and experience he had into 'the Imperial problem.' He was convinced that the best way to achieve this was as a South African colonist, 'because it is better that those who can should push the Imperial cause from the colonies. There are men enough like Jebb and Amery to push it from England.'[50]

48 Curtis to Milner, 31 Oct. 1908, box 77, Milner Papers
49 Much of this early discussion and reasoning by the kindergarten in South Africa was summarised in 'Memorandum of conversations which took place between a few English and South African friends at intervals during the summer of 1909,' GD40/17/11, Lothian Papers.
50 Curtis to Milner, 31 Oct. 1908, box 77, Milner Papers. Another interesting development at this time was Abe Bailey's offer to pay all Alfred Deakin's expenses if he would 'take up deliberately the role of apostle of Closer Union in the Empire' and tour the dominions, In-

The idea of having Curtis working for imperial union pleased Milner, and he quickly assured his young protege that there was much to be done. Although it might be impossible to see the outcome at the moment, there could be no doubt that there was 'no other political object of anything like equal importance'; it was 'for all Britons the great political question of the next twenty years.' Milner believed that the great difficulty would be to keep in touch with all the outlying dominions and he looked forward to having Curtis's help.[51]

Encouraged by this reply Curtis and the kindergarten discussed the matter at great length during the next few months.[52] Eager to put their recent knowledge and experience to work, they drew up a detailed proposal based on their South African experiences. In March 1909 Curtis forwarded it to Amery and Milner for consideration.[53] Comprehensive and carefully thought out, the proposal revealed both the strength and weakness of the new movement. The sincerity and concern behind the plan could not be questioned, but it also suggested a self-confidence bordering on arrogance that ultimately could only be self-deceptive. Men and institutions were to be used for imperial ends, and the suggestion was implicit throughout that they were willing to be used. No thought was given to the idea that not everyone in the dominions would share the movement's assumptions or reach the same conclusions. Their cause seemed so important and so obviously right that they questioned neither it nor their methods. The fact that Lionel Curtis drafted the proposal might account for this pervasive tone. He was all too apt to become mesmerised by his own brand of logic.

Curtis indicated that he was prepared, if it seemed desirable, to visit the other dominions 'as a sort of prospector'; the other members of the kindergarten were willing to act once more as an editorial committee and, in conjunction with friends in England, to draft 'a statement of the Imperial problem' for evaluation and criticism. Once such a statement had been prepared and more or less agreed to by those at the centre of the movement, the various people throughout the empire who were known to favour the pres-

dia, and the crown colonies. Bailey to Deakin, 11 Nov. 1908, mss 1540, Deakin Papers. Deakin refused because of Australian commitments. Deakin to Bailey, 18 Dec. 1908, ibid.
51 Milner to Curtis, 1 Dec. 1908, Curtis Papers
52 One such meeting was held in late December – early January 1909. Brand to Milner, 5 Jan. 1909, box 76, Milner Papers. For an indication of the extent to which the kindergarten, expecially Philip Kerr, came to be influenced in their thinking by problems of defence see the space given to defence matters in the early issues of *The State* (April, June, and July 1909).
53 Curtis to Amery, 29 March 1909, Amery Papers, quoted in Nimocks, *Milner's Young Men*, 134-6.

ervation of the imperial connection and who were in positions of influence could be asked to lend their support. Curtis believed there was considerable fluid sympathy about, but until a logical exposition of the threats facing the empire was prepared there was no way of crystallising it. As he travelled about the empire he would also attempt to locate in each country people who could be trusted to support the movement: 'The local editors are most important. Already I am getting hold of a series of local papers here whose editors will undertake to give common currency to the Imperial ideas ... We must also get hold of some trustworthy members in each legislature who will undertake to master the information placed at their disposal and to raise a debate every year on the estimates.'

Perhaps this second circle of supporters could be organised on the lines of the Closer Union Societies; but, drawing on his experience, Curtis advised Amery and other supporters in London not to be too hasty about establishing such groups: 'When you do I should lay much more stress on the quality than on the numbers of members it embraces. The active intelligent cooperation of a dozen men ... in each dominion is worth long lists of sympathisers who put their names on paper and do nothing else.'

Curtis also insisted on the need for a chain of publications throughout the empire to disseminate the ideas of the movement. Modelled after *The State* these monthly magazines could carry the gospel of imperial unity to leaders of opinion in all the self-governing countries of the empire.[54] However, if they were to remain free from the provincialism which would threaten the goals of the movement, centralised supervision would be essential. 'I think,' wrote Curtis, 'there should be an office in London to feed them with pictures and staff to make them readable and to look after the English "Ads."' Each local editor, besides the primary responsibility of publishing his magazine, would also be charged with passing on to the London office all local material which might be of use to his colleagues throughout the empire. Curtis believed Philip Kerr would be the man to run the central office, find the editors, and keep the whole thing going. The plan was admittedly complicated and expensive but it would be well worth it if colonial opinion could be educated. Once established, 'everyone concerned in the movement from Lord Milner downwards will have at their disposal a medium through which the same train of thought can be set in motion through all the self-governing colonies

---

54 In early December 1908 Curtis suggested to Richard Jebb that *The State* might be developed 'into a system of Imperial magazines published simultaneously in all the colonies but centering in England, through which people like H.E.[Milner] and Jameson might utter their thoughts to the Empire as a whole.' Curtis to Jebb, 6 Dec. 1908, box 1, Jebb Papers

of the empire at the same time.' Curtis appealed for an early meeting at which the plans could be examined in the light of conditons viewed from the centre of the empire.[55]

By the early summer of 1909 South African union was assured, and some of the kindergarten, having decided not to remain in South Africa, began to drift back to England. Curtis sailed in the first week of June and landed in London on the 26th while Brand and Kerr both left on the 30th. The kindergarten returned to England wondering whether sufficient money would be available for their new scheme. They need not have worried. The £2000 originally made over to Lord Selborne by Lord Salisbury for closer union work had not been needed in South Africa; it was now pledged to the kindergarten's imperial activities. Lords Selborne, Lovat,[56] Howick,[57] and Wolmer[58] all contributed; and Abe Bailey, generous as always, made an initial donation of £2500 and later an annual contribution of £500. The kindergarten's greatest source of wealth was the Rhodes Trust which agreed to match all other donations on a £ to £ basis. This arrangement lasted for almost four years and was terminated by the grant of a lump sum. Other backers came forward later in the year and gave varying but usually large amounts.[59] With their finances assured, the kindergarten set to work.

Early in May Milner, Amery, and Steel-Maitland had discussed the possibility of organising 'a small office to keep touch with all Imperial matters,'[60] and at the end of that month Milner had received a long letter from E.B. Sargant strongly recommending the formation of an imperial organisation modelled on the closer union societies;[61] the atmosphere was thus conducive to an extensive discussion of Curtis's scheme. On 2 July Milner

55 Although nothing was said in this letter to Amery, the kindergarten had discussed the possibility of Curtis becoming a member of the South African Senate and travelling around the empire in that capacity. By late August 1909, however, their opinion had changed and they urged Curtis to concentrate on organising the offices in London which, for the moment, was far more important. Also they believed that Curtis's chances of election were far from assured, especially if it was understood that he proposed being out of South Africa, or at least absent from the Transvaal, for a great part of the year. Duncan to Curtis, 23 Aug. 1909, copy, GD40/17/11, Lothian Papers

56 Lord Lovat (1871-1933); parliamentary under-secretary Dominions Office 1927-8; chairman of the Overseas Settlement Committee 1927-9; Rhodes trustee 1917-33

57 Lord Howick was Lord Selborne's son-in-law.

58 Lord Wolmer was Lord Selborne's heir.

59 Milner to Holland Martin, 20 July 1921, copy, box 97; and Milner diary, 31 Oct. and 1, 3 and 8 Nov. 1909, vol. 272, Milner Papers. Also Quigley, 'The Round Table Groups in Canada'

60 Milner diary, 7 May 1909, vol. 272, Milner Papers

61 E.B. Sargent to Milner, 30 May 1909, Box 167, Miler Papers

and Curtis huddled for a long talk about South Africa and the empire. As usual Milner was somewhat more cautious than the eager Curtis. He wanted more thought given to the nature and purpose of the magazine, to the duties of the overall co-ordinator, and to the overwhelming problem of finance.[62] Although the members of the movement considered these issues carefully at a meeting in mid-July, it would appear that Milner was not a primary force at this time; for on 12 July Amery wrote to Curtis suggesting that Milner be asked to attend a large meeting on 23 July and that he be sent a copy of a memorandum drawn up by Curtis.[63] This role of 'father-figure' would seem to be the one that Milner maintained throughout his relationship with the Round Table. Twenty-five years later John Dove discussed this point with Cecil Headlam[64] and Headlam prepared a statement with which Dove agreed:

Milner was entirely in agreement with the other members of the Round Table Group, that some form of organic union was necessary as the only means of securing the political ideals of the race – real nationality and self-government for those capable of exercising it, and for those not so capable, government in the interest of the governed themselves. But he was by no means equally convinced that the moment for pressing for it had arrived. Nor was he in complete agreement with the particular theories or details of the particular policies advocated by some of the younger men. He confined himself to giving his general support to the object of achieving organic union of the Empire in some form, some day: and to contributing, besides financial assistance, criticism and advice upon the proposals that were put forward ... But though not responsible for their views, Milner wished to give the young men their head, confronting them with a vital problem, and eager to see what they would make of it. Members of the Round Table 'Moot' ... tell me that at the time the attitude he deliberately assumed towards them was that of the Elder Statesman, already 'on the shelf,' but whose practical experience was wholly at the service of those to whom he had handed on the torch of Imperialism in its sanest form. The role played by Milner, in fact, in the discussions of the Round Table, and in the direction of its policy, so far as he did direct it, was that of President of an intellectual Republic.[65]

Shortly after the meeting on 23 July Robinson was compelled to return to South Africa and thus took no further part in the important meetings of Au-

62 Milner to Amery, 3 July 1909, Amery Papers, quoted in Gollin, *Proconsul in Politics*, 165
63 Amery to Curtis, 12 July 1909, copy, GD40/17/11, Lothian Papers
64 Cecil Headlam (1872-1934); author and director of examinations in the Civil Service Commission; among his books was *The Milner Papers*.
65 Headlam to Dove, 12 April 1934, copy, GD40/17/274, Lothian Papers

gust and September 1909.[66] But before leaving he wrote to Curtis urging him to consider the desirability of a 'short statement (for *private* and *very limited* circulation only) of *practical* steps which *can* be taken *immediately* in the direction of the "larger policy."' There was nothing to be gained by standing still while the 'egg' was being hatched.[67] A defence conference was already in session, and there would be a full-scale imperial conference in two years. 'Some of us,' Robinson explained, 'have to talk or write about these things in public *now*, while you are gathering your material, and we may be able to help you to keep them on lines which will fit in with (or at any rate not conflict with) our general scheme even before that general scheme has taken shape.' Robinson wanted Curtis to consider the possibility of drawing up 'a private guide to the faithful.' 'Will you,' he asked, 'talk it over with the "Silent Ones" and see what they think?'[68]

The 'silent ones' apparently thought that the time had finally come for a full-scale discussion of the movement's plans. By early August a major meeting had been arranged for September at Plas Newydd, Lord Anglesey's[69] home on the Menai Straits. Despite this rapid progress, or perhaps because of it, Milner was still inclined to be cautious. He disliked the idea of a large general meeting discussing fundamentals, and would have much preferred 'more basic discussion among the first movers in the scheme.' He did not expect anything conclusive to emerge from the Anglesey gathering.[70] Nevertheless, when it became apparent that the kindergarten was determined to hold the meeting and to treat it with some importance, Milner held a final working dinner on 26 August for Curtis, Marris, Kerr, and Steel-Maitland. It lasted until well past midnight.[71] Shortly afterwards a long memorandum summarizing the conversations of the past few months was drafted by Curtis for circulation at Plas Newydd.[72]

---

66 The meeting on 23 July took the form of a dinner by Jameson at the Bachelor's Club attended by Milner, Robinson, Brand, Curtis, Craik, Oliver, and Martin Holland. Afterwards there was 'a long and most interesting talk about the formation of a body of men in all parts of the Empire cooperating to bring about Imperial Unity.' Milner diary, 23 July 1909, vol. 272, Milner Papers
67 The term 'egg' referred to the major memorandum on the imperial problem contemplated by Curtis. The term was later used more freely to mean any one of the many memoranda prepared by the movement.
68 Robinson to Curtis, 26 July [1909], copy, GD40/17/11, Lothian Papers
69 Lord Anglesey (1885-1947); 6th Marquess of
70 Milner to Kerr, 4 Aug. 1909, GD40/17/11, Lothian Papers
71 Milner diary, 26 Aug. 1909, vol. 272, Milner Papers
72 'Memorandum of conversations which took place between a few English and South African friends at intervals during the summer of 1909,' GD40/17/11, Lothian Papers

The memorandum showed that the genesis of the movement was still being heavily influenced by the South African experiences of the kindergarten. Considerable emphasis was placed on the problems of imperial defence and foreign policy. It was pointed out that although the dominions were clamouring to negotiate for themselves with foreign powers, they still assumed no proportionate share of the burden of defence which was beginning to weigh heavily on Great Britain; 'so long as the burden of protecting all five is borne, with difficulty by the fifth alone, four of the five self-governing communities have not vindicated the claim they are making to be considered as sovereign nations.' It had been agreed by the group that an arrangement so discordant, in principle as well as in form, would break down under inevitable pressure. If the five states of the empire acquiesced in it they would 'drift towards disruption, with all the consequences that that entails.' Only some kind of union would ensure real nationality and self-government to those capable of exercising it. The time had come to enquire in a studious fashion what structural changes were necessary, and how they might be brought about.

The group had soon realised that it would be necessary to create an organisation to correlate and pursue a general plan in five different countries. It had been agreed that a beginning should be made by forming small groups in each dominion, members to be chosen personally by a representative of the London organisation. To ensure that the groups would be severally effective, a whole-time executive secretary 'of character and capacity' would have to be chosen by each. Concerted action between the groups would be secured by the periodic visits of an itinerate delegate and by correspondence with the central group in London which would undertake to collect, to digest, and to disseminate information. While the general plan was being evolved and in order to secure the eventual attention of the public and the press in the different dominions, *The State* should be continued in South Africa and similar magazines founded in the other dominions. These would be edited by the executive agent in each dominion, although much of the material required to popularise them could be supplied from the larger resources of the central group. Pending the settlement of a general plan they would advocate the need for a common understanding, provide the necessary information, and prepare the way for the acceptance of a common scheme. All these activities would have for their primary object the preparation by the central agency, in communication with the rest, of 'a full and reasoned statement of the Imperial problem, setting out the alternatives involved, the real import of disruption, the sacrifices necessary to avoid it, and the successive stages through which the ultimate goal is to be sought.' This statement would be compiled in such a way that each of the groups would be prepared to adopt and to issue it as its own menifesto; 'it must therefore be a creed to which all have contributed and all will subscribe.'

It had also been agreed that the 'Movement should avoid any savour of advertisement or mystery.' The organisation should be tacit, and until the groups were all agreed on a common policy all reference to its existence, whether in the press or on the public platform, would be premature. The kindergarten and their associates had considered whether it was desirable, and if so, possible, to keep the movement from becoming identified with the economic or military policies advocated by particular political parties. Although it was impossible to imagine that the principles of the Movement could ever be carried into effect without applying the driving force of party organisation, it was the general opinion that for the present it would be inexpedient to seek or to allow identification with any party. On the question of finance it was anticipated that an expenditure of something like £25,000 would be required in the first few years until the general statement was produced. In addition to this would have to be reckoned the funds, whether raised already or to be raised in the future, for the special purpose of conducting the magazines. It was hoped that, 'If the original promoters were prepared to contribute substantially each according to his means, men of wealth would follow suit with the larger contributions required'; in any event sufficient funds were already available to set the work in train.

With this memorandum in hand Curtis, Kerr, Brand, and Milner were able to keep control of the meeting held at Plas Newydd on the weekend of 4-6 September. Present besides themselves and their host Lord Anglesey were Oliver, Marris, Craik, Martin Holland,[73] Lovat, Howick, and Wolmer. Owing to some confusion Jameson, who had also been expected, did not turn up. After dinner on the Saturday a general conference was held which eventually divided into several groups to discuss different practical questions. The groups continued to meet successively on the Sunday morning, and Curtis, Kerr, and Milner were present at all of them. The plenary conference was then reassembled between tea and dinner and the results of the morning's discussions were reported and some general resolutions agreed upon. Milner, despite his initial pessimism, had to admit that 'We got a good deal settled.'[74]

---

73 Robert Martin Holland-Martin (1872-1944); director of Martin's Bank; born R.M. Holland, he took the surname Martin in addition to that of Holland by Royal License 14 August 1917.
74 Milner diary, 4-5 Sept. 1909, vol. 272, Milner Papers. Owing to Milner's protests the number at Plas Newydd had been held down.

The meeting that weekend, the most important held to date, benefitted from the fact that all those present had got 'a common jumping off ground in the conviction that permanent stability for the Empire was not to be found in the policy of alliances or in bonds of sentiment,' and certainly not in the perpetuation of colonial conferences.[75] They all realised that co-operation was capable of overcoming many obstacles, but only temporarily; sooner or later co-operation always broke down. The group therefore agreed that its main object was 'the discovery of some form of federation which shall be at once effective and acceptable – by comparison with disruption – to the various Dominions.' A necessary preliminary was to obtain accurate knowledge of the trend of influential thought in the dominions, for until 'the Problem' had been defined it would be impossible to say what particular solution would fit the case. As an initial step they decided to send Curtis, Marris, and Kerr, 'Les Trois Mousquetaires,' to Canada on 17 September.

In addition they agreed that until the situation was ripe for some constitutional measure every effort should be made to encourage the principle of co-operation, providing the Movement's future plans were not jeopardised. The members appreciated that 'organic unity would probably only be possible when people realised that the principle of cooperation had broken down.' They also elected to preserve their secrecy. When they considered Robinson's letter to Curtis of 26 July, asking what he and others of the press could safely advocate in their papers, the group decided that nothing should be published. They were not yet prepared to issue, even privately, a declaration of aims. The group then turned to the business arrangements. A finance committee was formed, consisting of Milner, Lovat, Oliver, and Holland with Kerr as secretary, and plans were made to establish an account at Holland's bank. Finally, it was agreed that an office should be opened in London in January 1910 with Kerr as whole-time secretary at £1000 a year, and that eventually Kerr would edit a quarterly for which he would receive an additional £600.[76]

The results of the gathering were relayed to Jameson by Milner the next day, and it was also Milner who gave final counsel to Curtis on 14 September, three days before 'Les Trois Mousquetaires' sailed for Canada on the first formal venture of the movement.[77] While Curtis, Kerr, and Marris were engaged in their Canadian work, Milner continued to meet reguarly

---

75 The following account of the Plas Newydd meeting is taken from two memoranda – 'Minutes of a meeting held at Plas Newydd, 4-6 September 1909' and 'Main and Subsidiary Objects,' GD40/17/11, Lothian Papers.
76 For the details of Kerr's duties see Oliver to Kerr, 16 Sept. 1909, ibid.
77 Milner diary, 6 and 14 Sept. 1909, vol. 272, Milner Papers

with the other organisers of the movement. Particularly important was a meeting between Milner and Lady Wantage[78] on 30 October to discuss the 'Kerr-Curtis scheme' which resulted in her promising 'substantial help.' Further talks were held with Rhodes's lawyer, B.F. Hawkesley[79] and his fellow trustees, Jameson and Lord Rosebery,[80] and with Sir Abe Bailey.[81] Undoubtedly 'the scheme' was discussed at length at such gatherings and important financial arrangements either concluded or tentatively thrashed out.

Curtis, Kerr, and Marris arrived in Canada armed with letters of introduction to well-placed Canadians from such friends as Edward Grigg[82] and Steel-Maitland. A letter from Steel-Maitland to John Willison was indicative of how the three men initiated their activities. Nothing was said of the Round Table or of any long-range plans for the empire. Curtis and Kerr were simply described as 'good Imperialists' who needed friends to talk freely with if they were to get a true impression of Canada.[83] Presumably, it was left to the judgment of the 'Mousquetaires' to decide whether or not to reveal anything of the group's activities.

On reaching Toronto in early November Curtis and Marris lost little time establishing contact with Willison whom they soon took into their confidence.[84] They acquainted the Canadian with their activities during the past year and told him of the recent discussions at Plas Newydd. They impressed upon him the urgency of settling the future relations between Great Britain and the dominions. Unless Great Britain was soon given assistance in mat-

---

78 Lady Harriet Sarah Lloyd-Lindsay Wantage (1837-1920); daughter of first and only Baron Overstone; wife of first and only Baron Wantage; husband died 1901
79 Bouchier Hawksley (1851-1915); lawyer; senior partner in Hollams, Son, Coward & Hawksley; legal adviser to De Beers Consolidated Mines Ltd; an original Rhodes trustee
80 Lord Rosebery (1847-1929); under-secretary for Home Office 1881-3; Lord Privy Seal 1885; chief commissioner of works 1885; secretary for European affairs 1886 and 1882-4; prime minister and lord president of the Council 1894-5; Rhodes trustee 1902-17
81 On 8 November Bailey held a dinner at the Ritz for Cawdor, Lord Leconfield, Lord Winterton, F.E. Smith, George Farrar, Otto Beit, Brand, Lovat, Oliver, and Milner. See Milner diary, 31 Oct. and 1, 3, 6, 8 and 10 Nov. 1909, vol. 272, Milner Papers
82 Edward Grigg, 1st Baron Altrincham cr 1945 (1879-1955); editorial staff *The Times* 1903-5; assistant editor the *Outlook* 1905-6; rejoined *The Times* 1908, resigned 1913; military secretary to the Prince of Wales 1919-20; private secretary to Lloyd George 1921-2; MP (NL) 1922-5; secretary to the Rhodes trustees 1923-5; governor of Kenya 1925-31; MP (Nat.C) 1933-45
83 Curtis to Willison, 3 Nov. 1909, enclosing Steel-Maitland to Willison, 27 Sept. 1909; also Grigg to Willison, 17 Sept. and 18 Nov. 1909, Willison Papers. Grigg's second letter is revealing: 'I am going out to Govt House tonight to wrestle with Curtis. Empire or no Empire, I mean to get to bed by 11 – so I hope you have left him weak and tractable.'
84 Kerr had by this time parted from his companions to pursue independent research. Butler, *Lothian*, 37

ters of defence the stability of the imperial structure would be threatened. As a result the empire would lose control of the sea, and the dominion's chance of realising a genuine nationality would be lost. Curtis and Marris suggested that the movement could be of great use but only if it were empire-wide. No organisation based solely in the United Kingdom would have any hope of success. It would almost inevitably be interpreted as a recrudescence of Downing Street and an attempt to interfere with colonial autonomy. It was vital that the dominions initiate matters.

In Willison, Curtis and Marris had a sympathetic audience. When he agreed that 'students in the Dominions should set to work to think out a common policy as a future guidance for their external relations,' Curtis and Marris broached the idea of a common journal for the purpose. The three men agreed that it should be a quarterly publication and that it should contain 'an article written in England which should aim at stating the whole imperial position as seen from the centre.' The essential feature of such an article should be its freedom from the influence of either of the political parties in England, and every effort should be made to prevent it serving the interests of either party. Willison was especially concerned that the article should aim at 'telling us in the Dominions what the actual facts were.' Curtis suggested that Kerr might be the man best qualified to write such an article, which could then be followed by one from Canada. Willison offered to write this himself, or get it written, and Curtis agreed to arrange for a similar article from South Africa while Marris saw no difficulty in his contributing one from India; as opportunity offered, they would arrange for similar articles from New Zealand and Australia and if possible from Egypt.[85] This was one of the most important meetings of the trip. It enabled Curtis to rethink and refine his concept of the journal and, in Willison, brought into the Canadian side of the movement a most able and influential figure.

But not everything went well on the journey. While they were in Canada considerable disagreement and a degree of tension grew between Curtis and Kerr. Kerr admired Curtis, but he found him single-minded to the point of being narrow-minded and doctrinaire, and he worried whether Curtis was thinking about the various matters confronting them with sufficient clarity and logic. The difference between the two men was largely one of temperament, and Kerr recognised this and realised how stimulating Curtis could be. Nevertheless, 'I know no man,' wrote Kerr, 'who has so big a furnace in his belly. It is so fierce that the fumes overwhelm his brain at times.' Kerr was

85 This meeting was recalled by Curtis the next year when discussing the nature of the journal with Kerr. See Curtis to Kerr, 21 July 1910, GD40/17/1, Lothian Papers.

also unable to share Curtis's mystical faith in the empire, his 'transcendental confidence that one is divinely inspired in one's political operations ... The empire is a noble thing but not fit to be a God. To unite it is part of God's work, and one which we are all called to help. But I cannot worship at its shrine alone.'[86]

Kerr had travelled to Canada with certain doubts about the feasibility of closer union. He did not see any reason 'to suppose that Canada will get further away from the United Kingdom, but for the life of me I can't see why it should want to get any closer. I don't see that we can offer her anything that the United States can't offer just as well, and there are certain obvious disadvantages in the surrender of autonomy which is entailed in the creation of an Empire organization. I am beginning to think that the publication of an Empire egg – the pistol policy – is impossible. If you forced Canada to choose now between Imperial Federation and independence, I think she would take independence.'[87]

A few weeks later he was more than ever convinced that matters could not be rushed. He had found Canadians lacking in perception about international politics, with little understanding of the United Kingdom, and with an 'almost universal want of knowledge' about the effects of a reorganisation of the imperial structure. Many seemed to think that a re-vamping of imperial machinery would interfere with local autonomy. While he had discovered a reasonably strong imperial feeling in Ontario, he found that both the Liberal and the Conservative parties appeared to cater to French-Canadian anti-imperialism.[88] It seemed obvious to him that the movement would have to find 'a scheme of Imperialism which appeals to men's imaginations ... Pure combination for defence is not enough.' He, for one, could not see 'the golden writing on the wall just at present.'[89]

His findings forced Kerr to write to the London group about his disagreement with Curtis:

Lionel believes that the only hope for the Empire lies in 'organic unity.' That is to say the creation of a central sovereign authority directly elected by the people of the Empire which shall control policy and services such as army and navy, and raise tax-

86 These remarks are quoted without reference in Butler, *Lothian*, 38.
87 Quoted without reference in ibid., 37.
88 This account of Kerr's reaction to Canada and Canadians is taken from an undated memorandum written shortly after his return to England in early 1910. Curtis and Marris also wrote memoranda but they have not survived. See P. Kerr, 'Undated Memorandum,' GD40/17/11, Lothian Papers.
89 Quoted without reference in Butler, *Lothian*, 37-8.

ation through its own officers. I think, now, that 'organic unity' of that kind is impossible, at any rate until science has revolutionised communication and transportation, and that to bring on a movement of that kind would be almost certain to break up the Empire ... Of course I am still a strong Imperialist. I am more convinced by my visit to Canada than I was before that the Empire is going to hang together and will become a strong vigorous and living entity. I am further convinced that there is an immense amount of work to be done in bringing that about. But I am also convinced that any attempt to fit the Empire into the constitutional ideas which have suited the United Kingdom and the self-governing colonies in the past is simply courting destruction.[90]

All the members of the movement shared Curtis's desire to strengthen imperial ties, but unlike him they did not have a firm opinion about the methods and the speed required. The difference of opinion that developed in Canada between Curtis and Kerr was only the first of many such differences that were to develop between Curtis and his colleagues. However, these conflicts within the movement were not confined to a Curtis vs 'The Rest' battleline, although such a division did tend to predominate. The members could usually agree on strategy but were often hopelessly divided over tactics.

Curtis, Marris, and Kerr finally returned to England in early January where each drafted a memorandum on their Canadian experiences. These were distributed in time for a meeting at Ledbury which lasted from 15 to 18 January. Many of the aims and future activities of the movement were finally decided upon at this meeting. It is therefore important to note who took part. Present were Duncan, Feetham, Hichens, Curtis, Marris, Brand, Craik, and Kerr – those who, with the addition of Craik and Hichens, had first discussed the project more than a year before in South Africa. None of their London friends or financial backers, not even Milner, attended. It would seem that the Ledbury group was the important nucleus of the movement who turned for advice to Milner and others only after the major decisions had been made.

At their meeting the group confirmed that the ultimate aim of the movement should be an organic union of the empire.[91] It was recognised that action towards the attainment of this end ought to be of two kinds: first, a scheme of union – if possible a constitution – should be prepared and eventually published 'as an answer to the objection that Imperial Union was impossible, and as the ultimate solution of Imperial problems towards which

90  Kerr to Brand, 1 Nov. 1909, ibid., 39-40
91  See 'Minutes of a meeting held at Ledbury January 15/18, 1910,' GD40/17/11, Lothian Papers

workers would direct their efforts'; and second, the encouragement of intermediate steps which would serve to educate public opinion 'in the truth about Imperial affairs and the necessity for them.'

The discussion which followed this definition of purpose turned first on the principles which should be embodied in the ultimate constitution of the empire. Although most of the group thought that the more important functions of the imperial authority would be executive rather than deliberative 'the necessity of providing for the public discussion of Imperial affairs in some representative assembly, the importance of avoiding the evils and even deadlock incidental to the discussion of Imperial affairs by the national legislatures, and the need of some representative assembly to which the executive should be answerable, seemed to require the reproduction of institutions of Cabinet and Parliament in the final Union of the Empire.' The majority of the members in this imperial parliament would have to be directly elected. This would avoid the discussion of imperial affairs in national legislatures which would result if secondary elections were held. It would also separate imperial and national interests at election time.

Since the need for the union of the empire had arisen out of external affairs it was agreed that the central organ for the empire should have sole authority to conduct foreign relations, to determine the nature, strength, distribution, and organisation of the defensive forces of the empire while possessing the power to raise the revenue required. The principle upon which the cost of the imperial services was to be distributed between the various states should be laid down in the constitution. The amount of the levy would be determined by the imperial government but should be collected by the local legislatures, except in cases of default, when the imperial government should have the power to impose taxation itself. It was also agreed that the imperial government should not only assume responsibility for India and the dependencies but should ultimately decide whether or not they were to be represented in the imperial legislature.

No further conclusions were reached on the ultimate form of union to be aimed at, and discussion turned to the intermediate steps which ought to be taken in that direction. The members agreed that 'the congestion of business in the Imperial Parliament prevented the proper consideration either of Imperial Affairs, or of external reforms,' and it was suggested that there should be a royal commission to consider the whole question of the devolution of power within the United Kingdom before any measure of home rule was accepted. They then recommended that the dominions should be encouraged to found local navies in order to inform themselves about imperial defence and that they should be associated with the imperial government in the negotiation of all treaties or arrangements affecting them. They also advocated an extension of the principle of preference, and urged a closer association of the agents-general with the imperial government. The members hoped that the general effect of these intermediate measures would be 'to concentrate attention on Imperial affairs, while the conviction that they were inadequate and unsatisfactory in themselves which would inevitably arise when their defects were exposed by practical experience would force home the contention of those who maintained that organic union was the only permanent solution of the Imperial problem.'

Finally, the position and work of the groups was considered. It was agreed that it was no longer desirable to maintain the movement as a tacit organisation. The fact that a number of persons interested in imperial affairs had raised enough money to conduct a thorough enquiry into 'the imperial problem' should no longer be disguised; however, it was decided not to reveal the amount of the funds nor the names of the contributors. It was also thought advisable that correspondence with the dominions from the office should be conducted as far as possible through the medium of local groups and not directly with individuals. The method of distributing information about foreign and imperial affairs and ideas and arguments about imperial union was also discussed, but not at great length. It was obvious that the group were still undecided about the exact form and purpose of a magazine. However, they were prepared to recommend that the simplest, most effective and least suspicious vehicle would probably be 'a quarterly journal devoted entirely to Imperial affairs, which would be sent to all Editors for review, and to which all workers and all important statesmen in the Dominions could be induced to subscribe ... At a later stage it might become the recognised organ of the groups in all parts.' Such a magazine would have a small sale and would probably be run at a loss. A more popular magazine with a larger sale would entail a greater expense and would place a far more severe drain upon the Round Table office.

Although Milner had not been involved in these talks at Ledbury, the group were quick to inform him and the other members of their decisions and to seek their advice.[92] On 23 January Milner, Oliver, Amery, and Lovat joined the Ledbury group in Milner's rooms to discuss the minutes of the meeting.[93] At this session organic union was accepted as the ultimate aim of the movement, but it was clear that not all the members were satisfied with

92  Milner diary, 14, 15, 16, and 20 Jan. 1910, vol. 273, Milner Papers
93  Milner diary, 23 Jan. 1910, ibid. See 'Minutes of a meeting held in London on January 23, 4-5 p.m.,' GD40/17/11, Lothian Papers.

the idea. It was therefore established that nobody in the movement was committed to accepting all the principles embodied in the minutes; equally, anyone could advocate some or all of them if they wished. This decision of January 1910 was to assume a major significance after the outbreak of war. As for the status and work of the group it was agreed that 'as little as possible should be said about its existence or the objects of its activities,' and that when asked 'members should explain that a number of individuals were making a study of Imperial relations and were conducting a magazine as a means of communicating ideas and information between persons interested in the British Isles and the oversea dominions.' It was also decided to ask Arthur Glazebrook to act as the movement's agent in Canada. These decisions were confirmed two days later, 25 January, at a second meeting of the group at the Rhodes Trust office.[94] Almost immediately Curtis left for South Africa where he began drafting a memorandum, based on his Canadian experiences, which was to serve as a basic introductory document for the formation of groups in the other dominions.

Thus by the end of January 1910 the Round Table movement was securely established in Great Britain. Its aims and methods were now reasonably clear and it was ready to embark on its overseas activity. However, there were still difficulties left to resolve. For example, it was quite apparent that the 'scheme,' as defined, still owed much to the ideas of Lionel Curtis. Not everyone in the London group was happy with this; men like Brand and Amery could not accept Curtis's stark alternative of union or disruption. Differences on this issue were to bedevil the movement for many years. Another matter which had not been satisfactorily settled was the role of the new quarterly, *The Round Table*. Was it to aim at a limited audience confined to Round Table groups throughout the empire – what Curtis wanted – or was it to be a popular magazine aiming at a much wider readership? The group continued to wrestle with these problems for some weeks. Finally, Philip Kerr drew up a memorandum on the quarterly and circulated it to the movement's supporters in the dominions.[95]

Curtis had left for South Africa before these intensive discussions on the nature and function of the quarterly were begun, and for some months he was unaware of the precise decisions of his colleagues. This led to a misunderstanding about the role of the magazine and later complicated matters for him in New Zealand. Moreover, once the London group had disposed of

---

94 Milner diary, 25 Jan. 1910, vol. 273, Milner Papers
95 Kerr's undated memorandum on 'The projected quarterly magazine' was enclosed in A. Glazebrook to Walker, 29 April 1910, Walker Papers.

the problem of the quarterly, they began examining and preparing memoranda on the British parliamentary system, anglo-dominion relations, and the various matters which could be profitably discussed at the Imperial Conference of 1911. Despite his absence Curtis was soon drawn into the London group's activities.

# 4
# The prophet's first mission

Curtis left for South Africa in January with the dual purpose of bringing the South African members of the movement up to date on developments in London and finishing the draft of the memorandum based on his Canadian experiences. He was followed to South Africa by Amery in mid-February, and until Amery returned to England in April there were innumerable discussions about imperial affairs and the role of the new organisation with Duncan, Feetham, Robinson, and Wyndham. Efforts were also made to draw others into the small circle in Johannesburg, and over the next few months a number of informal meetings were held.[1] By the beginning of June Curtis had completed his task in South Africa and was preparing to leave for New Zealand and Australia. He informed his mother on June 1st: 'I have just finished revising the last sheets of my Imperial memorandum to go to Philip to be printed by today's mail ... Union started here yesterday, which brings to a close the first chapter of our work. It is not three years ago since we published the Selborne Memorandum which set the ball rolling.'[2] His imperial memorandum, better known as the 'Green Memorandum,' was printed in interleaved form and circulated among his South African friends for criticism.[3]

1  Curtis to Kerr, 21 July 1910, GD40/17/11, Lothian Papers; Duncan to Curtis, 23 Nov. 1910; and Feetham to Curtis, 7 Dec. 1910, Curtis Papers
2  Curtis to his mother, 1 June 1910, copy, ibid.
3  The printed form of the 'egg' was known initially as the 'Green Memorandum' and then as the 'Annotated Memorandum.' It was later entitled 'Round Table Studies. First Series.' It will be referred to hereafter as the Green Memorandum.

The Green Memorandum was the first major document drafted by Curtis for the movement. It was designed to summarize the discussions and arguments of the previous two years and to provide potential recruits with a quick insight into the movement's assumptions and aims. It contained a lengthy survey of the issues confronting the British empire, an analysis of how they affected the dominions, particularly Canada, and a detailed plan of imperial federation. During the next year the Green Memorandum became a crucial instrument in the formation of the dominion groups.

In his opening pages Curtis made it clear that the movement considered the rise of a militant Germany a severe threat to the British empire and the strongest argument for a union of Great Britain and the dominions. Curtis distinguished between the English and the continental political and legal systems, claiming that the British constitution was an expression of the sanctity accorded to personal rights whereas the continental spirit, as a result of its military environment, was autocratic and inclined to impose the same standards on all men. He argued that Great Britain and the continent could not appreciate or comprehend each other's system, and furthermore that the profound antagonism between the two systems was the key to the interpretation not only of European history since the Middle Ages but to the present world situation.[4] Under her system Great Britain had sheltered and protected her colonies and had encouraged them to assume a virtual independence. This in time had proven a conspicuous success so far as their domestic affairs were concerned but in external affairs the colonies were still protected by Great Britain, at considerable cost to the mother country and with a loss of independence for themselves. Curtis noted the immense increase in productivity and power brought about by the federation of Germany and suggested that the time would soon come when Germany and many other states would be able to build and maintain stronger fleets than Great Britain which was staggering under the burdens of a parent state. It would be rash to suppose that the empire's superior strength at sea could rest indefinitely on the resources of such small islands. Moreover, if fleets stronger than those of England assumed control of the sea would the independence of the dominions continue to be the reality it now was? And without such independence could they achieve the status of nations at all? The real element in national greatness was not wealth nor even freedom, but 'the spirit begotten of freedom which rises to responsibility,' and it was 'in gathering difficulties of the Empire that the real opportunity of the younger nations lies.'[5]

4  Green Memorandum, 10          5  Ibid., 60

On examining the 'Effect of Canada's Position in the Empire on her Political Life,' Curtis concluded that in Canada, as in the other oversea dominions, the lack of responsibility for the safety of the whole structure had led to a reluctance to face such ultimate issues as the dominion's duty to the dependencies, and was preventing the proper political development of the community.[6] He was also critical of the concept of 'Imperial Cooperation,' pointing out that whenever a conflict developed between the two ideals of local autonomy and unity of the empire it was often reconciled by the assumption that 'the five independent democracies can be trusted to see eye to eye, and to work hand in hand in any measures required for the common safety.'[7] Curtis doubted that common action by separate governments could ever be fruitful. Moreover, the existing situation in the empire could not be left as it was, for Canada would soon be approaching Great Britain in population and strength. Was it conceivable that a population of twenty-five or thirty millions could leave the responsibility of handling issues which might plunge them into war to a government representing the electorate of Great Britain? He argued that foreign policy and defence were and always would be the primary function of a national government. How could a nation be truly a nation which did not have 'its own hand on its own rudder?'[8] As matters stood the dominions had never learned how continuous and heavy were the sacrifices necessary for national defense. Information was lacking, and passing naval scares or similar crises were not sufficient to provide it or to stimulate rethinking about an essentially false position of security. The protection afforded the dominions by Great Britain had enabled them to develop domestically, but it had meant that governments were chosen only with reference to internal issues and not to the safety of the country or the empire. This freedom from responsibility for the safety of the structure had cramped the moral development of the dominions and narrowed their outlook. If they were to become nations they would have to learn to accept their share of the imperial burden.[9]

Turning to the 'Effect of the Existing Imperial System on the United Kingdom,' Curtis argued that the institutions of the country were breaking down under the strain of domestic and imperial responsibilities. He referred to the terrible congestion in the parliamentary programme and the overwhelming administrative burdens and political pressures on the Cabinet minister. Severe physical and mental stresses were also evident in the British population brought about by overcrowding and maldistribution of money.

6  Ibid., 130-8
8  Ibid., 172-6
7  Ibid., 158-60
9  Ibid., 210

Lionel Curtis

Curtis pointed out that the only self-governing state of the empire with serious domestic problems was the United Kingdom, the only state whose domestic affairs were seriously entangled with those of the empire. The situation could be resolved either by the dominions separating from the empire and assuming the responsibilities of peace and war for themselves or by their assuming some of the imperial burden. To do neither would endanger not only the United Kingdom but the empire as a whole. But if it was agreed that the first step toward curing the malady was the separation of the domestic affairs of Great Britain from those of the empire that could only be done by Great Britain and the dominions conferring and acting together, not by one presenting the others with a *fait accompli*.

In a chapter entitled 'An Alternative,' Curtis sketched the details of a scheme for an organic union of the empire. He argued that no reform of the imperial constitution would be final or sufficient which did not provide the empire with a single agency clothed with full powers in peace and war and furnished with adequate resources. Since it could not be expected to depend on voluntary contributions it would have to have the power not only to request but to demand the supplies it required. 'Unless we give it the power to tax,' said Curtis, 'we shall not be establishing a Government at all, but only a conference of separate States. Government and taxation are, in fact, correlative to one another.'[10] In order to avoid any abrupt financial changes which might lead to economic disruption, Curtis suggested that the states of the empire contribute for the first five or ten years to imperial defence in the ratio of their average expenditure on defence for the ten years previous to imperial federation. This would provide enough time to establish machinery for assessing the national income of each state, a task which would best be performed by an independent and impartial assessment commission composed of members from each state. A revised assessment could be submitted every five years and the annual revenue required by the imperial parliament could be contributed by the states in those proportions. In order to collect the money Curtis suggested that 'the annual contribution for Imperial defence would form a first charge on the consolidated revenue of each State, and the amount would be transferred automatically to the federal account.'[11] In this way the authority of the state government would not be impaired and the power of the imperial parliament would be upheld.

Curtis also argued that since the duty of the imperial government was to ensure the safety of the empire as a whole, it would have to have absolute and unfettered control over the main striking force and over diplomacy. Indi-

10  Ibid., 254                              11  Ibid., 276

vidual states would be able to initiate agreements affecting themselves, but ultimate ratification should always remain with the imperial government. An exception to this was the regulation of tariffs. Curtis believed that when all the powers necessary for common defence had been secured to the imperial government all other functions and attributes of nationality should be reserved to the states, and tariffs were a crucial domestic concern.[12] Inseparable from defence, however, was the control of the dependencies and it was through the federal authority 'that all the white communities of the British Empire would share alike – in this the most solemn responsibility of the self-governing races of the world.'[13]

The new imperial parliament would be quite distinct from the one existing at Westminster. Its lower house would derive its authority directly from the electors of the empire and representation of each state would be based on its population and revised at each census. In the upper house the states would be accorded equal representation and Curtis envisaged each state being represented by thirty peers, ten retiring at the end of every five years. To ensure that the peers would be representative of the whole state rather than the majority, Curtis suggested that they should be chosen by proportional representation. He also considered that it would be necessary to have a tribunal to decide disputes that might arise over rights of legislation between the federal authority and the dominion governments. He suggested that the speakers in the houses of commons and assemblies throughout the self-governing empire become peers. In a federal parliament a judicial committee of the House of Lords would absorb the functions of the Judicial Committee of the Privy Council and become the supreme court of appeal for all the dominions. When, however, a constitutional question arose over whether a matter should be handled by the federal parliament it would be decided by the new committee, together with ex-speakers from all the dominions added for the purpose.[14] Since it would also be wise for the new federal parliament to come into contact with as many of its citizens as possible it should meet at various places throughout the empire. All the necessary records could be moved by ship and the presence of imperial statesmen in a community every five or ten years would be enormously beneficial for imperial unity and fervour.

All of these changes would mean the creation of a domestic government for the United Kingdom. The new federal government would deal only with imperial affairs and have nothing more to do with the internal affairs of the United Kingdom. Thus organic union would not be possible unless the people of the United Kingdom were prepared to accept the same status, so far as

12 Ibid., 310          13 Ibid., 294          14 Ibid., 332

their internal affairs were concerned, as Canada, New Zealand, Australia, and South Africa. Curtis believed this change to be the only one conducive to social reform in the United Kingdom as well as to the safety of the empire as a whole.

In a final chapter called 'The Path to Union,' Curtis re-emphasized that the British empire depended too much on the strength and direction of the mother country. This situation could not endure; if it did the dominions would find it difficult to foster the development of a genuine national spirit. Co-operation was not a solution, it did little more than conceal 'the actual insolvency' of the association as it existed. It was in fact a dangerous policy because 'by preserving and idolising the symbols of union, we encourage the delusion that we are equipped with the strength which can only be derived from unity itself.'[15] But the states of the empire could not 'slip into union' by a process of growth as some people suggested. An organic union of the empire would have to be fashioned deliberately and consciously by architects appointed for that purpose by the states themselves. Curtis called for an imperial convention to prepare an imperial constitution.[16]

In the interim, to facilitate the achievement of union, Curtis suggested that the dominions should begin to co-operate more with Great Britain in the foreign and imperial fields, thus gaining valuable experience. For instance, dominion ministers could be brought into closer touch with the Foreign Office, the Admiralty, and the War Office, and their staffs could be trained in conjunction with the staff of the Foreign Office. The ministers might also be summoned to the Imperial Cabinet whenever imperial affairs were under discussion; such as was done in the Committee of Imperial Defence [CID]. The dominion ministries would thus begin to find themselves in touch with the realities of the situation, and to understand the factors upon which the peace of the empire depended. Another advantageous step might be to grant dominion representatives in London, such as the high commissioners, life peerages and allow them to sit and speak in the Lords but not to vote. Such an arrangement would at least result in a periodic exchange of views on imperial matters and might serve to educate public opinion in the United Kingdom and the dominions.

Curtis's concluding remarks concerned the Round Table movement. He reminded the potential dominion recruits that many citizens in the empire were undecided between two alternatives, union or disruption, and it was at such a juncture 'that a few quiet but determined men in each of the states concerned may accomplish much by a patient and concerted inquiry.' In-

15  Ibid., 352                    16  Ibid., 358

itially the proper business of students would be to make opinion rather than to marshal adherents. The time for converting others had not arrived. For the present the task of the Round Table members would be to find the truth for themselves, and to be sure at the outset that they agreed about the ultimate object of their search. But, he warned, the truth about the future safety of the empire could not be one thing for Great Britain, another for Canada, a third for South Africa, a fourth for Australia, and a fifth for New Zealand. It had to be one for all alike.[17]

Armed with copies of the Green Memorandum and a number of the South African publications of the kindergarten, Curtis left for New Zealand in early June.[18]

According to the original arrangements made late in 1909 and early 1910, Curtis's first visit to Australasia was to be devoted to collecting the necessary information for an 'egg' on the two southern dominions and to making a reconnaissance for the kind of men who could be asked to join the movement. The formation of groups was to be left to a future visit. After his departure from England, however, the London group decided that the work had to be accelerated and that Curtis should not only gather information but in addition organise the Round Table groups in New Zealand and Australia during his initial visit.[19] Curtis was characteristically unperturbed by this change of plan and upon reaching Wellington on 29 June he plunged eagerly into his task.

New Zealand was the smallest and most isolated of the dominions. It had a predominantly British population and was traditionally considered to be the most loyal of the self-governing colonies, the least critical of Great Britain, and the most amenable to some form of closer union. Never uniformly shared, these attitudes had undergone a subtle change since the Boer War. The interest shown in the British tie was now based as much on peculiarly New Zealand concerns as upon any deep-seated loyalty to Great Britain and the empire. Nevertheless, New Zealanders were nothing if not realistic, and many of them were highly conscious of their vulnerable position in the South Pacific. Curtis had little difficulty interesting a number of prominent citizens in his arguments about defence and foreign policy and in his overall scheme.

17 Ibid., 388-94
18 Curtis also completed a separate pamphlet entitled *The Form of an Organic Union of the Empire* which he distributed with the Green Memorandum. There is a copy in the library of the Royal Commonwealth Society.
19 Curtis to Oliver, 15 Aug. 1910, copy, GD40/17/2, Lothian Papers

He stayed in New Zealand almost eleven weeks during which time he managed to organise major groups at Wellington, Christchurch, Auckland, and Wanganui, to form a smaller one at Dunedin, and to establish contacts at Napier, Peel Forest, Mount Peel, Palmerston North, Bulls, and Fielding. He made a point of choosing group members from the academic, business, legal, and farming worlds. In this way 'men of earnest and studious mind accustomed to search for truth for its own sake' were balanced by the 'practical man of the world' who was familiar with 'the idiosyncracies of unreasonable human nature.'[20] Curtis's technique was more or less the same everywhere he went, no matter if he were in a major city or a small hamlet. First, with the aid of introductions supplied by his English friends, he approached certain members of the community, usually finding that not more than half out of every dozen introductions he carried were of the right sort. When he had chosen the suitable few he decided who was 'the best man for the cause,' told him everything, enlisted his support, and then discussed with this 'leading spirit' other men who might be suitable. Curtis had often met some of those named, but nearly always there were a few who were considered as good or better to whom Curtis was introduced. Finally, when all these people had been sounded, Curtis invited them to dinner so that his proposals could be generally thrashed out.[21]

Although this appeared a humdrum way of setting to work, Curtis believed it to be far more effective than addressing a number of mass meetings. Such an approach would probably cause a great sensation but the effect would soon subside if there was no one left behind to keep it going. As Curtis explained to Lady Wantage: 'Surely the sounder method is to establish a small nucleus of men all imbued with the same truths and uttering them as a matter of their own personal conviction to their own people. Then there is no need for outsiders like myself to come forward at all. The movement springs up from inside each Dominion among the people themselves, and becomes their own spontaneous movement. Our function, as I understand it, is not to feed these countries with flour as it were, which is gone as soon as it is consumed, but to bring them seed so that they may grow the food for themselves and have no limit to the supply.'[22]

His methods were eminently successful in New Zealand. The Green Memorandum aroused considerable interest and enthusiasm among all

20 Curtis to Lady Wantage, 9 Sept. 1910, Curtis Papers
21 This account of Curtis's technique is taken from Curtis to Oliver, 15 Aug. 1910, GD40/17/2, Lothian Papers.
22 Curtis to Lady Wantage, 9 Sept. 1910, Curtis Papers

who read it, and the groups themselves, particularly the one in Wellington, were composed of serious-minded, dedicated, and often-times influential men.[23] Aided by letters of introduction from Marris, a New Zealander, Curtis had little difficulty making contacts. From the academic community he managed to attract Professors James Hight,[24] Francis Haslam,[25] and Thomas Blunt[26] of Canterbury College in Christchurch, Patrick Marshall,[27] professor of geology at Otago University in Dunedin, and T.H. Laby,[28] a brilliant young Australian scientist teaching at Victoria University College in Wellington. All of these men, especially Hight, who became the secretary of the Christchurch group and the author of the first New Zealand article in *The Round Table*, and Laby, who subsequently became a driving force in the Australian organisation after his move to Melbourne in 1915, were active in the early years in New Zealand, and did much to keep discussion alive in the university communities. From the business world Curtis drew such men as Harold Beauchamp (later Sir Harold Beauchamp)[29] of Wellington, already a prominent public figure, Henry Francis Wigram (later Sir Henry Wigram),[30] chairman of the *Lyttelton Times* and a Liberal member of the Legislative Council (Canterbury), Arthur Myers (later Sir Arthur Myers),[31]

23 Curtis's activities in New Zealand can be traced in the Curtis diary 1910: Australia and New Zealand, Curtis Papers. For a detailed description of the formation of the New Zealand groups see Kendle, 'Lionel Curtis and the Formation of the New Zealand Groups.'

24 James Hight (1872-1958); lecturer in political economy and constitutional history, Canterbury College 1901-6; director of studies in commerce, Canterbury College 1906; rector Canturbury College 1928; New Zealand representative World Economic Conference, Geneva 1927

25 Francis William Chapman Haslam (1848-1924); professor of Classics, Canterbury College 1879-1912; interested in colonial defence; president of Navy League

26 Thomas Blunt (1876-1950); born in England; went to New Zealand in 1901; professor of Modern Languages, Canturbury College, Christchurch

27 Patrick Marshall (1869-1950); lecturer in science, Lincoln Agricultural College, 1892-1901; lecturer and professor in geography Otago University 1901-16; headmaster Wanganui Collegiate 1916-22

28 Thomas Howell Laby (1880-1946); born in Australia; professor of physics, Victoria College, Wellington, to 1915; appointed professor of physics, University of Melbourne 1915

29 Harold Beauchamp (1858-1938); knighted 1923; director of the Bank of New Zealand; chairman Wellington Gas Co Ltd; director and chairman of many boards and companies

30 Henry Francis Wigram (1857-1934); businessman; chairman of the Canturbury Seed Co; director of the New Zealand Refrigeration Co; chairman (30 yrs) *Lyttelton Times* Co; mayor of Christchurch 1902; member of the Legislative Council from 1903; knighted in 1926

31 Arthur M. Myers (1867-1926); businessman and politician; chairman and director of many boards and companies; mayor of Auckland pre-1910; member of the House of Representatives 1910-21; minister of finance, railways and defence 1912; minister of customs, munitions and supplies in the National government 1915-19

a wealthy brewer and MHR for Auckland East, his brother Michael Myers (later Sir Michael Myers)[32] of Wellington, William Reece,[33] a leading ironmonger and former mayor of Christchurch, and Sir George Clifford,[34] a wealthy landowner and company director who became president of the Christchurch group.

Together the academic and business worlds yielded a fairly formidable nucleus but Curtis drew the largest membership from the legal profession. Of the lawyers who joined, Arthur Richmond Atkinson[35] and Heinrich von Haast[36] of Wellington and Downie Stewart[37] of Dunedin made the most vital contributions in following years. Two other prominent figures became involved during the initial weeks: Hector Rolleston,[38] the British imperial trade commissioner in Wellington, described by Curtis as a 'charming, kindly, helpful person' although 'no intellectual force,' was appointed convenor of the Wellington group and acted as the first treasurer of the dominion organisation; and S.A. Atkinson,[39] the younger son of the former New Zealand premier, Harry Atkinson, referred to as 'not brainy, but highsouled and tremendously keen,' was named dominion secretary and charged with the responsibility of transmitting all official papers of any interest to the London office. Curtis was confident that between Rolleston and Atkinson all the routine of the New Zealand organisation would be efficiently trans-

32 Michael Myers (1873-1950); lawyer and businessman; with Bell, Gully and Myers 1892-1922; chief justice 1929; KC 1922; KCMG 1930
33 William Reece (1856-1930); businessman; member of the firm of Edward Reece & Sons, ironmongery and hardware merchants; president of the Chamber of Commerce, Christchurch 1890; mayor of Christchurch 1900; chairman and director of many boards and companies
34 Sir George Hugh Clifford (1847-1930); businessman; chairman of the New Zealand Sheepbreeders' Association; founding member of Canterbury Frozen Meat Co; Chairman New Zealand Shipping Co
35 Arthur Richmond Atkinson (1863-1935); lawyer and journalist; member of the New Zealand House of Representatives 1899-1902; regular contributor to the *Evening Post* (25 yrs); New Zealand correspondent of *The Morning Post* 1907-11 and of *The Times* 1911-21
36 Heinrich von Haast (1864-1953); barrister and solicitor; member of the Board of Governors, Canterbury College; fellow and treasurer of the Senate, University of New Zealand; secretary of the Wellington group of the Institute of Pacific Relations 1929; delegate to the Shanghai Conference 1931; representative at the Banff Conference and the British Commonwealth Relations Conference, Toronto, 1933
37 William Downie Stewart (1878-1949); New Zealand politician and lawyer; mayor of Dunedin 1913-14; MP for Dunedin West 1914-35; minister of internal affairs 1921-3, of customs 1921-8, of finance 1926-8; attorney-general 1926 and acting prime minister 1926; minister of finance 1931-3; represented New Zealand at the Ottawa Conference 1932
38 No additional information was available on Hector Rolleston.
39 S. Arnold Atkinson; lawyer; died in action World War I, a prime mover behind the Round Table group in New Zealand until 1914.

acted. Colonel Edward Chaytor (later Sir Edward Chaytor),[40] a man with a distinguished record in the Boer War, joined the Wellington group and often advised Curtis during the latter's first weeks in New Zealand. Walter Empson,[41] former headmaster of Marris's old school, Wanganui Collegiate, became the Round Table agent in the Mount Peel district while William Montgomery,[42] a sheepfarmer in the Wairewa area of Bank's Peninsula, read the Green Memorandum with enthusiasm and later became one of the mainstays of the New Zealand organisation. One other who deserves to be mentioned is Edward Tregear,[43] the secretary of the Labour Department, and a long-time force in the New Zealand labour movement. Tregear was very much an oddity in the Round Table organisation, not only in New Zealand but elsewhere in the empire. For despite many efforts by Curtis and others few men with legitimate labour interests became members of the movement.

Of the various groups, Curtis believed the one in Wellington was by far the most vigorous. Although its average age of forty-five was slightly higher than that of the Christchurch group, it had only one member in his sixties and none in their twenties or thirties. It contained four lawyers, one military specialist, one academic, one politician, and in Arthur Myers and Hector Rolleston two men who combined political and business interests. To Curtis's mind the most impressive member was Arthur Atkinson. A lawyer with a flourishing practice, Atkinson was 'a considerable intellectual power' who did a great deal of leader writing for the Wellington *Evening Post* and the *Dominion.* He was also the New Zealand correspondent for the London *Morning Post* and later for *The Times* and was well acquainted with Richard Jebb and Fabian Ware. According to Curtis, he was 'one of the men who made opinion in New Zealand behind the scenes.' When the group was formed Curtis assured Atkinson that in his journalistic writings he was to feel free to ventilate any views of his own, and if the Green Memorandum

40 Edward Walter Chaytor (1868-1939); served in South African war with New Zealand forces; in 1914-18 commanded the New Zealand mounted brigade in Palestine and Egypt; commandant New Zealand forces in New Zealand 1919-24; KCMG 1918

41 Walter Empson (1856-1934); second master at Wanganui Collegiate School 1883-7; later headmaster Wanganui Collegiate

42 William Hugh Montgomery; born 1866; called to the bar at the Inner Temple 1888; member of the House of Representatives 1893-9; manager of the family estates at Little Ellesmere; member of the Board of Governors, Canturbury College, and of Christchurch Hospital

43 Edward Tregear (1846-1931); saw active service in the Maori Wars; entered civil service in survey department; on the creation of the labour department was appointed successively secretary of the Bureau of Industries 1891; chief inspector of factories 1891; and secretary of the Labour Department 1898; he retired in 1911.

had changed his views he was to consider himself at liberty to say what he thought. Curtis believed Atkinson would prove to be the best man to write the New Zealand articles for *The Round Table,* for he was 'the nearest counterpart that I can find in New Zealand to Willison ... the final settlement of the contributors must ... remain with the local people; but my suggestion will go some way towards settling their judgement.'[44] Curtis had his way, and during the next few years Atkinson wrote many of the New Zealand chronicle articles for the quarterly.

All the members of the New Zealand groups committed themselves to the general purposes of the Round Table movement. A few, such as von Haast or Laby, were convinced that imperial federation or some form of organic union was essential in order to resolve the imperial problem. Others, such as Montgomery or Downie Stewart, were more skeptical. But even they were sufficiently concerned and idealistic to believe that the Round Table method was well worth trying and its views worth examining. In fact, Arthur Myers of Wellington suggested that the Green Memorandum 'should be published and copies sent to all the prominent Ministers before the Imperial Conference next year, in order that the issues it raised might be discussed there.' Curtis, knowing that the London group did not wish to force the pace toward imperial union, pointed out that if the Green Memorandum were published it would merely go forth as representing the views of a few New Zealanders and South Africans. Since Canada and Australia were the keys to the whole situation, perhaps it would be wise to obtain support for the memorandum from a few Australians and Canadians before acting.[45]

While Curtis was in New Zealand, supposedly concentrating on forming a Round Table organisation, he was inevitably drawn into the activities of the London group. Only three weeks after his arrival in the dominion he received from the London office a number of copies of a pamphlet designed to advertise the new quarterly *The Round Table.* It was obvious that he and the London group held widely divergent views about certain aspects of the movement's activities – a situation aggravated by Curtis's prolonged absence from England and by the totally different conditions under which he and the London members were working. Curtis had long believed that if the imperial cause was to have any hope of success it had to be pushed from the dominions rather than from Great Britain. Therefore, during his first three weeks in New Zealand, he had been emphasizing the South African origins of the

44  Curtis to Kerr, 21 July 1910, GD40/17/1, Lothian Papers
45  For an expansion of this point, see Kendle, 'The Round Table Movement and the Conference of 1911.'

movement and passing himself off as a South African colonist. The arrival of the circular which tended to emphasize the importance of the London group now threatened to undermine this approach.[46]

On 21 July Curtis sat down and wrote a long letter to Philip Kerr outlining the principles which were guiding him in his missionary work in New Zealand. He started by revealing what function he thought the new quarterly should serve. From the beginning, he stated, 'I believed that it would be impossible to secure continuity from groups in five different countries and any uniformity of action between them unless there were established something in the nature of a common journal – that was my private reason for advocating a journal. My secondary reason was that I thought in time it could be made a vehicle for the wider circulation of a common policy, whenever the five groups found that they had been able to agree upon one.' The function of the journal had been discussed by Curtis, Marris, and Willison in Toronto, and it had been generally agreed at that time that the journal should initially, and perhaps primarily, be a medium of information; it certainly could not propagate a policy 'because as yet none of us have a policy to propagate.'

Now this particular idea is all important to my work, because the spectre which I am always having to exorcise, is the notion so easily provoked in the Dominions, that people are to be lured into some propaganda, the final upshot of which they do not see. The only way I can meet this is to show them the books we produced in South Africa, and to show them how again and again, as the results of study, we had to discard ideas which we had long held, e.g. in the case in which in the middle of the 'Government of South Africa' we renounced the federalism to which we had committed ourselves in the Selborne Memorandum and declared that our researches had driven us into the fold of unification. My line in dealing with people is, and must be, that we have as yet evolved no solution of the problem of our external affairs and that our whole experience in South Africa has taught us there, that if we sit down to get at the facts and to review them on their merits, we are likely, before we have done, to be brought to conclusions which we little anticipated. In the meantime, I say that I am not prepared myself to put forward any views except as hypotheses for discussion. When I put in front of them our Canadian Reports, I do so with this warning and coupled with a request that they may be read with the object of picking holes in them. When I speak of the proposed journal I emphasize that it cannot as yet propagate any policy; but is to supply a continuous fund of fact ...[47]

46 For Curtis's early conviction see Curtis to Milner, 31 Oct. 1908, box 77, Milner Papers; and for his method of approach while in New Zealand see Curtis to Kerr, 21 July 1910, GD40/17/1, Lothian Papers.
47 Curtis to Kerr, 21 July 1910, ibid.

Curtis also contended that in the later editions of the circulars no mention was made of the dominion articles, a facet of *The Round Table* upon which he had been 'laying the greatest stress.' In fact there was an indication that efforts were being made by the London group to obtain a circulation among *'a great majority of men of real influence* ... in order that *from the outset it may reach a large number of readers.'* Curtis believed this to be diametrically opposite to what had been decided before he left London. Although it had been understood that each member of the central group should quietly extend the circulation as opportunity offered, he thought it had been agreed that the first and most important object of the magazine for the present would be fulfilled if it were read only by the few dozen men who 'as an inner circle' were to take part in the work of study.

Furthermore, Curtis believed that the circulars conflicted 'with the primary conception as to the method of our work which has figured most largely in my own brain from the very outset, and upon which I have worked constantly throughout.' He said that his work in the dominions, as distinct from the London group's activities, had always been guided by the principle that the domestic government of the four self-governing dominions had, with the recent union of South Africa, arrived at a stage of finality and that henceforward they should begin to attend to their mutual relations and to their relations with the United Kingdom. In other words, the time had come when a forward movement should originate from the dominions themselves. Together the dominions had to work out a policy but they would have to be sure that it fitted in with the needs and conditions of the United Kingdom as well as the other dominions. It had therefore been agreed that a group should be established in the United Kingdom, and for geographical reasons that the journal should be printed and circulated from England by the English group. 'The central idea which I have been advocating throughout with reference to the London group, is that it is to be a common agent and clearing house of the four Dominion groups. It is for this reason that I am bound to represent the movement as originating from South Africa; whence in fact it does originate at least to the same extent as from England ... I represent the establishment of a similar group in England, rather as the outcome of a suggestion from South Africa, subsequently endorsed by the approval of friends we have made in Canada, and I feel that I can do so with perfect sincerity.'[48] After reading the circulars, however, New Zealanders would 'assume that the whole thing was engineered from England and was just a repetition of the pattern, so often attempted before ... a kind of mission to the Colonies prop-

48 Ibid.

agated and fostered from London.' To Curtis the alternatives were: to represent the movement as emanating from either (i) England or (ii) South Africa. Personally he believed the second method the best, and his experience in Canada and thus far in New Zealand strengthened this belief. Nevertheless, he thought either approach could be adopted with equal justification. But if the London group was taking one line and himself another an impression of insincerity was bound to be produced which would damage their work.

Curtis received no reply to his letter until late November, almost ten weeks after leaving New Zealand. Even then he was given little guidance, although Kerr did admit that 'nobody had thought out sufficiently clearly what the Magazine was to be like before you left England ...'[49] As it happened some of Curtis's arguments proved acceptable to the London group. In a memorandum prepared at the end of the year summarising the activities of the movement during the previous twelve months it was stated that *The Round Table* was designed to fulfil a double function: first, to serve as a means of correcting false impressions and misunderstandings about the attitude of the different parts of the empire in imperial matters; and second – and here is where Curtis's contentions had obviously had effect – to serve 'as a link between the students of the Imperial problem within ... the different groups throughout the Empire.'[50]

Curtis's sincerity cannot be questioned, but his close adherence to the principles outlined above often led to the charge that his methods were disingenuous. Even his close friend Lionel Hichens admonished Curtis for 'masquerading as a S. African.'[51] Nevertheless, in the weeks following his letter to Kerr, Curtis had little reason to change his methods and he continued to work with the same optimism and religious fervour which characterised everything he did. Writing to Oliver in mid-August Curtis assured him that although many New Zealanders seemed content with the present imperial relationship, whereby Great Britain assumed the burden of imperial defence, there was no need for despair, because at all times and in all places ... the whole dead weight has been lifted up by the strength and foresight of a very few. Seven thousand who had not bowed the knee to Baal were enough to save Israel and Sodom could have been saved if only ten just men could have been found.'[52] It was for such men that Curtis was searching in New Zealand.

In addition to forming the first New Zealand groups and attempting to

49  Kerr to Curtis, 14 Oct. 1910, GD40/17/2, ibid.
50  Undated 'Memorandum' surveying the work of the movement in 1910. probably written by Philip Kerr in December 1910, GD40/17/14, ibid.
51  Hichens to Curtis, 19 Dec. 1910, Curtis Papers
52  Curtis to Oliver, 15 Aug. 1910, copy, GD40/17/2, Lothian Papers

define the role of the movement and the function of the journal, Curtis was busy during his visit preparing a memorandum on the 1911 Imperial Conference for Lord Islington,[53] the newly appointed governor. Curtis had not gone to New Zealand with the intention of influencing the dominion's actions at the coming conference, and the most he had hoped for was a chance to speak privately with Sir Joseph Ward about imperial affairs in general. During his first three weeks in the country there had been little opportunity to talk at length with the premier and Curtis had really been too busy with his Round Table tasks to pursue the matter. Then on 19 July, two days before he left for the south island, Curtis had been approached by Islington and asked to prepare a memorandum on subjects which could be discussed at the conference.[54] Initially he was excited about the opportunities presented by Islington's request, and wrote in haste to London about 'bringing back the discussion to the real matters at issue';[55] but his ardour soon abated and by early August he was urging the governor to be discreet and 'to confine his public speeches for the present time to the line that the Imperial position was one which required conscious attention.'[56] While in Christchurch at the end of July Curtis worked on the memorandum, a task which he admitted had left him 'very little time for everything else,'[57] and, having finished a first draft, he had further meetings with Lord Islington on 6 and 7 August, the second lasting for almost one-and-a-half hours.[58] These sessions resulted in Curtis agreeing to refine and moderate his arguments, and to turn the final draft over to the governor before leaving New Zealand. Unknown to Curtis the members of the London group had also become interested in the 1911 conference and had set up a sub-committee to prepare plans which might usefully be considered by some of the delegates. Memoranda drafted on the constitution of the conference, the Dominions Office, and the Secretariat had been prepared by Leo Amery, Dougie Malcolm, and Philip Kerr. They were despatched to Curtis on 29 July, ten days after he had been approached by Islington. These did not arrive until early September, and in no way influenced the preparation of Curtis's memorandum.

53  Lord Islington (1866-1936); politician and administrator; MP (C) 1892-1905 and MP (L) 1905-10; in 1905 he crossed the floor of the House on tariff reform; member of London County Council 1898-1904; governor of New Zealand 1910-12; under secretary of state for the colonies 1914-15; under secretary of state for India 1915-18; chairman of the National Savings Committee 1920-6
54  Curtis diary, 19 July 1910; also Curtis to his mother, 4 Aug. 1910, Curtis Papers
55  Kerr to Curtis, 31 Aug. 1910, GD40/17/2, Lothian Papers
56  Curtis diary, 6 Aug. 1910, Curtis Papers
57  Curtis diary, 25 July 1910, ibid.
58  Curtis diary, 6 and 7 Aug. 1910, ibid.

By the time Curtis had succeeded in forming the Auckland group he had also completed his memorandum on the Imperial Conference for the governor and turned it over to him at the end of August[59] The memorandum was a strong plea for imperial unity and an indictment of voluntary co-operation. He argued strongly against separate action by the dominions in the naval sphere, believing that preparations for war conducted by five separate states on the principle of voluntary co-operation would only end in failure and ultimate ruin for the empire. Curtis believed that the dominions should assume more responsibility for, and become closer acquainted with, the complexities of external affairs, and he outlined a number of changes in imperial organisation which he thought might hasten the process. He suggested a separation of dominion from crown colony business, the creation of a secretary of state for imperial affairs, the establishment of a closer relationship between this secretary of state and the high commissioners, the enchancement of the responsiblities of the high commissioners, the appointment of dominion ministers for imperial affairs, and a constant dicussion of external affairs between ministers in the United Kingdom and the dominion representatives.[60]

A few days after turning this document over to Islington, Curtis received copies of the memoranda on the conference prepared in London. The most detailed and elaborate was Amery's and those by Malcolm and Kerr were brief and supplementary. Amery, of course, was the one man in the Round Table who had devoted a considerable amount of time during the previous five years to analysing the existing imperial structure and recommending changes; but it was not surprising, considering the many opportunities for an exchange of ideas, that Amery's arguments differed very little from those of Curtis and when they did it was usually only in matters of detail. Amery believed that the United Kindgom, as trustee for states fast approaching manhood, was 'morally bound to consult them, to consider their views, and in their own interests and in the future interests of the partnership to familiarize them with the conduct of ... our general policy of Imperial Defence ... and ... the main issues of foreign policy.' To bring this about he recommended the establishment of a secretary of imperial affairs and a dominions office, and advocated a more active secretariat. He also believed that dominion ministries for external affairs should be established which would keep in close

---

59 Curtis diary, 27 and 29 Aug. 1910, ibid.
60 L. Curtis, 'Memorandum looking at matters that may be discussed with advantage at the 1911 Imperial Conference,' GD40/17/13, Lothian Papers. See Kendle, *Conferences*, 135-6, for a fuller discussion.

and constant touch with the Committee of Imperial Defence and the minister of foreign affairs through their ministers for external affairs.[61]

In forwarding these documents to Curtis on 29 July, Kerr informed him that they were purely provisional, and that it must be understood that the preparations for the conference were 'a bye [sic] product of our activites.'[62] Nevertheless, 'The committee want you to read them carefully and do what you judge to be the best to promote the success of the next Conference ... The psychological effect on the population of the Empire of a joint Imperial Conference and Coronation may be very great, if things are properly managed ... Next year's deliberations and ceremonial may put the finishing strokes to the process of educating the democracies of the Empire up to the point when they will be ready to digest the real doctrine of organic unity which it is our main purpose to promote ...'[63]

Kerr thought it likely that whether the constitutional conference was a success or not 'a proposal for the solution both of the Irish and of the House of Lords questions by federating the United Kingdom' would be put forward by one or other party, or both together, in connection with the coronation. Thus, at the time of the conference the country might be 'buzzing with excitement at the prospect of a great constitutional change in the British Isles, with an obvious bearing on the Imperial problem ... It is therefore of the utmost importance that the next Imperial Conference should be properly managed':

We think therefore that it is highly desirable that you in Australia when talking to people like Fisher or Hughes, or similar important men should impress on them, as far as you think it judicious, the general views laid down in these memoranda ... if ... the Conference were to discuss the strategic needs of the Empire it would not be very long before the Dominions would realise far more clearly than they realise today the importance of unity in preparation and unity of control, with its obvious corollaries about constitutional unity ... if they discuss seriously matters like All Red Route, Shipping Combines, Cable Services, they will see the value of a Secretariat which will prepare material for them. And if the Secretariat were once created it would spend its time in trying to bring into line the views of the different parts of the Empire on com-

---

61 L.S. Amery, 'Notes on the Reorganization of Official Relations between the United Kingdom and the Dominions, and on the possible development of the Conference system,' GD40/17/13, Lothian Papers. Hereafter referred to as the Amery Memorandum. See also a memorandum entitled 'The Imperial Conference' probably written bv Kerr in November 1910, ibid.; and Kendle, *Conferences*, 136-9 and 141-5.
62 Kerr to Curtis, 29 July 1910, GD40/17/11, Lothian Papers
63 Ibid.

mon concerns, which now diverge mainly through ignorance ... So will you read these documents carefully and do what you can to further our objects.[64]

Although Kerr believed all these matters to be of rather secondary importance, he admitted that as practical steps they had 'great value, because one must either go forward or backwards. One cannot stand still. And until one is ready to deliver the great assault one must be content to win positions here and there, and thereby raise the confidence of the army as a whole.' When Curtis received this letter he was about to leave for Australia and had already committed himself to influencing action in New Zealand. He considered it most fortunate that the arguments in his memorandum differed so little from Amery's, and he had no hesitation in forwarding the latter to Islington in the hope that it would strengthen the Round Table case. Islington soon turned the two memoranda over to Ward, who had been considering the subject of conference resolutions with his ministers, and by late November a full text of New Zealand resolutions was forwarded to the Colonial Office. The drafting of the two most important, the second calling for 'Imperial representation of oversea Dominions with a view to furthering Imperial sentiment, solidarity and interest,' and the third suggesting a 're-constitution of the Colonial Office,' had obviously been greatly influenced by Round Table ideas.[65]

At about the time Curtis was studying the Amery Memorandum and deciding to turn it over to Islington, the London group became aware for the first time of Curtis's agreement with the New Zealand governor. They were so alarmed by Curtis's desire 'to bring back the discussion to the real matters at issue,' by placing in Ward's hands 'a new sort of Selborne memorandum,' that they wrote in haste to dissuade Curtis from committing himself or the movement too far.[66] Unless 'Ward and Fisher can put up a decent fight, and force the hands of Laurier, Asquith and Botha and Company and expose in all their nakedness ... the facts of the present imperial situation,' the London group thought it most unwise to force a discussion of imperial federation at the Conference. The movement would only be forced into publishing 'a half-boiled egg to which nobody has pledged his consent, instead of a real chicken, in the hatching of which people all over the Empire have taken their share.' It would be preferable if Curtis stuck to the original plan of preparing

---

64 Ibid.
65 See Kendle, *Conferences*, 141-5
66 Kerr to Curtis, 31 Aug. 1910, GD40/17/2, Lothian Papers; also Kerr to Curtis, 14 Oct. 1910, GD40/17/12, ibid.

a comprehensive memorandum on the imperial problem. Only when the case had been sufficiently prepared should a debate be forced at the conference level. If the right man could be found to state the case it might be all right, but Ward would be 'little up to the job.' It would be a pity to force a discussion on the real issues, only to get a resolution endorsed by Asquith, Botha, and Laurier to the effect that present arrangements worked very well and that no urgent step was necessary – which was precisely what would happen if a weak man were to start the discussion in the conference. Kerr reminded Curtis that 'if we wanted to get something *done* it would be another matter. We don't; we want to make people familiar with the idea of Federation, so that they will be all the more ready to swallow our gospel when it is published. Therefore in talking to Islington, Ward, or Fisher, I should recommend caution about the possibility of using the Conference as a lever to focus public attention on the attraction of Federation as the solution of the Imperial Problem.'[67]

Curtis, of course, was well aware of the movement's long-range plans and the danger of proceeding too rapidly. His initial reaction to the Islington request had been understandable, but he had soon realised the need for caution, and in his revised memorandum had not made any suggestions about imperial federation or an imperial council. But as Curtis and the London group were soon to discover, their restraint was to no avail. Ward was unfortunately given a copy of the Green Memorandum by one of the New Zealand members so that despite all their efforts the whole problem of imperial unity and federation was thrust into the limelight at the conference.

With his and Amery's memoranda safely in Islington's hands, Curtis's task in New Zealand was complete. He sailed for Australia on 13 September, leaving behind him the seeds of a strong organisation already turning its attention to the criticism of the Green Memorandum and to the preparation of articles for *The Round Table*. His trip to New Zealand had been most fruitful; not least because it had helped him gain much-needed perspective on dominion attitudes. Many of his findings were unexpected. He now realised that the majority of English visitors rushed through the dominions making little effort to be discerning. His own discoveries differed considerably from the usual reports: 'The startling fact I have to convey is, that the inhabitants of the Dominions ... are greatly indisposed to disturb any state of affairs which for the time being seems convenient or pleasant ... This leads me on to another unpalatable truth, that the majority of people in the Dominions are

---

67  Kerr to Curtis, 31 Aug. 1910, GD40/17/2, ibid.

thoroughly contented with their present situation. After all, they would be more than ordinary human beings if they were not, for the system is one which gives them all the material advantages of independent nations, while relieving them of the insurance which forms the first charge on the public revenue of such nations. With the Dominions, defense is just being accepted as a last charge.'[68]

Despite this reservation, Curtis was still hopeful and thought his task in New Zealand had been exceptionally easy. As he explained to Lady Wantage, 'New Zealand is like a fragment snipped off the southern counties of England ... It is the weakness of New Zealand that she has developed no separate national sense ...' He did not anticipate such rapid results in Australia.[69]

Australia was certainly a more aggressive and abrasive dominion than New Zealand. On this basis Curtis was probably right to expect difficulties in convincing Australians of the merits of his argument. But, in fact, Curtis found his work went remarkably well in Australia. The Australian dilemma was after all not so very different from that confronting New Zealand. It too was isolated and vulnerable and fearful of European and Asian interests to the north. Defence and foreign policy questions had been a matter of heated discussion in Australia for almost a decade before Curtis's arrival and in 1909 the Deakin government had agreed to build a separate navy – the first dominion to do so. Despite the initiatives of their governments, many Australians realised that in the event of war they would still be dependent upon Great Britain. This being so, they welcomed an opportunity for continued discussion of defence and foreign policy problems.

Curtis's major activity in Australia was the distribution of the Green Memorandum and the formation of groups. He did not become involved in influencing Australian government actions or proposals in any way. Although the London members obviously wanted him to bring some pressure to bear on Australian political leaders, Curtis decided very quickly after his arrival on 16 September that to broach the movement's conference proposals to Australians would be foolish in the light of recent developments in New Zealand: '... our best hope must be that Ward may absorb them and make them his own and put them forward as such, as I very much hope in the form of a despatch to be circulated to all the Premiers before the Conference. I believe that it would be a great mistake to attempt to repeat that operation

68  Curtis to Oliver, 15 Aug. 1910, copy, GD40/17/2, ibid.
69  Curtis to Lady Wantage, 9 Sept. 1910, Curtis Papers

here where there is no Lord Islington. It would never do for Ward to find, as he inevitably would find, that exactly the same proposals were being poked forward from a totally different quarter.'[70]

Curtis adhered to this policy, and the conference resolutions submitted by the Fisher government bore no resemblance to Round Table ideas; nor did the arguments produced by the Australians at the conference sessions.[71] The only major figure Curtis seems to have talked with at length about these matters was Deakin, whose attitude toward imperial organisation coincided in some respects with the movement's. But since Deakin was now out of power, having lost the 1910 election, and unable to influence government thinking on matters of either defence and foreign policy or imperial organisation, nothing substantial resulted.[72]

Curtis stayed in Australia until early December, and while there adopted the same technique as in New Zealand. He contacted certain individuals in Sydney, Melbourne, and Brisbane, held discussions with them, circulated the Green Memorandum, drew other men in, and eventually groups were formed. One significant difference between the New Zealand and Australian ventures was the assistance of John Dove, who had been sent out by the London group to help Curtis and to ensure that the movement was not committed too far in Australia. Obviously, Curtis's New Zealand activities had rather alarmed the London members. Dove arrived in Brisbane at the end of September, and together the two men established the framework of an Australian organisation.[73]

In forming the groups in Sydney and Brisbane Curtis and Dove had the valuable assistance of Lord Chelmsford,[74] the governor of New South Wales

---

70 Curtis to Kerr, 19 Sept. 1910, GD40/17/12, Lothian Papers
71 See Kendle, *Conferences*, 177-83.
72 Both Jebb and Amery had written to Deakin about Curtis's plans. Jebb to Deakin, 23 April 1910 and Amery to Deakin, 10 June 1910, MSS 1540, Deakin Papers. Curtis had two lengthy meetings with Deakin in October. He later presented Deakin with a copy of the Green Memorandum and discussed it with him in November. See Deakin's rough diary, 21 and 22 Sept., 18, 23, 25, and 30 Nov., and 5 Dec. 1910; also Curtis to Deakin, 19 Sept. and 6 Nov. 1910, ibid. Curtis also had talks with Andrew Fisher, the Labour prime minister, and with William Morris [Billy] Hughes, an old friend of Amery's; but he did not cultivate them. See Curtis to his mother, 20 Sept. 1910, Curtis Papers.
73 A fairly extensive account of Curtis's Australian activities is in the Curtis diary 1910: Australia and New Zealand, Curtis Papers.
74 Lord Chelmsford (1868-1933); fellow of All Souls College 1892-9 and 1929; member of London County Council 1904-5; governor of Queensland 1905-9; governor of New South Wales 1909-13; viceroy of India 1916-21; first lord of the Admiralty 1924; warden of Winchester College 1930-2; warden of All Souls 1932-3

who was an old friend of many of the kindergarten, and of Archbishop Donaldson of Brisbane.[75] On first being approached by Curtis, Donaldson, who had read Jebb's *Studies in Colonial Nationalism*, was rather skeptical, but after reading the Green Memorandum he completely altered his position and became a leading figure in the Brisbane group. Others who joined were J.W. Story[76] of the Queensland education department, Reginald Roe,[77] first vice-chancellor of the University of Queensland, Judge Shand[78] of Townsville, John Fairfax,[79] whose father owned the *Sydney Morning Herald,* and John Woolcock,[80] a young lawyer and parliamentary draftsman, later judge of the Supreme Court of Queensland.[81] In Sydney Jack Bridges,[82] a wealthy young sheep farmer, Robert Irvine,[83] the secretary of the New South Wales Public Service Board and professor of economics at Sydney in 1912, Mungo MacCallum,[84] professor of modern languages at Sydney University, Henry Yule Braddon (later Sir Henry Braddon),[85] the manager of

75 St. Clair George Alfred Donaldson (1863-1935); ordained deacon 1888, priest 1889; head of Eton mission 1891-1900; rural dean of Hornsey 1902-4; bishop of Brisbane 1904; first Anglican archbishop of Brisbane 1905-21; appointed Bishop of Salisbury 1921

76 No additional information was available on J.W. Story.

77 Reginald Heber Roe (1850-1926); headmaster Brisbane Grammar School 1876-1909; inspector-general of schools and chief education adviser to the Queensland government 1909-19; vice-chancellor University of Queensland 1910-16

78 A.B. Shand; BA (Sydney) 1884; leading member of the New South Wales bar; admitted 1887; appointed KC 1906

79 John Hubert Fraser Fairfax (1872-1950); newspaper proprietor and sheep breeder; director of John Fairfax & Sons Ltd, publisher of *The Sydney Morning Herald* and *Sydney Mail*; director of the Bank of New South Wales

80 John Laskey Woolcock (1861-1930?); called to the Queensland bar 1887; parliamentary draftsman 1899-1927; appointed judge of the Supreme Court of Queensland 1927

81 Others named by Curtis were Macdonald of the Mines Department and Robert Ramsey, a Brisbane businesman.

82 No additional information was available on Jack Bridges.

83 Robert Francis Irvine; born 1861; member of the Public Service Board New South Wales and special commissioner on housing of working men in Europe and America; appointed professor of economics, University of Sydney 1912

84 Mungo William MacCallum (1854-1942); appointed professor of English literature and history, University College of Wales 1879; held chair of modern languages, University of Sydney 1886-1920; acting-warden and warden 1923-4; vice-chancellor 1924-7; deputy-chancellor 1928-34; chancellor 1934-6; KCMG 1926

85 Henry Yule Braddon (1863-1955); businessman; KBE 1920; joined Dalgety & Co Ltd 1884, sub-manager Sydney 1904, manager 1906, superintendant for Australia 1914-28; commissioner for Australia in USA 1918-19; lecturer on business principles, University of Sydney 1907-18; appointed a member of the Legislative Council of New South Wales 1917; elected a member of the Legislative Council 1933-40

Dalgety's, George Wood,[86] Challis Professor of History at Sydney, Professor Edgeworth David,[87] the geologist, and young Cecil Nathan,[88] later a prominent wine and spirit merchant, were among the first members of the New South Wales group. Lord Chelmsford was particularly keen on the Round Table work and while he remained in Australia was a useful contact for the movement. Men such as Wood, David, and MacCallum, all academics, were to be the backbone of the Sydney group in its early years, and it soon became a much more vital organisation than the one in Brisbane.

But the most vigorous group in Australia, almost from the day it was formed in late November 1910, was the branch in Melbourne. There William Harrison Moore (later Sir William Harrison Moore),[89] professor of law at Melbourne University, and Frederic Eggleston,[90] a practising barrister, assembled a powerful and productive group, among them George Knibbs (later Sir George Knibbs),[91] the commonwealth statistician, and Ernest Scott,[92] later professor of history at Melbourne. Much of their success was due to the efficiency and dynamism of Harrison Moore and Eggleston, both firm believers in the imperial mission and both worried about the mounting

---

86 George Arnold Wood (1864-1928); Challis Professor of History, University of Sydney 1891-1928; author of *The Discovery of Australia* (1922) and *The Voyage of the Endeavour* (1926)
87 Tannatt William Edgeworth David (1858-1934); Australian scientist; professor of geology and physical geography, University of Sydney from 1891; in 1907 joined Shackleton expedition to Antarctic; reached South Pole 16 January 1909; CMG 1910; KBE 1920
88 Cecil Gibson Nathan; born 1889; manager and trustee of Cooper, Nathan & Co, wholesale wine & spirit merchants, importers and exporters
89 William Harrison Moore (1867-1935); CMG 1917; KBE 1925; born in London; called to the bar 1891; went to Australia 1893; professor of law and dean of the Faculty of Law, University of Melbourne 1893-1927; constitutional adviser to the government of Victoria 1907-10; Australian delegate to the League of Nations Assembly 1927-9
90 Frederic William Eggleston (1875-1954); knighted 1941; admitted to Victoria bar 1897; on staff Australian delegation to the Paris Peace Conference 1919; member of the Legislative Assembly 1920-7; minister for water supply and minister for railways 1924-6; attorney-general and solicitor-general 1924-7; Australian envoy and minister plenipotentiary to China 1941-4, to USA 1944-6
91 George Handley Knibbs (1858-1929); CMG 1911; knighted 1923; lecturer in surveying, University of Sydney 1899; acting professor of physics, University of Sydney 1905; commonwealth statistician 1906-21; director of the Institute of Science and Industry 1921-6
92 Ernest Scott (1868-1939); born in England; journalist on *The Globe* and other London newspapers; went to Australia 1892; on staff Melbourne *Herald*; member Victorian Hansard staff 1895-1901, and Commonwealth Hansard staff 1910-14; professor of history, University of Melbourne 1914-36; dean of the Faculty of Arts 1919-24; retired and elected emeritus professor 1936

German menace. These two men acted as the Australian convenor and secretary, respectively, in much the same manner as Atkinson in New Zealand.

In composition the Australian groups resembled those in New Zealand. They were heavily larded with academics and lawyers and leavened by a few businessmen, farmers, and civil servants. Curtis's and Dove's contacts were usually high on the political or social scale, which resulted in a lack of labour representatives in the discussion groups, a particularly incongruous situation in Australia. Nevertheless, the men who joined, or who were drawn in later, were all dedicated to the preservation of the empire. They believed, as did their counterparts in New Zealand, that a problem existed, that the empire was in danger, and that some attempt should be made to resolve the difficulty. Most of them favoured a closer relationship, although only a small number, fewer than one might expect, were actually out-and-out federationists.

By late November Curtis was beginning to think about his departure from Australia. When he had left South Africa in June he had intended to return to England via India and Egypt but he was now changing his mind: 'The cables from London made me feel that the ideas we are trying to propagate are beginning to work like leaven. I am almost beginning to fear their working too quickly there and getting ventilated before the Doms are ready for them. My own line was and is that movement for National Union should initiate from the Colonies first, not from England. If we can get a few colonials to preach these doctrines their own countries will listen to them in a way that they will not listen to doctrine thrown at them from England. This is making me feel that I better abandon my visit to India and come back by Canada so as to organise a few groups there en route and complete the circle of the organisation.'[93] He quickly decided that this would be the best course of action. Shortly after forming the Melbourne group, and after a final conversation with Deakin, he sailed for Vancouver in early December.

A few days after Curtis had left for Canada a 'Suggested Plan of Discussion' of the Green Memorandum was circulated to members of the Melbourne group.[94] It recommended a close chapter-by-chapter scrutiny with members continually asking themselves:

'Are we favourable to the maintenance and development of Imperialism as defined?'

'Do we favour the further development of the principle of Imperial co-operation and inter-imperial alliances as the best means of securing such Imperialism?'

93 Curtis to his mother, 6 Nov. 1910, Curtis Papers
94 G. Lightfoot to members, 16 Dec. 1910, Harrison Moore Papers

'Is some form of federation the only other alternative, short of disintegration and ultimate absolute independence?' and
'Ought we to support the proposed plan of Imperial Federation, or is there any other federal proposal worthier of our active assistance?'
Members were also asked to consider whether or not there was a fair prospect of the ultimate establishment of such a constitutional system, and whether the proposal was organically related to the past history of the empire and would evolve easily out of the existing system of co-operation.[95] A second memorandum entitled 'Provisional List of Subjects for Discussion' advised members to examine the proposed constitution and consider what should be the structure of a federal system.[96] By late January two meetings had been held and had not proven very satisfactory. In fact, many members considered them 'fruitless.' Frederic Eggleston, the secretary of the Melbourne group, took it upon himself to draw up a scheme of study and suggested that the group be divided into sub-committees, each with a definite area of investigation and each formulating conclusions to be presented to the group as a whole. In this way everyone would have a concrete problem to come to grips with and discussion would be concentrated.[97] Eggleston's initiative had a salutary effect and from mid-February 1911 the Melbourne group was finally at grips with the essential geo-political, military, and naval aspects of the imperial problem.[98]

By the time the Melbourne members had ironed out their early difficulties Curtis was engrossed in Canadian Round Table affairs. At one time, in August, he had been reluctant to go to Canada from Australia, and for two reasons. While in New Zealand he had become convinced that India and Egypt could not be left out of any comprehensive study of the imperiaal problem. As he explained his position to Oliver:

... when I was in England, I was sensible of a disinclination to touch the question of India and Egypt, but I tell you with the most absolute conviction, that we ... must face the question as to who is to be responsible for the great Dependencies under any new scheme of government which we put forward ... I am spending all the fragments of time I can get, on reading Indian history, because I feel instinctively that the collapse of British sea power means the collapse of British rule in India. The consequence of

95 'Suggested Plan of Discussion of Memoranda,' enclosed in Lightfoot to members, 16 Dec. 1910, ibid.
96 'Provisional List of Subjects for Discussion,' ibid.
97 Eggleston to members, 28 Jan. and 8 and 9 Feb. 1911, ibid.
98 See for example a memorandum outlining some tentative conculsions of the Melbourne group enclosed in Eggleston to Deakin, 22 April 1911, MSS 1540, Deakin Papers.

such a catastrophe seems to be so immeasurable, that I want to be in a position to try and trace them with accuracy and sobriety. I have not Marris with me here to handle men's imaginations about India and I cannot do it myself until I have had a look at the country, nor can I properly picture the kind of results which would follow from the collapse of British rule, until I have been on the spot and conversed with men like Marris ...[99]

Curtis did not believe that either he or the movement could get properly to work until they had tested their hypotheses in India and Egypt, as well as in the dominions, and he wished to delay a visit to Canada until the memorandum had been properly completed and the movement's attitude well defined on such a major issue.

In addition to this concern about the best way to prepare himself for his imperial mission, Curtis was conscious that in its present form the Green Memorandum might prove an irritant to many Canadians. He reminded his London friends that Canada was 'the one Dominion to which I cannot show the Egg in its present form; they are far too sensitive, and the criticisms on Canada would tend to alienate many of the people on whose support we must count. Before it can either be shown to Canadians or come near the stage of publication, the first part must be completely rewritten ... When I go to Canada I want to go with the memorandum in a form that can be shown to people like Willison and Sandford [sic] Evans without driving them into hostility ... It is the greatest possible mistake to suppose that I can do anything in the capacity of a whirlwind. The only real results I have ever produced in life are by calm, deliberate and rather slow work. Anything in the shape of Philip's meteoric rushes are wholly impossible to me.'[100]

In November, however, Curtis finally decided it would be wiser to return to England via Canada in order that the organisation could be completed. Curtis had always believed that imperial union should be initiated in the colonies, and to leave Canada without groups at a crucial stage in imperial development might prove disastrous for the movement's aims. Without waiting for the London group's advice he left for the northern dominion in early December.[101]

This change in plan raised rather an awkward problem. Although a

99 Curtis to Oliver, 16 Aug. 1910, copy, GD40/17/2, Lothian Papers
100 Ibid. William Sanford Evans (1869-1949); publicist and author; journalist first in Toronto and then in Winnipeg; editor-in-chief of the Winnipeg *Telegram* 1901-5; mayor of Winnipeg 1905-11; became a successful broker and investment dealer; represented Winnipeg in the Manitoba Legislature 1922-35; leader of the opposition 1933-6.
101 Curtis to his mother, 6 Nov. 1910, Curtis Papers.

number of Canadian friends had been consulted at length about imperial union and the formation of a quarterly magazine, they had not been informed about the Green Memorandum. As a result a magazine group existed in Canada but no 'egg' groups, and the Green Memorandum had not been distributed. This decision, taken shortly after Curtis's departure for South Africa, had been made when no one had thought out clearly either the role of the magazine or the relationship, if any, between the magazine and Curtis's general memoranda. It had also been designed to give Curtis the greatest flexibility in his choice of group members. Kerr now admitted that there was a risk involved: 'namely the risk that some of the people who are interested in the Magazine will object to the tests which you will apply before admitting them to the "egg" group.'[102]

While in Auckland in early September, Curtis had suggested to Kerr that Willison be sent a copy of the Green Memorandum and had enclosed a draft letter explaining to the Canadian its genesis and purpose: '... we wrote down what we saw in Canada, as it appeared to us, with cold-blooded frankness. Our first object is to get at the facts for ourselves; but to publish what we have written about Canada in its present form would merely excite intense indignation and blind people ... Canada has the strongest patriotism and feeling of nationalism of any of the Dominions we have visited, so is it most sensitive to criticism ... I don't know any born Canadian to whom I would dare show this document but you, but we badly want first class Canadian criticism on it in its present form. We should like to know how far you consider that what we have said is right, but it is infinitely more important to us that we should learn how far you think what we have said is wrong...'[103]

Kerr had thought this a useful letter, but before doing anything he had consulted Lord Milner, who had agreed that since copies of the Green Memorandum had already been distributed to a number of people in the other dominions one should be sent to Willison with Curtis's letter enclosed. Kerr had sent it off, but after discussing the matter with Brand realised he had acted hastily: 'At all costs we must avoid giving Glazebrook and Peacock the impression that we have either got secrets from them or are working behind their backs in Canada. We decided therefore that as a copy had gone to Willison it was absolutely necessary that we should give one to Peacock and Glazebrook also ... explaining ... that we sent it them because we know they

102 Kerr to Curtis, 14 Oct. 1910, copy, GD40/17/12, Lothian Papers. See in this connection Kerr to Sanford Evans, 6 March 1910, box: Corresp. 1908-17, Sanford Evans Papers; and Peacock to Shortt, 20 April 1910, Shortt Papers
103 Curtis to Willison, [nd], Willison Papers

will be interested in it and because we want their frank criticism, and that ... it must be treated as strictly confidential as for obvious reasons it would raise a howl if it fell into the hands of ordinary Canadians.'[104]

Kerr thought it might prove a very good thing that the three Canadians should have been taken into confidence so early: 'Up to the present of course they have not been told the full import of our activities, though they have a sort of idea that we are engaged on some measure of general inquiry.'[105] Copies of the Green Memorandum were therefore in Willison's and Glazebrook's hands when Curtis reached Canada in January. Edward Peacock,[106] who was to be a vital link between the Canadian and British groups in coming months, was in London during Curtis's Canadian visit and took no part in the Prophet's activities.

Although the London group left it to Curtis to decide whether or not to discuss the Round Table ideas on the Imperial Conference with men like Robert Borden,[107] Curtis appears to have adhered to his Australian decision and to have devoted all his time in Canada to the formation of groups and the discussion of the imperial problem. He did show Borden a copy of the Green Memorandum and succeeded in interesting the Conservative leader in the work of the movement, but did not approach any of the Liberal leaders. Generally, he tried to avoid including active politicians in the groups, for it had long been agreed among the London members that their work should be kept out of party politics. It is true that one prominent Conservative, Thomas White,[108] the general manager of the National Trust Co., was a founding member of the Toronto group but he soon withdrew on becoming the minister of finance in the new Borden government. Anyway, White was 'included as a person not disposed to favour the views put forward in the memorandum because we wanted to have brought to bear upon it the most acute criticism that could be obtained.'[109] Later in the year Curtis also showed the

104 Kerr to Curtis, 14 Oct. 1910, copy, GD40/17/12, Lothian Papers
105 Ibid.
106 Edward Robert Peacock (1871-1962); English master and senior house master Upper Canada College 1895-1902; with Dominion Securities Corporation of Canada and London 1902-15; director Light, Power and Traction Cos in Spain, Brazil, and Mexico 1915-24; director of the Bank of England 1926-46; director Canadian Pacific Railway; formerly director Baring Bros and Co; Rhodes trustee 1925-62
107 Robert Laird Borden (1854-1937); GCMG 1914; MP (Halifax) 1896-1904 and 1908-17; (Carleton) 1905-8; (King's county) 1917-21; leader of the Conservative opposition 1901-11; prime minister 1911-20; Canadian delegate to the Washington Conference 1921-2.
108 Thomas White (1866-1955); KCMG 1916; general manager of the National Trust Co to 1911; minister of finance 1911-19; retired from politics 1921
109 Curtis to Borden, 19 Dec. 1911, reel C246, Borden Papers

Green Memorandum to Martin Burrell,[110] new minister of agriculture, and to Colonel Sam Hughes,[111] 'my old Colonel, who for many reasons has the warmest possible corner in my heart,' but neither became members of the Canadian groups nor contributed criticisms of the memorandum.

During his February visit Curtis had a number of meetings and discussions with Edward Kylie, the young University of Toronto professor, who along with Arthur Glazebrook shouldered most of the administrative burdens in the early years of the Canadian Round Table. In addition he met and talked with Glazebrook, Sir Joseph Flavelle,[112] a prominent businessman, Sir Edmund Walker, the president of the Canadian Bank of Commerce, George Wrong,[113] professor of history at the University of Toronto, John Willison, Sir Robert Falconer,[114] the president of the University of Toronto, and Adam Shortt,[115] the historian and civil service commissioner. He also stayed a few days in Ottawa with Governor General Earl Grey where he was made welcome by Dougie Malcolm, Grey's newly appointed private secretary.

One important point should be made about the dominion members of the movement, especially the Canadians: most of them, while committed to a pan-Britannic ideal, were deeply concerned with the status of the dominions.

110  Martin Burrell (1858-1938); politician, librarian, author; MP (C) 1908-20; minister of agriculture 1911-17; secretary of state and minister of mines 1917-19; retired from politics 1920; parliamentary librarian in Library of Parliament, Ottawa, 1920-38
111  Samuel Hughes (1853-1921); KCB 1915; MP (C) 1892-1921; in 1897 became lieutenant-colonel commanding 45th Regiment volunteer militia; served in South African war 1899-1902; promoted colonel 1902; minister of militia and defence 1911-16
112  Joseph Wesley Flavelle (1858-1939); bart 1917; financier; president William Davis Co; vice-president Robert Simpson Co; chairman of the Royal Commission on the reorganisation of the University of Toronto 1905; member of the Board of Governors, University of Toronto; chairman Imperial Munitions Board 1915-20; chairman Grand Trunk Railway 1920-1; chairman of the Canadian Bank of Commerce and the National Trust Co
113  George MacKinnon Wrong (1860-1948); historian; lecturer in history and apologetics, Wycliffe College 1883-92; lecturer in history, University of Toronto 1892-4; professor of history and head of department 1894-1927; a founder of the Champlain Society, its editorial secretary 1905-22 and president 1924-8; in 1897 founded the *Review of Historical Publications Relating to Canada* which in 1920 became the *Canadian Historical Review*.
114  Sir Robert Alexander Falconer (1867-1943); ordained a minister of the Presbyterian Church in Canada 1892; lecturer in New Testament Greek, Pine Hill College, Halifax 1892-5; professor 1895-1904; principal of Pine Hill 1904-7; president of the University of Toronto 1907-32
115  Adam Shortt (1859-1931); economist and historian; assistant professor of philosophy, Queen's University 1885-92; professor 1892-1908; a civil service commissioner at Ottawa 1908-18; chairman of the Board of Historical Publications of the Public Archives of Canada 1918-31

All had a strong belief in the role Britain could play in the world and all were willing to support the mother country in that role, but even more important they realised that the dominions had to be given the opportunity to voice opinions in the inner councils of the empire. Admittedly, most of them were to the right of the political spectrum – very few men with labour or socialist leanings joined the movement – but despite their Toronto-, Melbourne-, and Wellington-based toryism it would be wrong to assume that the dominion members of the movement were arrogant imperialists interested in nothing but power and the strength and unity of the race. Their method of resolving the imperial problem was ultimately to be rejected, but at the time of their Round Table involvement this was not clear. For many of the Canadian members their interest in the movement's ideas was based primarily on Canadian rather than pan-Britannic needs. As early as 1903 Sir Joseph Flavelle, later a permanent member of the Canadian Round Table, suggested to an English friend that:

The whole character of an Englishman's family life and discipline helps to keep him from understanding the spirit of the distant sections of the Empire. His whole idea of the child, while he is a junior, is to keep him in junior's place ... Running all through your public men's ideas of the Colonies is the feeling that we are children, and as the father speaks for the child in England, and restricts him and keeps him in his place, and does not seriously consider his views upon any question, so your public men have treated your Colonies ... I am not able to believe that Canada, as one member of the family, with optimism, energy, growing wealth, and self-reliance, would consider it tolerable to tie herself to live permanently under such conditions. The sentiments of Empire would not be a sufficient tangible quantity to stand the rude shock of being constantly treated as a youngster whose interests were to be sacrificed for the good of Great Britain.[116]

Four years later Flavelle wrote in a similar vein about Englishmen and the empire to Willison: 'Even among the best of them, I fancy there has always been, consciously or unconsciously, a patronizing spirit, with occasionally some amusement at the over-heated bumptiousness of the lusty son of the Empire.'[117] Sir Edmund Walker, later the chairman of the Canadian Round Table organisation, was equally emphatic in declaring his allegiance. He wrote to J.S. Ewart,[118] the Canadian publicist and fervent nation-

116  Flavelle to J. Wheeler-Bennett, 30 Oct. 1903, copy, box 1, Flavelle Papers
117  Flavelle to Willison, 10 April 1907, copy, ibid.
118  John Skirving Ewart (1849-1933); lawyer and author; called to the bar 1871; practised in Winnipeg 1882-1904, in Ottawa 1904-33; author of *The Kingdom Papers* (1911-14) and *The Independence papers* (1925-30)

alist, that 'I am a Canadian first and an Imperialist subject to that ...' Nevertheless, he hoped for a closer relationship with Great Britain than did Ewart, although he confessed he did not know how it would be brought about: 'I am as restive as most Canadians under what remains of our dependent relations with Great Britain; as conscious of our humiliation in most matters settled for us by British diplomacy; as uncertain as to how far we would actually be protected in case of war; as ready for independence if no other honourable and bearable course is possible, but I am not sure that in time a closer relation and one in which we may share in some form in the government of the whole Empire may not be possible.'[119]

One man with whom Curtis spoke and to whom he showed the Green Memorandum was Adam Shortt. Shortt did not share Flavelle's and Walker's ultimate faith in some form of closer relationship with Great Britain but believed that Canada was inevitably moving towards independence or at least to complete autonomy. He also did not share Curtis's fear of Germany. After one discussion between Sir Robert Falconer, Curtis, and himself, Shortt scribbled in his diary that 'He is sure war threatens, I am not. This chief difference.' Three days later his opinion hardened: 'Had another long talk with L. Curtis. He is too anxious to divert everything into war measures, the only interest in Imperialism.'[120] This exchange revealed not only the unique problems that Canada and Canadians would provide the movement but also revealed something of Curtis's methods and personality. These were summed up early in March by Sir Edward Peacock in a letter to Shortt: 'Curtis is really a very useful fellow, and is going to have a great effect on things of that kind, I think, through his enthusiasm and his persuasive, persistance. I am glad that you are having some talks with him, because on some points I feel that he needs guidance and I know that your views are the ones which would put him right. In general he is sound enough but when he comes down to particulars he begins to get a bit dangerous through a wish to build the whole framework and exhibit it to the public for the sake of their education.'[121]

Despite encounters such as these, and although Dougie Malcolm believed the ground particularly 'thorny' in Canada, Curtis was well satisfied with his achievements. Building on the nucleus of Glazebrook's old 'Club,' Curtis formed a strong group in Toronto with Glazebrook as convenor; and

---

119 Walker to Ewart, 9 March 1908, copy; also Walker to Sir R.H. Inglis-Pelgrave, 29 Oct. 1909, Walker Papers
120 Shortt diary, 6, 18, and 21 Feb. 1911; and 'Memorandum of Lionel Curtis to Dr Shortt' summarising a conversation of 18 Feb. 1911, Shortt Papers
121 Peacock to Shortt, 3 March 1911, ibid.

in Montreal a number of men were assembled to study the Green Memorandum. Enthusiasm was high and after one important meeting George Wrong, who had been chosen chairman of the Toronto committee to study the defence and foreign policy problems, confided to his diary: 'If we can achieve anything our gathering tonight will be epoch-making in the history of the world. On beginnings so slight do great issues sometime depend.'[122] Dougie Malcolm, one of the original founders, was conveniently on the spot in case of difficulties but because of his position could not become too deeply or too obviously involved in the affairs of the Canadian branch.[123]

By early April Curtis was back in England attending a London 'moot,' having laid the framework of an empire-wide Round Table organisation. While the groups concentrated on studying the Green Memorandum and preparing articles, the London members turned their attention to the pressing problems of defence and foreign policy which were to be discussed in May at the Imperial Conference and which all the dominion members recognised as their one major common interest.

122  George Wrong diary, 15 Feb. 1911, Wrong Papers
123  Malcolm to Curtis, 12 March 1911, Curtis Papers

# 5

# Imperial defence
# and foreign policy 1909-14

Imperial defence and foreign policy were matters of crucial concern for the Round Table movement. They lay at the heart of the 'imperial problem' which the members had determined to study and, if possible, resolve. The naval scare of 1909 had hardened the kindergarten's conviction that some form of imperial union was essential, and in the years before the war the defence and foreign policy issue was seized upon and used as a focus of study and propaganda, particularly by its two leading figures Curtis and Kerr. It resulted in intense discussion and on occasion serious disagreement within the movement, but also led to three attempts by the members to direct the course of action in the empire. Much of the movement's attention was concentrated on Great Britain and on Canada, where they hoped they had an ally in Robert Borden, the new Canadian prime minister. The other dominions, with the exception of New Zealand at the 1911 conference, were little affected by the agitation of the London members.

The essence of the Round Table argument in those years was that the dominions could not call themselves nations, or pretend to be fully self-governing, as long as the control of defence and foreign policy and the decisions on peace and war, the most important for any state, remained with the United Kingdom government. Until the dominions either controlled or had some weight in the determination of foreign policy they would not be nations but dependencies. This could not be achieved by the separation of the dominions from the empire or by co-operation between the dominions and Great Britain, but only by imperial federation. The movement argued that if the dominions sent representatives to an imperial parliament they would not lose power or become more subordinate, but if anything would achieve greater respectability as nations

This concern for a unified approach to the problems of imperial defence and foreign policy forced the movement to define its concept of the British empire and, in turn, led to a comparison of British ideals and attitudes with those of Germany. This was done in a number of articles on the international situation published in the early issues of *The Round Table*. The majority were written by the editor, Philip Kerr, but they can be taken as representative of at least the London's group's opinion, because nothing was published in the quarterly in those early years which met with the profound disapproval of any member. The articles provide the first real statement, apart from the Green Memorandum, of the movement's beliefs and aims. It is interesting to note that they reflected much of Curtis's thinking on the imperial future. By mid-1911 Kerr and the other members were sufficiently alarmed by developments in Germany to accept, if only for the time being, their prophet's more alarmist thunderings.

In his article 'Foreign Affairs: Anglo-German Rivalry,' published in the first issue of *The Round Table* in November 1910, Kerr argued that 'the central fact in the international situation today is the antagonism between England and Germany ... the solution of this rivalry between the great military power of Europe, and the great sea-power of the world is the most difficult problem which the Empire has to face.'[1] To comprehend this situation properly it was necessary to understand the forces which had moulded the two nations. As Kerr saw it the spirit of individualism had grown to full maturity in the British empire; whereas on the continent the struggle for personal rights had been impeded by incessant warfare and the constant necessity of submitting to a rigid and uniform discipline. Personal freedom had had to be sacrificed to national liberty with the result that the continental spirit was very different from the British spirit; it accepted authority readily, and subordinated the individual to the will of the community. For Kerr, the continental spirit was most characteristically embodied in modern Germany where history had taught 'the bitter lesson that the citizen can only be free when the State to which he belongs is strong enough to guarantee his freedom.' The German people had never known the political liberty of the British subject or the American citizen; to their mind it conflicted with national interests. Just as the political organisation of the British empire was designed to promote the development of the individual, so the political organisation

---

1 [Philip Kerr], 'Foreign Affairs: Anglo-German Rivalry,' *The Round Table*, Nov. 1910, 7-40

of Germany promoted the efficiency and welfare of the state over the welfare of the individual. This antagonism between the British and German systems was reflected in their foreign policies. Kerr claimed, sincerely, that the primary concern of British foreign policy was to protect at all costs the unique British political system. It was essentially a defensive policy, for an aggressive and expansive policy was contrary to the whole spirit of England. On the other hand, the foreign policy of Germany was still the foreign policy of Bismarck, the incarnation of the Prussian spirit; one based on power and the will to use it. It was a relentlessly aggressive policy, recognising neither right nor justice beyond the orbit of German national existence.

Up to the late 1890s Germany's ambitions and power had rested almost entirely on her land forces, but by then it had become apparent that without sea-power her influence would be confined almost entirely to Europe. In 1898 and 1899 navy bills had been passed and in 1906 and 1908 large increases authorised; so that in 1910 the German navy act provided for the creation of thirty-eight dreadnought battleships and twenty dreadnought cruisers as well as thirty-eight other cruisers, 144 destroyers, and a number of submarines. Such a navy would make Germany enormously influential outside Europe. What, asked Kerr, was England to do? Obviously it would have to look to its naval defences. This was the key to the safety of the empire. If ever its supremacy became doubtful its full liberty would disappear. Kerr doubted if the arrangement reached at the 1909 Defence Conference, whereby each dominion was to retain separate control of its own fleet, was likely to be successful in withstanding a possible attack on the imperial system.

The London group also believed that the empire would be threatened if Japan ever decided to link arms with Germany. This she could easily decide to do if the various dominion immigration policies became too offensive, and she broke with England.[2] Until now the keynote of the relations between the imperial and dominion governments had been local autonomy. Experience had shown that where local interests were involved it was best to leave local authorities in charge. But, argued Kerr, Asiatic immigration and the future of the Anglo-Japanese Alliance were no mere local concerns; for they could not be handled effectively by any one part of the empire. No one dominion was strong enough to uphold the policy of Asian exclusion in its own territories in face of the force that could be brought to bear against it.

2 See particularly [Philip Kerr], 'The Anglo-Japanese Alliance,' *The Round Table*, Feb. 1911, 105-53.

Nor could England settle the future of the Japanese Alliance in the light of her own interests alone, because the dominions had it within their power to make the continuance of the alliance impossible by going to extremes over Asiatic immigration. It was therefore essential that Great Britain and the dominions agree upon a common policy in defence and foreign affairs.

What was this empire that was worth devising a common policy for, that was worth defending in common? For the founders of the movement it was not an empire in the generally accepted sense. Rather, it was a system of government based on personal liberty and the rule of law whose function was to afford its citizens the opportunity of self-development rather than to enlarge and glorify the state.[3] The success of institutions such as these had rested on the readiness of the British people to make the necessary preparations to repel attacks, and 'to uphold resolutely throughout their territories those conditions of peace, law and order which they believed to be essential to the enjoyment of true liberty.' The empire was the product of the individualist principles of the British race, and it had to be preserved because civilisation would suffer if it were to fail. 'It is only by bearing in mind what the Empire really is, by remembering that it is not an imperium but a system of government which gives peace to one quarter of mankind and better government to hundreds of millions of backward people than they could get in any other way, that it is possible to understand the real nature of the problem of imperial defence.'

At the moment, external pressure was more severe than at any time in one hundred years, and Germany was the primary cause. Its policy could not fail to be dangerous to the empire and all it stood for. Yet, while the external dangers of the empire were increasing, the system of defence by which its integrity had been so long preserved was breaking down. Great Britain was no longer able to maintain a preponderant navy on all the chief oceans of the world, and unity in foreign policy and defence was gradually being impaired. The safety of the imperial system could not be maintained much longer by existing arrangements. Great Britain alone could not indefinitely guarantee the empire from disruption by external attack, and it would be impossible for the dominions to set up independent foreign policies and defensive systems of their own without destroying the empire. It was obvious to the movement that the principle of complete local autonomy, admirable as it was for the internal politics of the empire, could not be applied to foreign affairs. The empire would disappear if any one of the five governments could involve it in war:

3  For these arguments see [Philip Kerr], 'The New Problem of Imperial Defence,' *The Round Table*, May 1911, 231-62. This was published on the eve of the 1911 conference.

The conclusion is inexorable. Either the nations of the Empire must agree to co-operate for foreign policy and defence, or they must agree to dissolve the empire and each assume the responsibility for its own policy and its own defence. There is no half-way house between the two positions. There is no third alternative. The present system cannot continue. It neither provides for the safety of the Imperial system as a whole nor for the safety of the Dominions within it. Somehow or other the nations of the Empire must agree upon the interests they are to defend in common and frame a policy towards foreign powers and a system of defence which they are all committed to support, or they will be faced with the necessity of providing by themselves for their own defence.

The London group recognised that it would not be easy to find a satisfactory method of imperial co-operation for foreign policy and defence. Many difficulties, prejudices, and traditions would have to be overcome. Great Britain would naturally be reluctant to part with any share of the control of policy, especially to young nations inexperienced in international affairs. But unless the dominions had a real share in the control of imperial policy, they would be driven to adopt policies of their own; no longer could they allow their foreign policy to be decided for them by a government which did not represent them. If co-operation was to exist at all, the dominions would have to have an effective voice in imperial policy.

The case in favour of co-operation in matters of defence and foreign policy was a strong one. In 1911 it had many supporters in both Great Britain and the dominions and it was still conceivable that some form of closer co-operation would emerge. The Round Table movement realised this and that is why they pressed their case so hard. But by putting it so dramatically – as a matter of union or disruption – they only damaged their credibility and revealed their lack of sensitivity to dominion feelings.

The group did realise, of course, that it would be too much to expect the Imperial Conference of 1911 to answer outright how the system of imperial co-operation in foreign policy and defence was to work; but they believed that it had a duty to reveal to people the difficulties involved, and to devise some machinery by which the various governments could keep in closer and more constant consultation than had been possible in the past. Four-yearly conferences, even supplemented by correspondence and cablegrams, were inadequate for the co-ordination and preparation of imperial foreign policy and defence. As Kerr pointed out:

If ... things go right [at the conference] all the Dominion Prime Ministers will come home in May feeling that they must make some arrangement by which they will be kept constantly informed about foreign affairs and defence, and the British Cabinet will propose the separation of the Dominions department from the Colonial Office and suggest also that to correspond with this change each Cabinet should depute one of their own Ministers to keep in constant personal touch with the new department as well as with the foreign and defence Ministers. We shall have to decide in the course of the next few months whether it is necessary to do anything more to bring about this result by public or private action here. Personally I am inclined to think that the less publicity the suggestion gets and the more personal influence can be brought to bear both here and in the Dominions to popularize the idea among those who have the power to carry it out, i.e. the Cabinets, the better, but circumstances must guide us. Broadly speaking we don't think that it is possible for the next Imperial Conference to do very much more than this itself, and we shall be well satisfied if this result is brought about. If a good despatch goes in from New Zealand, so much the better, because after the Conference it will tend to focus public attention on defence issues ...[4]

Despite their concern, the London group did not want to force the pace unnecessarily; and they were strongly opposed to the discussion of organic union or imperial federation at the conference. For the time being they wanted to prevent imperial union becoming a party-political issue in either Great Britain or the dominions. They preferred to establish *The Round Table* as a medium of information and instruction. After they heard of Curtis's activities in New Zealand they were quick to remind their more fervent colleague of the movement's task.[5] But Curtis had not been unaware of his duties while in the dominions. He had made no effort to make detailed suggestions about imperial union to any political leader in the three countries, although he had shown both Deakin and Borden copies of the Green Memorandum. Even when asked by Islington for advice about the conference he had simply outlined the major disadvantages of the existing co-operative system. When Amery's memorandum had arrived, it had proved to have no detailed discussion of an imperial parliament and had been passed on without fear of complications. The most the movement wanted at the conference was a general discussion of foreign affairs, and with Curtis's and Amery's memoranda in Ward's hands, and with a further memorandum by Amery in the hands of the special sub-committee of the Cabinet appointed to consider the programme and business of the conference, enough seemed to have been done.[6]

4   Kerr to Curtis, 22 Dec. 1910, copy, box 210, Lothian Papers. See also Philip Kerr, 'Subjects to be discussed at the Conference,' probably written in June or July 1910, enclosed in Kerr to Curtis, 29 July 1910, copy, ibid.
5   Kerr to Curtis, 22 Dec. 1910, copy, ibid.          6  ibid.

In most respects the Imperial Conference of 1911 was a disappointment for the members of the movement. Their hopes for a separation of the dominions department from the crown colonies department, the creation of a 'Secretary of State for Imperial Affairs' and an independent secretariat, and the widening of the powers of the high commissioners all met with the disapproval of Prime Ministers Asquith, Botha, and Laurier and of the Colonial Office, which fought tenaciously and successfully to retain the *status quo*.[7] The only real source of consolation was the forthright speech on imperial defence and foreign policy given to the dominion premiers by the foreign minister, Sir Edward Grey, at a meeting of the Committee of Imperial Defence. Amery had suggested such a speech in his original memorandum submitted to Ward in September 1910 and in his brief to the Cabinet subcommittee in December. He later noted with some satisfaction that 'my talks with Haldane and Grey had at last resulted in bringing the Dominions into confidential discussions on foreign policy and strategy.'[8] Amery was rather too optimistic about the 1911 CID meetings, for very little of real moment occurred and a common understanding in defence and foreign policy was not realised; however, it had been decided that henceforward the dominions would be accorded representation on the CID whenever a matter of defence or foreign policy directly affecting them was to be discussed. This provision was later to be of considerable importance to the movement.

The most disastrous development at the conference for the Round Table members was Sir Joseph Ward's rambling incoherent cry for an imperial parliament to control imperial defence and foreign policy. The movement's effort to avoid discussion of imperial federation at the conference had been unsuccessful. Unfortunately, a copy of the Green Memorandum, and possibly even the more detailed *The Form of an Organic Union of the Empire*, had been given to Ward by a New Zealand group member shortly before the premier left for England. His conference speech was based almost entirely on the ideas embodied in the memorandum. Not only had the London members thought the moment inopportune for any airing of 'the ultimate solution,' but they had believed Ward signally ill-equipped to handle any such proposal. Both they and Curtis had been at pains to avoid preparing the New Zealander too well. Their fears were more than justified by Ward's conference performance. In the words of Atlee Hunt,[9] head of the Australian

---

7 For an elaboration on Colonial Office preparations for the conference and the meetings themselves see Kendle, *Conferences*, chapters VIII and IX.
8 Amery, *My Political Life*, I, 373. See also Bennett, 'Consultation or Information?'
9 Atlee Arthur Hunt (1864-1935); CMG 1917; KBE 1925; New South Wales Lands Department 1879-87; admitted to the New South Wales bar 1892; secretary, Department of External

External Affairs Department, who was present during Ward's imperial council speech: 'Ward made a shocking mess of his Imperial Council proposals. His resolutions were faulty in design and badly constructed but his speech didn't even attempt to support them. Instead he wandered on for hours talking about an Imperial Parliament in a style that would have discredited a member of a fifth class debating society. There is of course a case to be made for a broad Imperial Federation and a fine theme it would have been for an idealist, but he not only did not rise to the level of his subject but he dragged it down into the depths and kept it sunk by the weight of his disconnected platitudes.'[10]

Milner regarded the conference proceedings 'as calculated to dishearten Imperialists everywhere,'[11] but Kerr was more optimistic. Although he deplored the vapourings of Ward, he believed that the conference, or at least the Committee of Imperial Defence, had come to grips with the problems of defence and foreign policy and had recognised the need for a unified policy.[12] He was probably more hopeful than accurate in this estimate, but it was true that many of the premiers had indicated the need for 'some machinery by which the Imperial Government and the Dominion Governments should keep in close consultation about foreign affairs and other matters between Conferences.' Kerr also recognised the strength of colonial nationalism displayed at the conference. He was reminded that any future attempts to solve the imperial problem would have to reconcile the claims of this nationalism with the claims of the empire. What exact form the new system would take Kerr did not say, but he did suggest that if the empire was to be preserved as a force for good in the world it should move along the path of imperial union. He felt the conference had given some hope in that direction.

Despite their failures at the conference of 1911, the Round Table retained their interest in a reorganisation of the imperial structure and continued to work for a common policy in defence and foreign affairs. They were spurred by the growing tension of the years 1911-14 and by the ever-increasing German menace. The movement was active in both the public and private spheres, carrying on a campaign of some intensity in *The Round Table* and *The Times*, and when possible attempting to guide the statements and ac-

Affairs, Commonwealth of Australia 1901-17; secretary, Department of Home and Territories 1917-21; public service arbitrator 1921-30; present at 1907 and 1911 imperial conferences.
10 Hunt to Deakin, 1 June 1911, MSS 1540, Deakin Papers
11 Milner to Walker, 15 June 1911, Walker Papers
12 [Philip Kerr], 'The Conference and the Empire,' *The Round Table*, Aug. 1911, 371-425

tions of well-placed men in Great Britain and the dominions. They had two major goals in the years following the conference. First, to try and bring about a unified imperial fleet, in which they favoured the contributory system rather than the fleet unit system. They caught the ear of Churchill and also had some impact, although probably not a decisive one, on Robert Borden, the new Canadian premier. Their second aim was to help establish a better means of conferring on common problems. After their failure at the conference, they no longer seriously attempted to restructure it. Instead they concentrated their efforts on extolling the merits of the Committee of Imperial Defence with the hope that it would gradually replace the conference as the central consultative organ in the empire. Once again the Round Table efforts in this matter were directed at Borden, although Edward Grigg did campaign strongly in *The Times* and efforts were made to talk to other dominion leaders. While the two goals were being pursued writers in *The Round Table* continued to provide articles on the European situation; and as the Agadir crisis or the Balkan war loomed, the quarterly provided its readers with a valuable background synopsis and an assessment of the future implications of each situation. A few of these articles were written by Kerr, but by late 1911 he was on the verge of a breakdown and did no serious writing for *The Round Table* until 1914. In fact for much of that time, October 1911 to August 1912 and January 1913 to March 1914, Kerr was out of England and the quarterly was left in the hands of Brand and Oliver.[13]

The London members had always been convinced that Canada was the key to the imperial problem; if the northern dominion could be convinced of the need for a unified system of defence, a common foreign policy, and a reorganised imperial structure, then perhaps the other dominions would follow suit. While Laurier was in office their efforts would so obviously end in failure that nothing was attempted; but when the Conservatives under Robert Borden were returned to power late in 1911 there was cause for optimism in Round Table ranks. Borden differed significantly from Laurier in his approach to imperial problems. He appeared to have a sounder appreciation of the realities of the international situation and of the dominion's position in the empire. He was as convinced a Canadian nationalist as Laurier but without the Liberal leader's basic prejudices toward imperial reorganisation. He had no intention of surrendering any of Canada's sovereignty, and the Round Table were mistaken if they thought they could ever

13 The articles by Kerr were: 'Britain, France and Germany,' Dec. 1911, 1-57; 'The Balkan Danger and Universal Peace,' March 1912, 199-245; and 'India and the Empire,' Sept. 1912, 587-626

truly interest Borden in imperial federation; but if Canada were to be automatically involved in Britain's wars then Borden wanted Canada to have a share in the formation of policy. Not to make this demand would in Borden's eyes be to subordinate Canada's true interests, to say nothing of her sovereignty.

When the naval scare had broken in March 1909, the Liberals under Laurier had advocated the establishment of a Canadian navy and during the winter of 1909-10 had succeeded in having their plan approved by the Canadian parliament. At first Borden had sympathised with the principle of a separate Canadian navy, but by the spring of 1910 he was beginning to have his doubts. He thought the naval programme proposed by the Naval Service Act of 1910 was inadequate. The purchase of two old training cruisers and the building of five cruisers and six destroyers over the next six years hardly constituted a vigorous response to the crisis facing the empire. And the omission of a dreadnought from their scheme seemed to suggest a complete Liberal failure to recognise that the crisis was, after all, a dreadnought crisis. Borden immediately suggested that Canada could better serve her own and the empire's interests if she contributed two dreadnoughts to the Royal Navy and sought a voice in the inner councils of the empire on matters of defence. He adhered to his position during the next eighteen months despite the opposition of the important Quebec wing in his party who, under the leadership of F.D. Monk[14] and in conjunction with disillusioned French-Canadian Liberals led by Henri Bourassa,[15] vehemently opposed any Canadian contribution to Britain for imperial purposes. After the Conservative electoral victory of late 1911, Borden stated his intention to repeal the Naval Service Act. Although he refrained from defining his exact programme at that time, his sympathy for a contributory scheme and some representation of Canadian interests in London was well known.

It was thus with considerable expectation that the Round Table movement made overtures to the Conservative administration. Lionel Curtis who had met Borden earlier in the year lost little time getting in touch with the

14 Frederick Debartzch Monk (1856-1914); MP, Canadian House of Commons, 1896-1914; leader Liberal-Conservative party in Quebec 1900-4; minister of public works 1911-12; resigned from the Cabinet in 1912 as a result of disagreement with his colleagues over government naval policy.

15 Henri Bourassa (1868-1952); journalist and politician; MP (Ind L) Canadian House of Commons 1896-1907; member Quebec Assembly 1908-12; MP 1925-35; a pronounced 'Nationalist'; founded Le Devoir 1910; editor Le Devoir 1910-32; outstanding political figure, orator, pamphleteer

new Canadian premier. In December 1911 he forwarded a copy of the annotated version of the Green Memorandum to Borden, and urged him to read and be guided by it.[16] Three months later, in March 1912, Curtis was again in touch, supporting Winston Churchill's suggestion that until the dominions settled their final relationship to Great Britain and the empire they should send representatives to the Committee of Imperial Defence. Curtis realised that if the first lord's proposal was implemented the dominions would have access to a vital channel of information. 'If you were to find yourself able to take up this offer,' he urged Borden, 'I have no doubt that Australia, New Zealand and ultimately South Africa would one by one follow suit.'[17] Despite Curtis's enthusiasm and Borden's interest in Round Table ideas, the strain and stress of his first session left the prime minister little time to ponder a scheme of co-operation in naval defence.[18]

Undaunted by this setback and anxious that dominion representation on the CID should be publicised, particularly in Canada, the London group conferred with Glazebrook and DuVernet who were visiting England. Glazebrook was advised to discuss Churchill's proposals with his colleagues, especially with Liberals Kylie and Wrong and Conservatives Leacock and Willison. It was essential that Churchill's ideas be followed up:

... the presence of Canadian representatives on that Committee would enable the Canadian Government to make its views heard by the British Cabinet in the most direct way possible, and what is of no little importance in a continuous way. Such an expedient would enable Borden ... to establish the Canadian Navy as an integral part of the British Navy for the time being, while Canada is making up her mind whether she ultimately intends to be of the Empire, or to go out of it ... the time has arrived when it is all important that your great Dominion should take the lead in saving the Empire. Winston Churchill has now opened a door. That is all that any British Minister can do. If Canada puts her representatives on the Defence Committee, the other Dominions must inevitably follow before long. All our governments will then begin really to understand the essential unity of Imperial defence the common responsibility for maintaining the peace of the world.[19]

Curtis suggested that Leacock should write an article for *The Round Table* in support of the scheme. Wrong, Glazebrook, Kylie, and Sir Edmund

16 Curtis to Borden, 19 Dec. 1911, reel C246, Borden Papers
17 Curtis to Borden, 17 March 1912, ibid.
18 Borden to Curtis, 3 April 1912, copy; see also Borden to Curtis, 6 and 9 Jan. 1912, ibid.
19 Curtis to Wrong, 12 April 1912, Wrong Papers

PUNCH, OR THE LONDON CHARIVARI.—July 17, 1912.

## THE KNIGHT OF THE MAPLE-LEAF.

Sir Borden. "LADY, AN THERE BE AN ARMAGEDDON OR OTHER SCRAP TOWARD, COUNT ME IN!"

Britannia. "SIR, I COULD DESIRE NO BETTER CHAMPION!"

Walker, who was apparently 'looming up more and more as a leading man,' discussed this idea at some length, but finally decided against it. Part of the reason for this decision was Wrong's belief that the Borden government was now prepared to listen favourably to Admiralty arguments:

... The Conservative 'workers' are beginning to see that a striking naval policy is 'good politics.' Nationalism in Quebec is practically dead and the Quebec Liberals, who are still supreme in the Province, are committed to a forward naval policy. The Liberals in Ontario are taking the same tone. ... The result is that if the Government takes a strong line the support of this in both parties will be overwhelming. There is, indeed, a chance that the naval question may be taken out of party politics.

... The present situation could not be more satisfactory from our point of view. Borden, who is developing considerable personal strength, will go to England soon. Hazen, the Minister directly concerned with the naval policy, is proving one of the strong men of the Cabinet. They go with an open mind and they will be anxious to fit in with whatever policy the Admiralty prefers. I have reason to believe that they are ready to appoint a Canadian member of the Defence Committee and to undertake at once to supply two 'Dreadnoughts' to the Imperial Navy. What they will offer, however, will depend very much upon what the Admiralty asks. Do what you can to get the Admiralty to ask what is *best,* and not merely what they think Canada will do. ...[20]

Stimulated by this information the London members wasted little time before presenting their case to the Canadian prime minister. Curtis arranged an unobtrusive meeting in Newmarket on the weekend of 20-21 July between Borden, his minister of finance, George Foster,[21] and leading members of the London group.[22] Although discussion ranged over 'several aspects of the Im-

20 Wrong to Curtis, 22 May 1912, copy, ibid. Also quoted in Eayrs, 'The Round Table Movement in Canada.' Shortly after this Wrong and Kylie embarked on a trip to western Canada, primarily to establish a network of groups on the prairies and at the west coast. They were considerably impressed by the seemingly widespread sentiment in favour of a 'strong Canadian naval policy'; a few days after Borden sailed for England Wrong sent him a synopsis of their findings. Wrong to Borden, 9 July 1912, reel C246, Borden Papers. Also at this time Steel-Maitland asked Willison to write 'from time to time on the trend of opinion in Canada' re the navy and the question of representation on an imperial body. He promised to pass the information on to Bonar Law, Milner, or Austen Chamberlain. Steel-Maitland to Willison, 23 May 1912, Willison Papers

21 Sir George Eulas Foster (1847-1931); KCMG 1912; professor of classics, University of New Brunswick 1873-9; MP (C) 1882-1900 and 1904-21; senator 1921-31; minister of marine and fisheries 1885-91; minister of finance 1888-96; minister of trade and commerce 1911-21; delegate to the Paris Peace Conference 1918-19; acting prime minister 1920

22 Curtis to Borden, 1 and 2 July [1912], reel C246, Borden Papers; and Curtis to Wrong, 24 July 1912, Wrong Papers; also Milner diary, 20 July 1912, vol. 275, Milner Papers

perial Question,' it happened that defence and foreign policy, particularly naval affairs, and the merits of the CID were the most important matters under review. Present besides Curtis were Milner, Jameson, Sir James Meston,[23] Brand Hichens, Perry, and Valentine Chirol,[24] who for years had been in charge of the foreign affairs department of *The Times*.[25] Borden next met with the Round Table on 10 and 11 August during a weekend visit to Cliveden, the home of Waldorf and Nancy Astor.[26] Astor had been closely connected with the members of the Round Table since early 1911, and the movement's meetings were often held in the great library at Cliveden or in his London house at 4 St James Square. On this occasion 'an interesting and somewhat controversial conversation respecting Empire affairs' resulted.[27] These two meetings were of undoubted importance in determining Borden's interest in the CID and confirming his opinion about imperial defence, but Round Table influence by itself would not have been sufficient to stimulate Borden's later actions. Of probably greater importance was Borden's presence at two CID meetings on 11 July and 1 August, his meetings with Maurice Hankey,[28] secretary of the CID, and Major Grant Duff,[29] Hankey's assistant,

23 James Scorgie Meston (1865-1943); 1st baron, cr 1919; entered Indian Civil Service 1885; financial secretary, government of the United Provinces, 1899-1903: adviser to the governments of Cape Colony and the Transvaal 1904-6; secretary, Finance Department, Government of India 1906-12; lieutenant-governor United Provinces 1912-18; represented India at the Imperial War Cabinet and the Imperial Conference 1917; finance member, Governor General's Council, 1919; retired 1919

24 Sir Valentine Chirol (1852-1929); knighted 1912; clerk in the Foreign Office 1872-6; director of the Foreign Department *The Times* 1899-1912; member of the Royal Commission on Indian Public Services 1912

25 An attempt was also made to have Bonar Law at the meetings but it proved unsuccessful.

26 Waldorf Astor (1879-1952); baron, cr 1916; 2nd viscount, cr 1917; MP (C) 1910-19; parliamentary-secretary to the prime minister 1918, to the minister of food 1918, and to the minister of health 1919-21; British delegate to the League of Nations Assembly 1931; chairman of the board of directors of the *Observer*; chairman of the Royal Institute of International Affairs 1935-49. Nancy Astor (1879-1964); MP (U) 1919-45; first woman MP to sit in the British House of Commons; married Waldorf Astor 1906

27 Borden, *Memoirs*, 367; also Curtis to Mrs Borden, [nd] and Borden to Curtis, 13 July 1912, copy, reel C246, Borden Papers

28 Maurice Pascal Alers Hankey (1877-1963); KCB 1916; 1st baron, cr 1939; secretary of the Committee of Imperial Defence 1912-38; of the War Cabinet 1916; of the Imperial War Cabinet 1917-18; of the cabinet 1923-38; minister without portfolio in the War Cabinet 1939-40; chancellor of the Duchy of Lancaster 1940-1; paymaster-general 1941-2; chairman and director various boards and companies

29 Major Adrian Grant-Duff (1869-1914); General Staff officer, War Office, 1906-9; assistant-secretary (military), Committee of Imperial Defence 1910-13

and his frequent discussions with Asquith, Grey, Seely,[30] Harcourt,[31] and Churchill, who also had read the Green Memorandum and had been recently cultivated by the London members.[32] When Borden returned to Ottawa in late August he took with him copies of the CID minutes of the 1911 and 1912 meetings, prints of the various memoranda circulated on those occasions, and a comprehensive memorandum on the 'Constitution and Functions of the CID' He was well equipped to inform his Cabinet of the CID's activities and to reach a decision on Canadian representation.[33]

The Round Table were pleased with the way things had gone in London, and believed that the summer had seen an 'amazing development of the idea of Imperial partnership brought about by Borden's visit and by his statesmanlike handling of the whole question, and by the growing realization of the seriousness of the naval position.' Amery informed Deakin that 'From Asquith downwards, all sorts of people, whom you found impervious to all argument and encrusted over with prejudice, are having their eyes opened and are talking with real eloquence, and I believe also with something approaching real conviction of the need for a true Imperial partnership. The meetings at the Imperial Committee of Defence seem to have been most practical and businesslike, and I gather from various quarters that Borden is likely to announce an emergency gift of three Dreadnoughts as soon as he gets back to Canada. This is a long remove from your old friend 'the French dancing master' as Jameson used to call [Laurier] ... I fancy that one of the outcomes of Borden's visit will be that some Canadian minister will be over a considerable part of each year in constant attendance at the Foreign Office and the Committee of Imperial Defence.'[34]

While the London group had been busy conferring with Borden in England,

30  Sir John Edward Bernard Seely (1866-1947); 1st baron, cr 1933, of Mottistone; MP (L) 1900-22 and 1924; under-secretary of state for the colonies 1908-10; under-secretary of state for war 1911; secretary of state for war 1912-14; under-secretary of state for air and president of the Air Council 1919; parliamentary under-secretary, Ministry of Munitions, and deputy minister of munitions 1918
31  Lewis Harcourt (1863-1922); 1st viscount, cr 1916; MP (L) 1904-17; first commissioner of works 1905-10 and 1915-17; secretary of state for the colonies 1910-15
32  Curtis to Churchill, 17 April 1912, copy, Curtis Papers. Wrong's letter of 22 May had also been sent to Churchill. Curtis to Wrong, 24 July 1912, Wrong Papers
33  Seely to Borden, 26 Aug. 1912, reel C246, Borden Papers. Copies of the memorandum are in reel C246, ibid., and in Cab. 4/5/1. Also Hankey to Harcourt, 27 and 28 Aug. 1912; and Harcourt to Hankey, 29 Aug. 1912, Cab. 17/101; also Borden to Seely, 29 Aug. 1912, reel C246, Borden Papers. For an elaboration of the CID meetings and the talks with cabinet ministers and civil servants see Kendle, *Conferences*, 201-5. See also Hall, *Commonwealth*.
34  Amery to Deakin, 29 July 1912, MSS 1540, Deakin Papers

two of its Canadian members, George Wrong and Edward Kylie, had initiated a project to take the naval question out of party politics in the dominion. Their activities coincided with a visit by Philip Kerr, who was returning to England after an extensive tour of the Middle East and India. He was soon drawn into their activities and immediately informed the London group of the situation. The plan called for the preparation of a memorial and its circulation at two large private dinners to be held in Winnipeg and Toronto. The dinners were being arranged by Vere Brown[35] in Winnipeg, and in Toronto by John A. Cooper,[36] the Conservative editor of the *Canadian Courier,* and G. Frank Beer,[37] a Liberal manufacturer, with Kylie and Wrong acting as intermediaries and advisers. 'To show you how far the movement is genuine,' Kerr wrote, 'I may say that Sir Edmund Walker on one side and Dafoe[38] on the other, have agreed to further the scheme.' Kerr assured his London friends that he had not engineered the movement: 'I know of it from travelling with Kylie. But I believe that success would materially advance the cause of organic union. ... I have throughout encouraged Kylie, but have taken the utmost pains to prevent anybody connecting me with the origin of the scheme . . . '[39]

While in Canada Kerr had discussed the naval question with men of various views. Although he recognised that his opinion was 'obviously not of much value,' he thought that the best chance of getting agreement between parties would be for Borden to do four things: first, give an immediate order for two or three dreadnoughts whose construction would last over four or six years; second, announce that these ships were to be Canadian ships, but that in view of the existing foreign relations of the empire and of Canada's past debt to England in defence, the British government would have a lien on the ships – that is, whenever the Admiralty asked for them to be placed in the North Sea, the Mediterranean, or anywhere else, they would go there instantly to form part of the Royal Navy for as long as the Admiralty re-

35 There was no biographical information available on Vere Brown.
36 John Alexander Cooper (1868-1956); editor of the *Canadian Magazine* 1895-1906; editor of the *Canadian Courier* 1906-20; pioneer of the motion picture industry in Canada
37 George Frank Beer; born 1864; partner Beer Bros, Charlottetown. 1886-97; treasurer Eclypse Whitewear Co, Toronto, 1901-13; 1st president Toronto Housing Co Ltd 1912; represented the Ontario government at the Imperial Health Conference, London, 1914
38 John Wesley Dafoe (1866-1944); journalist; parliamentary correspondent Montreal *Star* 1883-5; editor Ottawa *Evening Journal* 1885-6; on staff *Manitoba Free Press* 1886-92; editor-in-chief *Manitoba Free Press* (later *Winnipeg Free Press*) 1901-44; member of the Canadian delegation at the Paris Peace Conference 1919
39 Kerr to Curtis, 31 July 1912, copy, reel c246, Borden Papers

quired them; third, that if the Admiralty did not ask for them to be stationed outside Canadian waters, they would form the nucleous of a Canadian navy to be built up on the same lines as the Australian navy, and that all subsequent additions to Canada's naval strength would form part of a Canadian navy; and fourth, pending such constitutional changes as would provide for Canada having a real voice in determining the naval and foreign policy of the British empire, Canada should exchange views on foreign and naval policy with the British government through the CID. Kerr believed that a policy such as this could provide a basis for compromise between the Conservative and Liberal parties in Canada. Anyway 'there is an overwhelming weight of opinion in Canada in favour of doing something handsome *now* ... I write you this because I fancy you will just have time to tell Borden what is going on before he leaves, so that he can make any consequential arrangements with Winston that he thinks fit. You will also know by the time you get this whether the dinners have borne fruit.'[40]

The dinners were, in fact, quite successful, and after some subsequent negotiation the Winnipeg and Toronto organisations agreed to the wording of a memorial which read as follows:

We, the undersigned citizens of—, members of both political parties, unite in urgently representing to the Premier and Cabinet of Canada and the Leader of the Opposition:

1. That in our judgement it is the desire of the majority of the people of Canada that the Dominion should forthwith take her part in the naval defence of the Empire.

2. That capacity for self-defence being a necessary incident of nationhood, the Canadian people looks forward to equipping itself with all reasonable despatch with the necessary means of defence; and that the permanent policy of the Dominion should look to the establishment of a navy that will be worthy of our national aspirations.

3. That if international relations as disclosed by official information are such as to indicate the existence of an urgent situation, substantial evidence should be given forthwith of Canada's recognition of her responsibilities as part of the Empire; and that action taken in accordance with this idea should be of such a notable character as to be adequate in the light of the responsibilities of Canada, and of the exigencies of the case, and worthy of Canada's material wealth and prosperity.

40 Ibid. Curtis sent a copy of this letter to Churchill and probably discussed it with him on the weekend of 17 and 18 August at Cliveden, where both he and the first lord were guests. In forwarding the letter to Churchill, Curtis hoped 'that the attempt to bring about a concorde between the two parties which we have always urged upon them may still bear some fruit.' Curtis to Churchill, 12 Aug. 1912, copy, Curtis Papers

4.   That the motive animating Canadians is not to promote the military spirit as such, and, in particular, is not to render more acute the tension between Great Britain and any other Power; but to show in a practical way their belief that the effective maintenance of the British navy makes for the preservation of the world's peace, and to demonstrate unmistakeably the strength of the Oversea's resources which are available for the defence of the Empire.

5.   That it is highly desirable that the policy of the Dominion of Canada, both for the moment and permanently, with regard to this matter should not be or become a party question.

6.   That without delay an earnest effort should therefore be made by the Government, through friendly consultation with His Majesty's Opposition in Canada, to give such immediate action and to the Dominion's permanent policy, a form which, securing the adhesion of both parties, may remove the whole question of Imperial Defence from the domain of contentious politics.[41]

The memorial was sent to Borden and Laurier with no known effect on the prime minister; but Laurier objected to the very premise of the scheme, and asked Dafoe 'why such a memorial at all?' As far as he was concerned the Liberal had a policy on the naval issue and they should have stuck to it. There was nothing to be gained by signing a non-party or inter-party memorial.[42] In fact, no political truce was declared on the naval issue. After the autumn of 1912 the Round Table movement was never again directly involved in attempting to determine policy and action in Canada.[43]

While these discussions and activities were underway in Canada, the London group initiated a public campaign urging the replacement of the Imperial Conference by the Committee of Imperial Defence. Emboldened by

41  A copy is attached to the 3 Oct. 1912 entry in the Walker diary, Walker Papers; see also Walker diary, 31 July and 7 Aug. 1912; J.K. Atkinson to Dafoe, 19 and 21 Aug. 1912, and Dafoe to Atkinson, 22 Aug. 1912, reel M73, Dafoe Papers

42  Dafoe to Laurier, 23 Sept. 1912 and Laurier to Dafoe, 26 Sept. 1912. ibid.

43  While in Canada in October Milner spoke with Borden, Laurier, and Bourassa. He also corresponded with Bourassa about imperial problems. But he made no effort to influence Canadian affairs. See Milner diary for October 1912, vol. 275, Milner Papers; also Bourassa to Milner, 7 and 10 Oct. 1912, box 74; and Milner to Bourassa, 9 Oct. 1912, copy, box 169, ibid. Also Milner to Borden, 17 Oct. 1912, OCA Series, file 3A, Borden Papers. It should be mentioned that although the Round Table did not attempt to bring pressure to bear on Borden, nearly all the Canadian articles for the magazine were shown to Borden during 1912, a habit which Kerr, when he learned of it, deplored: 'I think that was a mistake. It does not seem to me that it is for politicians to decide whether articles are likely to cause ill-feeling or not. We must decide that for ourselves.' Kerr to Willison, 27 Nov. 1912, Willison Papers

their talks with Borden and by the support of Churchill, with whom Curtis and Grigg discussed the matter in early September aboard the *Enchantress,* they decided to publicise their ideas as widely as possible. The campaign opened with the inclusion of an article on 'Canada and the Navy' in the September 1912 issue of *The Round Table.* The first section, 'The Problem as it Appears from London,' was written by Edward Grigg and contained an analysis of the CID as an embryonic 'Cabinet of the Empire.'[44] According to Grigg, the time had come for the dominions, especially Canada and Australia, to demand some share in the direction of imperial foreign policy. In his estimation the CID, owing to its elastic constitution and advisory nature, would probably provide the best means of effecting such a change in imperial relations. If the dominions agreed to send cabinet ministers to sit as members of the committee, the first step would have been taken toward a 'Council of Ministers' for the empire. Grigg continued to argue the need for increased consultation in the columns of *The Times* which was now being edited by Geoffrey Robinson. Grigg had joined *The Times* in 1908, succeeding Leo Amery as the newspaper's expert in imperial affairs, and most of the leading articles on the empire published between 1909 and 1913 were written by Grigg.

*The Times'* and the movement's advocacy of the CID in preference to the conference, and of emergency contributions instead of dominion navies, met with the disapproval of Richard Jebb, a long-time student of imperial organisation, a close friend of many of the London group, and Grigg's cousin. Initially, Jebb had been attracted by the movement's efforts to bring about closer union, but gradually the Round Table's stance on the CID, on the conference, on defence, and on tariff reform alienated him and he quickly became the movement's most persistent and telling critic. At this time he was attempting to complete a third volume of his study of the conferences, but he abandoned it in order to devote all his energies to combatting what he feared were ideas and activities dangerous to the empire. His arguments were eventually marshalled and published in 1913 in *The Britannic Question,* a book written specifically to counter the Round Table movement, but during September and October 1912 he stated much of his case against the CID in a series of letters to *The Times.* Grigg responded to these and the result was a fascinating dialogue over the various merits and defects of imperial organisation and, in particular, of the Committee of Imperial Defence and the conference. Jebb's views on the contributory system of imperial defence and

44 [Edward Grigg], 'Canada and the Navy: The Problem as it Appears from London,' *The Round Table,* Sept. 1912, 627-56

on the Borden government's naval programme were also elaborated in letters to friends throughout Great Britain and the empire.[45]

Jebb knew that the concept of allied navies was anathema to many in Great Britain, particularly to those in the movement, and that a single federated navy was considered to be superior technologically and strategically. But if the principle of alliance was fully developed, as he believed it could be within the British empire, 'allied navies need not mean disjointed navies, but rather units in a combined naval scheme.'[46] He pointed to the Japanese Alliance as a dramatic refutation of the imperialist, centralist Round Table argument.[47] He believed Borden was liable to cause himself considerable trouble if he advocated emergency contributions, and did not take up a permanent naval policy on Australian lines.[48] Borden had allowed himself 'to be nobbled by the Imperial Federalists,' he said, who hated the Australian plan of fleet units.[49] Grigg, of course, disagreed. He pointed out that *The Times* had supported the development of the Australian navy in past years and would continue to do so, but conditions in the empire were in a perpetual state of transition and arrangements needed to be continually improved. The question had to be faced how the fleets were to co-operate. He believed Borden had thought out the problem and had reached the only sensible conclusion.[50]

Grigg put this point of view to his cousin, but Jebb would have none of it and said as much in a letter to Robinson. He explained that he and Fabian Ware had been watching 'with deep misgivings the reaction here to the old, hopeless Conservative kind of Imperialism; which is typified in the frantic encouragement of Borden's "emergency contribution" policy. Our own feeling ... has been that Borden, in his honest, unimaginative stupidity, is backing the wrong horse and is simply playing into Laurier's hands ...' He believed that the reaction would only serve to alienate many who might support a more liberal doctrine of imperialism, and he asked Robinson 'to do something to stem the tide; at least so far as to check the inevitable impression in the Dominions that the old, militarist Imperialism, with its schemes of cash contribution, centralised administration, and British ascendancy perpetuated ... is again paramount in England.' Jebb realised that

45 For a detailed study of the Jebb-Grigg debate in *The Times*, see Kendle, *Conferences*, 207-10
46 Jebb to C.H. Cahan, 6 March 1912, copy, box 1, Jebb Papers
47 Jebb to Cahan, 3 April 1912, copy, ibid.
48 Jebb to F. Ware, 30 July 1912, copy, box 3, ibid.
49 Jebb to N.M. Collins, 28 Aug. 1912, box 1, ibid.
50 Grigg to Jose, 3 Sept. 1912, Jose Papers

the Round Table members might be attracted by the contributory scheme because it seemed to necessitate a more formal system of representation than would be required if Dominion navies were developed, but he believed them wrong to think a contributory system would popularize imperial federation. On the contrary, the result might be to provoke a counter reaction inimical to the prospect of closer union in any shape.[51] Jebb contended that 'the whole principle of "emergency contribution" is out of harmony with the natural course of the evolution, and that forms of consultation which might seem adequate in a system of alliance ... will not prove equally acceptable when Canadian money or Canadian ships are to be administered by an extraneous Government. The only logical or final solution of such a situation would be Imperial Federation. But that solution obviously cannot be immediate; nor, in my own belief, can it be canvassed with any thoroughness without being found to conflict hopelessly with the natural [and healthy] tendencies of Dominion development.'[52]

Throughout October Jebb waged his battle against the Round Table movement and *The Times* and worked hard on his small volume, but during this period he did not entirely break off relations with members of the London group. One of his letters to *The Times* resulted in a dinner meeting with them. It was a revealing session:

... I dined and had a long confabulation with Lionel Curtis (who is now Beit lecturer at Oxford), my cousin Ned Grigg (who now, alas, lodges with Curtis) and other Round Tablers. In private they seem to me to make no bones about it, that they DO aim at displacing the Conference for the sake of getting an undivided Executive. But they daren't rub in that point too much in public – e.g. The Times, which is now Geoffrey Robinson (another vindication of Milner's famous Kindergarten) and Grigg. Privately they say that, as far as Borden and his 'emergency' policy is concerned, they really don't aim at giving Canada any genuine share of control, because it really doesn't matter. As the contribution is to be a 'gift' to the Imperial Government, that Government of course can dispose the ships as it pleases any time, and Canada would be helpless. But they think the 'information' to be had in the Defence Committee should be a useful 'education' to the Dominion Ministers, whom they regard as quite ignorant of the mystery of foreign policy ... as regards Borden's 'permanent' naval policy, they feel that when *that* comes the moment will have arrived for proper Imperial Federation. To which I am bound to reply that, if that is Borden's view, either

51 Jebb to Robinson, 27 Sept. 1912, copy, box 3, Jebb Papers
52 Jebb to Cahan, 26 Sept. 1912, box 1, ibid. For an elaboration of Jebb's view re the CID see Jebb to Amery, 22 Oct. 1912, box 1, and Jebb to Foster, 23 Oct. 1912, box 2, ibid.

the 'permanent policy' is postponed to the Greek Kalends in Canada, or else Borden makes way for Laurier. Personally I would prophesy the first alternative.[53]

In early December 1912 there was an indication that the Round Table movement might yet succeed. On 5 December Borden introduced his Naval bill, calling for a money contribution to the imperial navy for the construction of three dreadnoughts and for Canadian representation on the CID. Five days later the Colonial Office issued a general invitation to all the dominions to send representatives, but for various reasons this offer was rebuffed.[54] Borden's bill met with heated opposition in Canada, and was only forced through the House of Commons by the introduction of closure. It was then rejected by the predominantly Liberal Senate.

Despite this setback the members of the London group continued to press their point of view on overseas visitors, such as James Allen[55] of New Zealand and George Pearce[56] of Australia. Grigg wrote often and at length to Jose, and outlined the movement's arguments in *The Times*, while *The Round Table* printed a number of articles on various aspects of the defence and naval issue.[57] All the while Jebb continued to oppose Round Table assumptions and arguments in letters to various friends throughout Great Britain and the empire; and in his book *The Britannic Question* published in 1913 he levelled the most serious criticisms yet faced publicly by the group. But so far as the defence and foreign policy issue was concerned, Jebb was wasting his ammunition because the movement's hopes had been devastated when the Canadian Senate had rejected Borden's bill and when the dominions had rebuffed the Colonial Office despatch. The move toward imperial

53 Jebb to Deakin, 31 Oct. 1912, 'Jebb Correspondence,' Deakin Papers
54 See Kendle, *Conferences*, 212-14.
55 James Allen (1855-1942); GCMG cr 1926; MP Dunedin East 1887-90; Bruce 1891-1920; minister of defence 1912-20; minister of finance and education 1912-15; minister of external affairs and finance 1919-20; New Zealand high commissioner in London 1920-6; member of the Legislative Council 1927-41
56 George Foster Pearce (1870-1952); KCVO 1927; founder of early Australian labour organisations; president Trade Union Congress 1899; MP Commonwealth Parliament 1901-38; minister for defence 1908-9, 1910-13, 1914-21, and 1931-4; minister for home and territories 1921-6; minister for external affairs 1934-7; acting prime minister 1916; attended the Imperial Conference of 1911; represented Australia at the Washington Conference 1922; leader of the Australian delegation to the League of Nations Assembly 1927
57 See particularly 'Policy and Sea Power,' *The Round Table* March 1913, 197-231; and 'Naval Policy and the Pacific Question,' ibid. June 1914, 391-62. Also the various dominion and United Kingdom chronicle articles after December 1912 often contained synopses of opinion and developments in defence matters.

federation via either a common defence policy or by representation on the Committee of Imperial Defence had been seriously undermined by 1913. It had not regained momentum by the time war broke out a year later.

# 6

# Home Rule all round

In addition to their efforts to influence imperial defence and foreign policy, the London members were also intimately involved before 1914 in the discussions and manœuvres surrounding the most explosive issue in British politics – the Irish question. They believed that the Irish crisis might provide a means of obtaining a separation of domestic from imperial affairs, an essential step in the achievement of imperial federation. For four years the central group advocated 'Home Rule all round' as a solution to the constitutional difficulties of the United Kingdom.

'Home Rule all round,' known also as 'Devolution' or 'Federalism' depending on the occasion or the party affiliation of the would-be reformer, was by no means a new concept; it had been broached as early as the 1830s and had received much attention in the eighties and nineties at the time of Gladstone's two Home Rule bills, and again in 1904-5 when the Unionists considered establishing a central administrative organ in Ireland. At best, it meant the erection of four provincial parliaments with separate executives for Ireland, Scotland, Wales, and England responsible for essentially local matters, with an overall parliament sitting in London, elected on a population basis, responsible for general United Kingdom affairs such as postal services, customs, trade, defence, and foreign policy; at the very least, the scheme meant the devolution onto local government bodies, possibly provincial councils, of the more parochial problems considered at Westminster. 'Home Rule all round' attracted considerable interest in 1910 at the time of the constitutional conference, and again during the tempestuous months of 1913-14 when the United Kingdom hovered on the brink of civil war and any and all compromise solutions were of necessity being explored. On both occasions the London group were prominent advocates.

The Irish question was never raised during the early Round Table discussions and it was not until Curtis, Kerr, and Marris journeyed to Canada in late September 1909 that anyone in the movement gave it serious consideration. One of the movement's most ardent supporters in Canada, and later an intimate in London, was Governor General Earl Grey. Long an imperial federationist, Grey believed Ireland might provide the key to imperial union, and as early as February 1907 had suggested to Laurier that 'Ireland may still redeem her past by providing the excuse for Imperial Federation ...'; later, in writing to George Wrong, he maintained that 'My interest in the federation of the United Kingdom must precede the federation of the Empire.'[1] His experience in Canada had also convinced Grey that if an attempt was made to federate the mother country it would have to be 'on lines which will make Ireland, not into a Canada or Australia, but into an Ontario or Quebec.'[2]

During Curtis's stay at the governor general's residence in December 1909 Grey outlined his thoughts on Ireland and the empire. Writing to Curtis shortly after, he exclaimed that 'It was a *real* pleasure to me to have you in the House. I wish it were a Hive *always* filled with Imperial Bees; each of them, like the original Imperial Bee Napoleon, realising that they have a mission, and are in themselves, each of them, a little finger of the almighty!' He took the opportunity to reiterate his views on Irish and imperial problems:

My view is, and I give it to you as a bone to worry over with Kerr, Grigg and Willison ... that it is in the United Kingdom that the chief educational work has to be done.

Before the road is cleared for the Federation of the Empire we have to put the United Kingdom straight. The time is approaching, if it is not already here, for getting this work done ... Provincial Legislatures of the Canadian rather than the South African type for 1. Ireland 2. Scotland 3. Wales 4. England (4. North? 5. South?) with a Federal Parliament armed with powers of disallowance sitting in London.

1   Grey to Laurier, 12 Feb. 1907, copy, box 250, Grey Papers; and Grey to Wrong, 22 Feb. 1910, Wrong Papers
2   Grey to Lord Brassey, 5 March 1910, copy, enclosed in Grey to Jebb, 14 March 1910, box 2, Jebb Papers. Jebb replied: 'On the general question of federal government for the United Kingdom, as a final solution of the Home Rule trouble and as a step towards Imperial Federation, I am in substantial agreement with you.' Jebb to Grey, 24 March 1910, copy, box 2, ibid.

Each Provincial Unit to be represented in the Federal Parliament in proportion to its population ...
When the Irish are thus reduced in the Federal Parliament of the United Kingdom to their proper proportions we can begin to talk Imperial Federation.[3]

Curtis later acknowledged the impact that Grey's arguments had had on his thinking about imperial federation, and for almost a year he tended to argue that 'Home Rule all round' or 'Federalism' in the United Kingdom had to come before imperial federation.[4] This was to be one of the main bones of contention between the members of the movement for much of 1910, and was a primary reason why Home Rule for Ireland very quickly assumed far more importance for the Round Table than a 'pure' domestic issue. The second major reason why the Round Table involved itself in the Irish problem was the hope of resolving the chaotic state of affairs at Westminster brought about by congestion of business. By 1910 international and imperial problems and decisions concerning the fate of nations had to share the same parliamentary calendar with many trifling interests of only local importance. It was obvious that too vast a proportion of a minister's time was spent on irrelevant platform work and too little in administrative duties, while the Cabinet absorbed in the tactics of the immediate situation or in the discussion of foreign politics were unable to give more than perfunctory attention to the principal measures coming up from the departments. Moreover, the electorate was confused by the mass of issues facing it, and all too often voted without giving much thought to foreign and imperial issues.

Although these problems were given preliminary attention at the Ledbury meetings of January 1910, they were not discussed in detail until Curtis returned to South Africa.[5] There in early March 1910 a meeting took place in Pretoria of 'the available members of the kindergarten [presumably Patrick Duncan, Richard Feetham, and Peter Perry], Lady Selborne,[6] Lord Robert

3 Grey to Curtis, 14 Dec. 1909, copy, Grey Papers
4 Curtis to Kerr, 19 Sept. 1910, GD40/17/12, Lothian Papers
5 At the Ledbury meeting it had been decided that 'a preliminary enquiry into the effects of the congestion of business in the House of Commons should be made and that a sum of £50 be allotted for payment to some qualified person for collecting the necessary data – further action – if any – to be decided upon later.' See 'Minutes of a meeting held at Ledbury January 15/18, 1910' and 'Minutes of a meeting held in London on January 23, 1910, 4-5 p.m.,' GD40/17/11, ibid.
6 Lady Beatrix Maud Selborne was the daughter of the 3rd Marquis of Salisbury and the sister of Lord Robert Cecil.

Cecil[7] and Amery.' The basis of discussion was Curtis's proposals for the establishment of local parliaments for Great Britain and Ireland and 'in fact very little else was discussed.' Curtis's views met with considerable opposition, mainly on the ground that Ireland could not support the financial burdens involved in Home Rule. Everyone, including Curtis, finally agreed that the question of finance might prove a fatal obstacle, and that before going further it was desirable to get at the financial facts. Lionel Hichens was asked to conduct an enquiry into the matter; and after he and Jameson had been informed of the discussions in Pretoria, it was further decided 'That an effort should be made to secure the appointment of a Royal Commission to enquire into the whole question of congestion in Parliament and the Cabinet and the best means of remedying it.' Curtis and Hichens then drew up a rough draft of the terms of reference of the proposed commission which ran as follows: 'To enquire into the causes of the existing congestion of business in Parliament and the cabinet and to report how far it is practicable to remedy this defect. (a) By reorganising Parliamentary procedure (b) By delegating wider functions to existing local authorities (c) By creating local authorities for wider areas (d) By other means ...' In forwarding this information to Milner, Hichens hoped the commission would materialise; for it seemed to be the only way the whole question could be thoroughly ventilated. But whether there was a chance or not 'a small committee should be formed consisting of Oliver, Lord Robert, and myself to enquire into the financial effect of home rule upon Ireland ... I sail for England on April 6 ...'[8]

Before Hichens could reach England, the Round Table's chances of securing a royal commission appeared doomed. On 6 May King Edward VII died, and to avoid a disagreeable political crisis over the future of the House of Lords in the early weeks of a new reign a party truce was declared. On 16 June a constitutional conference assembled to find a solution for the conflict between the Lords and the Commons. It lasted throughout the summer and autumn, coming to an end after twenty-one meetings on 10 November. Under such circumstances it seemed hopeless to expect a royal commission to be created on the subject of Home Rule and the congestion of business in parliament. Nevertheless, the movement was determined to probe every ave-

---

7 Edgar Algernon Robert Gascoyne-Cecil, Viscount Cecil of Chelwood (1864-1958); 3rd son of 3rd Marquis of Salisbury; MP (C) East Marylebone 1906-10 (Ind C) Hitchin Division, Hertfordshire, 1911-23; parliamentary under-secretary for foreign affairs 1915-16; assistant secretary of state for foreign affairs 1918; a founder of the League of Nations
8 Details of the meetings in South Africa and the decisions taken are contained in Hichens to Milner, 21 March 1910, copy, GD40/17/11, Lothian Papers.

PUNCH, OR THE LONDON CHARIVARI.—October 26, 1910.

## THE NEW JOHN BULL.

AFTER THE PROPOSED "FEDERALISATION" OF THE BRITISH ISLES.

nue, and on 18 June Philip Kerr dutifully wrote to Lord Selborne in an oblique effort to influence the Unionist representatives at the conference.

He began cautiously by recognising that the Liberal government, because of its dependence on the Irish Nationalist vote, would find it impossible to appoint a commission on the single issue of Home Rule. Much the best chance would be for all the representatives at the conference to agree that not only was the constitutional machinery breaking down in the Lords but also in the House of Commons and the cabinet, owing to overloading. If assent could be gained to this proposition, then it should not be difficult to reach agreement on the appointment of a commission. As Kerr saw it, the net effect would be that the Unionists would have conceded the principle 'that Home Rule all round (including Ireland) ought to be investigated ... the Liberals would have assented to an arrangement which ... would necessarily involve the postponement of a Home Rule Bill until the Commission had reported,' while the Round Table would have secured an impartial investigation of the whole question of internal devolution, thereby leaving the way clear for the consideration of constitutional reform on its merits. Kerr prompted Selborne: 'I understand that you are in constant touch with the Unionist leaders in the Conference. Don't you think it would be worthwhile to suggest this as a possible solution of one of the difficulties.'[9]

Over a month later Kerr was still optimistic about the movement's chances, as he wrote to Curtis who was now in New Zealand on the second stage of his imperial journey: 'I believe that whether the constitutional conference is a success or not a proposal for the solution both of the Irish and of the House of Lords questions by federating the United Kingdom will be authoritatively put forward by one or other party or both together, in connection with the Coronation, so that it may be considered calmly and without party bias ... This will probably be in about a year's time ... For the moment we can do nothing. The general movement is now out of our control ...' Kerr thought it imperative that while in Australasia Curtis should impress on all prominent individuals 'like Fisher or Hughes' the general views on imperial organisation laid down in the various Round Table memoranda, for if plans for the constitutional reform of the United Kingdom did materialise it would be beneficial to have the dominion representatives at both the coronation and the 1911 Imperial Conference well-briefed on the broader implications.[10]

---

9  Kerr to Selborne, 18 June 1910, copy, ibid.
10  Kerr to Curtis, 29 July 1910, copy, ibid.

This was, of course, typical of Round Table methods – attempting to exert pressure behind-the-scenes in order to advance its schemes. But in this instance the movement failed, for it was unable to secure the appointment of a royal commission on congestion and had to satisfy itself with a private study. Some of the results were eventually published in article form in *The Round Table* in August and December 1911, and the whole study was issued anonymously as a book in 1912 under the title *An Analysis of the System of Government Throughout the British Empire.*[11] The only positive gain from these early plans was the findings of Cecil, Oliver, and Hichens, which bore fruit in the criticisms levelled by Amery and Cecil at the financial aspects of the Government of Ireland bill in 1912-14.

While the constitutional conference was in session the members of the Round Table had innumerable discussions among themselves about the importance of 'Home Rule all round' and the relationship between constitutional reform in the United Kingdom and organic union of the empire, matters which had been of increasing concern to the movement since Curtis's conversations with Earl Grey the previous autumn. Earlier in the year the group had generally agreed that 'Home Rule all round' was a step, perhaps a necessary one, on the road to imperial unity. In the following months many of them had second thoughts, particularly the financial expert Hichens and Unionists Amery, Cecil, and Steel-Maitland who saw 'Home Rule all round' as a first step in a process of disintegration rather than the opposite. Men like Oliver, Robert Brand, and Kerr, while not so pessimistic, were still more cautious than in January, especially Kerr: 'I have not yet made up my mind as to what constitutional reconstruction is necessary in the United Kingdom ... I always tell my cautious friends, like Hichens, that my sole object in helping the idea of Federalism along, is because discussions, such as have been going on ... are ploughing the hard soil so as to prepare it to receive our seed later on.'

Kerr agreed that 'federation' was a misnomer, for an imperial parliament would always remain supreme and under no scheme would there be a court to interpret the constitution. 'But it is a good fighting word to begin with. Devolution has noisome associations. Home Rule all round, worse. Federalism has been a success everywhere and people will therefore not be inclined to fight shy of the word.'[12] Kerr's main concern was to acquaint people with

11 For the articles see 'Colonial Neutrality,' *The Round Table*, Aug. 1911, 435-42; and 'The Congestion of Business in the House of Commons,' ibid., Dec. 1911, 58-95.
12 Kerr to Curtis, 10 Aug. 1910, copy, GD40/17/2, Lothian Papers

the idea of federation, so they would be 'all the more ready to swallow' the Round Table gospel when Curtis was ready to publish his general study. Until that time the movement should attempt to circulate the idea that federation was a plausible solution of the imperial problem; if this could be done to advantage 'under the shadow of Home Rule,' so much the better.[13]

Kerr was not loathe, however, to face the basic issues. In correspondence with Curtis he pondered whether or not it was possible 'to take a preliminary step towards Imperial unity before the Dominions are ready to be represented in a true Imperial assembly, by persuading the United Kingdom to entrust the imperial functions ... to a different assembly to that which conducts its national affairs.' Kerr did not believe it was; as long as Great Britain alone controlled the empire, national and imperial affairs would be so intimately connected that they would have to remain the responsibility of a single assembly. No scheme of devolution for the United Kingdom would produce the necessary division between imperial and national affairs; this would have to await the day when the dominions were ready to take their part in creating a true imperial body. 'Federalism for the Empire, and Federalism for the United Kingdom,' argued Kerr, 'are two entirely distinct ideas ... The Federation of the United Kingdom clearly is no necessary stage which must be passed before Imperial Unity can be achieved. The surrender of the Imperial functions can be made to an Imperial assembly just as easily by a unitary Parliament of the United Kingdom as by a federal Parliament.' Kerr recognised and, in fact, emphasized the educational value of a federal movement, but he believed the case 'conclusive against the moot committing itself to Federalism for the United Kingdom, and undertaking active work on its behalf as a necessary stage which has to be passed on the road to Imperial Union. Our energies must be concentrated on the Imperial side of the business direct.'[14]

By this time Lionel Curtis was also reconsidering many of his earlier ideas. Whereas he had once advocated the federation of the United Kingdom as a necessary preliminary to imperial federation he now, with his South African experiences in mind, urged his friends in London not to frame proposals for federating the United Kingdom until they had immersed them-

---

13 Kerr to Curtis, 31 Aug. 1910, copy, ibid.
14 Kerr to Curtis, 30 Sept. 1910, copy, ibid. This letter took the form of a memorandum which was circulated to Milner, Oliver, and Brand before finally being sent to Curtis on 7 October. Kerr planned to distribute an abbreviated and corrected edition to a larger 'moot' scheduled for mid-November at Blackmoor, the home of Lord and Lady Selborne. Kerr to Curtis, 7 Oct. 1910, copy, ibid.

selves in such problems as the restructuring of administrative bodies, the separation of powers, and the division of public revenues, and were sure that the scheme would work. At one time Curtis, much to the despair of Leo Amery, had also contemplated urging the union of New Zealand and Australia, possibly the separation of Western Australia from the commonwealth, and the union of Newfoundland and Canada, as essential steps to closer union. Now, having benefitted from his weeks in New Zealand, the prophet was inclined to agree with Amery that such a course of action would be dangerous to the movement: 'is it not wiser for us as imperialists to accept the units as we now find them, including the United Kingdom and to accept all the logical consequences of treating them as National units? ... Lord Grey at one time suggested to me that the Empire would not be ripe for considering Union until the Government of the United Kingdom had put itself on the same federal footing as Canada and Australia. I am very much open to conviction on this point, but my advice at present would be ... that we accept the Units as they are.'[15]

Thus by late September 1910 both Curtis and the majority of the London group were reaching similar conclusions, although for somewhat different reasons, about the relationship of 'Federalism,' or 'Home Rule all round,' to the ultimate question of imperial union. It was at this moment that the constitutional conference suddenly appeared in danger of breaking up over Irish Home Rule. Concerned by this development, a few members of the movement, including Kerr, decided to abandon their theorising in order to work for reform in the United Kingdom. The most active besides Kerr and Brand was F.S. Oliver. A Unionist and a much respected political thinker, Oliver had interested himself in the problem of constitutional reform from the early months of 1910. Shortly after King Edward's death he had had circulated among the more prominent Unionist peers a private memorandum advocating a compromise between the parties. A few weeks later, under the pseudonym 'Pacificus,' he had carried his campaign into the public sphere by publishing in *The Times* on 23 May and 6 and 8 June three cogent letters calling for a party truce.[16] With the assembling of the conference and the apparent success of his efforts, he had immersed himself in Round Table discussions, meeting frequently throughout the summer and autumn with other members of the movement. But as soon as the conference began to fail Ol-

---

15  Curtis to Kerr, 19 Sept. 1910, GD40/17/12, ibid.
16  Oliver's intermediary with the Unionist peers was Lord Salisbury, another intimate of the Round Table. See Gollin, *The Observer*, 193-4.

iver, with the backing of some of the moot, reinvolved himself, and during the hectic October and November days became one of the most forceful advocates of federalism.[17]

At first, Oliver attempted to win converts to the idea of federalism within influential Unionist circles; for it was the Unionists who were the most militant opponents of Home Rule, and a long memorandum entitled 'The Conference and Its Consequences' was sent first to Austen Chamberlain[18] and then to Balfour.[19] It is an interesting document and deserving of close attention. In forwarding his 'prolix jottings' to the Unionist leader early in October, Oliver revealed that 'Austen says they are rather wild – I'm not sure that he didn't say "*very*" wild." But Austen is a conservative, if ever there was one, and I am a Tory.' Oliver stressed that it would be 'a great imperial as well as a great national misfortune' if the conference failed to settle the constitutional issue, for the ordinary methods of general elections and parliamentary debates were unsuited for dealing with such problems. The method of settlement by consent and mutual compromise between leading representatives of various parties was the natural safety valve of popular government, and 'If you are ever going to make an attempt at Imperial Union this is the only possible method ...' He urged the summoning of a convention of a more representative character to consider the whole constitutional question and emphasized the foolishness of disregarding dramatic force in political affairs. 'The chance of getting the Irish question as well as the House of Lords question settled (amicably even!) in the year of the Coronation – possibly *before* the Coronation – would appeal to the popular imagination not only at home, but in our Dominions.' Although the Union-

17 By this time 'federalism' was being advocated in a number of influential quarters. In late July Gideon Murray, the Master of Elibank (succeeded his father as Viscount Elibank in 1927) outlined a plan to federalise the constitution to Harold Harmsworth who in turn spoke to J.L. Garvin, editor of *The Observer*. An article favouring a federal solution of United Kingdom difficulties first appeared in *The Observer* on 31 July and was succeeded by many others in following months. Garvin was not content to work solely through the medium of the newspapers, but continuously bombarded leading Unionists with lengthy letters and memoranda on the question of Ireland and 'Home Rule all round.' He also corresponded with Oliver, and to some degree the Round Table and Garvin pursued parallel courses with considerable effect. For a full account of Garvin's activities in 1910 see Gollin, *The Observer*, 168-234.

18 Sir Austen Chamberlain (1863-1937); MP (U); chancellor of the exchequer 1903-6; secretary of state for India 1915-17; member of the War Cabinet April 1918; chancellor of the exchequer 1919-21; secretary of state for foreign affairs, Nov. 1924-June 1929

19 The Memorandum, dated 28/9/1910, was enclosed in Oliver to Balfour, 11 Oct. 1910, Additional MSS 49861, ff1-25, Balfour Papers.

ist party could not champion Home Rule they could for patriotic reasons submit to it if a representative convention agreed upon such a policy. The Unionists could 'honourably surrender ... for the sake of ending a long and dangerous controversy, and also for the sake of bringing the hope of Imperial Union a stage nearer.'

Oliver did not believe that the grant of Home Rule to Ireland would necessarily mean Home Rule all round, that is, Home Rule for England, Scotland, and Wales as separate units, but it would obviously involve the creation of at least a single domestic parliament for the United Kingdom to deal with roughly the same subjects as those allotted to a domestic Irish parliament. Over this there would need to be an imperial parliament in which Ireland and the rest of the United Kingdom would be represented according to population. This body would be responsible for imperial affairs and would bear the same relation to the domestic parliaments of the United Kingdom and Ireland as the dominion parliament of Canada bore to the various provincial legislatures. Logically, in the final stage of development it would hand over its imperial duties to a purely imperial parliament, elected by the dominions as well as by Ireland and the United Kingdom; but, argued Oliver, 'it was needless to enter into this visionary problem at the present time.'[20]

The advantages of setting up two levels of parliament would be manifold. 'You will, I venture to prophesy, – have your Imperial Parliament sanely imperial – neither jingo nor peace-at-any-price. And your Domestic parliaments, though they will make their mistakes and rash experiments ... will tend ... to become composed more and more of men who are serious students of the particular set of problems with which they have to deal. And the consequence here also ... would be a gain for sanity. Quacks do not thrive in a company where things are fairly well understood.' There might be additional benefits such as the abolition of closure, 'the destroyer of Parliaments'; the abatement of the power of caucus, which insisted upon too great a sacrifice of principles; the relief of congestion in parliament; and the restoration of cabinet government – all of which might make it possible for the functions of the prime minister to be discharged 'effectively and with mastery once more by a mere human being, without the qualities of a demi-god and the nerves of a steam engine.' What had to be remembered above all else was the uselessness of talking to the other states of the empire about union as long as the existing confusion continued: 'For they can understand nothing clearly out

20 Here Balfour had underlined 'visionary' and noted 'Visionary not in a bad sense. I see this vision and believe in it.'

of the babel and only lose their tempers when they try to draw conclusions from our debates and elections.'

Balfour's reaction to this lengthy epistle is not known, but shortly after receiving it he was confronted with Lloyd George's plan for a coalition government, with its suggestion of devolution, and with a letter very similar to Oliver's from J.L. Garvin,[21] editor of *The Observer*, an equally ardent champion of federalism. Balfour's reaction to Oliver's ideas can perhaps best be determined from his reply to Garvin. He was in no mood to dicker over the Irish question, and his answer doomed any hope of either the Lloyd George plan or any scheme of federalism being accepted by the Unionists.[22] Balfour dealt initially and somewhat summarily with the imperial implications of 'Home Rule all round.' Was it not an illusion, he asked, to suppose that a federal constitution in Great Britain would be a step towards ultimately federalising the empire? Was it not a fact that federalism, as exhibited in the United States, Canada, and Australia, was a stage in the progress from separation towards unification; while federalism in the United Kingdom would be a step from unification towards separation? This was a telling point and one upon which the Round Table movement was not altogether clear; it had certainly not been considered by Oliver in his memorandum. Balfour dealt at greater length but no less decisively with the problem of Ireland, the solution of which was crucial to the Lloyd George plan and to any federal scheme. The Unionist leader had little faith in the Irish, and believed they would waste little time before defying the imperial parliament and establishing independence. For a party leader committed to the Union and to Ulster such an eventuality could not be ignored. Moreover, was Ireland to form one province or two? If the latter, the Irish Nationalists would not be satisfied. Either way, a federal solution seemed to raise as many problems as it solved. And what of England? Was there to be an English as well as a British parliament and executive in London or were Scotland, Wales, and Ireland to remain as they were while England was cut up into administrative districts? Nowhere could adequate answers be found to these questions; not in Garvin's letter or Oliver's memorandum nor in the multitude of newspaper and magazine articles and platform and parliamentary speeches which dealt with the subject. There was little chance that the Unionists could have been persuaded to change their minds even if federal plans had been more precise;

---

21 James Louis Garvin (1868-1947); editor *Pall Mall Gazette* 1912-15; editor the *Outlook* 1905-6; editor *The Observer* 1908-42
22 Balfour to Garvin, 22 Oct. 1910, copy, Additional MSS 49795, ff100-9, Balfour Papers. Garvin's letter to Balfour, 17 Oct. 1910 is quoted extensively in Gollin, *The Observer*, 213-15.

nevertheless, the scheme of 'Home Rule all round' was bedevilled throughout 1910 by some very fuzzy thinking.

Having failed with Balfour but by no means undaunted, Oliver decided to campaign once more in the public sphere. Using his adopted title, 'Pacificus,' he published a series of seven letters in *The Times* from 20 October to 2 November, expanding and emphasizing the various points made in his memorandum to the Unionist leader.[23] He directed himself primarily to the Unionists, urging them to agree to a national convention representative of all parties, so that a 'fresh inquiry' could be made into both the Irish question and general constitutional reform. He devoted his article of 31 October to Federal Home Rule, outlining a plan of four local parliaments and an overall United Kingdom body responsible, until such time as imperial union, for both United Kingdom and imperial affairs. Apart from emphasizing the supremacy of the imperial parliament there was little new in the article, and in fact nothing very novel in the whole series, but Oliver argued lucidly and cogently and it was the best public exposition thus far of the federalist position. It had, of course, no effect on the Unionist leaders whose minds were already decided, and only served to harden the attitudes of the rank and file who were much alarmed by the apparent suggestion that the Unionists should adopt Home Rule. Shortly after Oliver's last article appeared the constitutional conference broke down, and both the Lloyd George plan and the federalist solution for United Kingdom difficulties were abandoned – the former permanently, the latter as a public issue until 1912-14. The role of the Round Table throughout the sitting of the conference had been an important one; those of the movement who had involved themselves had been the best organised and, apart from Garvin, the most articulate of the exponents of federalism, and had not hesitated to use their influence with the Unionist hierarchy in an effort to steer that party into other channels. Their involvement, however, did reveal what many of them would have been reluctant to admit, but which was obvious to the outside observer – the wide gulf that existed between their ideas and day-to-day political realities on both the imperial and domestic stage.

Their failure forced the London group to reconsider their objectives. On 12-13 November, the weekend following the collapse of the conference, they assembled in strength for a moot at Blackmoor.[24] Every aspect of Round

23  See *The Times*, 20, 22, 24, 26, 28, and 31 Oct. and 2 Nov. 1910.
24  Those present were Milner, Kerr, Brand, Hichens, R. Martin Holland, Oliver, Lord Robert Cecil, Craik, Steel-Maitland, Amery, Lord Howick, and Lord and Lady Selborne. Entry

Table work was discussed but the first question to receive close attention was congestion in parliament. The members decided to proceed with the publication of the memorandum on congestion in the hope of proving 'that the present system is inefficient for Imperial affairs, and therefore also for local affairs,' and that 'the only adequate remedy ... is the devolution of some of the powers of the Cabinet and Parliament on to one or more other bodies.'[25] The second matter discussed in detail, and for which Kerr had prepared a memorandum, was whether any measure of federation or devolution within the United Kingdom was a necessary preliminary to imperial union. Leo Amery and Lionel Hichens, both of whom had always been dubious about the 'practical working' of 'Home Rule all round,' did not believe it was, and Milner was equally emphatic: '... speaking as an Imperial Unionist of the most advanced type, I certainly do not hold that the grant of any measure of 'home rule' to Ireland can be made a basis for the wider federation of the whole Empire. The problems are entirely different. *'Ireland'* like *'Canada'* might at first sight seem a step in that direction. But I believe myself it would be a step in the other – i.e. towards the dissolution of the whole. *'Ireland'* like *'Ontario'* on the other hand (the whole United Kingdom standing for Canada) may or may not be a good thing, but it clearly affords no jumping off ground for Imperial Federation ... No doubt any change in the constitution of the United Kingdom, the centre of the Empire ... must have important consequences for the Empire as a whole. But they will be indirect consequences.'[26]

Amery, Hichens and Milner were opposed in debate by Brand and Oliver who thought the others lamentable stick-in-the-muds.[27] The end result was a bland compromise; the moot concluded 'that in all human probability the two are not connected directly, though indirectly they are closely related,' and it was resolved not to discuss United Kingdom federation in the general

for 12-13 Nov. 1910, vol. 273, Milner Papers. Also Lady Selborne to Curtis, 17 Nov. [nd], Curtis Papers

25 Kerr to Curtis, 22 Dec. 1910, copy, GD40/17/12, Lothian Papers. This was marked letter #1 to distinguish it from another to Curtis of the same date. See also an unsigned and undated 'Memorandum,' written by Kerr after the moot, enclosed in letter #1. Articles on the subject of congestion appeared in the August and December 1911 issues of *The Round Table* and a book entitled *An Analysis of the System of Government Throughout the British Empire* was published in 1912.

26 For Amery's views see L.S. Amery to the editor, *The Times*, 1 Nov. 1910; for Hichen's, see Hichens to Curtis, 19 Dec. 1910, Curtis Papers; and for Milner's, see Milner to Balfour, 5 Nov. 1910, copy, Milner Papers.

27 See Hichens to Curtis, 19 Dec. 1910, Curtis Papers.

study being prepared by Curtis nor to use the funds or agents of the movement in promoting the measure.[28]

Although the decisions reached at Blackmoor were closely adhered to in following months, neither the constitutional problem nor federalism were entirely ignored by the movement, and Philip Kerr as editor of *The Round Table* arranged for regular surveys of the Irish situation to be included in the 'United Kingdom' section of the journal.[29] The articles ventured little that was original, and the writers appeared content to refine and harden the general conclusions of the movement. Federalism was presented as the obvious method of satisfying the aspirations of the Irish and of resolving parliamentary congestion by conceding 'Home Rule all round' in such local affairs as education, land, and local government, while retaining the existing parliament, representative of the population of the British Isles, for such matters as defence, foreign policy, and customs. The journal made it clear that federation of the United Kingdom had nothing to do with an imperial constitution, and could not be considered a first step toward imperial union. Even if parliament were relieved by some sweeping scheme of devolution its real incapacity as an 'imperial' parliament would remain; it would still be elected by the people of the British Isles voting on party issues which had little or no relation to imperial affairs. If the empire was to survive, warned *The Round Table*, its interests could not figure very much longer 'as counters in the party prize fight of the British Isles.'

Throughout 1911 Round Table moots continued to be held at regular intervals to discuss the movement's affairs, the most important being a large gathering at Blackmoor in October, but nothing of significance was agreed upon with respect to either the general constitutional problem or Home

---

28  See unsigned and undated 'Memorandum' enclosed in Kerr to Curtis, 22 Dec. 1910, #1, copy, GD40/17/12, Lothian Papers. A few weeks after this meeting Oliver's letters to *The Times* were published in book form under the title *Federalism and Home Rule* and were dedicated to 'Young Men who see Visions,' but as the decision to publish had been taken before the Blackmoor meeting and since there was no way of connecting 'Pacificus' with the Round Table movement, Oliver's action was not the direct rebuff to the counsel of the moot as would at first appear.

29  See particularly 'United Kingdom: The Revival of Home Rule,' *The Round Table*, Nov. 1910, 63-70; 'British Politics,' *The Round Table*, Feb. 1911, 154-67; and [F.S. Oliver], 'United Kingdom. Home Rule,' *The Round Table*, Dec. 1911, 112-29. For proof of Oliver's authorship of the December article see Oliver to Willison, Dec. 1911, copy, OC Series, file 44, Borden Papers.

Rule.[30] Naturally the members did not altogether relent in their efforts to spread Round Table ideas, and in August Lionel Curtis, recently back from Australasia and Canada, wrote at length to Waldorf Astor, a new recruit to the movement, outlining the moot's convictions on devolution and forwarding various memoranda for consideration.[31] Nevertheless, it was not until the early months of 1912 and the introduction of the Government of Ireland bill that the Round Table Members fully committed their energies once more to the problem of constitutional reform in the United Kingdom. For the next two years the Home Rule crisis was to be a dominant issue at Round Table gatherings. During the early months of the debate, and for much of 1913, the Liberal proposals were strongly criticised by Edward Grigg, who became co-editor of *The Round Table* in mid-1913, Curtis, Kerr, Brand, and Oliver. These criticisms were voiced in the Commons by Amery, Astor, Lord Robert Cecil, and Steel-Maitland, who was now chairman of the Unionist party, and in the Lords by Selborne. As the issue of Ulster became more dominant, Lord Milner, who had little faith in 'Home Rule all round,' became increasingly involved with Sir Edward Carson[32] in the cause of the Irish Protestants. Initially he was aided by one other Round Table member, Leo Amery, who became active in the Covenanter agitation. But in early 1914 when the United Kingdom began to drift inexorably toward civil war and Milner's intention became extreme, Amery recoiled and joined with Kerr, Grigg, Brand, Curtis, Astor, Hichens, and Lovat in urging a compromise solution. For much of the two years those of the movement who sought a peaceful end to the United Kingdom difficulties advocated 'Home Rule all round,' and it was in this vein that they began their attacks on Asquith's Government of Ireland bill in April 1912.

Asquith's bill established an Irish parliament of two houses, a House of Commons consisting of 164 elected members and a Senate of forty members. In addition, Ireland was to be represented in the parliament of the United Kingdom by forty-two members. The Irish parliament was given full power to legislate for Irish affairs with the exception of a certain number of specified subjects such as defence, religion, treaties, naturalization, trade with

30  For the dates of these meetings and those in attendance see Milner diary 1911, vol. 274, Milner Papers.
31  Curtis to Waldorf Astor, 14 Aug. 1911, copy, Curtis Papers
32  Sir Edward Henry Carson (1854-1935); MP (CU) Dublin University 1892-1918; Duncairn Division of Belfast 1918-21; solicitor-general for Ireland 1892; solicitor-general 1900-6; attorney-general 1915; first lord of the admiralty 1917; member of the War Cabinet 1917-18; leader of the Ulster Unionists

any place outside Ireland, merchant shipping, coinage, trade marks, copyright, and stamp duties, while other matters – the collection of taxes, the management of land purchase, old age pensions, national insurance, labour exchanges, savings banks, and the Royal Irish Constabulary – were reserved to the imperial government. In introducing his measure Asquith suggested that the government considered it 'the first step, and only the first step, in a larger and more comprehensive policy' which, in the interest of the United Kingdom and the empire, would emancipate the imperial parliament from local cares and local burdens.[33]

Appropriately, the first member of the movement to criticise the bill publicly was Oliver, who as Pacificus had a lengthy letter published in *The Times* on 30 April 1912.[34] Oliver fastened immediately on Asquith's suggestion that the bill might be the opening move toward a federal system. He pointed out that the first essential condition of a federal arrangement was that it should consist of not fewer than two units of an 'equal *status*' entirely independent of one another and with no mutual responsibilities. The second necessity was a federal parliament responsible for matters concerning the whole country and in which all units were represented fairly and equitably. This, argued Oliver, was 'the essence of a Federation, that the various Federal units should accept the leadership of a supreme Federal authority, and that they should neither make nor meddle in one another's domestic and local affairs.' Ireland could be freed to manage its own domestic affairs in two ways, by being granted her independence – which was inconceivable – or by making the United Kingdom a confederation; there was no middle course. Under the second method England and Scotland would have to have domestic parliaments as well as Ireland, for the conversion of the constitution of Great Britain could not be done piecemeal or by stages. The supreme parliament could not, 'by any ingenuity of man,' be made to perform its supreme functions and the domestic functions of any particular unit. An attempt to combine these two sets of functions in one body would inevitably lead to clashing and friction of the most mischievous character. This impossibility, contended Oliver, was 'precisely what the Government Bill attempts to accomplish ... if the Bill becomes law and is put into force it will break down; for it is a botched piece of work.'

These arguments were elaborated and emphasized in following months both in *The Round Table* and by various members of the movement through the press, in journals, and in parliament. A closely reasoned article entitled

33 5 Hansard (H of C), vol. 36, 11 April 1912, 1399-1426
34 'Pacificus' to the editor, *The Times*, 30 April 1912, See also 8 May 1912.

'Home Rule,' highly critical of Asquith's bill and favourable to federalism, appeared in the June issue of *The Round Table*, and the same month Arthur Steel-Maitland commented caustically on the financial aspects of the measure in the pages of *The National Review*.[35] The most outspoken member of the movement at this time both in the press and in parliament was Leo Amery. He wrote a series of seventeen articles for the *The Morning Post* on the Home Rule problem which he later published as *The Case Against Home Rule* (1912), and he rose repeatedly in the Commons during the session of 1912-13 to launch scathing attacks at the financial aspects of the bill and, more important from the Round Table point of view, at its supposed federal implications.[36] He tended to deny Ireland the status of a nation, and believed that she could find the fullest and best development of her national life within the wider union of the United Kingdom, as Scotland had. Although the idea of federalism was appealing in principle, Amery had never from the earliest discussions of the Round Table believed it practicable for the United Kingdom. To his mind what was urgent was not a division of powers between the government of the United Kingdom as a whole and its different parts but a division between the functions and duties of the British parliament as a parliament of the empire and its functions and duties as the central body of the United Kingdom. 'We want to set up, not local parliaments in the United Kingdom, but a local Parliament for the United Kingdom which will make the United Kingdom a Dominion parallel to the other Dominions, and thus enable the Dominions to join in the central government of the Empire, to federate with us in a real Imperial Council.' Anyway, what of Ulster? One could not ignore that problem simply by introducing a scheme of federalism which made no attempt to grapple with Ulster's unique position.[37] In 1913 Amery became increasingly involved in the Ulster cause and, with Milner, formed on the Irish question rather an extremist element within the movement.

While various members of the movement continued their public attack on Asquith's bill and attempted to promote the cause of federalism, Curtis

35 See 'Home Rule,' *The Round Table*, June 1912, 422-46; and A. Steel-Maitland, 'Finance of the Home Rule Bill,' *The National Review*, June 1912, 620-36
36 He also contributed two chapters on the 'Finance of Home Rule' and the 'Colonial Analogy' to a book on Home Rule written by leading Unionists and published to coincide with the introduction of the Home Rule bill. Amery, *My Political Life*, I, 398-9
37 For Amery's parliamentary comments see 5 Hansard (H of C), vol. 37, 30 April 1912, 1526-30; vol. 43, 28 Oct. 1912, 142-5; vol. 44, 25 Nov. 1912, 930-7; and vol. 46, 8 Jan. 1913, 1218-27. Lord Robert Cecil also spoke caustically of the bill. See 5 Hansard (H of C), vol. 42, 16 Oct. 1912, 1308-11; 23 Oct. 1912, 2280-1; 24 Oct. 1912, 2443-6; vol. 60, 6 April 1914, 1698-1706.

PUNCH, OR THE LONDON CHARIVARI.—May 13, 1914.

## THE SWASHBUCKLERS.

TORY DIE-HARD. "DOWN WITH HOME RULE!"

RADICAL EXTREMIST. "DOWN WITH ULSTER!"

JOHN BULL. "THIS SORT OF THING MAY AMUSE YOU, GENTLEMEN, BUT I'VE NO USE FOR IT. I'M NOT GOING TO HAVE CIVIL WAR TO PLEASE EITHER OF YOU!"

and Grigg were achieving a minor coup by gaining the ear of Winston Churchill who had introduced the second reading of the Government of Ireland bill in the Commons. Churchill had long been aware of Round Table activities, but it was not until April 1912 that the movement made any attempt to include him in their circle of favoured politicians. His position as first lord of the admiralty and his interest in the Irish problem demanded nothing less; so on 17 April Curtis sent him 'a carefully edited and selected copy of the green memorandum' for consideration.[38] It was well received by Churchill who allowed the relationship with the movement, particularly with Curtis and Grigg, to mature to the point where he sought their counsel repeatedly in following months on both defence and Irish questions. In August Churchill spent a weekend at Cliveden, resulting in long talks with Curtis,[39] and in early September Curtis and Grigg were Churchill's guests on the Admiralty yacht *Enchantress*. This was a unique opportunity for the Round Table, and the two men proposed 'to improve his mind laboriously all day long.'[40] Lady Selborne was more perceptive and certainly less sanguine. She cautioned Curtis: 'I hear you are going yachting with Winston. Take care of yourself. I have always an idea that he means to steal the moots clothes while they are bathing, and come out as the one true original Imperialist. I shouldn't tell him too much, but he is a friend to the cause worth cultivating because he is so clever. Let him do the talking as much as possible ...'[41]

A few days later it became obvious that Curtis and Grigg had done much more than listen. On 12 September Churchill devoted the greater part of a major speech in his Dundee constituency to a consideration of a federal system of government for the United Kingdom. In addition to advocating national parliaments for Scotland, Wales, and Ireland, Churchill suggested that more than one body be created for England. He feared an English parliament, whatever its functions and limitations, might be so powerful that it would become embroiled in disputes with the imperial parliament, thereby endangering the very existence of the state. To avoid such a clash Churchill thought separate legislatures might be granted to populous regions like Lancashire, Yorkshire, the Midlands, and Greater London. If necessary, ten or twelve such English bodies, all subordinate to the imperial parliament, could be created. For Churchill one of the strongest arguments for a federal system

38  Curtis to Churchill, 17 April 1912, copy, Curtis Papers
39  Curtis to Churchill, 12 Aug. 1912, copy, ibid.
40  Grigg to Willison, 5 Sept. 1912, Curtis Papers
41  Lady Selborne to Curtis, Sept. 1912, Curtis Papers

was the ease with which the dominions could then be associated in a central government of the empire. But the essential preliminary was Home Rule for Ireland.[42] Although Churchill spoke speculatively and not as a representative of Cabinet his speech had wide reverberations. Despite his neglect of Ulster and the rather grandiose nature of the scheme, he helped to make federalism a major talking point once more in party and intellectual circles; and it remained at the forefront of the political stage until the early summer of 1914. Much of the credit for this development must go to the Round Table movement who through two of its principal lieutenants had succeeded, as so often before, in influencing men and events from behind-the-scenes.

Throughout 1913 the Home Rule question gradually came to dominate the domestic political scene, and increasingly Ulster loomed as a barrier to a peaceful solution of the problem. Preparations were made by Protestant Ulstermen, backed by many prominent Unionists – of whom Milner was one – to obtain serviceable weapons to replace their hitherto symbolic wooden rifles. Late in the year a series of meetings between Bonar Law, the new Unionist leader, and Asquith broke up over the problem of excluding Ulster from the Home Rule bill leaving Bonar Law unimpressed with Asquith's rotund style. By the end of 1913 it seemed to many that the United Kingdom was on the brink of grave difficulties which only a scheme of federalism could possibly resolve. A concerted effort was made in late 1913 and early 1914 to advertise the merits of 'Home Rule all round' and, as was to be expected, many members of the Round Table were to the fore.

Since its success with Churchill in late 1912 the movement had confined its interest in Ireland to discussions at monthly moots and to statements on federalism in *The Round Table*.[43] The Round Table contention that the grant of a semi-independent parliament to Ireland was not an approach to

---

42  For an account of Churchill's Dundee speech see *The Times*, 13 Sept. 1912. Churchill was not unfamiliar with the federal solution and his enthusiasm was probably easily aroused. In February 1911 in a memorandum on devolution prepared for the Cabinet Churchill had considered it 'impossible for an English Parliament and an Imperial Parliament to exist together at the same time; however, a week later in another Cabinet memorandum he advocated the division of the United Kingdom into ten areas each with a legislative and administrative body elected separately from the imperial parliament which would remain unaltered. He favoured giving women the vote and the right to serve on these regional bodies. See W.S.C., 'Devolution,' 24 Feb. 1911, and W.S.C., 'Devolution,' 1 March 1911, CAB 37/105.

43  A particularly important moot on the Irish question was held on 30 Oct. 1913. For that and other such meetings see Milner diary 1913, vol. 276, Milner Papers.

federalism but a step in the opposite direction had been re-emphasized, and the argument that a federal solution meant 'the simultaneous creation of subordinate, national, or local parliaments throughout the whole of the United Kingdom' was further outlined.[44] Toward the end of the year the activities of the movement increased, and while Robert Brand and Grigg were embarking on another cruise with Churchill, Oliver in a small pamphlet entitled *The Alternative to Civil War* advocated holding a National Convention to consider a federal solution to the constitutional problem. Lord Selborne was no less outspoken, and in speeches at Newport, Isle of Wight, and Hyde, Cheshire, he maintained that the only possible solution to existing difficulties was a federal system decided upon not by party but by 'some national agreement.'[45]

The theme of a national convention became a dominant one in Round Table arguments during the next few months. In the December issue of *The Round Table* a writer on 'The Irish Question' pointed out that to pass the Home Rule bill in its present form would simply intensify an already fevered situation; only a non-party convention could resolve matters.[46] Even Leo Amery began to counsel moderation and wrote at length to Bonar Law at the end of the year to urge the summoning of a convention 'of at least twenty or thirty representatives of all views deciding questions not by a bare majority, but practically unanimously, i.e., by a two-thirds or three-quarters vote. Its reference would be to ascertain the possibility of a federal or devolutionary scheme for the United Kingdom and the reforms required to restore a working constitution.'[47] Amery developed his arguments in a series of anonymous articles published in the *Quarterly Review* in January, April, and July 1914, as well as in parliament, in letters, and in private conversations with Unionist leaders.[48] Oliver meanwhile continued his fight in the public arena with the publication in February 1914 of a well-argued pamphlet on *What Federalism is Not*, while Waldorf Astor, increasingly irritated by the die-hard atti-

---

44 'United Kingdom: The Home Rule Bill,' *The Round Table*, Dec. 1912, 98-133; see also 'United Kingdom. The Home Rule Bill,' *The Round Table*, March 1913, 318-29.
45 Grigg to Willison, 18 Oct. 1913, Willison Papers; and *The Times*, 11 Nov. and 3 Dec. 1913
46 See 'The Irish Question,' *The Round Table*, Dec. 1913, 1-67.
47 Amery to Bonar Law, 27 Dec. 1913, quoted in Amery, *My Political Life*, I, 437-9
48 See L.S. Amery, 'The Home Rule Crisis and a National Settlement,' *Quarterly Review*, Jan. 1914, 266-90; L.S. Amery, 'The Home Rule Crisis,' ibid., April 1914, 570-90; and L.S. Amery, 'The Home Rule Crisis,' ibid., April 1914, 570-90; and L.S. Amery, 'The Home Rule Crisis, ibid., July 1914, 275-94; also 5 Hansard (H of C), vol. 58, 11 Feb. 1914, 237-46 and vol. 60, 6 April 1914, 1730-8; and Amery, *My Political Life*, I, 439.

tude of many leading Unionists, urged J.L. Garvin to emphasize federalism in *The Observer*. Together Oliver and Astor held private tête-à-têtes with Lloyd George in order to sound Liberal opinions and to promote Round Table ideas.[49]

The climax of this varied activity came in April and early May 1914, at a time when party leaders were still stunned by the implications of the 'Mutiny' at the Curragh. In two separate instances leading members of the movement made every effort to direct, or at the very least to deflect, the drift of events. On the first occasion the initiative came from outside their ranks. In the March issue of *The Round Table* Edward Grigg had again proposed the summoning of a national convention and the consideration of 'Home Rule all round.'[50] This particular article caught the eye of Lord Roberts,[51] the senior field-marshal of the army, a much respected figure in military and Unionist circles and an ardent supporter of Ulster. Distressed by events at the Curragh, Roberts was attracted by Grigg's arguments and asked for further details. On 1 April Grigg drew up a memorandum reiterating the Round Table contention that the Home Rule bill should be abandoned and a federal solution considered. There followed the novel recommendation that the plan be reviewed by representatives of both major parties, preferably by elder statesmen whose stature would give a joint declaration added weight in political circles. The names suggested were those of Unionists Roberts and Milner and Liberals Lord Loreburn,[52] an ex-lord chancellor, and James Bryce,[53] a former ambassador to the United States. If the federal idea was sanctioned by such men, argued Grigg, then it might at long last be taken seriously. Roberts was much intrigued by these proposals and inclined to be well-disposed toward them, but obviously he could do nothing without Mil-

---

49  Oliver, *What Federalism is Not*; also Gollin, *The Observer*, 416-19. An important Round Table moot on the Irish problem was held at Oliver's home on 12 Feb. 1914, see diary entry for that date, vol. 277, Milner Papers.

50  [Edward Grigg], 'The Irish Crisis,' *The Round Table*, March 1914, 201-30

51  Lord Roberts (1832-1914); commander of forces in Ireland 1895-9; commander-in-chief, South Africa, 1899-1900; commander-in-chief 1901-4

52  Lord Loreburn, 1st earl, cr 1911, Robert Threshie Reid, 1st baron, cr 1906 (1846-1923); M.P. Hereford 1880; MP (L) Dumfries 1886-1905; solicitor-general 1894; attorney-general 1894; lord chancellor 1905-12

53  Bryce, 1st viscount, cr 1914, James Bryce (1838-1922); Regius professor of Civil Law, Oxford, 1870-1893; MP Tower Hamlets 1880; MP (L) Aberdeen S. 1885-1907; under-secretary of state for foreign affairs 1886; chancellor of the Duchy of Lancaster 1892; president of the Board of Trade 1894; chief secretary for Ireland 1905-7; ambassador to the United States 1907-13

ner; so on 2 April he forwarded Grigg's memorandum to him for consideration. As an active member of the movement, and in many ways its father-figure, Milner might have been expected to agree with Grigg's plan, but such was not the case. He had little faith at this juncture in any scheme of 'Home Rule all round,' and in fact was in no mood for compromise. On learning of Milner's attitude Roberts dropped the plan, and the first Round Table effort to influence the solution of the Irish problem was thus derailed, as it were, from within.[54]

The second Round Table effort to effect a compromise got underway while Grigg was still preoccupied with Roberts, and for the first few days he was dissociated from it. The initiative on this occasion came from three leading members of the movement, Hichens, Brand, and Curtis. During the first week of April the three men held long discussions with Bonar Law, Austen Chamberlain, and Carson, and, having met with some encouragement in all quarters, decided on 8 April to see Asquith.[55] Their meeting with the prime minister gave them no cause for pessimism and in the next three weeks, now aided by Grigg and Waldorf Astor, they drew Lloyd George, Lord Lansdowne, and Churchill into the discussions.[56] The scheme broached by the Round Table at these various meetings attempted to provide an alternative to placing Ulster under a Dublin parliament, and was patently federal in character. Home Rule was to be granted to Ireland (excluding Ulster) England, Scotland, and Wales, and an Irish national convention was to be assembled to see if terms of union between northern and southern Ireland could be arranged. Till then, Ulster was not to be allowed to govern herself without the permission of the Dublin parliament nor could she become an integral part of any other unit.[57] With this scheme in mind Churchill appealed to Carson in the Commons on 28 April to consider a federal arrangement; and Carson showed himself favourably inclined provided the six counties of Northeast Ulster were firmly excluded.[58] Against this background Curtis and his friends persisted in their efforts to get the various leaders in the same room for a discussion of the Round Table scheme. On 5 May

54  Grigg's memorandum is enclosed in Roberts to Milner, 2 April 1914, box 100, Milner Papers
55  See entry for 8 April 1914, Milner diary, vol. 277, ibid.; Lady Selborne to Curtis, 21 April 1914, Curtis Papers; also A. Chamberlain, *Politics from Inside,* 637. In recent months Chamberlain had been the one leading Unionist to consider federalism seriously.
56  See Colvin, *Carson,* 383; Hyde, *Carson,* 366; and Chamberlain, *Politics from Inside,* 639.
57  See Colvin, *Carson,* 382-3; and Hyde, *Carson,* 366.
58  5 Hansard (H of C), vol. 61, 28 April 1914, 1591; and 29 April 1914, 1747-53

they succeeded, and a meeting took place at Edwin Montagu's[59] house in Queen Anne's Gate between Asquith, Bonar Law, and Carson. It quickly became apparent that Asquith, because of his understanding with the Irish Nationalists, would not commit himself to any form of compromise settlement.[60] Despite this setback, the members of the Round Table remained optimistic, and for almost a week continued to act as intermediaries between party leaders. But on 11 May during a session with Milner they were told their scheme would come to nothing, and so it proved.[61] Although Asquith did introduce an Amending bill, it did not resolve the basic problem of Ulster, and neither did the hastily assembled Buckingham Palace Conference in July. Only war in Europe and a party truce finally saved England from domestic disaster in the summer of 1914. After the failure of their second attempt to effect a compromise, the Round Table, with the exception of Milner, ceased to play any further part in Irish affairs before the war.[62]

When members of the movement had first involved themselves in the Irish problem it had been for essentially imperial reasons. Home Rule for Ireland had been seen as a means of securing 'Home Rule all round,' which hopefully would have relieved congestion in parliament and separated local from national and imperial affairs. These aspects of the question had been emphasised by the movement in 1910, both in public and private, but in 1913-14 the emphasis was somewhat different; for the United Kingdom seemed in grave danger, and the need to solve immediate problems far outweighed any long-range effects. The primary concern of the movement in early 1914 was the maintenance of the union and the stability of the state, and 'Home Rule all round' or 'federalism' appeared to be the most suitable method; but at no time did this lead to a rejection of Kerr's earlier dictum that United Kingdom federation and imperial federation were 'two entirely different ideas' and should not be confused. As Curtis explained to Feetham

---

59 Edwin Samuel Montagu (1879-1924); MP (L) 1906-22; parliamentary secretary to the chancellor of the exchequer 1906-8; to the prime minister 1908-10; parliamentary undersecretary of state for India 1910-14; chancellor of the Duchy of Lancaster 1915; financial secretary to the Treasury 1914-16; minister of munitions and member of the War Committee 1916; secretary of state for India 1917-22

60 Hyde, Carson, 367

61 See entries for 5 and 11 May 1914, Milner diary, vol. 277, Milner Papers; also Chamberlain, Politics from Inside, 646-7. Oliver had begun to lose heart at the end of March and had taken very little part in the efforts made by his friends of the Round Table. See 'Pacificus' to the editor, The Times, 27 March 1914.

62 Lord Lovat did speak briefly in July in favour of a compromise. See 5 Hansard (H of L), vol. 16, 2 July 1914, 654-6.

shortly after the failure of the Round Table's second effort to effect a compromise: 'Bob Cecil, Grigg and I were indeed used as a kind of intermediary between the two parties who had ceased altogether to be on speaking terms. A scheme of federalism was only an incident in a vain attempt to get some settlement which would stave off the impending nightmare of civil war.'[63]

During those hectic years the movement was not alone in its advocacy of 'Home Rule all round,' for a number of individuals, particularly J.L. Garvin, brought considerable pressure to bear on party leaders. Nevertheless, the Round Table was the only highly organised pressure group to interest itself in a federal solution, and it played a major part in publicising the idea and in influencing events from behind-the-scenes.

Their involvement in the Irish question was a most beneficial experience for the London members; they had been forced to grapple with a dimension of the 'imperial problem' which the defence and foreign policy issue did not highlight – the relationship between imperial federation and devolution in the United Kingdom. To some extent their thinking had been clarified. However, the need to express their views had also revealed a basic lack of sympathy for the Irish nationalist position. This was an ominous indication that despite all their efforts the London members were out of touch with colonial opinion. They did not appreciate that their assumptions about the empire and its future were not necessarily shared by many in Ireland, in India, or in the dominions.

---

63  Curtis to Feetham, 24 June 1914, copy, Curtis Papers. Also Curtis to Feetham, 4 June 1914, copy, ibid.

# 7

# On the eve of war

By 1914 the Round Table movement was firmly entrenched in all the dominions. After Curtis's visit in 1910-11 a number of groups had been established in New Zealand, particularly at Auckland, Christchurch, Wellington, Dunedin, and Wanganui; in Australia at Melbourne, Sydney, and Brisbane; and in Canada at Toronto and Montreal. Since then efforts had been made to start groups in other major centres. By 1912 a group of about ten had been formed in Adelaide, and active groups in the United Kingdom existed in Glasgow and in the two main English university centres of Oxford and Cambridge. In South Africa the Johannesburg group was the only continuously active one, although a number of individuals in various parts of the country criticised the Green Memorandum and subscribed to *The Round Table*, as did many people in Great Britain. The most flourishing dominion organisation was in Canada where three junior groups had been established in Toronto, and active branches founded in Winnipeg, Edmonton, and Victoria as a result of an organising trip made by George Wrong and Edward Kylie in the summer of 1912.

The major preoccupation of all the dominion groups was the discussion of the various memoranda drafted by Curtis. They began by looking closely at the Green Memorandum, and attempted to reach conclusions about the imperial relationship and about the special problems of defence and foreign policy. They then considered the short volumes, *Australian Notes* and *New Zealand Notes*, compiled by Curtis, and by 1914 were also reading and commenting on successive instalments of his major report.[1] In addition to study-

1 This memorandum was referred to initially as the 'major egg,' then as 'Round Table Studies.

ing the imperial problem through the medium of Curtis's memoranda the groups, or at least some of them, were also responsible for the preparation of the dominion articles for the quarterly. In Canada this responsibility rested with the major Toronto group, and more particularly with Willison, although others such as John A. Stevenson,[2] at that time a journalist in Winnipeg, were often asked to write special articles or even particular sections of the regular Canadian article. In Australia this chore was supposed to be shared by the Sydney and Melbourne groups; but in those early years Frederic Eggleston, Ernest Scott, and William Harrison Moore, all of Melbourne, were primarily responsible. In New Zealand J.A. Atkinson drafted the majority of the articles, subject to the comments and criticisms of his colleagues, particularly those in Wellington and Christchurch; while in South Africa Patrick Duncan, Richard Feetham, and Hugh Wyndham, who were the heart and soul of the Johannesburg organisation, usually prepared the South African contribution.

Of the overseas groups the Canadian were the most prominent during these early years, owing to the importance of Canada in effecting any change in the imperial structure. Their contact with the London group was virtually continuous. After Curtis's departure in 1911 Dougie Malcolm and Earl Grey provided continuity for a few months. Lionel Hichens visited briefly in November 1911, and in the summer of 1912 Philip Kerr spent some weeks in the company of Wrong and Kylie on his way back from India. Hichens returned again in the autumn of 1912 and Brand and Milner both made flying visits at the end of the year.[3] Lionel Curtis made a major visit in late 1913 to confer with the leading members of the Canadian organisation about the purpose and direction of the movement. Nothing could have been more indicative of the importance of the Canadian groups and the weight attached to their opinions. In addition to receiving visitors from the central group many members of the Canadian organisation spent lengthy periods in London. Sir

Second Series.' It was privately circulated under the title *The Project of a Commonwealth* in 1915; it was published in 1916 unchanged but under a new title, *The Commonwealth of Nations*. This was done to avoid confusion with the shorter popular volume *The Problem of the Commonwealth* also published in 1916. See the end of this chapter and Chapter 8.

2  John Alexander Stevenson (1883-1970); journalist; called to the Manitoba bar 1910; editorial contributor to the *Winnipeg Free Press*; later Ottawa correspondent of the Toronto *Star*; chief Canadian correspondent of *The Times* 1926-40; editorial writer for the Toronto *Globe and Mail* 1940-6; Ottawa editor *Saturday Night* and Canadian correspondent of the *Guardian* until 1958; frequent contributor to *The Round Table*, the *Spectator*, and the *Quarterly Review*

3  One can follow the Canadian Round Table activities during 1912 in the Walker diary. See especially entries for 31 July and 3, 13, and 15 Oct. 1912. Also Kerr to Curtis, 31 July 1912, copy, reel c246, Borden Papers

Edmund Walker visited in the summer of 1911 and again in 1913, and dined and talked often with the moot. Arthur Glazebrook was a yearly visitor to England, where he had had his early education, and was always included in the major discussions of the London group. Vincent Massey,[4] a young lecturer in history at the University of Toronto, who had come under the spell of Kylie and Wrong, spent some time in England in 1911.[5] Edward Kylie himself was in London for much of July and August 1913. He met Milner almost immediately after his arrival, attended a moot dinner, and in mid-August spent two days at Milner's country home Sturry Court 'talking "moot" politics.'[6] Because of the ease and rapidity with which they could cross the Atlantic, Canadian members of the movement were the most frequent visitors to London; but they were not the only dominion representatives to make the journey. While Walker and Kylie were in London in 1913 a major discussion was held on 22 July between the central moot and representatives of all dominion groups;[7] and in early 1914 Laby and Atkinson of New Zealand had long conversations with the London members, particularly with Grigg.[8] Whenever a dominion member was in London on business he was usually invited to attend the moot, and in this fashion C.N.H. Macalpine, secretary of a Winnipeg group, was present at two crucial meetings on 16 and 24 April 1913 when the London members entertained potential financial supporters.[9] The leading South African members, Duncan, Feetham, and Wyndham, always attended meetings when in London.

This gravitation back to the United Kingdom underlined the central importance of the London group. No matter how extensive a dominion organisation happened to be, no matter who its members were, the intensity

---

4 Vincent Massey (1887-1967); lecturer in modern history, University of Toronto, and dean of residence, Victoria College, 1913-15; associate secretary of the War Committee of the Cabinet 1918; secretary, then director, Government Repatriation Committee 1918-19; president of Massey-Harris Co 1921-5; minister without portfolio 1925; Canadian representative in Washington 1926-30; high commissioner for Canada in London 1935-46; governor-general of Canada 1952-9

5 For Glazebrook's visits see Milner diary, 22 March 1911, vol. 274; 4 and 24 April 1912, vol. 275; 26 Feb. and 5 and 13 March 1913, vol. 276; and 29 May and 3 July 1914, vol. 277, Milner Papers. For Walker's visits see Walker diary, 28 June and 6 and 7 July 1911; and 26 May and 16 and 22 July 1913. For Hichen's 1911 visit to Canada see Walker diary, 7 Nov. 1911. For Glazebrook's introduction of Massey see Glazebrook to Milner, 22 Sept. 1911, box 169, Milner Papers.

6 Present at dinner were Milner, Selborne, Hichens, Brand, Grigg, Craik, and Lovat. Milner diary, 9 and 17 July and 16-18 Aug. 1913, vol. 276, Milner Papers

7 Walker diary, 22 July 1913, Walker Papers

8 Grigg to Laby, 14 Feb. 1914, Laby Papers

9 Milner diary, 16 and 24 April 1913, vol. 276, Milner Papers

and relevance of their deliberations, or even their local influence, the stimulus and to a great extent the directional influence of the Round Table movement was in London. During the initial years the kindergarten continued to be the most important element in the central group, but others drawn in after 1909 often played vital roles. Selborne, Jameson, and Bailey, particularly Selborne, attended most of the moots and general discussions, while Milner remained the movement's 'father figure,' and was consulted whenever major decisions or policy matters came up for review. But for much of the prewar period Milner was deeply involved in the Irish crisis, and many of his activities in that sphere were dissociated from the Round Table's. Leo Amery continued to attend moots during those years, and was the one member of the movement, apart from Geoffrey Robinson, editor of *The Times*, who maintained a close personal relationship with Milner. Amery was also the one man in the London group who differed most vehemently with the established Round Table policy of remaining aloof from both politics and the preference issue, and he had strong reservations about Curtis's scheme for organic union. As we have seen, F.S. Oliver had quickly become a vital member whose opinions were always respected and whose friendships with Unionist leaders were often of great value.

Lord Robert Cecil was also close to the London group, having been introduced to the movement in the summer of 1909 by his sister Lady Selborne.[10] He attended most moots and was a useful spokesman for the movement in the House of Commons. Waldorf Astor had joined in 1911 as a result of a friendship formed with Philip Kerr, and he and his wife, Nancy Astor, remained life-long friends of Kerr and the Round Table.[11] Lords Wolmer and Howick, after their initial involvement in the autumn of 1909, played relatively little part in the actual workings of the organisation, but Lord Lovat extended his interest and was soon speaking with a Round Table bias in the Lords. Four others from outside the central core who played influential parts before the war were Edward Grigg, Graeme Paterson,[12] Reginald Coupland,[13] and Alfred Zimmern.[14] The latter were two young Oxford

10  See Lady Selborne to Bob Cecil, 4 Aug. 1909, Additional MSS 51157, ff126-7, Cecil Papers
11  See Astor, *Tribal Feeling*, 54.
12  No additional information is available about Paterson.
13  Reginald Coupland (1884-1952); KCMG, cr 1944; fellow and lecturer in ancient history, Trinity College, Oxford, 1907-14; Beit Lecturer in Colonial History 1913-18; editor *The Round Table* 1917-19 and 1939-41; fellow of All Souls 1920-48 and 52-; Beit Professor, history of the British empire, Oxford, 1920-48; fellow, Nuffield College, 1939-50; member of the Palestine Royal Commission 1936-7; member of Cripp's Mission to India 1942
14  Alfred Zimmern (1879-1957); knighted 1936; lecturer in ancient history, New College, 1903; fellow and tutor 1904-9; staff inspector, Board of Education, 1912-15; Political Intelligence

academics who proved to be of considerable assistance to Curtis while he was drafting his memoranda. Coupland began attending moots in 1913, and Zimmern in the winter of 1913-14.[15] Graeme Paterson was a young man recently out of Oxford who helped with the quarterly and the general running of the central office.

One major triumph in 1912 was the appointment of Lionel Curtis to a fellowship at All Soul's and to the Beit Lectureship in colonial history at Oxford. This enabled him to use the facilities of the university and to meet young men such as Massey and A.L. Burt[16] who were to be vital to the success of the movement. Curtis launched an ambitious programme while he was at Oxford; for instance, in the summer of 1913 he dealt with the problem of imperial organisation from the administrative point of view. He had his students consider how the various departments which would be placed under a new imperial government would need to be organised after they had been separated from the United Kingdom government and rendered responsible to electors throughout the self-governing empire.[17] Some of the findings of this project were included as an appendix to the volume containing the Australian and New Zealand 'Notes' published in 1914. When Curtis gave up the lectureship that year he was succeeded by Coupland, who in 1920 became Beit Professor of colonial history at Oxford.

The relationship among the members of the London group seems to have been most congenial, and whatever differences of opinion developed, and there were often many, they were never allowed to interfere with friendships and fellow feeling. All of them looked to Milner for counsel and advice, and Milner's diaries for those years abound with entries concerning private tête-à-têtes with various members as they individually discussed the moot's problems and aims. But nothing is more apparent during this period than the dominating and persuasive presence of Curtis, his personality, and his ideas. The London group, and really the entire Round Table movement, tended to take their inspiration and stimulus from him. He was often exasperating, often wrong, often very badly wrong, but always stimulating and often inspiring. As Lionel Hichens once explained after a brief disagreement with

Department, Foreign Office, 1918-19; Wilson Professor of International Politics, University College of Wales, Aberystwyth 1919-21; professor of international relations, Oxford, 1930-44

15  Milner diary, 1913-14, vols. 276 and 277, Milner Papers
16  Alfred Leroy Burt (1888-1970); historian; Rhodes Scholar, Ontario, 1910; member of the Department of History, University of Alberta, 1916-30; professor of history, University of Minnesota, 1930-56
17  Curtis to Jebb, 14 April 1913, box 1, Jebb Papers

Curtis: 'You must not take my little criticisms too seriously because although I may differ from your line of action in certain respects yet after all the difference is only in regard to matters of detail & ... in all essentials of your work I am entirely at one with you & want to help you as much as I can ... may your work prosper as much as such unselfish devotion deserves. If any one can succeed in such a difficult task as you have set yourself you are that man. In any case you can't fail altogether & even if outward things seem to fail this remains that you have imposed a spirit into the kindergarten which they would never have had without you. But outward things won't fail; we shall go on & accomplish something worth doing even if we fall short of our highest aims.'[18]

The differences of opinion and approach which had developed between Curtis and Kerr in late 1909 in Canada remained a problem for much of the period. It was a continual worry to Kerr in particular, and he explained the situation to Brand in September 1912:

I haven't heard what happened at the Sept. 3-5 Moot. But I shall go down and stay with Lionel as soon as I can leave London and thresh things out with him. I'm damned if I see, just now, what part I am to play in the R.T. movement in future. Lionel's present idea really means that he is to go as a prophet with a new gospel of citizenship, plus a plan of Imperial Union, collect not more than 12 disciples – fanatics like himself – and preach the word to the British world, trusting to the truth winning its way in the end. That is one method I admit and not a bad one. But it is not the R.T. idea, which is rather the practical one of omitting everything which is non-essential, and trying to get as great a multitude as possible agreed upon one or two fundamentals in order that they may be put through as speedily as possible. Lionel too has much too much practical sense to be able to stick to No. 1 plan once he gets into active propaganda again. The real real danger is that he will start with a Number 1 gospel and find that it is entirely unsuited to No. 2 method. Whether we can get him to see reason before he starts I don't know ... However it is impossible for the R.T movement to go ahead, unless L. and I can find a working agreement so as to correlate our respective spheres. Morever my own future depends very much on what that movement is to be for the next year or two, and what part I am to play in it. So I must try and reach an understanding with L. before anything else. It won't be easy, and we shall both lose our tempers several times. But it must be done, and the best way is for us to be shut up together for a day or two until we have rubbed one another's corners off ...[19]

Whether or not Kerr and Curtis did manage to rub the corners off is dif-

18  Hichens to Curtis, 19 Dec. 1910, Curtis Papers
19  Kerr to Brand, Sept. 1912, quoted without documentation in Butler, *Lothian*, 51-2

ficult to say. But there is little doubt that Kerr's fears were shared by others, particularly Brand and Amery, and even by Coupland,who more than most shared Curtis's idealism about the empire. A perceptive, although somewhat unflattering, picture of Curtis at this time is provided by Violet Cecil, an observer of one of the moots at Hatfield House, the home of the Cecils: 'I lunched with the Round Table on Friday. I thought that I had better try and get in with them as they are all very well meaning and some of them are able. I sat next Hichens with Curtis within hail (he was on my other side making suitable talk with Pattison [sic] who was kind to him). I think I understand Curtis and that given time I might like him for his genuine and absolutely singlehearted devotion to a set of ideas, but I do not think him very intelligent, tho' in talk he showed rather more docility than his nose led me to think he possessed. Still I know that I can get on with him if I want to and if I can remember not to tell other people that I think him dull, all will be well. Of course he is all right with Nancy, who never leaves him to finish his sentence and never allows him to be sententious.'[20]

During these years moots were held both in London, either at the home of Brand, Grigg, and Curtis in Cambridge Square, or at Milners, the Round Table offices, the Astors, or the Rhodes Trust; and also at the various country homes of its members and associates, particularly at Blackmoor, the home of the Selbornes or at Kerr's lovely estate Blickling in Norfolk, as well as at Hatfield, Checkendon, and Cliveden. The moots varied in importance and in the amount of work accomplished. Oliver, for one, thought too much time was wasted at the gatherings in the country, and preferred the more businesslike meetings in London.[21] The moots in London were of two types: those assembled to discuss, criticise, and rephrase articles, and those called to discuss and plan the movement's ideas and actions on such specific problems as defence and foreign policy or the Irish question. Sometimes a single moot served both purposes, and often smaller private conferences were held. A letter from Lady Selborne to Lionel Curtis after a moot in November 1910 gives some sense of the atmosphere that prevailed: 'We had a very nice Moot last Sunday here, of which no doubt you will get full particulars from Philip. We missed you very much. Lord Milner took a very active part in the discussions. He is a very fine chairman – all his remarks are short & to the point. Amery and Steel-Maitland talk too much ... Lionel Hichens not enough – in fact he never hardly volunteered a remark. What he did say was dragged out of him by the Chairman who occasionally required information

20 [Violet Cecil] to Milner, 23 Dec. [1912], box 194, Milner Papers. Violet Georgina Maxse married Lord Edward Cecil in 1894; he died in 1918. In 1921 she married Lord Milner.
21 Oliver to Curtis, 23 May 1913, Curtis Papers

on some point of finance. Bob Brand is good in council, though he does not say much, & I thought Philip showed great ability ... Oliver is exceedingly clever, but one felt he was an amateur, compared with some of the others. A practical experience of the inside of government offices & Legislature gives a different atmosphere to the mind.'[22]

One of the primary purposes of a moot was to discuss the potential articles for *The Round Table*. The quarterly had begun publication in November 1910 under the guidance of Kerr, and by 1914 was highly regarded by its widely scattered readership. Its primary function was to provide information and 'food for thought,' and this it did by having in each issue three or four lead articles plus regular chronicle articles from the dominions. The lead articles were usually written by members of the London group, by Kerr in the early issues and by Brand and Grigg in the later ones. The journal naturally reflected the major concerns and interests of the central moot, with the result that virtually every issue had an article on some aspect of either the German menace, the international situation, or imperial defence, particularly naval defence. The Irish question also dominated the pages of the quarterly for a lengthy period, and India was given considerable attention. Other matters, such as the financial implications for the empire of a war, the history of the colonial and imperial conferences, and inter-imperial relations in general were given their due. Matters of particular interest, such as the Brisbane General Strike, the Graingrowers of Manitoba, the Indian question in South Africa, the Workers Educational Association, and the new regime in China were all covered in special articles; thus broadening the appeal of the journal and sharpening its comment.

The London group adhered as much as possible to the method of group preparation of articles, although many of them were drafted by a single man. Ten were done by Kerr before he had a nervous breakdown brought about by overwork and a crisis in religious belief.[23] After that many were initiated by Grigg. Overall, however, it can be said that they were group articles, for

22  Lady Selborne to Curtis, 17 Nov. [1910], ibid. Those who attended moots regularly were Robinson, Hichens, Oliver, Craik, Curtis, and Brand, who along with Kerr, Dove, and the South Africans, Duncan and Feetham, can be considered the central core. Often present were Martin Holland, Anglesey, Dove, and Waldorf Astor; while Malcolm, Marris, and Perry attended when they were in London. Amery, Peacock, and Steel-Maitland, all associates of the movement, do not seem to have attended many moots in those years. Important financial moots were attended on 16 Jan. 1912 by Lovat, Curtis, Milner, Hichens, Bob Cecil, Oliver, Brand, and Robinson; and on 24 April 1913 by Oliver, Brand, Curtis, Hichens, and Milner. Milner diary, 16 Jan. 1912, vol. 275; and 24 April 1913, vol. 276, Milner Papers. Also Milner to R. Cecil, 8 Jan. 1912, Additional MSS 51160, ff67-8, Cecil Papers
23  See Butler, *Lothian*, for a detailed treatment of this episode.

no article severely criticised by any of the members would have been allowed to appear as representative of group opinion. The dominion groups, particularly the Canadian and New Zealand branches, appear to have had difficulty following this format; and while in Canada in 1912 Kerr conferred at length with Glazebrook, Kylie, and Willison about the Canadian articles and the best methods of preparing them. On his return to England, Kerr was at pains to preserve the corporate method on sensitive subjects: 'We here now are trying to arrange that all articles dealing with controversial political subjects shall be read by two or three of us representing if possible different points of view, before publication. One nearly always finds that one's habit of mind or habit of writing unconsciously betrays one into phrases which are not intended to have a partisan significance, but which in point of fact are likely to produce that impression on the readers mind ...'[24]

Kerr was editor of *The Round Table* throughout the period, although during his absence from October 1911 to August 1912 Craik, Brand, and Oliver, aided by Paterson, guided the journal. Kerr's continued illness finally necessitated more permanent arrangements, and in June 1913 Edward Grigg left *The Times* to become joint editor of *The Round Table*. Grigg was sorry to leave Printing House Square but as he explained to Willison: 'I am so fully convinced that such energy as I possess can now be most usefully thrown in to Round Table work, that I have had no hesitation in coming to a decision. Kerr's illness has put a considerable strain on the Magazine Committee, and particularly on Craik, who has been combining the work of Editor with his duties at Scotland Yard, and a fresh hand is urgently needed ...'[25] Grigg also wanted to do something other than daily journalism, and 'The Round Table though its results at present are mainly a matter of faith has an appeal for me which nothing else can equal, and I can throw myself into it with a wholeheartedness which I have lost at Printing House Square.' Nevertheless, arrangements had been made with Geoffrey Robinson, the editor of *The Times,* for Grigg to continue to write and advise on imperial affairs. Grigg was not sure how long the joint arrangement could last; it certainly could not be permanent, but since the Round Table members valued the influence and information of *The Times* they hoped a reliable successor to Grigg could be appointed. 'Also the fact that I am still in any way connected with "The Times" is not for the world at large, since it would not be good for the Round Table to let the slightest suspicion grow up that its independence was tempered by any official relations with so powerful and (as Liberals

24 Kerr to Willison, 27 Nov. 1912, Willison Papers
25 Grigg to Willison, 29 May 1913, ibid.

think) so partizan an organ as "The Times." '[26] Grigg hoped Kerr would be well enough before the end of the year to resume at least some of the responsibilities, for they were growing so fast 'that we cannot keep pace without him.'[27]

The inner moot were at great pains to keep the journal non-political in accordance with their belief that the movement should not become attached either in Great Britain or the dominions to any political party. Although many friends and critics of the Round Table movement suggested at the time, as have others since, that this doomed the movement to ineffectuality, the members fervently believed in keeping the imperial problem a non-party issue, immune from the grubbing and prejudices of politics. This attitude toward politics was a holdover from their years with Milner in South Africa, and was most apparent in the manœuvres of the Round Table members over the naval policy in Canada and the Irish question. It is interesting that the one member of the movement who was deeply involved in the political arena disagreed with the inner moot's stance on the political question. Amery believed the Round Table should identify with a party, preferably the Unionists in England, the Conservatives in Canada, and with Deakin and his followers in Australia. Others of the group did not agree. Despite their caution it was obvious that the movement and its jounal were being identified with only one end of the political spectrum. In the words of the French-Canadian Rodolphe Lemieux,[28] the movement and its journal appeared to be 'a Jingo institution.' Lemieux, like many others, found the journal a useful one with lofty ideals, but, as he explained to George Wrong: 'I do not read it in the same light as you do. I find that almost all of the contributions on Canada are tainted with ardent toryism – The articles on South Africa are also biased ... There is an *inner circle* in that organisation – I know it, I *feel it* ... Of course he [Curtis] is one of Milner's disciples—he belongs to the Knitergarten [sic] and for me, such associations have a strong tory-Jingo flavour.'[29]

Many people shared Lemieux's opinion and in many respects it was true. To a French Canadian, or to an Afrikaner, or to an English-speaking dominion nationalist, the movement and its journal must have smacked of British interests and high-flown paternalism. This was the inevitable fate of liberal-

26 Ibid.
27 Kerr, however, was absent for much of 1913 and the early months of 1914.
28 Rodolphe Lemieux (1866-1937); called to the Quebec bar 1891; law partner of Honoré Mercier and Sir Lomer Gouin; professor of law, Laval University, 1896-1926; MP (L) 1896-1930; senator 1930-7; solicitor-general 1904-6; postmaster-general 1906-11; minister of marine and fisheries 1911
29 R. Lemieux to Wrong, 29 Aug. 1913, Wrong Papers

imperialists like the movement. Though they were to some degree in advance of their time in Great Britain, they still operated within a narrow range of racial stereotypes and with a false set of assumptions about dominion attitudes and political realities. The members of the London group believed deeply in the superiority of English civilization. They did not appear to appreciate that constant assertion of this superiority in their journal, either explicitly or implicitly, harmed their cause. It was ironic, however, that the group's association with Milner should have helped brand them; for they often disagreed with Milner and travelled paths he would never have ventured down. So, though there is considerable truth in Lemieux's point of view, in some respects it is unfair. If anything the Round Table movement were opposed to tory-jingoism. Even Curtis, the most ardent champion among them of organic union, believed in the role of the empire as a stabilising factor whose ideals could help lessen international tension. Theirs was certainly not a philosophy of might and expansion. And though many of them had more sympathy for the Unionists than for the Liberals, they were at pains to dissociate themselves from the Unionist party – the imperial party – in public and never had very great influence in private.

A good example of the movement's desire to remain aloof from politics was their avoidance of the issue of imperial preference, one of the most dynamic political footballs of the day. The leading members of the movement believed that to take a stance on the issue of preference would involve them in the feverish party warfare in Great Britain. To their mind their ends would be best served by not becoming identified with any faction.[30] Leo Amery thought this was to stage *Hamlet* without the Prince of Denmark, and Richard Jebb believed the movement had its priorities wrong. For him the path to closer imperial union lay initially through preference and not through common agreements and arrangements on defence. His marginal comments in his personal copy of the Green Memorandum are enlightening.[31] In connection with the Round Table attitude toward economics, which is stated fairly early in the book, Jebb wrote, 'You rule out economics as irrelevant to the science and art of state-making, which is like ruling out the principle of gravity from the science and art of engineering.'[32] Where the Green Memorandum read 'foreign policy and defence are the pimary function of a national government,' Jebb scribbled 'No: its primary function, generally

30  See especially Grigg to Willison, 8 Aug. 1912, Willison Papers
31  Jebb's copy of the Green Memorandum is now shelved in the library of the Institute of Commonwealth Studies, London.
32  Ibid, 79

recognised by it, has always been to see that its people are getting a livelihood, without which they cannot hold the rudder at all'; and where Curtis had argued 'Security against attack from without is the most vital of all wants,' Jebb had countered 'No – the most vital is physical sustenance, without which you cannot fight.'[33]

Jebb later argued in a personal letter to Curtis that economic co-operation was the necessary basis of communal activities:

Until we have established the principle and practice of economic cooperation we cannot tell how far we can or cannot go in the direction of cooperative foreign policy – since foreign policy arises from economic interests – and its corollary, defence ... The problem is by nature one of political-economy, whereas you are trying to treat it as one of politics divorced from economics, which can never be more than a paper divorce. I don't quite see ... what your next move is likely to be ... at the very least you are working up a splendid stimulus; the best we have had since Joe's campaign, and all the more useful in that it caters for the anti-Joe push. Apparently I am destined, when you take the field, to appear as an antagonist. But my position will be more comfortable than yours, for whereas you would regard the prevalence of my view as a catastrophe, I would regard the prevalence of yours with as much gratification as surprise. Give us a federal parliament – only I fear you can't – and the economic system would inevitably follow very soon.[34]

Almost from the beginning there were differences of opinion among the Round Table members over the preference issue, and Milner and Lord Robert Cecil, a Unionist Free Trader, were said to be 'widely divided.'[35] In late 1912 Leo Amery was heard to say that 'the table is so very round that there has never been an article on Preference.'[36] Apparently there was some thought given to including a passage by Oliver on the subject in the December 1911 issue, but in the end it was omitted. Oliver, an ardent tariff reformer, had discussed the matter at some length with Curtis and Kerr. He informed Willison of the result: 'The wise youths of the "Round Table," whom I occasionally serve, have decided – and I fully agree with them – that it is better to omit the ... passage from my article upon United Kingdom affairs in the December issue. Their reason is that the policy of the "Round Table" is to keep its hands free from partisanship in the matter of Tariff Re-

33  Ibid., 73-4 and 101
34  Jebb to Curtis, 27 Dec. 1911, copy, box 1, Jebb Papers
35  Lady Selborne to Curtis, 17 Nov. [1910], Curtis Papers. Cecil's views on the preference issue and the difficulties they caused him can be followed in the Cecil Papers, Additional MSS 51159.
36  [Violet Cecil] to Milner, 23 Dec. [1912], box 194, Milner Papers

form. My words – bearing as they do the unmistakeable signs of sympathy with the movement – might have awakened doubts among those of "the brethren" at home and overseas, who are favourable to organic union, but who, for one reason or another, are attached to the principles of Mr Cobden.'[37]

Unaware of the central group's caution Richard Jebb believed that Philip Kerr, in his article 'Britain, France and Germany' in the December 1911 issue of *The Round Table*, had recommended the abandonment of preference by the Unionist party. His quick rejoinder in *United Empire* did not please Kerr, who maintained that the movement was not anti-preference, but was pursuing a policy of fiscal neutrality. 'As you know,' wrote Kerr, 'we have studiously avoided taking sides in the tariff controversy, because ... we believe that we can do more good by ventilating the non-tariff case for Imperial Union among Free Traders who regard every argument coming from a Tariff Reformer as suspect.'[38]

Jebb remained unconvinced; and for much of 1912 and 1913 he continued to attack the Round Table movement for attempting to subvert the Unionist party's policy on preference. He saw their supposed activities on the tariff reform issue as part of their campaign to concentrate attention on the Committee of Imperial Defence and on the issue of defence and foreign policy. Jebb attributed the dropping of the food duties by the Unionists in the winter of 1912 to the attempts by the Harmsworth press to 'stampede' them. He believed that *The Times* was 'practically identical with the Round Table,'[39] and argued that the article in the March 1913 issue of *The Round Table* on 'The Unionists and the Food Taxes' invited Austen Chamberlain to abandon the policy of tariff reform: 'I do not impute any actual intrigue to them, for I have no inside knowledge. But undoubtedly it was the influence of their ideas, particularly in the case of the Harmsworth press. The new editor of *The Times*, Geoffrey Robinson, is one of them, and I think a rather weak fellow anyway. My cousin, Ned Grigg oscillates between them and me, but lives under their roof nowadays.'[40]

Jebb undoubtedly had a right to be suspicious of the London group, but there is little evidence to suggest that they attempted to exert any pressure on the Unionist politicians over the tariff question. *The Round Table* during

---

37  Oliver to Willison, ? Dec. 1911, copy; also Oliver to Willison, 7 Dec. 1911, copy; and Willison to Oliver, 15 Dec. 1911, copy, oc series, file 44, Borden Papers
38  Kerr to Jebb, 26 Feb. 1912, box 2, Jebb Papers
39  Jebb to Colonel James Allen, 31 Jan. 1913, copy, box 1, ibid.
40  Jebb to Deakin, 23 March 1913, mss 1540, Deakin Papers

this period carried only two pertinent articles. One, a section entitled 'An Alternative Government' in the September 1912 United Kingdom article, simply commented on attitudes in the United Kingdom toward the idea of food taxes; and the other, the article in the March 1913 issue entitled 'The Unionists and the Food Taxes,' was essentially a survey of events leading to the dropping of food taxes from the Unionist platform.[41] Neither of these articles was directly propagandist, although one can detect a sympathy with the decision to drop the food taxes. Similarly, Jebb's suggestion that the movement was using *The Times* and the Harmsworth press in their campaign appears unfounded. Geoffrey Robinson admittedly was the editor, but it is doubtful that the movement was sufficiently influential or powerful to direct the attitudes and arguments adopted by 'The Thunderer.' It is true, however, that many members of the movement were ardent Unionists with many close friends in central Unionist circles, and no doubt this did arouse Jebb's suspicions. But Jebb's attitude toward the movement on this issue seems to have been partially motivated by pique that such a useful and powerful instrument as *The Round Table* was deliberately ignoring, even denying, his major premise.[42] Moreover, it must be remembered that Kerr was away from England at this time and thus not able to exercise any real influence on the nature or tenor of articles. *The Round Table* was being run by Brand, Oliver, and Craik, and Oliver would certainly have been opposed to any article undermining the preference policy of the Unionists. And Grigg, one of the suspected ones, was 'rather distressed' by the article of March 1913. He found it '... a splendid piece of writing, but it treats the whole crisis in a vein of a witty cynic laughing at a comedy of intrigue. It neither allows for the strong movement of feeling (quite apart from tactical considerations) which put the food taxes out of court for the moment, nor does it suggest that the food taxes controversy was anything but an isolated discussion conducted in a political vacuum. Of course such an account is extremely misleading.'[43]

Whatever this criticism might suggest about the way *The Round Table*

41  See 'An Alternative Government,' *The Round Table*, Sept. 1912, 689-708; and 'The Unionists and the Food Taxes,' ibid., March 1913, 232-76. Oliver did attempt to solicit Robert Cecil's support in an effort to sway Austen Chamberlain in favour of preference. Cecil did not bow to Oliver's pleas. See Oliver to Cecil, 31 Dec. 1912 and 3 Jan. 1913, Additional MSS 51090, ff1-4, Cecil Papers.
42  See Jebb to Amery, 20 May 1912, copy, box 1, Jebb Papers, for a general summary of Jebb's attitudes on imperial organisation and closer union. Jebb's views were still the same ten years later; see Jebb to Brookes, 12 May 1923, 'Jebb Correspondence,' Deakin Papers.
43  Grigg to Willison, 12 Feb. 1913, Willison Papers

was produced, it certainly does not indicate any plot on the part of the central group. Furthermore, Leo Amery, a respected figure in Round Table circles, was adamant on the need 'for the economic factor in union,' and would have opposed any Round Table attempt to subvert tariff reform. But his letters of the period do not suggest a Round Table intrigue.[44] The articles in *The Round Table* did not deserve the burden of responsibility Jebb placed upon them. Undoubtedly the movement's decision to remain aloof from politics and to avoid the preference issue was in theory well-founded; but in fact it harmed their cause because it removed them from the centre of power, and gave them no instrument within the fabric of the United Kingdom or the dominions through which they could achieve their ends. This, in part, accounts for the eventual failure of the movement.

While these discussions were going on within the moot, Lionel Curtis was preoccupied with the preparation of the major 'egg' which was to contain the movement's philosophy and its recommendations on the imperial question. This major memorandum was really the essence of the movement's work; and its preparation, added to all his other tasks, such as the completion of 'Australian Notes' and 'New Zealand Notes,' taxed Curtis's resources to the limit.

The pace was relentless. After his return to England in 1911 Curtis pushed himself hard, working from 7.30 AM to 5.00 PM every day, when he knocked off even if he felt 'as fresh as a pea.'[45] By January 1912 the Australian volume and an annotated version of the Green Memorandum were completed and on their way to the dominions.[46] But the strain had been too much and two years' continuous and unrelenting toil finally had their effect. At the end of 1911 Curtis was taken ill. He did nothing until mid-February 1912 when he was permitted to work only on the understanding that he cut down severely. Working at a reduced pace he completed the New Zealand volume by June 1912, and was finally able to turn his attention to the major report.[47] This took most of his time over the next two years, but when war

44 Amery to Willison, 6 Jan. 1913, ibid.
45 Curtis to Duncan, 8 Aug. 1911, Curtis Papers. Curtis did try to enlist Feetham's assistance in the summer of 1911, but without success. See Duncan to Curtis, 27 Aug. 1911, ibid.
46 Curtis had originally planned to prepare a revised edition of the Green Memorandum, but on reading the criticisms and the comments that poured in he decided they should be the common property of all the groups. The index alone took Curtis two months to complete. See Curtis to Kylie, 2 Feb. 1912, copy, Willison Papers.
47 Copies of 'Australian Notes' and 'New Zealand Notes' are in the library of the Royal Commonwealth Society, London.

broke out in 1914 the main outlines had been established and a number of chapters circulated for discussion and criticism.

It was during these two years that Curtis and the London group worked out what they referred to as 'the principle of the commonwealth.' It was the closest that the movement came to defining its aims; and all its activities, especially those of the London members, were directly related to 'the principle.' Without some knowledge of it, it is impossible to understand the movement. Essentially, 'the principle of the commonwealth' was the belief that responsibility for public affairs had to be assumed by an increasing number of citizens to an ever increasing degree. It meant 'entrusting sovereignty to all those whose sense of duty to their fellow citizens was strong enough to justify the trust.'[48]

The ideas behind the principle were not Curtis's alone, but were threshed out and agreed to in discussions by the London group in which Curtis, Kerr, Oliver, Zimmern, Coupland, and Ramsey Muir[49] made the major contributions. Alfred Zimmern was particularly useful as he had already made an intensive study of the ideas of citizenship in the Athenian city-state and had published his book *The Greek Commonwealth* in 1911.[50] Nevertheless, the final definition of 'the principle of the commonwealth,' as one finds it in *The Project of a Commonwealth*, *The Commonwealth of Nations*, *The Problem of the Commonwealth*, *The Round Table*, and various unpublished memoranda, was given by Curtis. In private correspondence, Kerr always credited Curtis with defining the principle, although he often wrote about it himself with much more sophistication, especially during the war, when he continually contrasted it to prussianism and later to bolshevism. For some years the members of the London group had compared the British and German systems of government, and had examined and juxtaposed the philosophy of state held in both countries. The definition of 'the principle of the commonwealth' owed much to this stimulus, as much perhaps as it did to

48  Curtis, *The Project of a Commonwealth*. 181
49  Ramsey Muir (1872-1941); historian and politician; lecturer then professor of modern history, University of Liverpool, 1899-1913; visited India 1913 and Germany 1914; among his books were *Nationalism and Internationalism* (1916); *National Self-Government* (1918); and *A Short History of the British Commonwealth*, 2 vols. (1920-2).
50  The first 119 pages of what became *The Project of a Commonwealth* (1915) and *The Commonwealth of Nations* (1916) were circulated to the groups by late 1912. It abounds with definitions of the commonwealth and 'the principle of the commonwealth.' On page 43 Curtis cites the section in Zimmern's book (pp. 179-83) which dealt with 'The Elements of Citizenship' and 'Liberty, or the Rule of Empire.' The first use of the term 'commonwealth' in *The Round Table* was in an article entitled 'The Spirit of the Coronation' published in the August 1911 issue, 426-34.

Fichte and Kant, to the Hamiltonian ideas outlined by Oliver, and to the philosophic idealism of Oxford and T.H. Green.[51] Kerr, Zimmern, and Coupland also publicised the principle in various essays and public addresses. Although it became the guideline of Round Table activities, it was not endorsed by all the members of either the London or dominion groups. The ethical idealism underlying it was never seriously questioned, but the doubtful history and gross generalisations indulged in by Curtis were subjected to considerable criticism within the movement.

Underlying 'the principle of the commonwealth' was a definite concept of the function of the state and the role of the citizen. For the London members the quickening principle of a state was a sense of devotion, an adequate recognition somewhere in the minds of its subjects that their own interests were subordinate to those of the state. The bond which united them and made them collectively a state was 'dedication.' Its validity, like that of the marriage tie, was at root not contractual but sacramental.[52] Obligation and not privilege, duties and not rights, lay at the root of citizenship; they were the foundations upon which every healthy and progressive state had to build its communal life. It was an obligation owed not to a monarch or to an abstraction labelled 'the State,' but to the whole body of one's fellow citizens, organised as a community in obedience to law. Each citizen was bound by an obligation to which he could recognise no limits, 'an obligation which requires him to sacrifice everything – property, and, if necessary, life itself – in the interests of the commonwealth.' It was in the general good of the community that his own particular good was to be sought, and to neglect the public interest in the pursuit of his own was to grasp at a shadow and ignore the substance.[53] But while obligation was the primary essence of citizenship, liberty was its essential correlative. If a citizen was bound to obey the law, the movement believed he should also have an equal voice with his fellow citizens in determining what the law should be.[54] This did not necessarily mean universal suffrage.[55] People should never be entrusted with their own gov-

---

51 Like so many others of their time at Oxford, Curtis and Zimmern had been exposed to philosophic idealism by Green's disciples at Balliol and other colleges. For an article on the empire as 'an ideal of moral welfare' see 'The Ethics of Empire,' *The Round Table*, June 1913, 484-501, probably written by Zimmern. Also Zimmern's article on 'Education and the Working Class,' ibid., March 1914, 255-79
52 Curtis, *The Project of a Commonwealth*, 181
53 Ibid., 23. For a further elaboration of this 'principle of service' see three articles in *The Round Table* by Philip Kerr: 'The Foundations of Peace,' June 1915, 589-625; 'The End of War,' Sept. 1915, 772-96; 'The Principle of Peace,' June 1916, 391-429.
54 'The Imperial Dilemma,' ibid., Sept. 1916, 688-712
55 Curtis, *The Project of a Commonwealth*, 181

ernment before they were fit for it.[56] But in the most advanced communities, where the sense of service had developed into a strong sense of responsibility for the general welfare, the task of framing the law ought to be in the hands of citizens who would amend it and control it through elected representatives. It followed that all citizens that had the necessary qualifications – an intellectual capacity for judging the public interest and some moral capacity for treating it as paramount to their own – ought to be admitted to a share in the formulation of the rules of society.[57] In such communities, not only was the law far better adjusted to the needs of the whole body of citizens, but true liberty was realised because the ctizens themselves determined the laws which governed the conditions of their social life. For the movement, it was this idea of liberty coupled with the rule of law as opposed to the rule of the individual which distinguished a commonwealth from other states.

Curtis believed that the most distinctive form of 'the principle of the commonwealth' had evolved in England. It was the citizens not the king, Cabinet, or parliament who were the mainspring of government in the United Kingdom; it was with them that the true sovereignty lay. And in the British empire, the allegiance of the people of the United Kingdom and of all its dependencies was due to the same paramount authority. Supposedly all of them were citizens of one comprehensible state where government was based on 'the principle of the commonwealth.'

But, asked Curtis, were the British justified in describing their empire as a state or even a commonwealth? From the international point of view it was a state; but viewed from within it lost the character of a state, and failed to realise the principle of a commonwealth. In the general government of the empire the dominions exercised no voice whatever while the imperial government had no power to command their resources for the maintenance of the imperial commonwealth.[58] Thus, viewed from without, the British empire was a single state with a single government; but viewed from within, the British empire was not a true commonwealth. It was an English empire governed by the United Kingdom. Its common affairs were controlled solely by the people of the British Isles through the same Cabinet and parliament responsible for the domestic affairs of the United Kingdom. The imperial constitution therefore offended against the canons of the commonwealth. The sense of common obligation had grown weak because the first principle

56 [Lionel Curtis], 'A Practical Enquiry in to the Nature of Citizenship in the British Empire and into the Relation of Its Several Communities to Each Other' (London 1914), 20
57 Curtis, *The Project of a Commonwealth*, 10-12
58 Ibid., 4-8

of liberty, the sharing of power and responsibility in common, had been in-fringed.[59] The British empire was 'a commonwealth which excludes from a share in its government an increasing proportion of citizens in no way less qualified for the task than those whom it admits to it. It is a state, yet not a state; a commonwealth, yet one which fails to realise an essential condition of the principle which inspires it. Can it continue in this condition, and if not, is it to develop the structure of a state and to fulfill the conditions of a com-monwealth, or is it to be broken up into a number of states?'[60] The people of Great Britain and the dominions would have to decide whether, in the last analysis, their final allegiance was due to the commonwealth as a whole or merely to the territory in which they lived. For Curtis that was 'the Imperial Problem, the final enigma.'[61] Until it was resolved the British empire would remain 'not a commonwealth, but the project of a commonwealth.'[62]

Despite its weaknesses Curtis believed 'this project of a commonwealth' the noblest enterprise yet conceived in the cause of liberty. It had united 'the divers families of mankind' without using despotic means and had given a wide degree of stability to the world.[63] The British people had included com-munities drawn from every level of human society under a single system of law and government without, like the Romans, completely destroying the 'principle of the commonwealth'; in doing so they were answering to 'the greatest need of humanity in the present age.'[64] Curtis and his colleagues agreed that it would be a tragedy for mankind if the British commonwealth did not survive. For them it was a guarantee of peace and civilized progress which no other system of government in the world could replace. It was needed in order to maintain 'some ordered scheme of relations between great masses of human beings, who cannot as yet govern themselves, and the civ-ilized races of the world at whose mercy they lie.'[65]

Although the movement generally agreed with Curtis's definition of 'the principle of the commonwealth,' many of his more sensitive colleagues were concerned by his historical and philosophical generalisations. Curtis's habit

59 'The Imperial Dilemma,' *The Round Table*, Sept. 1916, 688-712
60 Curtis, *The Project of a Commonwealth*, 17
61 Ibid., 705
62 [Curtis], 'A Practical Enquiry,' 7
63 Curtis, *The Project of a Commonwealth*, 177
64 [Curtis], 'A Practical Enquiry,' 68. The chapter 'The Opening of the High Seas' in *The Project of a Commonwealth* has excellent material on Curtis's attitudes toward India, the de-pendencies, and the commonwealth's responsibilities.
65 [Curtis], 'A Practical Enquiry,' 150

of bending history to suit his thesis was naturally annoying to the more scholarly of his friends, but this was not the major problem. Many of them – such as Brand, Amery, and Coupland – disliked Curtis equating the British empire-commonwealth with a state and suggesting that only it should have full sovereignty. They feared that undermining the sovereign authority of the democratic state would be 'a positive retrogression in the political life of the world, and a serious danger to the cause of real freedom.'[66] The same doubts occurred to outside observers. Fabian Ware, who received copies of the first instalment of the major 'egg' in late 1912, expressed his concern to Jebb:

The strength of the Round Table is in its anonymity and its (apparent and, I believe, real) disinterestedness. They ought to be fought ... in the same way. The Round Table volume of studies I have just received is the most respectable misguided unselfish effort I have ever seen. Their history is wicked – how *dare* they do this sort of thing. It is really poisoning the wells. I am pulled up at every page – always doubting their conclusions and, where I have any little knowledge, *knowing* them to be wrong ... A little more Grote & a little less Dicey, Bryce & Freeman ... & they would have been more trustworthy. Damn it if England is guided by the Round Table she becomes permanently second-rate intellectually among the great nations. But the influence of this sort of publication – the result of infinite pains is not to be underrated.[67]

The London members continued to grapple with Curtis's memoranda right up to the outbreak of war; but it was not until 1915-17 that they squarely faced the difficulties raised by his writings.

However, one problem did receive their attention: How was the movement to present its writings to the world? The original idea had been that the various Round Table groups should regard themselves as sub-committees of a commission of inquiry, and that they should all attempt to agree on a draft report. By 1913 Curtis had begun to realise the practical impossibility of such a course. When he raised the issue with his London colleagues it was decided that no final decision should be made until Curtis had discussed his memoranda and the future of the movement with the leaders of the Cana-

---

66 Excerpt from a letter from Coupland to G.L. Beer, quoted in Beer to Glazebrook, 24 Dec. 1917, copy, Willison Papers. See also a 'Memorandum' by Glazebrook on the philosophy of the movement dated 19 May 1917, copy, Walker Papers; and Beer to Glazebrook, 25 May 1917, copy, ibid.
67 Ware to Jebb, 24 Dec. 1912, box 3, Jebb Papers. Deakin was more complimentary. See Deakin to Curtis, 24 Feb. 1913, copy, MSS 1540, Deakin Papers

dian groups. Their judgement was respected and their support was essential if the movement was to have any success.[68] Curtis spent much of October and November 1913 in Canada. He held numerous meetings with Glazebrook, Kylie, and Massey and spoke to a large gathering of the Toronto groups. Curtis's conversations with the Canadians were of crucial importance to the movement. They not only determined his actions during the next three years, but resulted in a misunderstanding which when discovered in 1916 had serious ramifications for the movement.

Curtis told the Canadians that it now seemed impossible to prepare a memorandum agreeable to all the groups. While Massey, Glazebrook, and Kylie appreciated the difficulties involved, they pointed out that a report containing only Curtis's conclusions would be equally unsatisfactory. They argued that the Canadian groups could not be asked to agree to Curtis's report without placing the founders in a false position. In order to ensure that the problem would be studied from every angle, men of every variety of opinion had been persuaded to join the groups 'including some who would repudiate the name of Imperialists.' The suspicion and hesitation of many had been overcome only by assuring them that in joining the Round Table movement they would be committed to nothing beyond a study of the imperial problem. These members would be embarrassed by the publication of a report, even if approved by a majority. They 'would feel that they had helped to give prestige to an organisation which was promulgating views opposed to their own.'

These arguments seemed convincing to Curtis. After discussion with the Canadians he decided to draw the attention of all the Round Table groups throughout the empire to the difficulty during his scheduled speech to the Toronto groups in November. He would admit quite frankly that the original conception was now unworkable, and that a different procedure for giving the results of the inquiry to the public would have to be worked out. Discussing this with his friends, Curtis explained that as far as he was concerned the future relations of the dominions to the United Kingdom could only be based upon one of four different principles, the *status quo*, independence, co-operation, and organic union. He believed independence or organic union were the only real alternatives, and his report would favour union. Curtis proposed to make his opinions known to the groups at large in his speech, and to urge that members who favoured one of the alternatives should frame reports in support of their views. At a meeting held in Massey's

68 Minutes of a moot, 25 Sept. 1913, Curtis Papers

rooms in Burwash Hall shortly before he was to speak, Curtis asked Glazebrook, Kylie, and Massey what course he should pursue if, when his own
report was completed, no reports had been prepared in favour of the other
alternatives. Curtis reminded his friends that he had only engaged in the
study as a prelude to action, and he had asked others to join only on that
basis. He made it clear that if and when his own report was completed others
had not been produced, or were not even in sight, he would definitely not
abstain from action.

In reply to this Massey, with the support of Glazebrook and Kylie, made
a novel suggestion. His idea was that Curtis should produce the report over
his own name and on his own responsibility, and that at no time should the
Round Table organisation be asked to adopt it. This, Massey argued, would
leave it open for some members of the movement to form a new organisation
for the avowed purpose of supporting the general conclusions of Curtis's report. Massey insisted very strongly that no attempt should be made to convert the existing Round Table groups from an organisation formed for study
to one designed for propaganda. Those who agreed with Curtis's conclusions would have to start anew with a totally different organisation and a
new name. This was a completely fresh suggestion and not one to be acted
upon hastily. Curtis decided to discuss it with the London group before committing himself. In any event he found it difficult to accept the idea right
away, since it 'was so contrary to the impersonal traditions of our work.'
Curtis deliberately avoided mentioning the matter to the groups in his
speech at Senate House, University of Toronto on 18 November.[69]

In his speech Curtis outlined the nature of the major 'egg,' now being referred to as 'Round Table Studies.' It was to be divided into three volumes,
and each volume would be sent to the groups in several instalments. The first
volume would deal with the past, and would be an attempt to show how and
why 'the British Commonwealth' had come into being. The second volume
would deal with the present, and would be a survey of each of the different countries included in 'the great Commonwealth' in order to see what
kind of community it had become by reason of its position, and to gauge
what its position was. Essentially the object of the second volume would be
to provide those engaged in the Round Table inquiry with a statement of
contemporary facts so as to better examine the imperial problem. Curtis referred to the tentative studies of Canada, Australia, and New Zealand which

---

69 The account of these meetings is taken from a long historical letter, Curtis to Massey, 28
March 1916, copy, Walker Papers.

had been submitted to the groups for criticism, and indicated that further studies of Great Britain, South Africa, India, Egypt, and of the African dependencies were being prepared 'by men closely acquainted with these countries and qualified to speak of them.' He pointed out that since the future of 'the British Commonwealth' – this was a very early public use of the term – had to be viewed in its relation to the world outside it, the second volume would end with a study of its foreign relations. The third volume would deal with the future and would stand alone; so that those who could not afford the time to follow the inquiry through the first two volumes would only need to read volume three. It would open with an introduction which would summarise the conclusions arrived at in the previous volumes.

Curtis then outlined what he believed were the four alternatives facing the empire, indicated his faith in organic union, and then emphasized – as previously agreed with Massey, Glazebrook, and Kylie – that any one who believed in the alternatives of independence, co-operation, or the *status quo* should prepare a report showing how such a method would work. He argued that the Round Table movement would have done an invaluable work if it succeeded in elucidating the possible alternatives and in placing them, first, before its members and then before fellow citizens throughout the empire. His experience had also shown that the original idea of having someone draft a final report based on all previous memoranda and criticisms would have to be rethought. In the first place, the movement could not really work like the ideal royal commission because all the groups could not meet under one roof to discuss the report as a whole; and besides it 'would need magic to charm into verbal unanimity several hundred men all accustomed to think freely for themselves.' Furthermore, said Curtis, the Round Table inquiry had been conducted this far by men of all shades of opinion, and if 'the majority of the groups in each Dominion agreed to adopt the report as I have foreshadowed it and then with the prestige of the "Round Table" behind them, proceeded to advocate it as their creed, the minority might very well feel that their cooperation had been used to give prestige to an organisation which, after they had retired from it, was being used to propagate views directly contrary to their own.'[70]

Later that night, at a further meeting with Kylie, Glazebrook, and Massey, Curtis was asked to submit a rough draft of volume III of 'Round Table Studies' to the Canadian executive as soon as possible, so that it could be considered by their groups while Curtis was completing volumes I and

70  The above is taken from Curtis, *The Round Table Movement*.

ii.[71] On his return to England, he had his Toronto speech circulated to all the Round Table groups in the empire, and soon received a number of similar requests for a preview of volume iii.[72] At a special meeting on 9 March 1914 Curtis informed the moot of his discussions with the Canadians and of the various recommendations which had resulted from the circulation of his speech. It was agreed that Curtis should prepare a skeleton of volume iii in time for discussion at Whitsuntide.[73] After a feverish effort Curtis managed to complete this so-called 'Strawberry Memorandum' in time for a meeting of the moot at Cliveden during Whitsun 29-30 May 1914.[74]

At this meeting Curtis revealed that while drafting the skeleton of volume iii he had reached new conclusions about the whole nature of the movement's enquiry and the way it should be presented to the public. He now thought his previous idea of drafting volume iii to make it stand by itself was wrong and should be abandoned. It would be much better if the imperial problem and the changes necessary to resolve it were initially presented to the public in a short popular volume. The three-volume 'Round Table Studies' would still be prepared. But it would be a detailed study of the past, present, and future of the empire whereas the shorter volume would be 'a statement of the problem as it was, is and must remain so long as the British Empire remains the project of a commonwealth and until its people have decided to complete that project and to realise the Commonwealth.'[75]

Curtis's proposals were discussed at the Cliveden meeting, initially with the whole party and then more intensively on the Saturday with Milner, Grigg, and Kerr.[76] The group arrived at two principal conclusions.[77] First, on a motion by Glazebrook who had come over especially for the meeting, it was decided to circulate the draft of volume iii to all groups for the purpose of study and criticism during the following year. Second, the group conclud-

---

71  Curtis to Massey, 28 March 1916, copy, Walker Papers
72  Preface to [Curtis], 'A Practical Enquiry'
73  See minutes of a moot held 9 March 1914, Curtis Papers
74  The members had assembled in strength for the crucial discussions; present with the Astors were Milner, Kerr, Brand, Oliver, Craik, Grigg, Malcolm, Amery, Zimmern, Arthur Glazebrook, and Atkinson, the New Zealander. See Milner diary, 10 March and 29 and 30 May 1914, vol. 277, Milner Papers.
75  For Curtis's recommendations see L. Curtis, 'Note by the Draughtsman,' 29 May 1914, attached to Part iii of the rough draft of volume iii. Copy in the library of the Royal Commonwealth Society, London
76  Milner diary, 29 and 30 May 1914, vol. 277, Milner Papers
77  The account of the meeting is taken from Curtis to Massey, 28 March 1916, copy, Walker Papers.

ed, primarily on the basis of Curtis's arguments, that it was not possible to produce a volume for the general reader by attempting to summarise the results of the whole inquiry. It would be far too dull and detailed. Instead, 'Round Table Studies' would be finished in accordance with the original plan; and a separate popular report would be produced dealing with that aspect of the question which immediately concerned the dominions. Having gained the support of the London group, Curtis set to work and by August 1914 had put the final touches on the draft of volume III. It was immediately circulated to the groups for discussion.[78] When the war broke out in Europe Curtis had also completed and circulated four instalments of volume I and had begun to outline the shorter popular volume, soon to be entitled *The Problem of the Commonwealth*.

78 This was 'A Practical Enquiry.' It was marked for private circulation only. There is a copy in the library of the Royal Commonwealth Society, London.

# 8

# 'The Problem of the Commonwealth'

*One trouble about my friends of the Round Table is that they are all so serious and take themselves so. The issue of this book is something so momentous that it is debated as though the whole world were hanging on it.*[1]

The outbreak of the war in August 1914 brought no immediate dramatic changes to the Round Table movement, but it did serve to stimulate their work. In New Zealand and Australia, and particularly in Canada, interest in Round Table affairs increased, and small groups were soon established in outlying rural communities in all three dominions. Efforts in this direction had been going on in Canada since Curtis's speech in November 1913; and mainly through the work of Vincent Massey groups had been set up in Newfoundland in the spring of 1914.[2] The war shocked many previously disinterested people into an awareness of imperial and international problems, and both Laby in New Zealand and Kylie in Canada found it 'a very good time for Round Table work.'[3]

Even in South Africa the war had a beneficial effect. Early in 1914 there had been some fear that the organisation would completely collapse, a prospect which Curtis found 'too terrifying to contemplate.' Curtis had urged Feetham, Duncan, and Wyndham to enlarge their circle of acquaintances and place the organisation on a firmer footing. He advised Feetham, who

1 Steel-Maitland to Glazebrook, 28 May 1916, copy, Walker Papers
2 Kylie to Willison, 20 April 1914, Willison Papers
3 Kylie to Laby, 16 Oct. 1914, Laby Papers

had been acting as organising secretary, to concentrate on obtaining a good South African article, for its soundness would attract members. Feetham had apparently thought of establishing worker's educational association groups, and Curtis approved: 'I personally shall not mind your leaving Round Table groups on one side for the present if you can really put yourselves into the Round Table magazine and get the w.e.a. really going. Groups organised in the spirit of the w.e.a. will read the Round Table and the Round Table studies of their own accord.' By June a small study circle had been established in South Africa which resembled the old Fortnightly Club of kindergarten days, and after August 1914 it continued to discuss Curtis's memoranda and to submit a chronicle article.[4] Despite this renewed activity the South African branch remained the weakest of the dominion organisations.

The outbreak of war caused some heart-searching among the members of the London group. Four weeks after Great Britain declared war, Curtis advised Hichens to stay with Cammel Laird, and thought 'Robin should stay with the Times.' Similarly, he did not believe Grigg could do anything in the ranks to compare with what he could do 'in the Dominions and with the working classes by keeping the Round Table going. Because of Philip's health there is no one alive who can do such service in this direction as Ned.'[5] As for himself, the coming of war posed certain problems. Although the main outlines of his work were on record and available to students, he had not yet completed the three volumes of 'Round Table Studies,' the short popular volume, or the outline of the imperial constitution. The fact that the war had broken out sooner than the movement had expected only increased the need for their work. Admittedly no one could tell when the war would come to an end, but anyone could see that if the British commonwealth continued to exist at its close the constitutional problem which the Round Table groups had been organised to study would become vitally important. It would cease to be academic, if it ever had been, and would become the dominant question of practical politics. To Curtis it was of the utmost importance to get some document finished which 'would serve to prepare the public mind for the crisis which was rushing upon us.'[6] But at forty-two he felt 'as fit to fight as a man of thirty' and believed his duty 'lay with theirs' now that his work was so far advanced. He was prepared to go immediately but would wait until the popular volume and volume II of 'Round Table Studies' were

---

4 Feetham to Curtis, 26 March 1914; and Curtis to Feetham, 17 April and 4 June 1914, copies, Curtis Papers
5 Curtis to Hichens, 30 Aug. 1914, copy, ibid.
6 Curtis to Massey, 28 March 1916, copy, Walker Papers

completed. After that only a positive order from the moot to take the results to the dominions would prevent him enlisting. Curtis felt he could be an example for younger men.[7] Nothing is more revealing of Curtis's deep religious convictions and sense of duty than his heart-searching over his enlistment. He was dedicated to his Round Table work and all that he believed it stood for; but at a time of acute national crisis he could not decide whether his work, and what it might mean in the long run, should come before direct service for his country. The London group finally managed to convince Curtis that his duty lay with the movement and with further research into imperial problems, and he decided not to enlist. A year later Lionel Hichens reassured Curtis that he had chosen correctly.[8]

During the early stages of the war most of the London group remained at their current tasks. Robinson stayed at *The Times*; Oliver and Hichens in business; Brand with Lazard Brothers; and Kerr and Grigg with *The Round Table*. Lord Milner continued his life of discussion and negotiation behind the scenes, until he was brought in as chairman of the food production committee in the spring of 1915 by Lord Selborne, who had been named president of the Board of Agriculture in Asquith's coalition. Amery became involved in the recruitment programme under Kitchener at the War Office. But he was soon overseas, and spent the first six months of 1915 in Flanders and the Balkans. Back in London in July he met continuously with Milner, Oliver, Robinson, Carson, and Roberts to discuss and promote National Service.[9] This was the nucleus of the so-called Ginger Group which began to meet in January 1916 on every Monday evening. Waldorf Astor, Lloyd George, Henry Wilson,[10] Philip Kerr, and Jameson also joined the discussions occasionally. The primary purpose was to analyse the way Asquith was running the war; and, if possible, to help bring down the government.

Although a number of leading members of the movement were intimates of the Ginger Group, their activities were dissociated from it. This crossover of personnel between two extremely important behind-the-scenes groups is a good example of how difficult it is to discriminate between the interests and purposes of individual members and the activities and purposes of the movement as a whole. In this instance, however, the evidence suggests that the empire-wide movement did not become involved in British domestic wrangles, and that *The Round Table* did not become identified with party or fac-

7 Curtis to Hichens, 30 Aug. 1914, copy, Curtis Papers
8 Hichens to Curtis, Nov. 1915, ibid.
9 Milner diary, 1915, vol. 278, Milner Papers
10 Sir Henry Hughes Wilson (1864-1922); field-marshal; KCB 1915; saw action Burma 1885-9; South Africa 1899-1900; World War I 1914-15; director of military operations 1910-14; assistant chief of General Staff to Lord French 1914; field-marshall 1917

tion. Moreover, Amery, who was the prime mover behind the formation of the Ginger Group, had begun to drift away from the movement as Curtis's conclusions and arguments became clearer. Although he remained associated with the London group throughout the war, he was never again as deeply involved as he had been in 1908-14. In May 1916, only four months after the Ginger Group began to meet, Amery was off again to the Balkans. When he returned in December he found a Lloyd George government in power and Milner a member of the War Cabinet. Milner, as always, was the father-figure of the group and he continued to advise the London members, but he was active in many facets of British political and public life during the war which had nothing to do with the movement.

As can be seen the movement did not survive the war unscathed. Grigg soon enlisted in the Grenadier Guards, and in November 1915 Brand and Hichens were sent to Canada by Lloyd George, the minister of munitions, in order to arrange for the efficient production of armament. On their advice Borden appointed Joseph W. Flavelle, a leading member of the Canadian Round Table group, as chairman of the Ottawa based Imperial Munitions Board. Brand became the British munitions representative in Washington, and was out of England for months at a time. Perry was placed in charge of the financial operations of the board, and was based in Canada for the remainder of the war.[11] In December 1916, with the changeover of government, the movement lost Kerr and Astor to Lloyd George's 'Garden Suburb,' and Amery to the War Cabinet Secretariat under Maurice Hankey. The situation was much the same in the dominions. Many of the leading New Zealand and Australian members enlisted; and in Canada Edward Kylie, the backbone of the organisation, went off to camp in 1915.

In the early months of the war, however, the British and dominion groups remained fairly stable, and were able to function much as ever. As a result Kylie, Walker, and Willison in Canada, advised and encouraged by the London group, urged Borden to advocate the holding of the imperial conference scheduled for 1915. Despite a lengthy correspondence and the publication of an article on the subject by Grigg in *The Round Table*, the conference was postponed.[12] In Australia in 1915 the Melbourne group agreed that the pub-

11 Another Round Table man, Lloyd Harris of Brantford, Ontario, became the Canadian representative to the Imperial Munitions Board in Washington.
12 Kylie to Borden, 5, 12, 14, 26 and 29 Jan. 1915; Borden to Kylie, 6, 12, 13, and 27 Jan. 1915; Walker to Borden, 10 and 13 Jan. 1915; Borden to Walker, 12 Jan. 1915, reel c246, Borden Papers. Kylie to Walker, 6 Jan. 1915; Walker to Kylie, 18 Jan. 1915, copy, Walker Papers. See [E. Grigg], 'The Dominions and the Settlement: A Plea for a Conference,' *The Round Table*, March 1915, 325-44.

lic should be taken into the fullest possible confidence about the war effort and recommended a review of government censorship policies. They also suggested that a government secret service should be appointed, that the administration of the Defence Department should be streamlined, that the government should economise, that men should be transferred from public works into war work, and that large numbers of officers should be trained. They planned to send a deputation to the government to put these points once the necessary statistics had been assembled, but there is no evidence to suggest that this action was ever taken. By 1916 the Melbourne group was concentrating its energies on reorganising the Round Table activities in Victoria.[13]

Much of the attention of all the Round Table groups and members during the first two years of the war was focused on Curtis's memoranda. After making his decision to remain with the movement, Curtis concentrated on revising volume I of 'Round Table Studies.' By mid-1915 all the instalments were completed and reprinted in one volume and privately circulated among the groups under the title *The Project of a Commonwealth*.[14] Curtis also began work on the short popular volume. This was finished by October and proof copies were distributed to the London group.

The book, entitled *The Problem of the Commonwealth*, was divided into two sections. Part I was called 'What the Problem Is.' In it Curtis outlined the origins and growth of self-government in Great Britain and the dominions, examined the progress made by the dominions in the spheres of tariffs and immigration, and then revealed how the dominions had stopped short of complete self-government in the fields of defence and foreign policy. In Part II, 'The Conditions of its Solution,' he argued that the dominions had to have more control of defence and foreign policy. This could best be achieved by creating an imperial parliament, responsible to all the electors in the self-governing empire, which would control defence, foreign policy, and the decision of peace or war, and have the power to raise revenues for imperial purposes. The amount owed by each dominion to the imperial war chest would be decided by a permanent judicial commission of assessors who would regularly determine the taxable capacity of each member state. The manner in which the money was raised in the dominions would be left to each individual government. In the last resort, assuming a dominion de-

13 See 'Report of Round Table Committee,' Sept. 1915; and 'Round Table Resolutions Passed at Meeting on 28.IX.15,' Harrison Moore Papers.
14 There is some evidence that Curtis was also considering a propaganda campaign in Canada in the spring of 1915. The idea was probably never considered seriously, and nothing came of it. See Glazebrook to Milner, 15 Feb. 1915, box 140, Milner Papers; also Lady Selborne to Curtis, 22 June 1915, Curtis Papers.

faulted, the imperial parliament would have the power to collect the taxes itself from the individual citizens in the defaulting dominion. Curtis also argued that it was impossible to exclude the dependencies from the jurisdiction of the new parliament because foreign policy and the dependencies were inseparable. The dominions, therefore, would have to agree to assume a responsibility for the dependencies. In order that all these matters could be thoroughly discussed and decisions reached he recommended the holding of an imperial convention. Throughout his book Curtis made it clear that he thought the only alternative to organic union was independence for the dominions – that is, the disruption of the empire.

It was a compact, well-written book which covered every aspect of the imperial problem. The portion on the imperial parliament was especially cogent, as was intended. Curtis was convinced that the greatest stumbling block to the achievement of organic union would be taxation. He also realised that very few people had actually thought out all the implications of union. In order to provoke the necessary analysis and debate Curtis had deliberately stiffened his proposals.[15] The reaction within the movement was probably more dramatic than he had intended. His book, particularly the section on taxation, came close to splitting the London group and had a disastrous long-term impact on the movement's work.

The London group assembled in strength in early October to consider their next step now that the short popular volume had been completed.[16] They decided to circulate the book as quickly as possible to the dominion groups, but not to publish it. Wartime did not seem an appropriate moment to launch their federation campaign, particularly with a document as hard-hitting as Curtis's. Many of the London group doubted the tactical wisdom of Curtis's proposals. Even Milner who, on first reading it, thought the book raised 'no unnecessary issues' and was 'admirably suited for the purpose for which it is intended,' changed his mind.[17] Now he feared a serious split in the London group's small nucleus. He hoped that from a middle position he could hold the diverging views together, but he thought Curtis should take a closer look at his taxation and constitutional suggestions.[18]

But it was not only the taxation section that caused distress in London.

15 For Curtis's reasoning see Curtis to Borden, 6 Nov. 1915, oc series, file 212, Borden Papers.
16 Present besides Curtis were Milner, Brand, Hichens, Dove, Oliver, Marris, Malcolm, Zimmern, Amery, Kerr, Coupland, and Chirol. Milner described it as a 'Very long discussion' which he continued personally with Curtis on 13 October. Milner diary, 7 and 13 Oct. 1915, vol. 278, Milner Papers
17 For Milner's initial reaction see Milner to Curtis, 6 Oct. 1915, Curtis Papers.
18 Milner to Curtis, 27 Nov. 1915, ibid.

Ramsey Muir and Valentine Chirol objected violently to the short volume because Curtis had not provided for the representation of India in the future imperial government. As far as Curtis was concerned both these and Milner's criticisms were somewhat irrelevant. He had simply taken 'the plain question how a British subject in the Dominions was to get the same degree of self-government that a British subject in the United Kingdom had,' and had confined himself to showing 'by almost mathematical reasoning' that the thing could not be done unless people were prepared to face 'three or four changes of a kind distasteful to them.' Curtis admitted going into some detail over finances, but had not set out to build the framework of an imperial constitution. That was something reserved for the last volume of the main report. As far as the moot and the division of opinion in it was concerned, Curtis contended that 'its value surely arises to a large extent from its mixed character, because if Imperial Union were advanced by an organisation which consisted exclusively of Olivers it would be lost in the Dominions and among the working classes from the outset. A movement which consisted of Zimmerns and Couplands would probably lose touch with hard realities.' Curtis believed such a combination was worth holding together, although it probably needed a man like Milner to do it.[19]

At this particular moment in his life Curtis was obsessed by the need for a federal union of the British commonwealth, and he continued to defend his work against the critics with all his inimitable fervour and elan.[20] But he was not always alone, and it pleased him to see Lady Selborne and Philip Kerr becoming, as he believed, 'such real democrats': 'I, belonging to the lower middle class, believe more and more firmly every day in aristocracy as understood by Aristotle ... I believe in trusting political power to all who are fit to exercise it, plus as many more as can be given the vote without endangering the state too much. It is in this last point, perhaps, that I go further than Aristotle went and approach you and Philip. You will not get more people fit for political power until you entrust more of them, before they are quite fit, with the power.'[21]

By the end of 1915 copies of *The Problem of the Commonwealth* were circulating freely in Canada among members of the movement, and had also been forwarded to certain prominent politicians. Borden had been sent a

19 Curtis to Milner, 29 Nov. 1915, ibid. At this time Curtis revealed that he was 'up to his eyes in the India chapter in order to get it rough hewn before Marris went.'
20 For an amusing and characteristic example of Curtis's monomania in 1915, see Toynbee, *Acquaintances*, 129-30.
21 Curtis to Lady Selborne, 8 Dec. 1915, copy, Curtis Papers

copy by Curtis in November, and Glazebrook forwarded a copy to Mackenzie King in January 1916.[22] The book had also been examined by Zebulon Aiton Lash,[23] vice president of the Canadian Bank of Commerce, a confidant of Borden, and a close friend of Sir Edmund Walker. Although not formally a member of the movement, Lash took a great interest in the imperial problem and often acted as an intermediary between the Round Table and the Canadian prime minister.[24] He was rather taken aback by *The Problem of the Commonwealth.* Basically, he agreed with Curtis's aims but differed over methods. He believed many of Curtis's conclusions were unanswerable, and if logic alone could solve the imperial problem there was little he could add. But Lash did not believe that the subject could be treated logically beyond a certain point. The interests concerned were so diverse and so many difficulties would arise that logic and reasoning would have to bow to practicalities. Many problems would only be overcome by compromise. He was particularly concerned by the financial proposals, and wrote to the London group advising them to leave the taxing powers in the hands of the dominions.[25]

Lash was not the only Canadian who was disturbed by *The Problem of the Commonwealth.* Borden had very early expressed some concern over the taxation proposals, and when the volume began to be discussed intensively in Canada during January and February that section, plus the one dealing with the dependencies, aroused the most intensive debate.[26] These reactions

22  Curtis to Borden, 6 Nov. 1915, oc series, file 212, Borden Papers; and Glazebrook to King, 7 Jan. 1916, King Papers
23  Zebulon Aiton Lash (1846-1920); lawyer; called to the bar 1868; deputy minister of justice, Ottawa, 1872-6; chief counsel for Canadian Bankers' Association, Canadian Bank of Commerce and the Canadian Northern Railway
24  For instance, Lash was very interested in preparing a draft of an imperial constitution for Borden's use. He discussed this with Brand, Hichens, and Perry in December 1915, and they had dcided to co-operate. The draft constitution was forwarded to Borden in March 1916. Sir Edmund Walker's copy is preserved in his papers with an attached explanatory note by Lash. See Walker Journal, 30 Dec. 1915, Walker Papers. Also Lash to Borden, 16 Sept. 1915; Borden to Lash, 21 Jan. 1916, oc series, file 135; and Lash to Borden, 22 Jan. and 9 March 1916, oc series, file 308, Borden Papers
25  Lash's criticisms of *The Problem* were contained in a long twenty-four page double-spaced typed letter to Brand. Lash to Brand, 14 Jan. 1916, copy, Walker Papers
26  For Borden's reaction see Curtis to Borden, 6 Nov. 1915, oc series, file 212, Borden Papers. The Montreal group provides one of the best examples of the manner in which the Canadian groups approached their task. After an initial meeting on 12 January 1916 the group held eight meetings at two-week intervals during which they examined Curtis's book chapter by chapter. The greatest stumbling blocks, as expected, were taxation, the dependencies,

were were not altogether unexpected, of course, for Curtis had made the financial proposals intentionally stiff in order to elicit discussion. But the Canadians had been giving considerable thought to the expansion of their organisation, and to the possible circulation of a petition calling for a convention to discuss the imperial problem. They feared that a book as controversial as *The Problem of the Commonwealth* would make it difficult to broaden the base of their organisation and to bring in men of all opinions from across the country.[27]

In London there were similar fears. There the greatest fuss was also over the financial proposals.[28] Apparently Curtis was willing to moderate his arguments, but was opposed by some of the moot. Steel-Maitland supported Curtis: 'I have told Curtis that I agree with him, rather than with Brand and Philip Kerr, who appear to me to be of the ascetic kind and to want us all to put on hair shirts and feel the prickles just for the sake of feeling them, even though other clothing would suit the purpose of the weather just as well.'[29]

Brand was probably not as intractable as Steel-Maitland supposed. He had always recognised the necessity of conforming to public opinion in Great Britain and the dominions. So if a plan was operable he was prepared to adopt it even if in the long run it could only be considered a step toward the final goal. As far as Brand was concerned the most pressing need was to educate a largely ignorant public about the empire and its problems. Only then could proper conclusions be reached.[30]

While the book was being heatedly discussed at regular meetings of the London moot,[31] a difficulty arose which eventually forced the hands of the movement and precipitated a trend of events the members had been anxious to avoid. A copy of *The Problem of the Commonwealth* somehow found its way on to the editorial desk of *The Toronto Star*, resulting in a lead article by John Lewis,[32] the Liberal editor, strongly opposed to the idea of giving any central imperial body the authority to tax the Canadian people. This article forced the movement to consider the immediate publication of *The Problem*

and the creation of and representation in an imperial parliament. See File: Round Table-
 – Montreal Group – Minutes – 1916 – Meetings – 1-5, 7-9, Walker Papers.
27  Glazebrook to Milner, 18 Jan. 1916, copy, Glazebrook Papers
28  The London group had found Lash's criticisms especially worrying.
29  Steel-Maitland to Glazebrook, 24 Feb. 1916, copy, Walker Papers. See also 'Memorandum on "The Problem of the Commonwealth" by A.S/ M,' Jan. 1916, Steel-Maitland Papers.
30  Brand to Walker, 22 Feb. 1916, Walker Papers
31  See Milner diary, 29 Jan., 3 Feb., 2 and 9 March 1916, vol. 279, Milner Papers.
32  John Lewis (1858-1935); journalist; for many years on staff of the *Globe*

*of the Commonwealth* on the grounds that only direct action would prevent such mischievous journalism.[33] Brand, for one, was quick to advocate such a course of action; particularly after the Canadian journal *University Magazine* also wrote a review of *The Problem*.[34] It had not been the London group's intention to publish the book so soon, perhaps not until after the war, but since the movement's ideas were now being prejudiced by the publication of extracts taken out of context the time had obviously come for a change of plan. Therefore in February 1916, at about the same time that they were closely examining and criticising the final chapters of the book, the London moot began discussing the feasibility of publishing it. They were well aware of the implications of such a decision. As Brand explained to Lash, 'We recognise fully the immensely difficult nature of the problem and the danger of strong opposition to any idea of any Imperial body having taxing powers. At the same time, most of us feel that in any discussion of the whole problem it is necessary to face facts and that the worst policy of all would be to put forward some sham which is certain to be riddled by criticism. If our reasoning is sound it will gradually make its way.'[35]

The Canadian Round Table executives were not so sure.[36] They believed Curtis's taxation proposals would produce a revulsion of feeling in Canada which 'would seriously injure the Cause.' At the end of February they had reached a firm decision, and Massey as secretary was left to explain it to the London group.[37] The Canadians were unanimous in thinking it inadvisable to publish the book as it stood, particularly with the second part intact. It was already in the hands of nearly everyone who could help the movement and if necessary could still be circulated privately. There was little or nothing to be gained by publication, and probably something to lose. As Massey pointed out the book was 'rather an esoteric production – what in Canada we call "highbrow."' Moreover the elaboration of a cut-and-dried scheme,

---

33 Copies of the article had been sent to Brand and Curtis by Lash and Glazebrook. Lash to Borden, 9 March 1916, oc series, file 308, Borden Papers; and Massey to Curtis, 21 Feb. 1916, enclosed in Massey to Walker, 23 Feb. 1916, Walker Papers

34 C.W. Colby, 'Topics of the Day,' *University Magazine*, Feb. 1916, 6-8

35 Brand to Lash, 23 Feb. 1916, copy, Walker Papers

36 The Canadian executive consisted of Glazebrook, Willison, Falconer, Walker, Wrong, Massey, Frank Beer, Hugh Scully, secretary of the Canadian Manufacturers Association, H.V.F. Jones, the assistant general manager of the Canadian Bank of Commerce, and Colonel Reuben Wells Leonard, engineer, financier, and philanthropist who had been chairman of the Canadian National Transcontinental Railway Commission 1911-14.

37 Massey to Curtis, 21 Feb. 1916, copy; and Massey to Curtis, 1 March 1916, enclosed in Massey to Curtis, 2 March 1916, copy, Walker Papers. The only absentee from the crucial meeting was Colonel Leonard.

or even of definite financial proposals, would only discourage those who would otherwise be the first to realise that Canada's status in the empire was unsatisfactory and needed to be altered. As Willison had pointed out, if the Canadian group intended to ask the political leaders of Canada to advocate an imperial convention to discuss closer union then it should not attempt to instruct them publicly by detailed proposals such as those in the second half of *The Problem*. The material would probably be far more welcome and more closely considered if placed in their hands privately. Furthermore, even if the book were published in Curtis's name, and that of the Round Table movement were carefully excluded, many people would still associate the volume with the movement. 'There is no question in our minds,' wrote Massey, 'that a considerable number of men who are members of the various Round Table groups throughout the country would feel embarrassed in being, in a sense, committed to a certain form of centralisation which they could not conscientiously follow.' Massey believed it was necessary to take 'the most scrupulous care to prevent the Round Table name – whether on paper or in the minds of people – from being associated with any movement other than one devoted exclusively to search for political truth, and as far as possible removed from anything in the nature of the propaganda of any definite scheme of government.' Massey reminded Curtis and the London group that the executive was speaking for Canada, and since Canada was the strategic dominion in Round Table plans its political peculiarities had to be given consideration.

As a way of resolving the difficulty the Canadians suggested that Part I of *The Problem* be published as soon as possible under the auspices of the Round Table. The only addition required would be a chapter to round off the argument and to advocate an imperial convention. 'There is no doubt [argued Massey] that such a publication would be entirely in accordance with the Round Table idea, which has always been to encourage the study of present conditions, to expose the unsatisfactory status of the Dominions and to call for some solution. It has never promulgated any particular scheme, and had concerned itself only with the statement of the "Problem" proper. Such a volume would commit no member of the Round Table to anything new; it would stand as a tangible result of a movement which has often been criticised as leading nowhere; and it would give a reason for the summoning of such a national conference on closer imperial unity as we are now deliberating upon in the Moot ...'[38]

---

38 Glazebrook supported these arguments and in a separate letter reminded Kerr that the Canadian group had three classes of persons to deal with. First, there were those members

The Canadian proposals puzzled Curtis. He found it difficult to harmonise them with the considerations outlined so explicitly by Massey, Glazebrook, and Kylie in November 1913. In a lengthy letter of 28 March Curtis reminded Massey of those earlier crucial discussions, during which Massey had suggested that Curtis publish his conclusions over his own name and on his own reponsibility, so that those within the movement who agreed with him could form a new organisation to promote Curtis's ideas without endangering the student nature of the original groups.[39] 'You will understand my surprise,' wrote Curtis, 'at now being asked to produce a statement of the problem coupled with a demand for an Imperial Convention as a manifesto of the whole Round Table organisation.' Curtis admitted that the idea of publishing Part I with an additional chapter demanding an imperial convention might have been possible if it had been pursued from the outset, but it was not really a wise idea and certainly not one that he personally would have been willing to adopt. Curtis pointed out that both the first draft of volume III of the major report and the short popular volume *The Problem of the Commonwealth* were designed to facilitate the line of action proposed by the Canadians in 1913 and adopted by the London group. 'I was to publish my report when finally completed on my sole responsibility with such a preface as would make it clear that I was speaking for no one in the Round Table but myself. Anyone, whether inside or outside the Round Table groups, was then to be free to form a new organisation in support of its general tenor without committing themselves to any of its details.' For this reason Curtis had ended both books with the argument that no real step towards making the dominions responsible for foreign affairs could be taken

---

of the Round Table groups who were 'thoroughly enthusiastic and willing to go the whole distance'; then a second class of men – quite well represented by the Canadian moot – who would 'privately subscribe to the whole scheme minus the taxation scheme which none of them believe in,' but who were publicly inclined to proceed with caution. And thirdly there was the general public to which the Round Table movement ultimately had to appeal. Glazebrook was convinced that if the book were published as it stood two things would happen: 'First it would have an insignificant sale and secondly the details contained in the solution would be the subject of very bitter and sustained attack from all the autonomist organs, and the plan as a whole would be seriously injured by details that were not essential or not absolutely essential.' In making these assertions Glazebrook revealed that he had the support of George Louis Beer, the Round Table's principal American confidant and correspondent. Glazebrook to Kerr, 14 March 1916, copy, Walker Papers; also Beer to Glazebrook, 20 March 1916, copy, Walker Papers

39 Curtis to Massey, 16 March 1916, copy, ibid.

without an imperial convention being assembled to consider the problems and difficulties involved. To narrow the issue even further, Curtis had suggested that the summoning of a convention should be the work of the existing imperial conference. In this way he had sought to create a common ground for everyone who sincerely desired to resolve the imperial problem without at the same time forcing them to agree to any of his arguments. '... never till this moment,' argued Curtis, 'has it been suggested that any member of the Round Table, or of any new body formed for the purpose of propaganda, was to be bound not to raise or discuss the conditions of union in public until a Convention had met and issued its report.'

Curtis explained that as the short volume stood it was a final statement of his own views. There had been no intention to publish it until after the war, primarily because the British public was distracted by the controversy over compulsory service. Since that particular question had now been settled, and since the Canadians seemed in favour of action, the London group had reconsidered the matter. But they had never suspected that the Canadians would oppose Curtis publishing the report on his sole reponsibility. 'Surely,' said Curtis, 'we could scarcely be expected to realise that you had abandoned all the views you had urged upon me in 1913 and now wished to convert the Round Table into a militant organisation?' Curtis reminded Massey that,

the original Moot was a group of personal friends who all believed that organic union was the only alternative to disruption. That belief we felt was so important that we resolved to ask men of all varieties of opinion throughout the Commonwealth to consider and discuss our reasons in detail, with a view to submitting to the public whatever final conclusions we reached ... But never since we agreed upon my address to the Toronto group in 1913 have we supposed that this original group could commit the groups all over the Dominions, containing as they do, men of every shade of opinion, to a militant propaganda in favour of organic union ... I think you will excuse us therefore for thinking that the new committees consisted of men who were prepared as soon as my report was published to form a rallying point distinct from the old groups for all those who were ready to demand the reconsideration of the Imperial constitution. Inevitably we thought that your call for public action implied the immediate publication of my report in the manner proposed by yourselves, agreed upon by us and formally announced to all the groups in all the Dominions.[40]

Curtis maintained that the whole book should be published as originally

40 Ibid.

planned. It was essential in time of war to create public awareness, and to pass from 'the stage of inquiry to the stage of action.' Moreover, since some of the arguments from *The Problem of the Commonwealth* had appeared in *The Toronto Star*, the *University Magazine*, and also in *Land and Water*, an English publication with a circulation of some 40,000, it would be misleading and damaging, in fact 'fatal,' to the movement to publish only one-half of the book. 'My colleagues here,' revealed Curtis, 'without exception, were of the opinion that the book should be published as soon as possible.'

At this stage Curtis was strongly opposed to the war-time formation of militant groups in favour of organic union. He did not want the Round Table organisation to become propagandist. There was a greater need for public inquiry and education, and the movement was suited for that purpose. He did, however, believe that with the publication of *The Problem* the Round Table organisation should begin to conduct its inquiry in a more public way. This was yet another reason why he wanted any volume setting forth views different from his to be made generally available.[41]

By this time Curtis had decided to publish *The Problem of the Commonwealth* under his own name and to assume sole responsibility for it. As a concession to the marked division of opinion within the London group he slightly modified the financial chapters. Otherwise the book stood as originally written.[42] It was published in May 1916. In taking this action Curtis had Milner's support. Milner admitted ' – though I am bound to confess that I did not always think so – that it might have been wiser to confine "The Problem" to the *statement* of the problem, which could hardly, I think, have been better done than Curtis has done it; and not to have entered in such detail into suggestions for a new Imperial constitution, especially with regard to the raising of the future Imperial revenue. I can quite understand that Curtis' proposals – about which there has been very considerable difference of opinion among ourselves here – will give a *considerable* shock to many people in Canada, and that opposition will centre on this particular point.'

41  See also Curtis to Kerr, 24 April 1916, GD40/17/3, Lothian Papers, in which Curtis re-emphasised that the Round Table groups were 'sociétés d'études' which 'never have been and never can be based upon a fundamental agreement about the Imperial Problem. Such an agreement may and indeed must form a basis upon which some different and future organisation can be founded to advocate Imperial Union. But that organisation cannot be identified with the Round Table groups.'

42  Steel-Maitland later wrote to Glazebrook about these last frenzied meetings: 'As you know,' he noted, 'some of the financial part was watered down from the first print. Several of the Round Table were against any modification, and I was one of the few who were in favor of it. I see no reason for making things stiffer than is necessary.' Steel-Maitland to Glazebrook, 28 May 1916, copy, Walker Papers

But the decision had now been made, 'And I am not sure that in the long run, it will do any harm to have what may in some quarters be regarded as a rather extreme statement of the imperialist solution put before the world.' Milner believed the time had come, or was near at hand, when definite proposals for imperial unification had to take the place of vague general propaganda. And since he was convinced that 'nothing less than full partnership [was] the only ultimate possibility,' and since he wished to have that clearly enunciated, he thought Curtis might as well be allowed 'to open the ball in his own way.' 'Of course, there will be an outcry and very likely the first effect will be to rally the very formidable forces which are opposed to any general Imperial Union. But, sooner or later, that outcry has got to be faced. There will be a long controversy, and he would be a bold man who would venture to predict the result. It depends upon so many things – above all on the further course of the war – which are quite incalculable. But I don't see that anything would be gained by holding back the statement of the case for what I may call a radical solution. It is a very strong statement, certainly of fundamental principles. It will at any rate crystallise a controversy which cannot forever be left in its present vague and indefinite state.'[43]

In mid-April Curtis left for Canada on the first stage of yet another imperial journey with the initial purpose of explaining, defending, and publicising his book, and with the long-range goal of proceeding to India to initiate Round Table work there.[44] While in Toronto he stayed with Vincent Massey, and in conversations with Alice Massey began to understand why the Toronto group had changed its opinions so drastically since 1913. Apparently, when Kylie had been in charge of the Canadian organization he had succeeded in convincing Glazebrook and Massey of the merits of discussing the imperial problem from all angles, and of dissociating themselves from any particular solution. It seemed, however, that neither Glazebrook nor Massey had ever had a real change of heart; while Sir John Willison had never really understood that 'our object never has been to manœuvre politicians, but simply to educate public opinion by turning a dry light on the whole position, *and especially on our own position.*' Both Willison and

43  Milner to Glazebrook, 8 March 1916, box 144, Milner Papers. See also Milner diary, 2 and 9 March 1916, vol. 279; and Milner to Walker, 22 April 1916, copy, box 170, ibid.
44  Curtis landed in New York on 20 April 1916 where he spent some time with George Louis Beer discussing the possibility of forming a Round Table branch in the United States. The idea of establishing groups was quickly abandoned but Beer agreed to continue writing articles for *The Round Table* about American politics. See Kerr to Beer, 3 March 1916, copy; and Beer to Kerr, 20 March 1916, copy, Walker Papers; also Curtis to Kerr, 24 April 1916, GD40/17/3, Lothian Papers.

Glazebrook had ignored the principle that when the time came for an active propaganda of organic union 'some organisation absolutely distinct from the Round Table must be constituted for the purpose.' Curtis informed Kerr that 'Vincent just takes the colour from the people with whom he happens to be.' Thus, when Kylie joined the army the result had been 'inevitable.' Glazebrook had unconsciously swung back to the position he had earlier urged, and Massey had followed. They had 'clean forgot the principle that the Round Table Groups could never be converted into an Imperial Federation League.' Under the name of the Round Table they had instituted a moot into which had been introduced men who had never been in close touch with Round Table work. And Glazebrook and Massey, having themselves forgotten never explained that the Round Table was an organisation including men of all opinions which existed 'for the purpose of compiling and publishing reports on the Imperial Problem as a preliminary to forming militant organisations.'

To Curtis it seemed that Glazebrook, Massey, and Willison had shut their eyes to the fact that many men who had been Round Table members from the beginning did not agree that secession was the only alternative to organic union; and that as Round Table people they could not be committed to such a conclusion. More dangerous still was the assumption on the part of the Canadians that no one but the movement had seen or really understood the imperial problem. Curtis thought this was nonsense. Men like John Dafoe, the editor of the *Winnipeg Free Press*, and John Lewis of the *Toronto Star*, had seen it quite clearly without ever reading the Round Table reports. They would be able to ask all the questions the movement had raised. Curtis feared that the movement's six-years' work would be discredited 'by failure to adhere at the critical moment to the principle of absolute candour upon which our methods have been based from the outset.'[45]

Shortly after his arrival in Toronto, Curtis met with the Canadian exec-

---

45 Curtis to Kerr, 27 April 1916, ibid. While in Toronto Curtis also learned of some unfortunate aspects of the visit by Brand and Hichens the previous December. Apparently preoccupied with their work for the Munitions Board, the two men had hurt the feelings of the Canadian group during their hurried trip, and in some instances had given considerable offence, particularly to Glazebrook. Glazebrook complained bitterly that Brand had never given him half-an-hour's conversation in private on Round Table matters. 'Aristocrats like Bob,' he fumed, 'with their total want of sympathy are almost fatal to the unity of the Empire.' Unfortunately Brand had also been 'absolutely uncompromising' with Walker, and had left the impression that 'Canada must either receive Imperial tax-collectors or else get out of the Empire.' Imagine, said Curtis, 'the effect on men who had been allowed by Glazebrook to drift into thinking that they were honourably committed to defending any opinions we published.'

utive to discuss *The Problem of the Commonwealth*.[46] The discussion was intense and protracted but ended in the conclusion that Curtis should publish over his own name the modified version of the short volume. During May and much of June Curtis took the opportunity to learn more of the Round Table organisation in Ontario. He also helped the Toronto group to prepare plans for a Canadian convention and to draft a memorandum calling for an imperial convention. Obviously the Canadian organisation was about to undertake the more public airing of imperial problems that Curtis had urged. While he was in Toronto the Canadians made changes at the executive level necessitated by the untimely death of Edward Kylie earlier in the year. A committee was formed under the chairmanship of Sir Edmund Walker to handle all the Canadian Round Table affairs.[47]

On 21 June Curtis and Wrong embarked on a journey to the west coast to enable Curtis to speak at Canadian Club meetings in the chief centres of the West and to meet members of the various western Canadian Round Table groups. Wrong, who had made a similar journey with Kylie in 1912, went along as general handyman and diarist. After meetings and speeches in Winnipeg, Regina, Saskatoon, Edmonton, Calgary, and Vancouver, Wrong and Curtis parted on 5 July, the latter to go on to New Zealand, and the former to return to Toronto by way of California.[48] Before they separated the two men drafted a report on the Round Table organisation in Canada.[49] In their opinion 'the movement ought to be centralised, and also decentralised.' There should be a central office requiring the whole time of at least one clerk in which all the necessary information would be collected. Also the dominion should be mapped out in provinces or groups of provinces and one man made responsible for each area. They suggested that the organisation in the prairie provinces should be centred in Edmonton while Vancouver could remain the headquarters for British Columbia.

In order to correlate the activities of the western and eastern groups Curtis and Wrong recommended the holding of a convention to discuss both the imperial problem and the means by which the groups were to be organised

---

46  Walker Journal, 29 April 1916, Walker Papers. Present during the session at Walker's home were Willison, Wrong, Massey, Osborne, Leonard, Beer, Jones, Glazebrook, and Walker.

47  For Curtis's meetings with the Canadians to discuss the memorandum see Walker Journal, 15 and 27 May 1916, Walker Papers.

48  'Notes of a Journey to the Pacific Coast in company with Lionel Curtis June-July 1916 by George M. Wrong,' Wrong Papers. See also Walker to Glazebrook, 2 Aug. 1916, copy, Walker Papers.

49  'Report of Professor Wrong and Mr Curtis on Their Western Journey July 1916,' Walker Papers

throughout Canada. Such a convention was 'badly needed in order to give unanimity and cohesion in the movement and to get the different elements in various parts of Canada in close touch with one another.' They argued that Prince Edward Island should not be left out, nor should the groups in Newfoundland founded by Vincent Massey. Curtis and Wrong emphasized that at the convention a clear-cut scheme of organisation should be worked out and adopted. They specifically recommended that all future groups should be organised for the purpose of studying *The Problem of the Commonwealth* and *The Commonwealth of Nations.* In that way a large number of people throughout Canada would become familiar with the issues at stake in readiness for the time when Canada had to decide whether to demand or take part in an imperial convention. Wrong and Curtis believed that a vast amount of political confusion could be avoided by this system of organised self-education carried on during the war; especially since 'the rapidly increasing number of men who are determined on full self-government within the British Commonwealth will come to know of each other's existence and be able to form an organisation to fight for what they want at the shortest possible notice.' They urged that the Toronto group waste no time expanding the Canadian organisation.[50]

Curtis had been in Canada three months on this occasion – his fourth trip to the dominion since 1909, Glazebrook, on the eve of Curtis's departure, thought the trip had been a success;[51] and certainly if one looks at the decisions reached concerning *The Problem*, the memorandum, and the Round Table organisation in the few weeks that Curtis had been in the northern dominion one cannot but appreciate the dynamic effect of the man.[52]

Curtis arrived in New Zealand late in July and stayed four weeks. He left at the end of August for Australia, where he spent eleven weeks before going on to India in early October. His primary tasks in the two southern dominions were to meet the members of the Round Table groups, to give public lectures on the history and purposes of the movement, to advocate a more wide-

50 In a separate letter to Glazebrook Curtis underlined the need for a wide-flung network of groups in Canada so that every constituency would be permeated with Round Table men; for him this was 'the task of the next twelve months' and in spite of the number that had gone to war he believed with typical Curtis fervour that Canada was 'full of men eager to be used.' Curtis to Glazebrook, 5 July 1916, copy, Walker Papers
51 Among other things it resulted in the offer of $1000 a year to the Round Table by Colonel Leonard which was eagerly accepted. Kerr to Colonel Leonard, 24 Aug. 1916; and Leonard to Kerr, [nd], copy, Curtis Papers
52 Glazebrook to Milner, 5 and 16 June and 11 July 1916, copies, Glazebrook Papers

spread inquiry into the imperial problem, and to arrange for the distribution of *The Problem of the Commonwealth* and *The Commonwealth of Nations*.[53] Since the decision to publish *The Problem* had already been taken, Curtis did not discuss the merits of the case with the New Zealanders and the Australians, but simply requested that the book become the focus of a wide-ranging analysis of the imperial question. Nothing is more revealing of the relative positions of the dominion groups within the Round Table movement than the manner in which the decision to publish *The Problem* was reached. The whole matter was thoroughly thrashed out with the Canadians before the final decision was made, but there is no evidence to suggest that either the New Zealand or the Australian groups were consulted in the same way. This was partly due to the ease and rapidity with which ideas, arguments, and men could cross the Atlantic, but essentially the importance of Canada to the success of the movement's plans accounted for the disparity.

In New Zealand Curtis discovered that *The Problem* was being widely read and, in general, favourably received. One group member, W.B. Matheson, believed it was 'a great piece of work, far above ordinary politics. Real statecraft only made poss by the unselfish and loyal work of the RT since it existed. It is a clarion call for honest and able leadership.'[54] The appearance of the book had led to the suggestion that an open letter calling for an imperial convention and signed by prominent New Zealanders should be forwarded to the Asquith government. Curtis supported the idea, but after a general meeting of the New Zealand Round Table groups in Wellington on 12 August it was abandoned owing to lack of interest. Matheson, a prime mover behind the scheme, was bitterly disappointed with his colleagues: 'The matter was too evidently a secondary business with most of them. Their own affairs coming first.'[55] But the meeting was not a complete waste, certainly not for Curtis, and the following resolutions were passed:

1   ... we welcome the publication of Mr. L. Curtis's book 'The Problem of the Commonwealth,' and recommend its general perusal as a guide to the solution of the important questions urgently pressing within the Empire: and without identifying ourselves with every conclusion arrived at by the writer, we agree that some form of closer union is essential.

53   The latter book, really *The Project of a Commonwealth*, had been published in July. It had been retitled to avoid confusion with *The Problem of the Commonwealth*.
54   W.B. Matheson diary, 15 June 1916, Turnbull Library, Wellington
55   W. B. Matheson diary, 12 Aug. 1916; also entries for 27 and 31 July and 11 Aug. 1916

2   ... we agree that the people of the Dominions should have a voice in questions involving foreign relations and the defence of the Empire, and should accept their share of responsibility.
3   ... for the furtherance of these objects, we consider that a representative Imperial Convention should be held.[56]

A most important facet of Curtis's trip were the public speeches he made in all the major centres in New Zealand and Australia. Since the London group had now decided that the movement's work should be more widely publicised and efforts made to broaden its impact, Curtis took great pains over the speeches and made sure that all members of the press were given advance copies, so that there could be no danger of misconstruction or misinterpretation. There were two speeches. One, on the history of the movement and the need for common action in foreign affairs and defence through the medium of an imperial parliament, was delivered to large groups of carefully selected men and women, usually Round Table members and their friends and acquaintances. The other was based more on the ideas in *The Commonwealth of Nations* than on *The Problem of the Commonwealth*, and was delivered to mass public audiences ranging in numbers from 200 to 600. In this speech, Curtis emphasized the disparity between the British and German systems of government, argued that freedom meant self-government and mutual responsibility, and claimed that the United Kingdom and the dominions had a mission to perform in the world if they would first unite in accordance with 'the principle of the commonwealth.' Curtis, who one editor described as 'a well-set up youthful looking Englishman, whose speech reveals the characteristic marks of English culture,'[57] was generally well received by the press, and congratulated for presenting a stimulating and incisive discussion of the imperial relationship. Not all agreed with his conclusions, but the 'ability and earnestness of the missionary' were recognised and appreciated.[58] Only one New Zealand newspaper made any effort to come to grips with Curtis's statements, and this was *The Auckland Star* in its issues of 17 and 19 August. The editor, T.W. Leys,[59] recognised that New

56  *New Zealand Times*, 14 Aug. 1916. Curtis was, of course, present at this meeting. Sir George Clifford was in the chair. Matheson diary, 12 Aug. 1916
57  *New Zealand Times*, 1 Aug. 1916
58  For editorial comment on Curtis's New Zealand speeches see *The Dominion*, 12 Aug. 1916; *The Lyttelton Times*, 2 and 5 Aug. 1916; *Otago Daily Times*, 4 Aug. 1916; *The Press* (Christchurch), 2 and 5 Aug. 1916; *New Zealand Times*, 9 Aug. 1916; *The Wanganui Herald*, 15 Aug. 1916.
59  Thomas Wilson Leys (1850-1924); sub-editor *Auckland Star* 1972-6; editor *Auckland Star* 1876-1921

Zealanders owed a debt of gratitude to Curtis for clarifying many issues, but he was not prepared to endorse either Curtis's conclusions or his assumptions. He did not believe that the rigid alternative of organic union or independence really existed, and he thought Curtis had 'seriously understimated the strength of the public or national prejudice against centralised imperial control, especially in fiscal matters.' Curtis was committing the common fallacy of treating a scientific principle as a positive law; '... because he believes that he has found indications of certain tendencies in the growth of nations and empires in the past, he insists that our own Empire and its constituent parts must and shall follow these tendencies to their necessary logical conclusion.' But it was no good arguing from a general principle of self-government; one had to look at material realities. The editor believed Curtis was too dogmatic. To harp continually on his two alternatives was misleading and dangerous. This was a shrewd appraisal of Curtis and his ideas, certainly the best levelled at the prophet in New Zealand and one of the most searching ever levelled in print at the movement. Unfortunately it seems to have had little effect, for Curtis continued to deliver exactly the same speeches in Australia without attempting to meet the criticisms of *The Auckland Star*.

Curtis landed in Australia on 26 August, and during the next eleven weeks spoke in Sydney, Melbourne, Adelaide, and Brisbane. Once again he distributed advance copies of his speeches and gave a number of interviews, and the Australian press faithfully recorded his words. The editorials that appeared were generally uncritical, and no paper approached the level of the Auckland commentary.[60] In addition to making speeches Curtis visited all the major groups in Australia and was present shortly after his arrival at a general meeting in Melbourne of representatives of the Sydney, Melbourne, Adelaide, and Perth groups.[61] The meeting passed a number of resolutions concerning Round Table work in Australia. They registered their approval of Curtis's decision to publish *The Problem*, and while not endorsing all its

60 For Australian coverage of Curtis's speeches see *Sydney Morning Herald*, 9, 13 and 16 Sept. 1916; *The Daily Telegraph* (Sydney), 9 and 15 Sept. 1916; *The Brisbane Courier*, 20 Sept. 1916; *The Telegraph* (Brisbane), 21 Sept. 1916; *The Argus* (Melbourne), 26 Sept. 1916; *The Advertiser* (Adelaide), 3 October 1916; *The Register* (Adelaide), 3 Oct. 1916.

61 See Curtis, *Notes on the Progress of the Movement in Australia*, copy, Harrison Moore Papers. Also Minutes of Joint Meeting of Groups, 30 Aug. 1916, ibid. Presdent were G.H. Knibbs (chair); Curtis, Denison Miller, Professor J.T. Wilson and Meredith Atkinson (representing the Sydney group); R.S. Hawkes and Mr Young (Adelaide); A. McDonald (Perth); General Foster, R.H. Garran, A.T. Strong, E. Northcote, J.G. Latham, J. Sanderson, O.M. Williams, Professors Harrison Moore, Osborne, Picken, and Laby, C.H. Wickens, and G. Lightfoot (Melbourne).

conclusions agreed to foster the study of the book as a working basis for a scheme of organic union. They also decided to bring out an Australasian edition of the book in order to avoid waiting months for shipments from London. A publication committee was subsequently established under the chairmanship of the commonwealth statistician G.H. Knibbs. The committee, with help from Curtis, succeeded in getting the special foreword signed by one New Zealander, the Hon. Mr Justice Hosking,[62] and a number of prominent Australians, including Sir Edmund Barton,[63] a former prime minister.[64]

The meeting also agreed to extend the number of groups and to encourage co-operation between groups, in order that public opinion could be adequately developed. It was decided to establish a fund to finance the general activities of the movement as well as any campaign that might be considered necessary, such as a series of lectures by university members of the Round Table groups on the history of self-government in the British commonwealth. In conjunction with this it was agreed to establish a central office in Melbourne with a paid secretary in order to organise the movement and stimulate effort. It was left to the Melbourne group to investigate the question of a fund and the duties and employment of a secretary. The representatives also agreed to discourage strongly any tendency to give the movement in Australia, or any section of it, a colouring of party politics, and so far as was practicable the groups were to be chosen so that all parties and classes were represented in the study of the problem. At this meeting T.H. Laby, who had recently returned to Australia from New Zealand, was appointed acting dominion secretary for Australia in the absence of Eggleston

62 John Henry Hosking (1854-1928); solicitor and barrister; KB 1925; in practice in Dunedin 1875-1914; took silk 1907; appointed judge of the Supreme Court 1914
63 Sir Edmund Barton (1849-1920); Australian statesman; member of the New South Wales legislature 1879-87, 1891-4, 1898-1900; speaker of the assembly 1883-7; member of the Legislative Council 1887-91 and 1897-8; leader in Australian federation movement; first prime minister of Australia 1901-3; appointed a judge, Australian High Court, 1903
64 See Curtis to Kerr, 4 Sept. 1916, and Curtis to Barton, 11 Sept. 1916, copies, Curtis Papers. The Australian foreword read: 'In heartily recommending this book to the attention of Australasian readers, we do so without necessarily identifying ourselves either with its conclusions or with the arguments by which they have been reached. The issues raised, however, are of such vital importance to the future of the self-governing Dominions that they should be thoroughly understood and carefully considered ... while the war is in progress, the subject [should] be studied as widely as possible and without reference to existing party divisions.' In addition to Barton and Hosking it was signed by Knibbs, J.T. Wilson, W.M. MacCallum, J.C. Watson, W. Harrison Moore, and H.Y. Braddon.

who was at the front, and C.H. Wichens [65] was appointed dominion treasurer.[66]

Before closing, the meeting rejected a resolution by Laby 'That in the opinion of the Conference it is desirable that some form of organic union should be adopted so that the Dominions may appropriately share with the United Kindgom the moral and financial responsibilities for peace and war,' but did adopt one recommending that an imperial convention between the United Kingdom and the dominions be held at the end of the war to consider the question of inter-imperial relations. In a meeting of the Melbourne group in early September it was decided to add a further resolution to the effect that in future 'Groups be organised with the ultimate object of advocating a form of organic union for the Empire.' It was also agreed that the new groups should be known as 'Centres' and should be formed by university extension lecturers, each centre to decide whether it would be comprised of men or women, or both; whatever the composition, no centre was to exceed fifteen in number. Their object would be to study closely *The Problem of the Commonwealth*, and each was to finance itself or appoint a secretary to maintain contact with the secretary of the state group. When each new centre was formed the history and objects of the movement were to be explained.[67]

The decisions reached at these two meetings bear the clear imprint of Curtis and his experiences in Canada. The hope was that both Canada and Australia, and presumably New Zealand, would have a wideflung network of groups whose purpose would be to study *The Problem* in the hope of acquiring a better understanding of the imperial question and of formulating some conclusions. The Australian developments were an integral part of Curtis's plan to educate the public more widely by the spread of groups and by the greater outside activity of those groups.

After his trip through Canada, New Zealand, and parts of Australia, and despite some of the criticism directed at him, Curtis was more than ever convinced by September 1916 that the Round Table case was unanswerable. Nevertheless, he still had doubts about the future:

Hitherto the Round Table has done its work at what you might call fire-side meetings

---

65 Charles Henry Wichens (1872-1939); entered government service in Western Australia in 1897; joined the staff of the Commonwealth Bureau of Census and Statistics 1906; supervisor of census 1911, 1915, and 1921; commonwealth statistician 1922-32
66 Curtis to Kerr, 4 Sept. 1916, Curtis Papers
67 Minutes of meeting, 11 Sept. 1916, Harrison Moore Papers

– and our danger is that we should fail to emerge from that stage, and fail to convert the fire-side movement into a great national organisation. It is merely a question now of getting people to read *The Problem of the Commonwealth*, and if possible *The Commonwealth of Nations*, and then to get as many of the readers as possible to meet together in groups and thrash it out with one another till they really get a grip of the issues at stake. A great move was beginning when I left Canada ... But it is vital that it should be done now ... people will find themselves voting on this question at the first election after peace is declared, and it is high time that they should begin asking themselves how they are going to vote. Canada ... is the determining factor ... of the future, and the whole British Commonwealth rests in their hands to make or mar.[68]

By the time Curtis left Australia for India in early October the Round Table organisations in the dominions were entering a new, more public, phase brought about by the publication of *The Problem of the Commonwealth* and *The Commonwealth of Nations*. But one important aspect of the movement's work still remained to be studied – the position of India and the dependencies in the imperial framework. This problem had never been far from Curtis's mind during the previous six months, and one of his unofficial duties while in the dominions had been to sound opinion on the delicate subject of Asian immigration for the new viceroy of India, Lord Chelmsford. He had had discussions with Borden and with various Canadian officials, and had also talked with 'Billy' Hughes about the matter at the very height of the referendum crisis in Australia.[69] By September 1916 Curtis was increasingly preoccupied with the task awaiting him in the sub-continent. He outlined his thoughts to Henri Bourassa, the French-Canadian leader:

To me the course of human history is one long process from bondage to freedom and whenever I try to analyse what freedom is I am brought up against the principle of responsibility. Freedom surely is the antithesis of anarchy. It must mean that men are subject to the rule of law, but it must also mean that the men who obey that common law are responsible for its making and its administration ... if free nations are to survive they can only do so by realising something more than a National State, that is to say a human state ... I look forward with a sure and certain hope to a time in centuries

68  Curtis to Major Mason, 16 Sept. 1916, Curtis Papers
69  See Curtis to Lord Chelmsford, 2 Nov. 1916, confidential, Dept. of Commerce and Industry and Emigration, Dec. 1916, National Archives of India. Also W.M. Hughes to Curtis, 25 Nov. 1916, copy, in Malcolm Lindsay Shephard, 'Memoirs,' Commonwealth Archives, Canberra. I owe the latter reference to L.F. Fitzhardinge of the Australian National University. See also Yarwood, 'The Overseas Indians.'

to come when the whole world will be included in one such Commonwealth. Such a consummation can only be attained by a series of steps ... the first and greatest step is that which lies before us now: to pass from the stage of the merely National Commonwealth to one which includes a quarter of mankind – and that can be done by converting the British Empire into a true international Commonwealth ... I am on my way to India to study that part of the problem ... the future problem for the European races is to extend that freedom to the majority of mankind who do not at present enjoy it. That, behind and back of everything else, is why the free nations of this Commonwealth must all unite in trusteeship for the future of India. To make India free we have got, by a slow and gradual process, to renovate the soul of the Indian people, to enable them to rise to a true nationality of their own.[70]

Curtis landed at Bombay on 24 October.

70  Curtis to Bourassa, 2 Sept. 1916, copy, Curtis Papers

# 9
# Study or propaganda?

Curtis's visit to the dominions and the publication of *The Problem of the Commonwealth* resulted in a number of changes in the Round Table movement. The dominion branches, particularly those in Canada and Australia, embarked on a drastic reorganisation in an effort to make a wider and more public appeal. For some months before Curtis's visit the Canadians had been giving some attention to the organisational difficulties created by the war, but only in late 1916 and early 1917 did they really come to grips with them. The appearance of *The Problem* added to their determination to redirect the movement's activities. As many had feared, the book aroused a considerable uproar in Great Britain and Canada. Although other books on the same theme, such as Basil Worsfold's *Empire on the Anvil* and Percy Hurd's *A New Empire Partnership*, appeared at much the same time, it was Curtis's book that was singled out for criticism, perhaps because it was the most logical, pungent, and uncompromising. Despite all efforts to dissociate the book from the movement, most commentators viewed it as a statement of Round Table ideas and policy. The introduction of the Curtis book into the debate over the anglo-dominion relationship dramatically altered the original position of the movement, and forced some hard thinking within its ranks about the methods and aims of the whole organisation. The members in England, Canada, and Australia, and to a lesser degree those in New Zealand and South Africa, were compelled to decide whether the movement's role as a study organisation could be continued or whether it should openly advocate a specific solution. By early 1917 these matters were being widely debated. The meetings and decisions of the Imperial War Cabinet and Imperial War Conference in London during March, April, and May 1917 only deepened the movement's introspection.

While Curtis was preparing to leave Canada in early July 1916, Arthur Glazebrook was already arguing that the publication of *The Problem of the Commonwealth* 'closes the period of study and opens a period in which private work must more or less give place to an educational movement to be extended to the public in general.'[1] The difficulty was that the war had changed the Round Table situation in Canada. When the war began there had been about thirty-five groups in the dominion composed of some three hundred men, but these had been reduced almost to skeletons by the call of war.[2] Although a number of new men had joined, the groups had only remained alive by going over old ground. Naturally the older members had become impatient and had begun to discuss a more public appeal. But this also involved problems. The early groups had been composed of a rather select body of men to whom a more or less high level of study was agreeable. To broaden the appeal would mean dealing with 'a progressively less educated set of people.' It would demand the development of new seminar techniques and the recruitment of men skilled in stimulating discussion and organising groups. It would require 'simplicity and a sympathetic understanding of the man in the street.' Glazebrook and the Toronto group believed G.A. Warburton of the Canadian YMCA who had a reputation for exceptional organising ability was the man they wanted for the new and demanding role. Glazebrook wrote at length to Warburton about the movement and its aims, and received a favourable response. When it was thought Warburton would pass through England in late 1916 on his way to India for a short visit, Glazebrook supplied him with a number of letters of introduction to members of the central moot. However, there was apparently a change in Warburton's plans, for he proceeded directly to India. On his return to Canada he remained attached to the YMCA, although he did engage in some Round Table activities.[3]

In late August, while the Canadians were considering the recommendations of Wrong and Curtis and still hoping to acquire Warburton on a full-time basis, Arthur Glazebrook received a letter from the London group which frankly admitted that 'whether we like it or not the Round Table situation is being changed as a result of the publication of *The Problem of the*

---

1 Glazebrook to Warburton, 3 July 1916, Flavelle Papers
2 See Glazebrook to Milner, 8 March 1917, box 144, Milner Papers.
3 Glazebrook to Kerr, 4 July 1916; Glazebrook to Milner, 4 July 1916; and Glazebrook to Peacock, 4 July 1916, copies, Walker Papers

*Commonwealth* and *The Commonwealth of Nations.*[4] While the movement's immediate purpose remained the same, 'to complete an enquiry into the Imperial problem and to conduct a review whose main purpose is to afford information and exchange news,' it was becoming increasingly difficult to avoid coming to grips with the idea of imperial federation. It was impossible to keep away from the crux of the imperial problem now that the two books had been published. It was therefore essential that the movement 'should have a clear understanding as to what the policy of the Round Table as an inter-imperial as opposed to a local organisation should be.'

With this in mind the Canadians began to grapple with the problem of reorganisation. Some groups had already been formed, three alone in Vancouver, and a few had devised elaborate schemes of work.[5] But much was lacking, particularly in the Maritimes and in the West where the Dafoe influence was strong. A hard winter's work lay ahead for the Toronto group. An agreement had to be reached about the imperial convention memorandum which had been in preparation since the spring, and a decision made about the extent and limit of Round Table activity in Canada. Should the Canadians engage in propaganda, such as the promotion of Curtis's book? Or should they simply remain an organisation devoted to bringing before the public the importance and the nature of the problem to be solved?[6]

By late October the Canadians had taken a number of significant steps. It had been decided to employ a secretary and to establish a Round Table office, located for the time being in Victoria College, University of Toronto. The secretary chosen was Walter Bowles, a don of residence at Victoria and a divinity student with the charge of a small church in Toronto. Vincent Massey had high hopes that Bowles, a man dedicated to the ideals of the Round Table and possessed of considerable enthusiasm and organising ability, would place the affairs of the Canadian branch on a more systematic and permanent basis. A stenographer was also hired, and these various changes increased the expenses of the Canadian organisation some $3500 per year. Massey thought this an unimportant problem when compared with the increased efficiency. In the past neither he nor Glazebrook had been able to give the Round Table the continued and concentrated effort which it needed.[7] As for the memorandum, definite progress was also made. Frank

---

4 See, first, Kerr to Glazebrook, 24 Aug. 1916, enclosed in Glazebrook to Walker, 13 Sept. 1916; and, second, Kerr to Glazebrook, 25 Aug. 1916, enclosed in ibid., Walker Papers.
5 See G.F. Scott to Glazebrook, 24 Sept. 1916, copy, ibid.
6 See a circular letter Glazebrook to the groups, 19 Sept. 1916, Curtis Papers.
7 Massey to Curtis, 30 Oct. 1916, ibid.

Beer took it to the West and succeeded beyond the 'fondest hopes' in getting the signatures of many leading Liberals. He failed, however, on one or two important instances because the memorandum still contained a reference to *The Problem of the Commonwealth*.

It had been obvious for some time that the book was causing considerable concern in Canadian political centres. For many its appearance had simply confirmed long-held suspicions about the movement. John Dafoe wrote in this vein to George Wrong:

I have no doubt that the Canadian Round Table circles are precisely what you describe them to be, an organisation for inquiry; but I have never regarded the members of the movement in London as other than protagonists of a somewhat clearly defined idea. I have considered their assumption of the open mind as, to put it frankly, lacking in candour. They have had from the outset the intention that the inquiry should result in the apparent endorsement of their own scheme for Empire consolidation, which they have held from the beginning. What Mr. Curtis is advocating now as the claimed result of years of inquiry he believed in and advocated some years ago ... I have regarded the Canadian members of the Round Table as persons who were being shepherded along a definite path to a predetermined end, and I have thought that many of them were thus being shepherded so skilfully that they realised neither the road that [they] were travelling, nor the goal to which they were tending ...[8]

Although many in the Canadian organisation would not have agreed with Dafoe, they could not afford to ignore his remarks, and all references to *The Problem* were removed from the memorandum in order that a larger number of signatures could be obtained.[9] But this alone did not settle whether the movement should remain a study group or become purely propagandist. While the Canadians did not want to be committed to Curtis's book, or to any other particular solution, they did wish to adopt a more public stance so that they could reach a wider audience with their imperial message. If anyone wanted to advocate a specific solution then new machinery, divorced from the movement, would have to be set up.[10]

These Canadian suggestions were discussed in London at a special meeting in November 1916 attended by Kerr, Hichens, Brand, Flavelle, and Peacock. The outcome was a lengthy letter to Glazebrook suggesting that a

8 Dafoe to Wrong, 16 Oct. 1916, Wrong Papers. See also Lash to Borden, 1 Nov. 1916, oc series, file 308, Borden Papers.
9 Massey to Curtis, 30 Oct. 1916, Curtis Papers
10 See Massey to Kerr, 4 Nov. 1916, copy, ibid.

Round Table convention representative of all the dominions be held in London soon after Curtis returned from India.[11] The letter, drafted by Kerr, was the first really solid statement by the London group of developments within the movement since the war, and the first real recognition of the difficulties confronting the Round Table as a result of the publication of *The Problem of the Commonwealth* . Apparently the London group agreed with the Canadians and with Dafoe that the movement was liable to come under suspicion on the ground that it lacked candour. The position had now been reached where some members of the Round Table movement held clear-cut and definite conclusions about the proper solution of the imperial problem while a great many others were still in the preliminary stage of investigation and doubt. Since *The Round Table* was being edited by those who had clear views, the quarterly often contained definite conclusions in principle; conclusions for which neither the quarterly nor the movement openly stood as yet. The London members agreed that this state of affairs could not continue because 'it laid the whole Movement open to the charge of bad faith.' It would be necessary to make a clear line of demarcation between those who had made up their minds one way or the other about the broad principles on which the imperial problem had to be solved, and those who had not done so and who were anxious to keep an open mind while continuing their studies and investigation. The latter set of people would go on with groups, but the first set of people would form themselves into an association which stood for certain definite and clear-cut principles about the imperial problem.

On considering the content of such a platform, the London group had agreed with Curtis's main conclusions: first, that the 'empire (commonwealth)' should remain united; second, that the dominions should share in the control of defence and foreign policy; and third, that the best way to achieve this would be to create a federal parliament directly responsible to the people of the 'empire (commonwealth)' with authority to raise money directly for its purposes. It seemed to the London group that these were the essential principles upon which the majority of those who had taken part in the Round Table movement could agree. They had then decided that this majority and *The Round Table* quarterly should as soon as possible make it clear that 'they intended to stand for their principles, until the goal was either lost or won.' Such a stand would not commit them to immediate imperial federation, nor would it prevent them from approving and working for any intermediate steps that might be contrived. But it would commit them to keeping their view steadily in front of the public by means of speeches and

11 Kerr to Curtis, 22 Nov. 1916; and Kerr to Glazebrook, 22 Nov. 1916, copy, Curtis Papers

writings and to working against any step which might tend to lead away rather than toward their ultimate goal. They made it quite clear to the Canadians that Curtis's book, *The Problem of the Commonwealth*, 'could not be the common ground partly because it went into too great detail, and partly because there is a good deal of disagreement about some of its propositions even among those who accept its main conclusions.'

These decisions raised the question of what was to happen to the existing Round Table groups. The natural thing to do, said Kerr, would be to create a new body under the name of 'the Commonwealth Society.' Admission to the society would depend upon the acceptance of the broad principles outlined above. This step would not be in the least inconsistant with the continuance of the movement known as 'the Round Table movement'; for that study movement could continue, 'passing through itself, so to speak, a steady flow of students who would at the end of their studies and deliberations, either join "the Commonwealth Society" or some other league which advocated some alternative solution.' The only difficulty was *The Round Table* quarterly which would clearly stand for the principles of the new society. Its name could not be changed without destroying a large part of its circulation. Yet it did not seem logical that *The Round Table* magazine should defend the views of 'the Commonwealth Society' while the Round Table groups remained purely student groups. The alternative seemed to be to dissolve the old Round Table groups and restart them on the new principles, or to discard the Round Table name altogether except for the magazine. The London group had been unable to reach a decision on this thorny problem. However, they had agreed that 'it was impossible for the Round Table movement to remain, merely a student movement, that those of us in all parts of the Empire, who have made up our minds on fundamentals, must come out and say so publicly (without in any way stopping the study process going on at the same time), and that we ought to meet and take counsel together as to what these fundamentals were and how we should declare the faith which was in us, without any unnecessary delay.'[12] Kerr asked Glazebrook and the central Canadian group to give careful consideration to his letter during the winter, and to prepare for a convention in 1917.

This was the first firm indication that the London group realised what serious organisational and ideological problems it faced as a result of the war and the publication of *The Problem of the Commonwealth*. Nevertheless, the letter revealed how very little the London members seemed to have learned about the developments in the dominions during the war. To state so

12 Ibid.

explicit a faith in imperial federation was perhaps bad enough; but to simply abandon the details and not the general principles of Curtis, and then to suggest that by doing so one had cleansed oneself of the Curtis stigma, was extremely narrow-sighted. However, the decision to rethink the aims and organisation of the movement was a necessary one given the anomaly of the Round Table's position by late 1916.

During the winter the Canadians continued to prepare their memorandum, finally publishing it and calling for additional signatures on 10 February 1917. It read as follows:[13]

Of late years many Canadians have turned their attention with increasing interest to the question of their relation to the British Commonwealth. Since the war the feeling has grown that the present status of this country will be reconsidered after peace has been declared. Canada and the other Dominions have pledged their resources for the preservation of the Empire, and to establish a lasting and honourable peace. These facts point to the conclusion that in future the Dominions should share in determining the policy by which that peace may be kept. We unite, therefore, in urging a full discussion of the subject without delay, and we venture to suggest herein certain broad premises on which we have no difficulty in agreeing:

I Canada has shown her determination to preserve and strengthen the ties which now bind her to Great Britain and other portions of the British Commonwealth.

II Effective organisation of the Empire must not involve any sacrifice of responsible government in domestic affairs or the surrender of control over fiscal policy by any portion of the Empire.

III But it is an inevitable development of responsible government in the Dominions that they would assume their proportionate share in the defence of the Empire, and should have a voice in determining its relations with other States.

IV We think, therefore, that as soon as circumstances permit, political leaders throughout the Empire, irrespective of party, should meet to consider the problem.

The memorandum was widely distributed, and in March an overseas edition was circulated among the Canadian armed forces in Europe.[14] By late May over one thousand signatures had been obtained from both Liberals and Conservatives, although it had been met with suspicion in Quebec. 'Our

13 See 'Memorandum issued by the Round Table in Canada for Publication in the Canadian Press,' 10 Feb. 1917, vol. 794, Laurier Papers. There are also copies in the Milner, Steel-Maitland, and Walker Papers.

14 See 'Overseas Edition of the Memorandum Issued by the Round Table in Canada March 1917,' box 170, Milner Papers. The decision to prepare this version was made by the Canadian executive on 28 Feb. 1917.

harmless Memorandum,' noted Walker, 'is referred to in the French press of Quebec as a "dangerous imperial manifesto."'[15] Despite their failure to gain the support of French Canada the Canadian executive were pleased with the general response to the memorandum, and quickly issued a number of pamphlets explaining various aspects of Round Table work. The most important, *The Round Table in Canada: How the Movement Began: What it Hopes to Accomplish*, contained lengthy extracts from a speech by Kerr to the Toronto groups in 1912.[16] The executive also decided to have a public meeting, and this was duly held in Convocation Hall at the University of Toronto on 27 April 1917. Walker presided, and among the speakers were Joseph Flavelle and Newton Rowell,[17] the leader of the Ontario Liberals. Walker was well satisfied with the gathering, but *The Globe* was critical in its comments, and the Canadians resigned themselves to the fact that the Toronto newspaper would oppose every effort to publicise their aims and ideals.[18]

While the Canadians were thus making rapid strides in the early months of 1917 to adapt the Round Table organisation in Canada to a more public and educational role, the Australians, particularly in Melbourne, were beginning to establish contacts throughout Victoria and to plan for additional 'centres' of study and discussion.[19] The Victorians prepared a circular letter, and took great pains to define as accurately as possible the history, interests, and aims of the movement, emphasizing the need for examination by Australians of the critical problem of imperial relations. Both the Canadian and Australian organisations began to think seriously about forming a new society for the purpose of definite propaganda. Some members in both countries, however, were a little taken aback at the drastic changes envisaged, and

15 Walker to H. Bell Irving, 26 April 1917, copy, Walker Papers. Copies were also sent to Laurier and to Borden, who was in London attending the Imperial War Conference. Laurier's response was most unfavourable. He interpreted the memorandum as further proof that 'Canada is now governed by a junta sitting at London, known as "The Round Table," with ramifications in Toronto, in Winnipeg, in Victoria, with Tories and Grits receiving their ideas from London and insidiously forcing them on their respective parties.' Quoted in Skelton, *Life and Letters*, II, 510
16 Glazebrook to Milner, 8 March 1917, box 144, Milner Papers
17 Newton Wesley Rowell (1867-1941); called to the Ontario bar 1891; member of the Ontario Legislature 1911-17; leader of the Liberal party in Ontario 1911-17; MP 1917-21; president of the council in the Union Government 1917-20; appointed chief justice of Ontario in 1936
18 See Walker Journal, 27 April 1917 and Walker to Cronyn, 2 May 1917, copy, Walker Papers; and Warburton to Willison, 30 April 1917, Willison Papers. Also minutes of executive meetings, 28 Feb. 1917, enclosed in Bowles to Walker, 2 March 1917, Walker Papers
19 See undated and unsigned draft letter in Harrison Moore Papers; also an unsigned letter, 26 Feb. [1917], ibid.

were concerned about the future of the movement. Glazebrook, for one, admitted that he was worried 'about what seemed to me the over-emphasis on the point that relations could not stay as they are. I am afraid that we have in effect more or less forced a dilemma ... However, I suppose that risks must be taken, and we cannot do away with what has been done.'[20] These doubts were soon to be brought to a head by the decisions of the Imperial War Conference being held in London.

The meetings of the Imperial War Cabinet and the Imperial War Conference were held on alternate days between 20 March and 2 May 1917. It was a momentous occasion in the history of the empire-commonwealth, and one which had both immediate and long-range consequences for the Round Table movement. The Imperial War Cabinet was a unique constitutional body quite unlike the existing Imperial Conference. It was composed of the British War Cabinet, the dominion prime ministers or their representatives, and delegates from India. It had executive and not merely deliberative powers. It made decisions on the conduct of the war and on the major issues of foreign policy. It has usually been argued that the outbreak of war and the meetings of the British War Cabinet stimulated the movement to great efforts to bring about imperial union. The war had certainly affected the movement and had forced them to think about the ultimate solution of the imperial question much sooner than they had expected, but it had only been an unfortunate perversion of their arguments that had driven the movement to agree to the publication of *The Problem*. They had not envisaged public propagation of their ideas until after the war. Similarly with the meetings and decisions of the Imperial War Cabinet and the Imperial War Conference. Far from emboldening the Round Table members and spurring them to greater efforts to influence men and events in Great Britain and the dominions, the developments in early 1917 forced them to take stock of their situation and to reevaluate their role, something they had long realised would be necessary but which they had never had the time or the heart to do.

It has also been argued, although not so often or by so many, that the movement was influential in having the Imperial War Cabinet summoned, and that it was instrumental in shaping the course of the meetings. It is true that many of the central moot were well placed. Milner had become a member of the War Cabinet formed by Lloyd George in December 1916, and he had supported the idea of an Imperial War Conference with representatives from the dominions and India. But this idea had been in Lloyd George's

20 Glazebrook to Milner, 8 March 1917, box 144, Milner Papers

mind for some time and the decision can not be attributed entirely to the influence of Milner.[21] On Milner's suggestion Leo Amery became an assistant secretary in the War Cabinet Secretariat under the direction of Maurice Hankey. He was to play an important role in preparing the agenda for the meetings, and has claimed a major part in shaping the decision to invite the dominion leaders to attend the Imperial War Cabinet.[22] Two other members of the central group were also intimately involved. Waldorf Astor and Philip Kerr had joined Lloyd George's 'Garden Suburb' in December 1916. Kerr, who had turned over the editorship of *The Round Table* to Reginald Coupland in order to join Lloyd George, was particularly useful while the meetings were on. It would be difficult, however, to justify the suggestion that the movement controlled the Cabinet or the conference, or even vitally affected them. Even if one admits the influence of Milner and Amery in December 1916, it has to be recognised that they were but two voices in a rising chorus all of whom were arguing the right of the dominions to be consulted. The time, the mood, and the man, Lloyd George, happened to be right in late 1916.[23]

The impact of Amery, Kerr, and Astor behind-the-governmental scenes was minimal. They played useful roles in preparing and shaping agenda, but had no personal influence during the meetings.[24] Milner, of course, was in the thick of things, and as chairman of a sub-committee on non-territorial peace terms set up by the Imperial War Cabinet he made a valuable contribution to the smooth functioning of the meetings. Another Round Table man, Sir James Meston, was one of the three Indian assessors who attended Cabinet and conference meetings. Neither Milner nor Meston made an effort to introduce Round Table ideas into the discussions. In fact Milner from the time of his appointment to the War Cabinet in December 1916 had little time to spare for the essentials of the movement. He continued to correspond with the faithful Glazebrook, but more than ever was a valued commentator on Round Table affairs rather than an intimate contributor. Where the movement was important, and where Kerr and Brand in particular were useful, was in arranging informal dinners at which the dominion and Indian leaders met members of the movement as well as other prominent figures in English

21 See Gollin, *Milner*, 395-6
22 Amery, *My Political Life*, II, 91; also Amery to Jebb, 27 Dec. 1916 and 3 Jan. 1917, box 1, Jebb Papers. Also Cook, 'Sir Robert Borden'
23 See on this point Beloff, *The Imperial Sunset*, I, 214-15.
24 See Milner diary, 16 and 17 March 1917, vol. 280, Milner Papers, for Milner's meetings with Walter Long, the colonial secretary, Curzon, Austen Chamberlain, Hankey, Lambert, and Amery about the conference agenda. Also Cook, 'Sir Robert Borden'

political and social life. But it was the central group which learned most from these private tête-à-têtes, not the overseas representatives. The Round Table members were left with valuable insights into dominion and Indian attitudes toward the imperial relationship.

During the sessions of the Imperial War Cabinet and the Imperial War Conference, Milner met regularly with the 'Ginger Group' and with members of the central moot.[25] On 13 April the moot held a dinner for William Massey,[26] the prime minister of New Zealand, and Sir Joseph Ward his coalition partner, and again on 20 April for Meston and his two Indian colleagues, Sir S.P. (Lord) Sinha[27] and the Maharajah of Bikanir.[28] Finally, on 4 May when the meetings were over Smuts was the guest of the evening.[29] Milner found the Cabinet meetings and the private discussions very beneficial; 'without leading to definite results we have all got to understand one another better. Personally I feel that I have learned a good deal from these men, especially perhaps from the Indians.'[30]

Kerr also thought the conference discussions and the private meetings of

25 He talked to Grigg, Kerr, Smuts, and Amery on 24 March and on 4 April dined with Selborne, Oliver, Brand, Kerr, Herbert Fisher, Zimmern, Coupland, and Frederic Eggleston. See Milner diary, 24 March and 4 April 1917, vol. 280, Milner Papers.
26 William Ferguson Massey (1856-1925); New Zealand statesman; member of the House of Representatives 1894-1925; leader of the opposition 1903; prime minister 1912-25; New Zealand representative at the Imperial War Cabinet and the Imperial War Conference 1917-18; at the Paris Peace Conference 1919; the Imperial Conference 1921; and the Imperial and Economic Conferences 1923
27 Sir Satyendra Prassano Sinha (1864-1928); knighted 1914; 1st Baron of Raipur, cr 1919; called to the bar 1896; barrister, Calcutta High Court; advocate-general, Bengal, 1907-9, 1915-17; represented India at the Imperial War Conference 1917 and at the Imperial War Cabinet 1918; under-secretary of state for India 1919-20; governor of Bihar and Orissa 1920-1
28 Maharajah of Bikanir (1880-1943); assumed full ruling powers 1898; represented India at the Imperial War Cabinet and the Imperial War Conference 1917; represented India at the Paris Peace Conference 1919; leader of the Indian delegation to the League of Nations Assembly 1930; represented India at the Imperial Conference of 1930; delegate to the Round Table Conference 1930-1 and 1931
29 Present to meet the New Zealanders were Hichens, Kerr, Malcolm, Robinson, Oliver, and Milner. Present to meet the Indian delegation were Oliver, Brand, Coupland, Kerr, Malcolm, and Milner. Present to meet Smuts were Milner, Selborne, Oliver, Brand, Kerr, Dove, Herbert Baker, Malcolm, Coupland, and Eggleston. See Milner diary, 13 and 20 April and 4 May 1917; also 26 March, 9, 16 and 30 April; and 7, 14, 21, and 29 May 1917, vol. 280, Milner Papers.
30 Milner to Glazebrook, 21 April 1917, box 144, ibid. When it had first been suggested in 1915 that India be represented at any future imperial conference, the London group had quickly supported the idea in a vigorously argued article enittled 'India and the Imperial Conference,' The Round Table, Dec. 1915, 86-119.

the moot, particularly that with the Indians, had been productive. Never again could the Indians themselves be omitted from major imperial gatherings.[31] The dominions had also been involved in the most intimate consultation and had had access to all the most secret documents, and 'have had a real and effective voice in determining general instructions which should be given to the British Government as representing the view of the Empire in regard to peace terms.'[32] The most important development, as far as Kerr was concerned, was the effect the meetings had had upon the general imperial problem. He referred to a speech by Borden made to the Empire Parliamentary Association on 2 April, in which Borden had suggested that in the Imperial War Cabinet might lie the answer to the constitutional problem which had bedevilled imperial statesmen and theorists for years.[33] He believed this was 'the most important speech which has been made by a responsible statesman about Imperial relations since Joe Chamberlain's death.'[34] Kerr had sought Borden out after the meeting and had suggested to him that while the Imperial War Cabinet should continue in its present form the Imperial War Conference 'should blossom into meetings of Parliamentary delegates chosen by some system of proportional representation so as to include representatives for the opposition, at which general Imperial questions and proposals for joint action for legislation prepared by the Imperial Cabinet should be discussed in public.' He had argued that if the Imperial Cabinet principle were to continue it was vital that there should be some body at which there could be free public speech about imperial problems and in which representatives of the different parts of the empire could meet and learn about one another's point of view, without having on their shoulders the responsibility of office. He believed that Borden had generally agreed with these arguments although he had 'emphasised in the strongest possible manner the inadvisability of trying to force any system of Imperial Federation in the period immediately following the War. He said that any such propaganda might, in his opinion, do infinite harm. On the other hand he saw in the new constitutional machinery which has now been put into existence ... the nucleus which might eventually give us the Imperial Institutions we require ...'[35]

The Round Table had, of course, supplied Borden with most of their memoranda, and Lash had also forwarded his ideas and a draft constitution

31 Kerr to Curtis, 23 April 1917, copy, GD40/17/33, Lothian Papers. Also Coupland to Curtis, 22 May 1917, Curtis Papers
32 Kerr to Curtis, 24 April 1917, Curtis Papers
33 See text in Amery, *My Political Life*, II, 107; also Borden, *Memoirs*, II, 691-3.
34 Kerr to Curtis, 24 April 1917, Curtis Papers
35 Ibid.

to the prime minister before he had left for London.[36] Borden had made no attempt to use this material, or to raise Round Table ideas, when imperial constitutional relations were examined at the Imperial War Conference.[37] Despite this setback, the results were still very agreeable to many in the movement. The members of the Imperial War Conference decided that the dominions should not be automatically committed to war when they had no responsibility for imperial foreign policy, and agreed that the readjustment of constitutional relations could best be determined at the end of the war. On 16 April they passed the famous Resolution IX to that effect, placing on record their view that 'any such readjustment while thoroughly preserving all existing powers of self-government and complete control of domestic affairs, should be based upon a full recognition of the Dominions as autonomous nations of an Imperial Commonwealth, and of India as an important portion of the same, should recognise the right of the Dominions and India to an adequate voice in foreign policy and in foreign relations, and should provide effective arrangements for continuous consultation in all important matters of common Imperial concern, and for such necessary concerted action founded on consultation, as the several governments may determine.'[38]

This crucial resolution is a landmark in the constitutional development of the commonwealth. It formally recognised that the dominions and India had achieved a status quite distinct from their pre-1914 condition. The two men

36 Borden had also discussed 'the matter of Imperial reorganisation with special reference to the Curtis scheme' with John Dafoe who had found their views very similar. Dafoe to Sir Clifford Sifton, 12 Feb. 1917, copy, Dafoe Papers
37 However, Borden did broach a federal solution to his British colleagues in private meetings. Walter Long, the colonial secretary, wrote to Borden in mid-April commenting: 'I have been thinking over the scheme you outlined to me and I hope you won't mind if I write you unofficially and as a friend. The misfortune is that nearly all our "would be Alexander Hamiltons" know nothing of our People, nothing of the House of Commons, [and] I really believe do not care much for either. Some questions occur to me. 1. Who is to preside over the Imperial Assembly? 2. How are the members to be selected? 3. What is to follow from their deliberations? 4. If they are to have no power how long would they care to meet and do nothing but talk? I have been in our House for 37 [years], first joined a Gov. 31 years ago and a Cab. 22 years ago; and have been a close student of Parliament and of the People and I feel confident that this scheme would command no support worth having. I believe best plan for the present is. a. To make Impl War Cab. permanent so far as this is possible; i.e. announce that any P.M. or Minister sent over by the P.M. to represent him shall be a member of the Cabinet b. To get each Dom to think out and propose some scheme for representation ... and to meet to discuss the proposals at end of War.' Long to Borden, 15 April 1917, OC series, file 317, Borden Papers
38 Quoted in Dawson, *Development of Dominion Status*, 175

primarily responsible for drafting the resolution were Borden and Smuts.[39] The leading members of the London group soon had an opportunity to discuss the whole subject with Smuts when the South African was their guest at dinner on 4 May.[40] A vivid account of this meeting has survived in a letter from Frederic Eggleston to Thomas Laby, the secretary of the Australian organisation.[41] Eggleston had been in England for some months and had seen a great deal of the London members. They had been kind to him and he liked them immensely. 'Coupland is a somewhat prim individual very academic. But Kerr is a most attractive man. He looks very tired as if he were working hard ... Brand seems to me more of a man of the world than any of them, Curtis included; he is not so much of the apostle type. Has more savoir faire and yet is most charming ... Milner did not impress me ... I think he has lost his punch and at any rate he is a frightful Tory and the only virtue of a Tory is his punch. Oliver you have met. He has a fine sensitive face but takes knowing, is very reserved. Zimmern I liked ... he is most amiable.'[42]

At the dinner on 4 May discussion had soon turned to the results of the Conference, and naturally the Round Table were anxious to hear Smuts's views. The general, according to Eggleston, 'showed no disinclination to talk but how far he disclosed his mind I cannot say. He seemed quite enthusiastic on the scheme. You felt that he had considered the Round Table objections and had persuaded himself that the resolutions were sufficient.' For Eggleston the most remarkable part of the meeting was the attitude adopted by Kerr and Brand who, much to Coupland's astonishment, simply accepted Smuts's point as sufficient for the time being. 'Coupland kept quiet but attacked them afterwards and it was evident that they had made up their mind that the Round Table would welcome the resolutions of the Imperial War

---

39  For a fuller account of this important episode see Borden, *Memoirs*, 667-77. See also Brown and Bothwell, 'The "Canadian Resolution."'
40  See Borden to Willison, [nd] enclosed in Willison to Walker, 18 May 1917, Walker Papers, in which Borden replied to a letter from Willison of 16 May 'inviting me to express sympathy with the proposals embodied in "The Round Table" petition ... Shortly after reaching Great Britain I called into formal conference Mr Massey, General Smuts, and Sir Joseph Ward. After several meetings the form of resolution as finally proposed by me was adopted. I moved it in the Conference and it was carried unanimously. The British Government, to whom I had previously submitted the resolution, heartily concurred in its details. It embodied everything in the petition except the fourth paragraph. In speaking on the resolution to the Conference I expressed my opinion that the representatives from each unit of the Empire should include all recognised political parties. This would have been embodied in the resolution except for an objection, which seemed well founded, from South Africa.'
41  Eggleston to Laby, ? May 1917, Laby Papers
42  Ibid.

Cabinet [sic] and without giving up their views do their best to see them realised. They laughed to think what Curtis "the prophet" as they call him would say.'[43]

Coupland argued that the cardinal point of the Round Table thesis was the inefficiency of consultation and the need to effect organic union. Coupland realised that it would be impossible to bring this about immediately, and he knew it would be better to take what they could; nevertheless, he did not like going back on Round Table teaching. Eggleston was inclined to agree, and thought Kerr and Brand should have taken a more positive stand with Smuts:

... the defects of cooperation should always be borne in mind and be brought out on every appropriate occasion. When Smuts was there it was peculiarly appropriate to give him something to think about, to put into his mind some of the dilemmas which the Round Table have been raising. So that they could be working in his mind and fructifying. It was to my mind a great mistake to let him go away with the idea that what had been done satisfied the Round Table and met their objections. I have no sympathy with Imperialism and I have very little faith in the capacity of British statesmen to manage Imperial problems but from the very first I have realised the absolute soundness of Curtis's proposition that there is no such thing as effective cooperation and where we in Australia are so helpless we have to take the risks of union to get the protection of Great Britain rather than to trust absolutely and for all time to the rotten reed of cooperation.[44]

Kerr and Brand were only being realistic in adopting 'a wait and see' attitude. They were both acutely aware that the anglo-dominion relationship had undergone considerable and unforseen changes during the war. Coupland, too, came to realise this. He was distressed by the general belief that there was no immediate prospect of organic union, but he was forced to admit that 'that belief has emerged very definitely and universally from the meetings of the Imperial War Cabinet.' Probably because he had not visited Canada, he had underestimated dominion nationalism which the war had intensified rather than weakened. 'The future,' he wrote to Curtis, 'seems to depend more than ever on a deeper understanding by British citizens all over the world of what their citizenship means and of the value of the British Commonwealth to humanity.'[45] As Sir Edmund Walker perceptively commented, 'Whether we like it or not, we must work along the lines of least resistance if we are to succeed.'[46]

43 Ibid.                                          44 Ibid.
45 Coupland to Curtis, 22 May 1917, Curtis Papers
46 Walker to H. Bell Irving, 26 April 1917, copy, Walker Papers. Curtis tried to reassure Cou-

During late spring and early summer the London group held a number of meetings to discuss Round Table activities in the light of the developments at the Imperial War Cabinet and the Imperial War Conference. They decided to publish an article by Kerr in the June issue of *The Round Table* entitled 'The New Constitutional Developments in the Empire' which outlined the significance of the recent meetings and decisions and emphasized their value to imperial development.[47] They also reaffirmed their decision to hold a convention of Round Table representatives either in London or Canada to discuss the future of the Movement.[48] In order that such a convention would be as representative as possible they advised each dominion organisation to hold a conference to choose its delegates. The convention would now meet as soon as possible after the war rather than in 1917 as originally suggested, but certainly before the next imperial conference. They wanted the convention to be 'free to dissolve the movement altogether, to continue it as a purely student organisation or to reconstitute it as a society of people holding definite views' about the solution of the imperial problem. A memorandum to this effect was drafted by Kerr and accepted in principle by the moot for despatch to the dominions. Before being circulated it was forwarded to Curtis for criticism. Such a crucial decision could not be made without his involvement.[49]

This memorandum indicated that the Round Table movement was passing through yet another stage of development. The war, the publication of *The Problem of the Commonwealth*, and the decisions of the Imperial War Conference had dictated a drastic reassessment of the *raison d'etre* of the movement – its very existence was now being questioned, or at least discussed. As Kerr pointed out to Curtis, the dominions would appear at a peace conference 'in the spirit which will *more and more* resist the assertion of any superior authority or influence on the part of the British Government. They are tending more and more to conceive of the Empire as five nations deliberating on equal terms round a table at which India will also be repre-

pland; see Curtis to Coupland, 23 May 1917, copy, Curtis Papers. See also on this point Lash to Walker, 25 Aug. 1917, Walker Papers; Milner to Glazebrook, 21 April 1917 (two letters), copies, ibid.; and Milner to J.L. Garvin, 27 May 1917, copy, box 167, Milner Papers.

47 See Coupland to Curtis, 22 May 1917, Curtis Papers; also [Philip Kerr], 'The New Developments in the Constitution of the Empire,' *The Round Table*, June 1917, 441-59. Another article in this issue entitled 'The Education of the Citizen,' 460-90, was written by Sir Henry Jones, a philosophic idealist and a disciple of T.H. Green.

48 Coupland to Curtis, 9 July 1917, Curtis Papers

49 Kerr's draft letter of 29 June 1917 was enclosed in Coupland to Curtis, 9 July 1917, ibid.

sented.'[50] Under these circumstances the movement was obviously compelled to re-examine its aims.

While the draft memorandum was on its way to India the London members continued their discussions, but were unable to reach any further decisions until Curtis had been heard from. In Canada and Australia plans proceeded for reorganisation, circular letters were drafted, and the Canadians pondered what they could do in the fevered political atmosphere of 1917. They finally decided that common sense dictated a minimum of public involvement in the emotional political questions of the day, particularly conscription.[51] In late July the Australians held a major conference with representatives present from New South Wales, Victoria, and South Australia. A number of resolutions were passed reaffirming the Round Table's role and stressing the need for a convention after the war. It was agreed to continue to support the discussion of *The Problem of the Commonwealth*, but not to commit their groups or any member to it. They did agree, however, that seven years of study indicated that the imperial conference system would not be adequate for consultation in the future, and they recommended 'the ultimate adoption of some form of closer union.' In the meantime every effort would be made to counter misunderstandings and misstatements about the empire and the Round Table.[52]

In late July Robert Brand visited Toronto on war business and met briefly with Massey to discuss Round Table affairs. He briefed the Canadians about the recent London discussions and looked over their offices in Toronto.[53] During this visit Massey admitted that the Canadian Round Table was not very aggressive. Apart from the war, which had always hampered its efforts, the conscription crisis made it unwise to attempt any undue publicity. The existing groups were carrying on fairly satisfactorily, new groups were occasionally being formed, and the work of quiet propaganda was being conducted uninterrupted from the central office in Toronto; but

50 Kerr to Curtis, 21 July 1917, copy, GD40/17/33, Lothian Papers
51 See J. Sanderson to Harrison Moore, 12 July 1917, and undated circular letter re Round Table groups and reorganisation, Harrison Moore Papers. Also Bowles to Walker, 16 July 1917 with enclosure, 16 July 1917, Walker Papers
52 Minutes of Conference of Groups held 28 July 1917, Harrison Moore Papers. See also Report of the Activities of the Australian Round Table during 1917, Harrison Moore Papers. H.Y. Braddon presided at the conference held in Melbourne. Others present were T.H. Kelly and Professor Peden of New South Wales; President Jethroe Brown and Professor Mitchell of South Australia; and J.G. Latham, W. Harrison Moore, E. Northcote, and O.M. Williams of Victoria; plus T.H. Laby, acting dominion secretary, and C.H. Wichens, dominion treasurer.
53 Massey to Coupland, 30 July 1917, copy, box 169, Milner Papers

the organisation was lagging in the maritimes and on the prairies, and the services of a travelling secretary with very special personal qualities were still required.[54] Had it not been for the chaos in domestic politics, Massey thought the Canadians would have continued in their search for such a man; but it was out of the question for the moment. As he admitted to Coupland, '... it is becoming more and more apparent to me at least that there is a very large minority in Canada which is distinctly apathetic with regard to the Empire, and is so provincial in its outlook as to become hostile to any definite action, not only to strengthen the bonds of Empire, but even to preserve them ... I wish you were not so far away. To be able to "grouse" even at the telephone to a sympathetic friend is better than complaining at long range. Do write again as soon as you have a chance. You need not wait for anything to say – we just need comforting in Canada at present.'[55]

By early October Curtis's reply to Kerr's letter had been received in London. Although he disliked drawing up 'articles of faith' to which members of the Round Table would be asked to subscribe, Curtis had no major objections; and on 18 October Coupland forwarded to all the dominion secretaries Kerr's memorandum calling for a major Round Table convention as soon as possible after the war.[56] When Curtis returned to England six months later no further decisions had been reached about the future of the movement.

54 After a brief inspection trip to the West, Frank Beer advised Walker that 'There is no doubt whatever that the Round Table has received "a blackeye" in Winnipeg and it is useless to press *just now* for the creation of study groups in this district.' G.F. Beer to Walker, 2 June 1917, Walker Papers
55 Massey to Coupland, 30 July 1917, copy, box 169, Milner Papers
56 Curtis to Kerr, 28 Aug. 1917, GD40/17/33, Lothian Papers; and Coupland to secretary of the Round Table group, 18 Oct. 1917, Harrison Moore Papers; also enclosed in Massey to Walker, 15 Nov. 1917, Walker Papers. Curtis thought the movement should confine itself to research and discussion until the war was over; only then should it decide whether or not to become propagandist. See Curtis to Laby, 2 Jan. 1918, Laby Papers.

# 10
## India

When Curtis arrived in London in April 1918 he had been absent from England for two years. For the previous eighteen months he had been in India deeply embroiled as an adviser and commentator on the constitutional discussions raging in the subcontinent. He had not gone to India with this intention, but simply with a desire to learn more about the country and its problems before drafting the Round Table volume devoted to India and the dependencies. He had gradually been drawn into a more active role. As a result the movement through the medium of its major spokesman was able to add its voice to those clamouring for the grant of self-government to India.

The position of India and the dependencies in the empire had concerned the central moot for well over a decade, ever since 'The place of subject people in the Empire' had been discussed by the kindergarten in South Africa.[1] In those days they held, like most of their generation, severe views about the capacities and potential of 'the backward peoples' of the world. They had, for example, little faith in the Indian's capacity for self-government, and had recommended a long-term British supervision of Indian interests. As Curtis put it to his colleagues: 'However desirable self-government might be in the-

---

1 A paper by this title, 'The place of subject people in the Empire,' was read by Curtis to a regular meeting of the Fortnightly Club on 9 May 1907. Six months earlier, on 15 November 1906, Howard Pim had read a paper on 'The Question of Race.' The originals are in the library of the University of Cape Town.

ory it is no more in the nature of the [Indian] people, than it is in the nature of a billiard cue, to stand on end without support.'[2] Even if a few did manage to reach a position of intellectual equality, the majority would not. The kindergarten could therefore see little point in allowing the black and white races to mingle in the various countries of the empire. They suggested a policy of segregation. The British should 'aim at the separation of the two races into different areas'; the whites into the temperate zones and the blacks into the tropical zones. The races would then 'develop on their own natural lines' within their own territories.[3] Needless to say, little consideration was given to the place of India in an imperial parliament.

During the next few years many of the London group modified some of their views on India and 'the subject races.' This was partly due to greater experience but mainly to a deeper consideration of the imperial problem. Lionel Curtis attributed the change in his own opinions to conversations with William Marris. While the two men were visiting North America late in 1909 Marris had argued passionately that 'self-government ... however far distant was the only intelligible goal of British policy in India.' Coming shortly after the Morley-Minto reforms had been announced – by which Indian membership in the provincial legislative councils and the Imperial Legislative Council was increased – this fervent affirmation by a respected member of the Indian Civil Service left a deep impression on Curtis: 'So far I had thought of self-government as a Western institution, which was and would always remain peculiar to the peoples of Europe ... It was from that moment that I first began to think of "the Government of each by each, and of all by all" not merely as a principle of western life, but rather of all human life, as the goal to which all human societies must tend. It was from that moment that I began to think of the British Commonwealth as the greatest instrument ever devised for enabling that principle to be realised, not merely for the children of Europe but for all races and kindreds and peoples and tongues.'[4]

There is little evidence that India was discussed extensively in the Round Table meetings of early 1910 but by the end of that year both Curtis and Philip Kerr were beginning to wonder if in fact it was true that the educated and highly intelligent Indian was really unfitted to govern his own people.[5]

---

2 Curtis, 'The place of subject people'
3 Ibid.
4 Curtis, *The Dyarchy*, 42
5 See undated 'Memorandum' by Kerr, box 210, Lothian Papers; and [Philip Kerr], 'India and the English,' *The Round Table*, Nov. 1910, 41-57. Also Curtis to Oliver, 16 Aug. 1910, copy, GD40/17/2, Lothian Papers

Other members of the London group also recognised that the problem of India was tending to assume a different complexion; no longer was it 'merely that of the proper governance of India itself with a due regard for the interests of the Indian peoples, but it is also that of a possible readjustment of the relations between India and the rest of the British Empire in closer accordance with the interests alike of India and of the Empire as a whole.' Nevertheless, they still believed that India was unfitted for self-government. They could conceive of changes in the government of India which would make for efficiency but the immediate grant of self-government was not one of them. They did not feel there were enough educated Indians.[6]

By late 1911 the moot thought Indian and middle eastern affairs sufficiently important to send Philip Kerr to India through the Middle East. He left England in November 1911 and returned in August 1912. An important aspect of his mission was to gather and prepare material for a Round Table memorandum on India.[7] The visit was a crucial one for Kerr and the movement, for it convinced Kerr of the necessity of recognising India's claims and advancement. He now believed that the task of the British empire in India and the dependencies was 'the gradual education of the backward peoples within the Empire, so that they may come to govern themselves; and may ultimately come to be self-governing dominions within the British Empire ... If we manage to create in India a self-governing, responsible Dominion, and if India, when it is responsible and self-governing, elects to remain within the British Empire, we shall have solved the greatest difficulty which presents itself to the world today. The coloured peoples are going to progress and the future progress of the world hinges on whether there is going to be a long renewal of the world-old feud between east and west, black and white, and whether we can find a system based on mutual give-and-take which will enable them to live in peace and goodwill together.'[8]

Kerr, Marris, and Meston were able to convince the London group of the need for a reappraisal of their position. Thus far the group had tended to concentrate on the relations between Great Britain and the dominions. They

6 These views were expressed in an undated memorandum entitled 'India' probably written by Chirol, box 210, ibid. Milner was one who was doubtful. In 1908 he suggested that 'the idea of extending what is described as "Colonial Self-Government" to India, which seems to have a fascination to some untutored minds, is a hopeless absurdity.' Milner, 'The Two Empires,' *Proceedings of the Royal Colonial Institute* (1907-8), 333. See also Chirol, *Indian Unrest*, 332-3.

7 See Curtis to Kylie, 2 Feb. 1912, copy, Willison Papers.

8 Philip Kerr, 'The Meaning of the British Empire,' 30 July 1912. A speech given to the Canadian Round Table groups; printed in full in *The Round Table in Canada* (Toronto, Feb. 1917)

now realised that the Indian problem could not be arbitrarily set aside, but demanded continuing attention. The first major Round Table discussion of Indian affairs was held in late 1912. It lasted several days and was attended by various Indian officials including Marris and Meston.[9] This was the beginning of a coherent study of India by the central moot which in later years resulted in their being able to play a vital role in Indian constitutional development.[10]

Although no actual minutes of this meeting remain it is possible to follow the main points of the discussion from various extant memoranda prepared by Kerr, Marris, Meston, Craik, and Malcolm.[11] It is clear from these documents that the group members were by no means united in their approach; it is also evident that they had still not rid themselves of all their earlier views about 'the backward peoples.' The group had to answer two fundamental questions: should India be represented in an imperial parliament? and should India be granted self-government? Discussion of these issues quickly plunged the group into an assessment of the fundamental purpose of the movement and into a debate over tactics.

Although by this time all the members could agree on the basic aim of imperial union, men such as Malcolm and Craik were not sure that they could accept the arguments of Kerr and Curtis, enshrined in the 'principle of the commonwealth,' that Indians were fellow citizens of the commonwealth and would eventually share in its government. This quite logically led them to oppose Indian membership in an imperial parliament; but they also opposed representation on tactical grounds, and here they had Martin Holland's support. They were afraid that the dominions would strongly oppose India's inclusion in an imperial parliament. To make such a suggestion might endanger the success of the movement. This narrower view of the

9 Curtis, *Dyarchy*, 48-9. Others present were Curtis, Kerr, Craik, Malcolm, Chirol, and Martin Holland.
10 An article entitled 'Hindus and Mohammadans' appeared in the May 1911 issue of *The Round Table*, 299-312, but it had nothing to do with India and the Empire. See also a commentary article 'India,' ibid., Dec. 1911, 181-97.
11 See Philip Kerr, 'Memorandum on the representation of India,' June 1912, GD40/17/3, Lothian Papers; W.S. Marris, 'Memo on India and the Empire,' June 1912; Sir James Meston, 'Memo on India and the Empire,' June 1912; Sir Valentine Chirol, 'Memo on India,' July 1912, Meston Papers, MSS Eur F136/10. Also G.R. Craik, 'Note on the Principle of Indian Representation,' July 1912, and D.O. Malcolm, 'Memorandum,' July 1912, Curtis Papers. Kerr's views were also reflected in [Philip Kerr], 'India and the Empire,' *The Round Table*, Sept. 1912, 587-626. Curtis's views were contained in his 'Note on Philip Kerr's Indian Memorandum,' Curtis Papers. The 1912 discussions have received excellent coverage by Mehrotra, *India and the Commonwealth*, 79-83; and by Ellinwood, 'The Future of India.'

movement's purpose was opposed by Meston, Marris, Chirol, Kerr, and Curtis who met the arguments on two fronts: the philosophical and the tactical. Kerr pointed out that the movement had to disabuse itself of the idea that India could be dismissed under the label dependency. It was an empire as large as Europe, containing almost as many people. It would be a profound mistake for the movement to forget its educative mission; to do so would only endanger the long-range achievement of a true commonwealth. Curtis was also convinced that Craik and Malcolm were wrong. He reminded his friends 'that a "commonwealth" governing a dependency without having as its main object the training of the inhabitants of that dependency up to the status of citizens in order to enable them to assume the full rights and duties of citizenship, was acting like a despot and proving itself false to the law of its being ... Indians should be regarded as fellow-citizens of one super-commonwealth with ourselves, and that to prepare them first for the control of their sub-commonwealth and finally for an equal share in the control of the super-commonwealth should be our guiding principle.'[12]

Strangely enough, when it came to a discussion of what form representation in an imperial parliament should take, Curtis joined with Craik and Malcolm in opposing immediate representation. He did so on the grounds that India was not self-governing. However, he and Malcolm did favour the presence of Indian assessors in the imperial parliament. Curtis was not so far removed from the general consensus as one might have expected given the passionate defence of India's interests by Kerr, Marris, and Meston. When it came to the actual numbers that India was to be permitted, the three men suggested only token representation. Meston and Marris wanted it kept to a small number, perhaps only two or three, while Kerr recommended that only one Hindu and one Mohammedan, chosen by the elective members of the Imperial Legislative Council, should sit in the imperial parliament. This was a very conservative response, and indicated how much even the more enlightened members of the moot were out of touch, perhaps out of sympathy, with Indian nationalist opinion. On this issue the group's practical suggestions did not match their theories.[13]

The question of self-government for India raised fewer problems. The

12 Curtis, 'Note on Philip Kerr's Memorandum,' cited in Mehrotra, *India and the Commonwealth*, 83
13 One commentator on Kerr's memorandum was E. Molony, an Indian Civil Service official from Benares, who argued, in essence, that India should be given more representatives than Kerr suggested because in fifty years India would be 'ripe if not for complete self-government at least for a very considerable increase in her power of self-government.' The same argument was put in a slightly different way by a second ICS official, W.H. Buchan of Ben-

majority of the group, including Curtis, now accepted this as a necessary aim of the commonwealth and an appropriate goal for the movement. Even Craik and Malcolm were not opposed to the idea although they would probably have preferred to see greater self-government for the Government of India than for India itself. Only Chirol remained opposed to the idea in principle. He disliked talking about long-range political goals for India, fearing that it would create unnecessary unrest in the subcontinent.

For the London group to have reached this degree of unanimity before the war on the issue of self-government for India was a remarkable achievement. At that time very few other men in Great Britain or the dominions were prepared to think in those terms. One commentator has argued that the Round Table's doctrine of the principle of the commonwealth 'represented almost a revolution in imperialist thinking. It rejected the current imperialist dogma that non-white communities were incapable of self-government and that they should remain satisfied with good British government.'[14] This is certainly true; but one should not be too euphoric about the movement at this stage. The members found it relatively easy to agree about the abstract, but were far less ready to see a substantial implementation of their ideas. They still lacked faith in the Indian's capacity for self-rule; self-government was to be a very long-term goal. Milner's 'two empires' had not altogether disappeared from Round Table memoranda and certainly not from Round Table minds. Chauvinists and paternalists that they were, the London members still viewed with calm the vision of the white man – an Englishman – shepherding the Indian along the path to self-government. The goal was there for India to reach, but the decisions about pace and method would be British decisions not Indian.[15]

The 1912 meeting secured the question of India's place in the empire on the movement's agenda. But as yet it was not at the top of the list. During 1913 it was decided that the movement should concentrate primarily on anglo-dominion relations. For the time being the problem of India remained a secondary consideration.

India's generous military and financial response to the outbreak of war in Europe in 1914 disrupted this cautious mood. It was suddenly and dramatically demonstrated that India was willing and able to shoulder a con-

gal. See E. Molony to Curtis, 3 June 1912, and W.H. Buchan to Curtis, 11 June 1912, Curtis Papers.
14 Mehrotra, *India and the Commonwealth*, 83
15 See in this connection Curtis, *The Project of a Commonwealth*, 155, 173-4, 176-8; and Curtis, 'A Practical Enquiry,' 1-25 and 63-72.

siderable portion of the empire's war burden. The tempo of constitutional debate increased, and soon Indians of all political hues were clamouring for the extension of self-government to India and for a policy declaration by the British. For the next three years these demands were widely debated in India and in British government circles.[16]

The London group were quick to respond to the change in atmosphere.[17] In 1915, while Curtis was completing *The Problem of the Commonwealth*, other members of the London group were attempting to draft the Indian chapters for volume II of the major 'egg.' Five sections were envisaged: I India through the ages; II The Western World; III The Clash between the new West and the East; IV British rule in India; V The Future: (a) The place of India in the Commonwealth and (b) The future in India itself. In the Lothian papers there exists a draft of the first section, but only a small part of section II, hardly anything of section IV, and nothing of the rest. There are no suggestions in this material of a specific scheme, only an indication that the movement thought it vital that India remain within the empire for the good of mankind. The British commonwealth could then act as a bridge between East and West.[18] While the draft chapters were being thrashed out by Kerr and others of the London group, a series of fortnightly meetings between the group and a number of India Office officials was also arranged. They met continuously throughout the autumn of 1915 and those usually present were Curtis, Kerr, Reginald Coupland, Sir Lionel Abrahams, then in charge of financial questions at the India Office, Sir William Duke,[19] M.C. Seton,[20] C.H. Kisch,[21] J.E. Shuck-

16 For an excellent treatment of these issues see Mehrotra, *India and the Commonwealth*, 56-106.
17 James Meston soon warned the London group of the need for careful consideration of India's position, so that reliable material would be available on the British side to offset the 'preposterous' claims of Indian politicians. He admitted that the presence of Indian troops in the fighting line in Europe 'has precipitated a claim for something akin to colonial self-government which we have long anticipated, but which we had hoped to keep quiet for another generation.' Meston to Curtis, 16 May 1915, copy, Meston Papers, MSS Eur F136/11. For Curtis's sympathetic replies see Curtis to Meston, 16 July and 25 Sept. 1915, ibid.
18 P.H.K., 'An Outline of the Indian Chapters,' 2 June 1915, GD40/17/16, Lothian Papers
19 Sir William Duke (1863-1924); entered Indian Civil Service 1882; lieutenant-governor Bengal 1911; member of the Council of the Governor of Bengal 1912-14; member of the Secretary of State's Council 1914-20; permanent under-secretary of state, India Office 1920-4
20 M.C. Seton (1872-1940); entered the India Office 1898; secretary, Judicial and Public Department, 1911-19; assistant under-secretary 1919; deputy under-secretary 1924-33
21 C.H. Kisch (1884-1961); entered India Office 1908; private secretary to the permanent under-secretary 1911 and to the parliamentary under-secretary 1915; private secretary to the secretary of state for India 1917-21; secretary, Financial Department, 1921-33; assistant under-secretary 1933-43; deputy under-secretary 1943-6

burgh,[22] and Meston.[23] The group agreed that India's response to the the war indicated that 'the country was riper than had been supposed for a further instalment of reform,' and that it would be fatal to do nothing about India's relationship to the empire.[24]

'Clearly India must move,' wrote Curtis, 'but whither?' Curtis thought it dangerous and useless to discuss practical steps until the Round Table members were clear in their own minds about the goal of England's policy in India. There was general agreement among them that it should be 'self-government,' but they were uncertain about the precise meaning of the term. The group finally agreed to assume that the goal toward which India 'should be consciously and earnestly helped by her rulers should be self-government within the commonwealth' on lines similar to those travelled by the dominions. However, they were still convinced that India could not advance immediately to full responsible government because the electorate on which government would be based was not yet properly trained to make such important decisions. What was the alternative? The London group's answer was a principle now known to the world as dyarchy. The Round Table members asked:

Could not provincial electorates through legislatures and ministers of their own be made clearly responsible for certain functions of government to begin with, leaving all others in the hands of executives responsible as at present to the Government of India and the Secretary of State? Indian electorates, legislatures, and executives would thus be given a field for the exercise of genuine responsibility. From time to time fresh powers could be transferred from the old governments as the new elective authorities developed and proved their capacity for assuming them. Powers already transferred could also be recalled whenever elective authorities had shown themselves unable to exercise them properly.[25]

The proposal presumed the coexistence of two authorities in the same areas: one, responsible for certain specified functions to local electorates; the

22 J.E. Shuckburgh (1877-1953); entered India Office 1900; assistant secretary, Political Department 1912-17; secretary 1917-21; transferred to the Colonial Office 1921; assistant under-secretary 1921-31; deputy under-secretary 1931-42

23 Curtis, *Dyarchy,* xx; Mehrotra, *India and the Commonwealth,* 84; and Curtis to Sir Stanley Reed, 13 Nov. 1951, Curtis Papers

24 Earlier in the year the group had discussed the draft of Curtis's *The Problem of the Commonwealth* with Austen Chamberlain for two days at Blackmoor. Curtis to Meston, 16 July 1915, Meston Papers, MSS Eur F136/10. In September Curtis discussed with Chamberlain the manner of India's representation at a postwar imperial conference. Curtis to Meston, 25 Sept. 1915, ibid.

25 Curtis, *Dyarchy,* xxiii

other, responsible for all other functions to the British electorate through the secretary of state and the Government of India.

When the suggestion was first broached to the group it was rejected by those with experience of Indian administration as without precedent, and dangerously inapplicable to Indian conditions. Most of the arguments later raised against the scheme in India were suggested at these meetings. The suggestion was then set aside by the group, but when all other avenues of investigation proved fruitless they were forced to consider whether the objections to dyarchy were insuperable. They reasoned that before the arguments against the principle could be tested it would have to be reduced to a definite scheme and considered in detail. Sir William Duke undertook to prepare a plan of specific devolution using the government of Bengal as his model. He produced a scheme which was printed and circulated to the group who then retired to Oxford, and in the old bursary of Trinity College spent three days in early 1916 in detailed discussions. It was then completely recast by its author. None of the group were very pleased with the result, but no other alternative had been found during months of deliberation.

The memorandum was originally scheduled to be circulated to all the Round Table groups in Great Britain and the dominions in the autumn, and to be used by Curtis during the final drafting of volume II of the major 'egg'; but by early 1916 Lord Chelmsford, the newly appointed viceroy of India, was becoming aware that it would soon be necessary to make an announcement to the effect that Great Britain was looking forward to the advance of India toward self-government. Before such an announcement was made he was anxious to have a clear idea of the changes that would be necessary. Chelmsford had been governor of New South Wales in 1910 and had helped Curtis found Round Table groups in Sydney and Brisbane during the latter's first visit. On hearing that the London branch of the movement was studying the question of India, he asked to see the results. The request came shortly after the completion of Sir William Duke's first draft. Since it might have proved embarrassing to Chelmsford to have the Duke memorandum circulating even privately, the central moot decided not to forward it to the dominions but simply to send a revised copy to the viceroy. This was done in May 1916. In 1917, when Montagu's visit to India was announced and the governors of the Indian provinces were asked to prepare proposals, the memorandum was reprinted by the Government of India and circulated with other papers for their information. It came to be known as the Duke Memorandum, but was not published until 1920 when Curtis included it in his volume *Dyarchy*.[26]

26 For the above account see Curtis, *Dyarchy*, xxi-xxvii. Also Curtis to Reed, 13 Nov.

In his memorandum Sir William Duke outlined the structure of the Government of India and examined what changes could be made within the existing framework. He concluded that improvements in the system of election to the Legislative Council and changes in the method of selecting the Indian Executive Councillors – in other words, reforms along Morley-Minto lines – would not by themselves bring Indians any closer to a responsible position in the provincial governments. Furthermore, if wholesale additions were made to the membership of the Legislative Council it would mean a complete transfer of power to an elected majority, far too radical a reform under existing conditions. The alternative was to create in selected provinces responsible Indian executives side by side with the existing executives, and gradually to transfer the functions of government to them.

Using Bengal as his example Duke suggested that a responsible legislative council might be given immediate control of the departments of education, local self-government, and sanitation. Others such as registration, co-operative credit, agriculture, forests, and public works could be transferred at a comparatively early stage. The degree of control transferred and the time of transfer would be settled by the imperial government. Duke and his associates recognised that finding sufficient revenue for these purposes would be difficult. But he made it clear that the new executive would have control of the revenue for the specific departments transferred to it. Other means of raising revenue would have to be explored. In his concluding section Duke attempted to counter probable criticisms of the scheme. He conceded that there was a risk involved in transferring powers. Inefficient administration might result, as well as nepotism and corruption. But a beginning had to be made, and presumably the Indian people would be willing to submit to some loss of efficiency 'in return for being allowed to arrange matters according to their own views.'[27] A start on the road to self-government had been made by Morley and Minto by allowing Indians to exercise an influence on the executive through the legislature, but continued dependence on that method was subject to serious drawbacks. Under that system the Indians were developing their critical faculties at the expense of their constructive faculties. Without responsibility they had no reason to devise means to advance their ends. But under responsible government a new role would open up, and progress toward full self-government would be accelerated.

Chelmsford was pleased to receive the Duke memorandum, and sent copies to all his legislative councils and to the heads of the local governments.

1951; and Curtis to Milner, 29 Nov. 1915; Kerr to Curtis, 19 May 1916, Curtis Papers. For the 'Duke Memorandum' see Curtis, *Dyarchy*, 1-37

27  Curtis, *Dyarchy*, 33

Kerr informed Curtis, who by now had left for Canada, that Chelmsford 'and his Executive have been giving some consideration to the matter and are apparently working out the solutions on somewhat different lines. He is therefore anxious we should not publish our memorandum as, [in Chelmsford's words], "it would embarrass us considerably if a rival policy were set forth with all the prestige of the Round Table behind it."'[28] Valentine Chirol, who had not taken part in the discussions leading to the Duke memorandum owing to his absence in India, had some doubts about the Round Table proposals: 'I am rather sorry the Round Table committed itself to proposals which I doubt very much any one would have advocated whose practical experience had not been mainly confined to Bengal the worse [sic] province in India from that point of view. I don't believe however that a diarchate of that sort would work even in Bengal.'[29] And in October Kerr was forced to admit that the Duke memorandum was 'not finding much favour in high circles.'[30]

Curtis had left England shortly after the Oxford meetings, and had taken no part in the subsequent discussions with Chelmsford over the Duke memorandum. He arrived in India in October 1916 after a strenuous trip through Canada, New Zealand, and Australia where he had devoted some of his time to gathering information on dominion attitudes toward asiatic immigration which he subsequently forwarded to Chelmsford in November 1916.[31] Curtis's visit to India was a logical outcome of the stage at which the Round Table had arrived in its work. As Sir James Meston had so often emphasized, books on India obtainable in England were usually twenty years out of date. A visit to India was essential if Curtis wanted to prepare a reliable volume. He arrived in Bombay on 24 October and stayed with Sir Stanley Reed,[32] editor of *The Times of India*, who introduced Curtis to a number of ICS officials.[33] A week later he left with Reed for Delhi where he spent a few

28  Kerr to Curtis, 25 July 1916, Curtis Papers
29  Chirol to Kerr, 26 July 1916, copy, ibid.
30  Kerr to Curtis, 1 Oct. 1916, ibid. There is some evidence that Curtis had drafted some of the Indian chapters for volume II of the major report before leaving for Canada in April 1916 because in late October Kerr informed Curtis that only Seton had read them and rather hurriedly. 'Duke, Abraham and Shuckburgh have had the memo all summer and have not had time to deal with it.' Kerr to Curtis, 24 Oct. 1916, ibid.
31  Curtis to Chelmsford, 2 Nov. 1916, *Confidential*, Department of Commerce and Industry. Emigration Dec. 1916, National Archives of India, New Delhi. See also Curtis to Chelmsford, 2 Nov. 1916, Chelmsford Papers, MSS Eur E264/3.
32  Sir Stanley Reed (1872-1969); joined the staff of *The Times of India* 1897; editor of *The Times of India*, Bombay, 1907-23; MP (U) 1938-50
33  Curtis's India diary 1916, Curtis Papers

days at the Viceregal Lodge with Chelmsford. From Delhi he went on to Simla where he was the guest of Claude Hill,[34] a member of the Viceroy's Executive Council. Here Curtis saw Chirol and also met Sir Sankahan Nair,[35] the Indian member of the Viceroy's Council. Finally, Curtis reached Allahabad with Chirol on 11 November and was greeted by Meston at Government House.[36]

Throughout these weeks Curtis talked continuously and at length with a variety of British officials and many Indians gleaning information about India and her current feelings and attitudes. His discoveries led him to decide on a change in plan. Originally, he had thought of spending the winter in India collecting information, opinions, and materials and of returning to England in the spring of 1917 in order to write. But 'During the three weeks between my landing and arrival at Allahabad I came to the conclusion that the task I had undertaken here was so formidable that I could not hope to do justice to it if I left it in the spring. I felt that I must write the first draft of what I was going to say in India itself in order to discuss it with men on the spot. The importance of warning my colleagues not to expect my return to England in the spring was the consideration which overshadowed all others in my mind. Sir James Meston was intensely busy, but he devoted an hour at once to discussing this question with Mr. Marris, Sir Valentine Chirol, and myself, and in helping me to frame a programme of my movements. They all agreed emphatically that I should remain in India during the summer to write.'[37]

The result of this decision was a letter to Kerr dated 13 November 1916 in which Curtis explained his change in plans, and emphasized the need to approach the thorny and delicate problem of India in the most comprehensive manner. It would be the one aspect of the movement's work which would be subject to the greatest and most searching criticism.[38] Curtis had the letter printed in bulk for circulation to his friends in the United Kingdom and the

---

34  Sir Claude Hamilton Archer Hill (1866-1934); joined the Indian Civil Service in 1887; resident, Mewar 1906-8; agent to the Government of Bombay 1908-12; ordinary member of the Executive Council of Bombay 1912-15; ordinary member of the Viceroy's Executive Council 1915-20

35  Sir Sankaran Nair (1857-1934); judge of the High Court, Madras; member of the Madras Legislative Council; member of the Council of State, Government of India, Delhi; member of the Council of the Secretary of State for India 1920-1

36  While in Allahabad Curtis met a small local Round Table group which had recently been formed, and in December discussed the formation of groups at Calcutta and Nagpur. See Curtis's India diary 1916, Curtis Papers.

37  Curtis, *Dyarchy*, 50-1

38  This letter is printed in full in Curtis, *Dyarchy*, 51-7.

dominions. Unfortunately, this private letter somehow became public, and abstracted sections were circulated among the crowds attending the meetings of the Indian National Congress and the All-India Muslim League at Lucknow in December 1916. The letter, which was paternalist in tone and injudiciously mentioned Meston and Marris by name, raised a storm of protest in India and propelled Curtis's name to the forefront of public attention.[39] When he had arrived in the country Curtis had had no intention of taking part in public controversies, but the circulation of a disastrously abstracted private letter compelled him to reply at length. He did this in March 1917 in his famous 'A letter to the People Of India,' in which he outlined the ideals and goals of the movement and re-emphasized the Round Table's intention to promote self-government for India.[40] This whole episode was a crucial and unforeseen development for the movement.[41] As Curtis later pointed out: 'If this private letter had not been abstracted and published it is highly probable that I should have left India as I intended, without taking any part in the controversies then distracting the country. My studies of Indian government privately circulated would scarcely have attracted public notice. The results when afterwards published in England would probably have come too late to affect practical issues, so rapid had been the movement of events.'[42]

By the time Curtis drafted this letter his research had confirmed his conviction that 'a further advance on the path traced by the Minto-Morley reforms would lead to disaster,' and more than ever he was convinced that the principle outlined in the Duke memorandum should be pursued. He did not believe that a scheme adopted by the Indian National Congress and the Muslim League at Lucknow in December 1916 would work. He had no quarrel with their desire that 'definite steps should be taken towards self-government' nor that India should have equal status with the dominions in an imperial body; but he thought their other suggestions unworkable. These

39 Austen Chamberlain, the secretary of state for India, admitted to Chelmsford that the publication of Curtis's letter had not made the calm consideration of India's place in the empire any easier. He thought Curtis's letter indiscreet and dogmatic: 'I am doubly sorry for this, for though Curtis's ways irritate me, he is a most unselfish apostle of Empire and a genuine enthusiast devoting himself wholeheartedly to public service.' See A. Chamberlain to Chelmsford, 26 Jan., 27 Feb., and 16 March 1917, MSS Eur E264/3, Chelmsford Papers.

40 This 'Letter' is printed in full in Curtis, *Dyarchy*, 38-95.

41 One result was Chelmsford's ban on civil servants becoming members of Round Table groups. This seriously undermined the establishment of an effective network in India. See A. Chamberlain to Chelmsford, 16 March 1917 and Chelmsford to A. Chamberlain, 20 April 1917, MSS Eur E264/3, ibid.

42 Curtis, *Dyarchy*, xxx

were provincial autonomy, four-fifths of the central and provincial legislative councils to be elected, not less than half the members of the central
and provincial governments to be elected by their respective legislatve councils, the executives to be bound to act in accordance with the resolutions
passed by their legislative councils, and the secretary of state for India to
have the same relationship with the Government of India as the colonial secretary had with the dominions.[43] It was clear from this that Curtis was out of
touch with the depth of feeling in India. He was still convinced that Indians
were incapable of assuming so much responsibility right away. It offended
his deep-seated belief in the differences between European and Asian civ-
ilizations. It ran contrary to his self-righteous, educative zeal. He was determined to secure adherence to what for him seemed a more sensible way,
but for Indians appeared a lesser way.

In March 1917 he discussed the Congress-League scheme with
Bhupendra Nath Basu,[44] a member of the Indian Legislative Council and
one of the authors of the scheme. Basu argued that India should be given
self-government on lines suggested by the Morley-Minto reforms; the
scheme was an attempt to suggest a way that it could be done. In the days
following this discussion, Curtis drafted a lengthy letter in which for the first
time he outlined his ideas for the extension of responsible government to India. While he now agreed that an early pronouncement in favour of self-government would be wise, he wanted it tied to a specific scheme.[45] In brief, he
advocated a division of powers between the central and provincial governments, and the transfer of some of the provincial powers to a responsible
executive. The Provincial Legislative Council would sit in two capacities;
first, as an advisory council convened to discuss all matters of provincial
government; and, second, as a responsible body to deal with the functions
and revenues transferred to it. It was in this letter to Basu that Curtis first
used the term dyarchy to distinguish between 'advisory' and 'responsible'
functions. In preparing the final draft, Curtis received advice and criticism
from Chirol and William Hailey, then the chief commissioner of Delhi, both
of whom agreed that dyarchy was the only viable alternative to the status
quo (now clearly unacceptable to all sides) or rapid advance toward self-government. The letter was forwarded to Basu in early April 1917, and copies
were sent to Indian and British friends for criticism. They responded so well

43 For the Congress-League scheme of December 1916 see Curtis, *Dyarchy*, 90-5.
44 Bhupendra Nath Basu (1859-1924); member of the Bengal Legislative Council; also of the
   viceroy's Legislative Council; president of the Indian National Congress at Madras 1914;
   member of the Council of the Secretary of State for India 1917-23
45 See Curtis to Coupland, 19 May 1917, copy, MSS Eur F111/438, Curzon Papers.

that Curtis sent copies of the letter, and selections from the comments, to the Government of India and to all the provincial governments in July and August.[46]

Shortly after completing his letter to Basu, Curtis began drafting his 'Indian Studies.' These were based on a mass of notes gathered in the previous six months. When completed these memoranda were circulated for criticism and then revised. Meston assisted Curtis in revising the first study, entitled 'The Structure of Indian Government,' which dealt largely with the United Provinces of which Meston was then lieutenant-governor. It was circulated in June 1917; the second, 'Land Revenue,' in July; and the third, a further look at 'The Structure of Indian Government,' in August.[47] Most of this work was done in Naini Tal, United Provinces, where Rushbrook Williams,[48] a fellow of All Souls and professor of history at Allahabad, gave Curtis considerable assistance.[49]

While Curtis was hurriedly preparing his pamphlets, the British government finally bowed to enormous pressure and reached a decision about British policy in India. On 20 August 1917 Edwin Montagu,[50] who had succeeded Austen Chamberlain as secretary of state for India in July, declared in the British House of Commons that 'The policy of His Majesty's Government, with which the Government of India are in complete accord, is that of the increasing association of Indians in every branch of the administration, and the gradual development of self-governing institutions, with a view to the progressive realisation of responsible government in India as an

46 When Edwin Montagu reached India in November he also received a copy. Curtis, *The Dyarchy*, xxxi-xxxv; for the letter to Basu of 6 April 1917 see Curtis, *Dyarchy*, 96-124; for the comments see Curtis, *The Dyarchy*, 124-200. See also Curtis to Lord Willingdon, 23 May 1917, copy, Curtis Papers. One who did not respond favourably to Curtis's scheme was Lord Selborne. He thought Curtis was putting the British in a position where they would have to grant self-government even though no evidence existed to prove that India was capable of it. Selborne to Coupland, 23 June 1917, enclosed in Curtis to Chelmsford, 24 May 1918, MSS Eur E264/15, Chelmsford Papers
47 For these studies and appended criticisms see Curtis, *The Dyarchy*, 201-325. Also Curtis, *Dyarchy*, xxxv-xxxvi
48 Laurence Frederic Rushbrook Williams (1890-    ); lecturer in mediaeval history, Queen's University, 1913-14; fellow of All Souls 1914-21; university professor of modern Indian history, University of Allahabad, 1914-19; director, Central Bureau of Information, India 1920-6; foreign minister, Patrala State, 1925-31; adviser to the Indian States Delegation to the Round Table Conference 1930-1; a delegate to the Round Table Conference of 1932; editorial department *The Times* 1944-55
49 Curtis to Coupland, 23 May 1917, Curtis Papers
50 Edwin Montagu's house had been used by the Round Table during the interparty negotiations over the Irish crisis in 1914.

integral part of the Empire.'[51] Montagu announced that he would soon be travelling to India for talks with the Government of India and with Indians about the implementation of the new policy. He made it clear, however, that advance would be in stages, and that the British would remain the final judges of the speed and manner of progress.

Despite these qualifying remarks Montagu's statement laid down quite clearly that the aim of British rule in India was to grant, in time, parliamentary self-government on the dominion model to the subcontinent. Coupled with the inclusion of India at the recent meetings of the Imperial War Cabinet and the Imperial War Conference and the decision to include her in all future discussions of imperial constitutional relations, Montagu's announcement marked a turning point in Anglo-Indian relations. The immediate effect was a bitter controversy in the Indian and British press about the speed with which self-government should be attained. The extreme positions adopted so alarmed a number of moderate Indians and Englishmen in India that they began to search for a basis of agreement between the various elements. By now Curtis's name was well known. His 'Indian Studies' were being widely publicised, and in some quarters acclaimed. The pamphlets attracted the attention of the moderates who invited Curtis to assist them in framing a scheme for submission to Montagu. Lord Sinha, recently back from London where he had attended the meetings of the Imperial War Cabinet and Imperial War Conference, offered his home in Darjeeling as a meeting place for the initial gatherings of Curtis and the moderates. During these sessions Curtis became convinced that the existing provinces of India were too large and unwieldy for dyarchy to work well in them.[52] He proposed a subdivision of the provinces, and recommended that this be done before the transfer of powers. His views were accepted and incorporated in the twelve points of agreement signed by sixty-four Europeans and ninety Indians. A Joint Address containing the twelve points, and outlining a scheme of reforms using the United Provinces as a model, was then submitted to Chelmsford and Montagu shortly after Montagu's arrival in India in November.[53]

51  For the text see Smith, *The Oxford History of India*, 780; and for the discussions leading up to it see Mehrotra, *India and the Commonwealth*, 99-104.
52  This point had been drawn to Curtis's attention by Kerr in July. Kerr was convinced that the first step toward an effective federal structure would have to be a division of the provinces. See Kerr to Curtis, 21 July, 2 Oct., and 8 Dec. 1917; and Curtis to Kerr, 28 Aug. 1917, GD40/17/33, Lothian Papers.
53  Curtis, *Dyarchy*, xxx; xxxvi-xxxix; for the Joint Address see Curtis, *Dyarchy*, 326-56.

Publication of the address and the scheme resulted in violent controversy and bitter attacks by Nationalists who wanted the British to accept the plan outlined at Lucknow in December 1916. Curtis believed that the Lucknow scheme was inadequate. He also knew that no one would abandon it quickly. But since it was desirable to have the alternative clearly stated before the Congress meeting in Calcutta in December 1917, Curtis outlined the defects of the Congress-League scheme, the merits of a subprovincial system, and the overall advantages of dyarchy in a series of letters later entitled 'Letters to the People of India on Responsible Government' which were printed and circulated to all the Indian papers. When a number of papers abused this method by printing sections out of context, the 'Letters' were published in book form shortly before the Congress meeting in December 1917.[54] When the Joint Address had originally been presented to Chelmsford and Montagu, Curtis had talked to them privately for a few minutes; and when 'The Letters' were published he went to Bombay in December, at their invitation, to discuss the contents of his book.[55]

When Edwin Montagu arrived in India in November 1917 to make an on-the-spot study of possible reforms he had read all the available material on the subject, including the memorandum prepared for the Round Table by Sir William Duke who had accompanied him to India. His newly formulated opinions tended to follow diarchic principles.[56] Shortly after arriving he read Curtis's recent writings, and decided that the prophet's scheme was the best he had seen. On the whole the two men differed very little, although Montagu thought Curtis was inclined to confuse constitutional reform with geographical redistribution. He did not think Curtis's subprovincial plan workable, and found that Curtis had given insufficient thought to the problem of finance. Apart from this there was not a great deal to choose between them. Montagu and Curtis were both committed to responsible government and to a transfer of powers; the difficulty would be to thrash out the details. During the next six months Montagu saw numerous deputations, interviewed dozens of the Indian political leaders, and negotiated and wrangled endlessly

---

54　For the full text of the 'Letters' see Curtis, *Dyarchy*, 357-466. An English edition was published in May 1918. See Curtis, *Dyarchy*, 467-76 for the introduction to the English edition.
55　For the background to the 'Letters' see Curtis, *Dyarchy*. xxxix-xli.
56　For Montagu's months in India see Montagu, *An Indian Diary*. Duke had also managed to keep Montagu supplied with additional material favourable to dyarchy; this despite his lack of faith in Indian politicians and administrators. See Duke to Kerr, 25 Aug. and 1 Sept. 1917, F/91/1/6 and 7, Lloyd George Papers.

with Chelmsford, the governors, the princes, the members of his delegation, and with the Viceroy's Council, especially Sir C. Sankaran Nair and Sir William Vincent.[57] By early 1918 Montagu's nerves were badly frayed and everyone associated with the delegation was overworked and tired. The atmosphere was electric and Montagu and Marris, the drafter of the report, were continually at odds.

During these months Montagu met Curtis on nine separate occasions, the first time on 1 December in Calcutta. Today, wrote Montagu, 'I ... had my first introduction to the great Curtis. We spent an hour together. At last here was a person unprejudiced, keenly interested, properly equipped. I spoke to him with complete frankness, and although, of course, he prefers his scheme, he is quite prepared to see mine adopted. I am bound to say that he convinced me that an official majority is a thing which cannot be tolerated. I wish he sometimes made a joke; I wish he sometimes viewed things from some other attitude than that of Curtis, the empire-builder ... It was a satisfactory talk. He did not convince me that you could practically subdivide the provinces now, but of course our two schemes are so similar that it really does not matter.'[58]

The two men met again briefly on 7 December, and had a long discussion over lunch on 12 December. Montagu found Curtis on this occasion 'a strange mixture of impossible inhumanity and soundness,' but there was no doubt in Montagu's mind that 'Curtis and I see thoroughly eye to eye and he is going to be most helpful, and he is a valuable acquisition because he holds in the hollow of his hands the *Times* and Lord Milner.'[59] Curtis conferred again with Montagu and Chelmsford in Bombay on Christmas Eve, and Montagu tried to point out weaknesses in the Curtis scheme, especially the failure to create sufficient machinery for the avoidance of friction between A subjects (reserved) and B subjects (transferred). The discussion only served

---

57 Sir William Henry Hoare Vincent (1866-1941); entered Indian Civil Service 1887; served in Bengal in various capacities; secretary in the Legal Department, Government of India, 1911-15; member of the Executive Council of the lieutenant-governor of Bihar and Orissa 1915-17; member of the Governor General's Council of India 1917; vice-president of the Council 1921; member of the Council of India 1923-31

58 Montagu, *An Indian Diary*, 76

59 Ibid., 89, 101. Montagu later told a story about Curtis. Apparently 'Curtis had developed a desire to become a Hindu; he had summoned some men from the Central Provinces and told them this; they said: "No man not born a Hindu can become a Hindu." He said, quite characteristically: "Oh, nonsense; any man can change his religion." So they promised eventually to consult the Pandits at Benares, and the reply came back: "Mr Curtis must feed a thousand Brahmans every day for a year. At the end of the year he must commit suicide, and then possibly in his next incarnation he may become a sweeper."' Ibid., 214

to convince Montagu of the merits of his own ideas where they differed from Curtis's.[60]

By early January the formal hearing of evidence had been completed, and by the end of the month the meetings with Indian leaders and the governors and heads of provinces were also over. Montagu had three more talks with Curtis during this period and by 1 February was satisfied that they agreed on all things.[61] But on 4 February Curtis suddenly became greatly despondent, and thought that the greater part of the scheme should be dropped because it would never be accepted by the British government. The secretary of state was already having great difficulty in convincing some of his colleagues of the merits of the scheme but he had always relied on Curtis's support and goodwill. Coming on top of everything else Curtis's reaction was almost too much for Montagu's frazzled nerves. He became very depressed and worried about the outcome of Curtis's attitude. Curtis soon infected Duke and Marris with his doubt, and all that Montagu had struggled so hard to achieve seemed to be slipping further and further away. Curtis and Montagu talked at length on 6 February with little result:

[Curtis] appears to have been thoroughly frightened by something or other, and begs me to drop most of my proposals. At this eleventh hour he beseeches me: 'We are standing on the edge of the most frightful calamity.' Have you ever been talked to in this strain by the Round Table? I like Curtis very much; I thought he was so closely in accord with me, and I am deeply disappointed at this new turn of affairs. He appears to have had a letter from Chirol expressing alarm. He appears to be afraid that Curzon and Milner will say to Lloyd George: 'We cannot support this.' He is afraid I shall be driven to resignation, in which case he says there is nothing but martial law possible in India; that there must be no delay in completing my proposals; that the larger they are the less chance there is of getting them through, therefore they must be small. Indian public opinion does not matter; those whom I think will support me are going to turn and rend me; no scheme has a chance, and so on. I went back to the Council in a fit of deep depression ... [later in the day] I went to see Curtis, to whom I had given to read my notes for my report – more gloomy than ever, more certain of disaster than ever. It is the most depressing circumstance, which has nearly driven me to the verge of suicide, because up till today Curtis has seemed to be a supporter of everything we proposed ... Really it is black Wednesday, if ever there was one.[62]

The following day Marris began drafting the report with Montagu still in the depths of gloom: 'Well, things may look brighter, but I must say they

60 Ibid., 141          61 Ibid., 164, 231-3, 236          62 Ibid., 246-7

have never looked worse.'[63] Despite everything work proceeded on the report, and when Montagu saw 'the holy man, Curtis' again on 19 February the latter was 'infinitely happier' with the way things were going; and the two men parted friends.[64] During the next few weeks delay intruded and mid-March found Montagu and Marris struggling to get the report finished, and growing ever more tired in the process. Montagu wanted the report to express his ideas and conclusions, and his alone. He was not prepared to listen to Marris's objections or tolerate his procrastinations. Nothing is more obvious than that the Montagu-Chelmsford Report owed more to Montagu than to anyone else, certainly more than to Curtis, Marris, or even Chelmsford. It should be said in Marris's defence that he was grossly overworking himself, often staying up all night wrestling with a difficult section. But this did not lessen Montagu's annoyance, and on 18 March he lost his temper with Marris 'who seemed to be in a funk about everything, and had been so impressed by Vincent's arguments as to actually say that he did not feel justified in writing the report unless he was allowed to write what he thought of it. I never heard such nonsense. I told him he was a hack, and had got to express only our views.'[65]

On 26 March 1918 everyone moved to the viceroy's summer quarters at Dehra Dun, and Montagu waited impatiently for Marris to complete the draft: 'the melancholy Marris is worshipping his melancholy gods in his melancholy tent, and more or less willingly, but never cheerfully, drafting what he is told to draft.' During the first two weeks of April Montagu and his party 'spent almost every day without exercise continuously from ten in the morning till eight at night in revising the report – Chelmsford, Duke, Marris and I. Chelmsford has sat through the whole proceedings ... confining himself to such speculations as to whether the Government of India is a plural or singular noun. Marris has fought consistently for the right to say disagreeable things about people: I have fought to avoid it.' The report was finally completed on 21 April 1918 and Montagu returned to England, arriving in mid-May.[66]

Curtis had arrived back a month earlier, having returned on the advice of the London group who believed he should be in London when Montagu's proposals were presented to Parliament. Curtis had left India in late February, when Marris was well into the initial draft, with the feeling that his last months in India had been most productive. He claimed to have more peace of mind than he had known before.[67] But in July 1918 shortly after the publi-

63 Ibid., 248       64 Ibid., 266       65 Ibid., 330       66 Ibid., 343-4
67 See Kerr to Curtis, 8 Dec. 1917; Curtis to ?, 20 Feb. 1918; Milner to Curtis, 8 April 1918, Curtis Papers. See also Curtis to Laby, 25 May 1918, Laby Papers, in which Curtis said: '...

cation of the Montagu-Chelmsford Report, he admitted to Neville Chamberlain[68] that though he agreed in outline with the recommendations of the Report he felt they needed considerable revision in detail.[69] Montagu noted in mid-June that 'I have got the *Times* quite easily. Chirol, who is writing for the *Times* has been bitten by Curtis with the Two Governments plan for the Provinces. I had him and Roberts to lunch and I think weakened him.' Montagu found that the other Round Table members were inclined to agree with him, especially Philip Kerr, 'who has much influence with the Prime Minister, being strongly a supporter of our alternatives.'[70]

When the Montagu-Chelmsford Report was published in July there were various demands for postponing study of the whole question until after the war. Despite his doubts in India Curtis now disagreed with this view, and in a letter to *The Times* on 22 July 1918 urged the immediate appointment of the Franchise and Functions Committees which had been recommended in the report.[71] Committees to formulate schemes for the franchise, the separation of Indian from provincial functions, and the powers to be transferred to responsible ministers were despatched to India in late 1918 and subsequently amalgamated as two sub-committees under the general chairmanship of Lord Southborough. Questions of franchise were dealt with by one under Southborough himself, and those concerning decentralization and transferred powers by the second under the chairmanship of Richard Feetham, now a member of the South African legislature. In January 1919 the India bill had still to be drafted, and both Curtis and Montagu were in Paris; but both men could not keep the Indian problem from their minds. Montagu wrote to Chelmsford on 4 February about the reforms: 'Curtis is conducting an uncompromising campaign in favour of undiluted dyarchy. Oh these men who live above the clouds on the mountain tops, confident in the sordid imperfections of their fellow men and rightly convinced of the integrity of their own soul.'[72]

This Joint Address led to my seeing a lot of Chelmsford and Montagu and eventually I spent my last month in India at Delhi at the Viceroy's Camp while they were drafting the report ... all I can now say is that I am thoroughly satisfied with the results.'

68 Arthur Neville Chamberlain (1869-1940); lord mayor of Birmingham 1915-16; director-general of National Services 1916-17; postmaster-general 1922-3 and paymaster-general 1923; minister of health 1923, 1924-9, and Aug.-Nov. 1931; chancellor of the exchequer 1923-4 and 1931-7; prime minister and first lord of the treasury 1937-40

69 Curtis to N. Chamberlain, 18 July 1918, copy, GD40/17/33, Lothian Papers

70 Montagu to Chelmsford, 15 June 1918, quoted in Waley, *Edwin Montagu*, 167

71 For the text of the letter see Curtis, *Dyarchy*, 477-81.

72 Montagu to Chelmsford, 4 Feb. 1919, quoted in Waley, *Edwin Montagu*, 195

In the summer of 1919 a Joint Select Committee composed of seven MPS and seven members of the House of Lords under the chairmanship of Lord Selborne was appointed, and heard witnesses and evidence during July, August, and October 1919. Curtis's evidence before this committee was requisitioned in late August, just before the summer recess, giving him an opportunity to summarise his position in a lengthy memorandum which he submitted when giving oral evidence in October.[73] Despite its length the memorandum contained nothing new. Although Curtis took exception to some of the details of the proposed bill, and once again advocated a subdivision of the provinces, he generally agreed with the scheme and defended the gradual extension of responsible government to India. He was satisfied with the Government of India Act of December 1919 which admitted elected Indians to a new central legislature and introduced 'dyarchy' in the provinces.[74] Matters such as education, public health, agriculture, and the extension of local government were 'transferred' to the control of Indian ministers responsible to an Indian electorate while law and order, finance, land revenue, control of the press, and famine relief were 'reserved' to the provincial governor and his executive council. The act also enlarged the provincial legislatures and extended the franchise.

With the passage of the act Indian affairs ceased to be a major concern for the movement. As for the part played by Curtis and the movement in 1916-19 it was one of considerable importance. Although Montagu arrived in India with his own scheme more or less outlined, it was one which had been framed after reading a number of documents, particularly the Duke memorandum. Also, though Montagu's proposals differed very little from Curtis's, the latter's scheme had been published long before Montagu arrived in India, and everyone to whom the secretary of state subsequently spoke was aware of it and had been forced to come to grips with it. It had unquestionably helped sharpen the thinking and arguments surrounding Indian constitutional reform. Montagu himself was always highly conscious of Curtis's ideas and attitudes, a situation heightened by the presence of Meston, Marris, and Duke, all Round Table associates and supporters of Curtis's ideas. However, when it came to the actual drafting of the report Marris had little positive influence and Curtis had left India before the real work began.[75]

73 For the text of Curtis's memorandum see Curtis, *Dyarchy*, 482-552.
74 Curtis to Kerr, 28 Aug. 1918, Curtis Papers. Curtis to Lothian, 6 Aug. 1930, GD40/17/247, Lothian Papers
75 Throughout the war and continuously after it articles or political commentaries on India were published in *The Round Table*. See particularly 'The Montagu-Chelmsford Report,' Sept. 1918, 778-802; and 'Constitutional Reform in India,' Sept. 1919, 706-19.

PUNCH, OR THE LONDON CHARIVARI.—JUNE 25, 1919.

## A REDRESS REHEARSAL.

OUR MR. MONTAGU *(practising on dummy)*. "THE LATEST LINE IN WESTERN HEAD-WEAR, SIR, AND, IF YOU WILL ALLOW ME TO SAY SO, VERY BECOMING TO YOU. THANK YOU, SIR, AND THE NEXT ARTICLE?"

Since the idea of dyarchy was first analysed in an organised way at Round Table meetings, the movement and Curtis must be considered partly responsible for its ultimate acceptance and embodiment in the 1919 act. Curtis himself did an immense amount to publicise the idea of dyarchy both in India and Great Britain and to educate the Indian public about responsible government. What neither he nor the movement seemed to realise, however, was that dyarchy fell far short of Indian expectations. To Congress and the Muslim League it was little more than a gratuitous insult. For them the whole scheme smacked of paternalism and a want of confidence in individual Indians. Curtis and his colleagues did not understand this reaction. The same lack of perspective which prevented them from appreciating the motives of Irish nationalists hampered their approach to India. The London group had always failed to realise how much they were out of touch with local feeling in the overseas empire. They believed in an imperial mission of guidance and education. To the Indians and the Irish, and later the Africans, this civilizing mission smacked of hypocrisy and racialism. Trusteeship left them cold. The London group never properly understood this simple truth.

# 11
# The peace and after

The German peace overtures of October 1918 and the resulting armistice of 11 November had surprised the Round Table movement. The war had not been expected to end much before the summer of 1919, and the members of the central group had given little thought either to the terms of peace or to the possible effect of a peace settlement on the Round Table organisation. They had no detailed plans and no time to prepare any, and their efforts during the peace conference were therefore minimal. Even though Milner as colonial secretary and chairman of the commission appointed to draft the mandates, Kerr as private secretary to Lloyd George, Curtis as an adviser to the British delegation, and Lord Robert Cecil as chairman of the Supreme Economic Council were in important positions, there is no evidence to suggest that they ever asserted Round Table ideas. Nor did Latham,[1] Eggleston, and Garran[2] who were all members, in various minor capacities, of the Australian delegation.[3] George Louis Beer,[4] the movement's principle American

1 John Grieg Latham (1877-1964); GCMG 1935; called to the Victorian bar 1904; lecturer in logic, philosophy, and law, University of Melbourne; member of the Australian delegation Paris Peace Conference 1919; member of the House of Representatives 1922-34; attorney-general 1925-9; and 1931-4; deputy prime minister, minister for external affairs, minister for industry 1931-4; chief justice, High Court of Australia, 1935
2 Robert Randolph Garran (1867-1957); GCMG 1937; knighted 1917; called to the New South Wales bar 1890; secretary, Attorney-General's Department 1901-32, and solicitor-general 1917-32; accompanies W.M. Hughes to the Paris Peace Conference 1919
3 For Garran's recollections of Paris see Garran, *Prosper the Commonwealth.*
4 George Louis Beer (1872-1920); historian and publicist; lecturer in history, Columbia College, 1893-7; regular contributor to *The Round Table* 1915-18; in 1917 joined 'The Inquiry';

associate, was also in Paris as the American expert on colonial affairs, and did on occasion consult Curtis and Cecil about trusteeship and the mandate system. There is no doubt that Beer respected the advice and suggestions of his English friends, but he was very much his own man, and had formulated most of his ideas on colonial problems before leaving the United States. Neither Beer's efforts and successes nor his failures can be attributed to the movement.

All this is not to suggest that the London group did not have some positive ideas about the meaning of the war, and the sort of world they wanted to see emerge after it was over. They were especially concerned with the creation of a concert or league of nations, and the establishment of some system of trusteeship for the protection and guidance of the Turkish and German colonies. In neither instance was the movement the first organisation to express itself on these matters nor were its member particularly original in their ideas. The British Labour party did much more to champion the idea of colonial trusteeship than the movement, while the idea of a league of nations was generally in the air during the war, especially after the publication of President Wilson's Fourteen Points in January 1918.[5] Nevertheless, the movement's continuing interest in these matters, and the fervour and idealism with which it expressed its commitment, gave an added impetus to both concepts, and on one occasion – the publication of Curtis's article 'Windows of Freedom' in the December 1918 issue of *The Round Table* – gave a definite fillip to the idea of a mandates system. The movement had its major wishes fulfilled when both a League of Nations and a mandates system were established by the Peace Conference. But otherwise the end of the war only added to the difficulties which the movement had been experiencing since 1916. The creation of the league, the granting of individual membership in it to the dominions and to India, and the desire of all the dominions after the war to concentrate on their own problems, rather than on those of Europe or the commonwealth, brought the movement's difficulties to a head and forced its members to make the major decision that had been awaited since 1917.

chief of the colonial division of the American delegation, Paris Peace Conference; member of the Mandates Commission; exponent of Anglo-American co-operation

5 For the activities of the British Labour party see Winkler, *The League of Nations Movement*. Leonard Woolf published a book on *International Government* in 1916 which was extensively used by the British government in preparing its proposals for the Versailles conference. For this and Woolf's relationship with Curtis in the latter stages of the war see Woolf, *Beginning Again*, 183-93. See also Egerton, 'The British Government.'

The movement's attitude toward a peace settlement and the postwar situation was based on the principle of the commonwealth and was outlined during the first two years of the war in the pages of *The Round Table*, mainly by Philip Kerr. In his articles Kerr made it clear that the allies had to win a decisive victory over Germany and thus defeat Prussian militarism; only then could the postwar world be shaped along democratic lines and a concert of nations formed. Although he wrote often and repetitively on this subject, Kerr never outlined detailed plans for such a concert and neither did his colleagues.

From the beginning of the war the movement argued that permanent peace could not be imposed on the world by any one dominant national power.[6] Some nations would always revolt in the name of liberty. Equally, peace would never be assured simply by establishing an international council. In a crisis certain nations would refuse to recognise a superior foreign will. It would therefore be necessary to try and reconcile nationalism and liberty. The first step would be to secure in the peace settlement the fullest possible recognition of the rights of nationalist minorities and small independent states. But the cult of the little-nation school ought not to be pressed too far; smallness was a disadvantage both to the small nation itself and to all larger neighbour states. It was obvious to the movement that the larger and fewer the national sovereignties the fewer the points of friction, the simpler the issues, and the easier the acceptance and application of common ideas. Logically, the final step would be the creation of a world state. It would end war because it would extend the obligation of service from a race or a nation to mankind, because it would create a responsible and representative political authority which would consider every problem presented to it from the point of view of humanity and not from that of a single state or people, and because when that authority had embodied its decision in law it would be able to call upon the citizens of the whole world to obey it; and, if need be, to enforce obedience to it.[7]

Kerr was sufficiently realistic to know that for the time being the movement's goal was not practical politics. But he and his colleagues felt there was undeniable good sense in aiming at the creation of an international system based upon the principle of law, rather than acquiescing in a return to an international system based on the balance of forces. One would lead to a closer association between the great nations, and the other back to war. Be-

---

6 For the first public discussion of the problem by the movement see 'Nationalism and Liberty,' *The Round Table*, Dec. 1914, 18-69.

7 This argument was best developed by Kerr in 'The End of War,' ibid., Sept. 1915, 772-96.

lieving this, the London group argued that any political gathering after the war would have to have three characteristics.[8] It would need to include leading statesmen from all the great powers or it would fail in its purpose; it would have to meet at regular intervals and have a proper constitution because the idea of co-operation would gradually lapse as the nations became preoccupied with their own affairs; and the constitution would have to be such that even the most controversial question could be brought before it. The only body which could meet these needs would be a concert of nations. Its essential principle would be that its members, while surrendering none of their sovereign independence, would recognise that they were partners in a greater unity who had to deliberate together in order to promote the welfare of the whole. The concert would not be a parliament and would have no legislative, executive, or military power, and no member-state would be bound by anything save its own voluntary assent to a treaty or agreement. Although the concert would not always ensure peace, it would be the beginning of the end of war.

All through the group's arguments ran the idealism of the principle of the commonwealth. The members, especially men like Zimmern, Kerr, and Curtis, were convinced that the world could learn a great deal from the British system of government. For this reason they continually used the British commonwealth as an example of the world state they envisaged. For them the British method of uniting nationalities freely within a larger unit, which secured their common interests without denying their individual rights, appeared the only sure road of progress towards a policy in which the rights of all peoples would be securely fixed.[9] Undoubtedly the movement had a noble aim. Certainly Kerr and his colleagues sincerely believed in it. But their analogy would not have stood up to close examination. In this, as in so much else, Kerr and Curtis had grossly idealised and inflated the imperial experience. It is doubtful that many people in the commonwealth would have thought of it in quite the same way.

From December 1916 Philip Kerr was kept busy as Lloyd George's secretary. His duties absorded him and he had little time to write for *The Round Table*; however, he did remain a member of the editorial committee, attended moots when he could, and kept up a protracted correspondence with

8 [Philip Kerr], 'The Harvest of War,' ibid., Dec. 1915, 1-32; [Philip Kerr], 'The War for Public Right,' ibid., March 1916, 193-231; and [Philip Kerr], 'The Principle of Peace,' ibid., June 1916, 391-429
9 The movement's ideas were outlined in many articles in *The Round Table*; see especially [Philip Kerr], 'War Aims,' Sept. 1916, 607-13; [Philip Kerr], 'The Making of the Peace,' Dec. 1916, 1-13; and [L. Curtis?], 'The Imperial Dilemma,' Sept. 1916, 688-712.

members all over the globe, particularly with the wandering Curtis. Kerr's departure meant far fewer references to 'the peace and after' in the quarterly, and little additional comment on the role of the commonwealth. Coupland, the new editor, shared many of the ideals of Kerr and Curtis, but was inclined to be a more prosaic writer. Few of the lead articles had the same idealistic flavour and fervour as in Kerr's day as editor. The only continuing comment on the concept of a league was that of George Louis Beer in his articles on the United States. He carefully followed the organisation and progress of the 'League to Enforce Peace,' which had been established in the United States, and the various declarations of President Wilson; however, his articles were more political chronicles than interpretive or suggestive essays.[10] For over a year there was virtually no comment from the English or dominion writers, and no evidence to suggest that the central group was devoting any of the few moots it was able to assemble to an examination of the peace settlement or the projected league of nations.

This situation changed during 1918. By the beginning of the year, Philip Kerr had formed definite opinions on the shape of a future league, and he was supported by the majority of the London group. He believed it should be a functional, consultative body based on the development of the agencies of allied wartime co-operation, particularly the Supreme War Council. He did not favour a postwar league held together by solemn covenants and resting on sanctions.[11] These ideas were in keeping with an important body of British opinion which believed – unlike Woodrow Wilson and various pro-league pressure groups – that a league based on obligatory collective international action infringed the doctrine of national sovereignty. Throughout 1918 this viewpoint was given considerable coverage in *The Round Table*, and was the major contribution of the movement to the debate over the league of nations.[12]

10 See particularly [G.L. Beer], 'The United States and the Future Peace,' ibid., March 1917, 285-317; and [G.L.B.], 'America's Entrance into the War,' ibid., June 1917, 491-514. Kerr did not write again for the quarterly until June 1918, and then on 'The Irish Crisis.'

11 For Kerr's views see Maurice Hankey's diary entry for 6 December 1917, Roskill, *Hankey*, I, 469.

12 Lloyd George was attracted by Kerr's arguments and in December 1918 succeeded in convincing the War Cabinet of their merits. But Lord Robert Cecil, the British representative in negotiations with Woodrow Wilson, favoured a league based on the principle of sanctions. Therefore, despite a last-minute attempt by Lloyd George to dissuade Cecil – using material prepared by Kerr – it was the Wilson-Cecil concept of the league which triumphed rather than that favoured by Lloyd George and the Round Table movement. See [P.H.K.], 'League of Nations,' GD40/17/54, Lothian Papers; and Lord Cecil's Diary for the British Delegation, Paris, 31 January 1919, Additional MSS, 51131, Cecil Papers. For a comprehensive treatment of Britain and the creation of the league see Egerton, 'The British Government.' Perti-

A second major war-time interest of the movement was the future of the defeated powers' colonies, especially those of Germany. The members of the Round Table had long been concerned about the relations of East and West. They had often argued that the superior position of the European in the world involved not a privilege but 'a special obligation to serve' the lesser races in order to help them bridge the civilisation line.[13] Before the war Curtis claimed that the portion of humanity that could not govern itself was a trust of all civilised nations – especially of the British commonwealth which, he claimed, most understood the meaning of freedom and liberty.[14] He did not believe that 'the backward races' should be treated as instruments but as ends in themselves, and should be included in the commonwealth and recognised as co-heirs of self-government. They might, as yet, be unequal to the task, but in time they would rise to it.[15] Early in the war Philip Kerr added his voice to Curtis's. Mankind, he pointed out, was 'divided into a graduated scale varying infinitely, from the zenith of civilisation to the nadir of barbarism.' But just as there were differences in the level of civilisation, so there was imposed upon the more civilised peoples the duty of helping their backward neighbours to rise to the highest level. The advanced nations must assume responsibility for the government of the backward people, and educate them to such a point of civilisation and self-control that they would be able to maintain law and order, liberty and justice for themselves. But the government of dependencies was a trust; therefore dependencies could not be treated as the preserve of the ruling powers. All other nations would have to have an equal title to trade and communication with the dependency subject to whatever restrictions were necessary for the welfare of the inhabitants. As the world was knit closer together this principle of the open door would be of increasing importance. Although the responsible nation would obviously have to be free to impose whatever dues were necessary on foreign commerce in order to protect the prosperity of the dependency, it clearly must not take advantage of its position of trust. Kerr argued that 'The peoples responsible for the government of dependencies are trustees not for themselves only, nor

nent articles in *The Round Table* are: [R. Coupland], 'Freedom and Unity,' Dec. 1917, 85-99; 'The victory that will End the War,' March 1918, 221-37; 'The Unity of Civilisation,' Sept. 1918, 679-84; and [A. Zimmern], 'Some Principles and Problems of Settlement,' Dec. 1918, 88-113. Kerr did not comment on the war and the peace conference until September 1919 in 'The Harvest of Victory,' and not until March 1920 did he consider 'The British Empire, the League of Nations and the United States.'
13  See particularly Curtis, 'A Practical Enquiry.'
14  Curtis, *The Project of a Commonwealth*, 173-4, 176-8
15  Ibid., 690-1

for the inhabitants only, but for all mankind. Their function is to uphold the banner of liberty and civilisation and progress in these backward parts until their inhabitants can do so for themselves. To fail or falter in this work is to betray a trust which is laid upon them ... The duties of trusteeship are not fulfilled merely by the introduction of law and order, education and material development. The only real justification for alien rule is that it should lead to the elevation of the backward peoples in the scale of civilisation more rapidly and at less cost of needless suffering than any other way.'[16]

By 1915 Kerr was drawing attention in the pages of *The Round Table* to the problems which might arise over the disposition of the German and Turkish colonies if the Allies should win. What was to be done? Kerr suggested that those peoples incapable of governing themselves should be administered by a world government until they were sufficiently educated. As for those states higher in the scale of civilisation, it was not an easy decision; but it would seem that the external relations and such internal acts as would affect the rest of mankind would have to be controlled from above until the states were admitted to a share of the responsibility for world government. It would be pointless to admit them immediately, but 'to deprive the intermediate peoples of the responsibility of self-government would be to set back the hands of the clock of progress.'[17] Two years later, in December 1917, George Louis Beer, now a member of the special organisation known as the 'Inquiry' established by President Wilson to prepare for future peace negotiations, was advocating a mandate system under which 'the state exercising sovereignty in Africa is proceeding under an international mandate and must act as trustee primarily for the nations and secondarily for the outside world as a whole.'[18] At the same time Kerr was writing to Smuts in a similar vein: 'Personally I am against handing back the colonies, but I am of this opinion because I am sure it is contrary to the best interest both of the inhabitants and of the world that they should be given back to a nation inspired by Prussian ideals, and because I think it is better in every way that they should be attached to a neighbouring free power, e.g. German South West Africa to South Africa, or to a power which has a great colonial experience, e.g. Britain or France, or be internationalised.'[19]

During the early months of 1918 Beer continued to prepare the American

16 Philip Kerr, 'The Political Relations'
17 [Philip Kerr] 'The End of War,' *The Round Table,* Sept. 1915, 772-96; also [Philip Kerr], 'The Foundations of Peace,' ibid., June 1915, 589-625
18 Quoted in Gelfand, *The Inquiry,* 232
19 Kerr to Smuts, 14 Dec. 1917, printed in Hancock and Van Der Poel, eds., *Smuts Papers,* III, 576-7

position on the colonial question and to elaborate his ideas about a mandate system; he was aided to some extent by newspaper clippings and memoranda forwarded at his request by the Melbourne branch of the movement.[20] He discussed these questions, and the possibility of the United States accepting mandates in Africa in correspondence with Curtis, Coupland, and Lord Eustace Percy,[21] an associate of the movement, during the summer of 1918.[22] When it became clear that the war was near its end Kerr, who had been kept informed of Beer's activities, became greatly concerned about the manner in which the problem of politically backward peoples would be treated at the peace conference. A particular worry was the attitude of the United States. He outlined his concern in a lengthy letter to Lionel Curtis in October 1918.[23] The difficulties, as Kerr saw them, arose from the fact that there was a fundamentally different concept in regard to the matter between Great Britain and South Africa on the one side, and the United States and Canada and to some extent Australia on the other. He elaborated to Curtis:

I need not of course expound our view as to the necessity for some civilised control over politically backward peoples because you were the first person to propound it. Briefly it is that the inhabitants of Africa and parts of Asia have proved unable to govern themselves, not because they were inherently incapable of maintaining any kind of stable society if left to themselves, but because they were quite unable to withstand the demoralising influences to which they were subjected in [sic] some civilised countries, so that the intervention of an European power is necessary in order to protect them from those influences and give them time and opportunity in which to establish a form of self-government which is strong enough to withstand them. The American view ... is quite different. America still has a childlike faith in the virtues of democracy and *laisser faire* and, unfortunately, Wilson who today is absolute dictator of American public opinion appears to share this view.

Kerr thought this situation a difficult one because it would hamper the disposition of the German colonies and the Belgian Congo. But of most concern was the need, in the face of the still existent demoralising influences and

20 Coupland to Laby, 25 May 1918, Laby Papers
21 Eustace Percy, 1st Baron Percy of Newcastle, cr 1953 (1887-1958); politician and educationist; joined the diplomatic service 1909; Washington embassy 1910-14; Foreign Office 1914-18; assistant to Lord Robert Cecil at the Paris Peace Conference 1919; MP (C) 1921-37; minister of health 1923-4; president of the Board of Education 1924-9
22 Shotwell, *At the Paris Peace Conference*, 90 n2. Shotwell was also a member of the 'Inquiry.'
23 Kerr to Curtis, 15 Oct. 1918, Curtis Papers

new scourge of Bolshevism, for the Western powers to make themselves definitely responsible 'for seeing that the disorders which are likely to follow this war in these backward lands do not go beyond a certain point.' Kerr believed the extent of this work after the war, 'sometimes known as the white man's burden,' would be so vast that it would not be accomplished unless the allies shared it. But America appeared to have no understanding of the problem, but rather believed 'that the assumption of this kind of responsibility is iniquitous imperialism.'

You can see what an immense difference it is going to make whether America comes to learn its responsibility in regard to this matter quickly or slowly. If they are slow in learning we shall be condemned to a period not only of chaos in these backward countries but of strained relations between the various parts of the English-speaking world. On the other hand if only we can get into the heads of Canadians and Americans that a share in the burden of world government is just as great and glorious a responsibility as participation in the war, you at once remove the last great barrier to an Anglo-Saxon understanding and give to the whole English-speaking world a common task in the execution of which they can cooperate.

Kerr wanted Curtis to go to the States and talk to journalists and politicians, and even to Wilson if he could, in order to familiarise them with an aspect of the peace problem 'of which they are up to date absolutely unconscious.' But Curtis was too busy to leave England. Instead, he devoted some of his energies in late 1918 to preparing an article on the subject entitled 'Windows of Freedom.' It was published in the December issue of *The Round Table*, and outlined both the principles of a trusteeship system and reminded the United States of its responsibilities.[24] What, asked Curtis, was to be the effect of the victory on Asia, Africa, and the hundreds of Pacific islands? In the end, of course, 'the effect must be that they too will achieve the arts of governing themselves.'[25] But how soon that end could be reached would depend upon a right understanding by the free nations of the delicate and complex nature of the problem, the crux of which lay in the fact that none of the territories outside Europe detached by the war from the German and Turkish empires could in the near future provide peace, order, and good government for themselves. How to provide government for these territories was, so Curtis believed, 'the most difficult of the questions which the Conference has to face.' Curtis thought anyone wanting to solve this problem

24 [Lionel Curtis], 'Windows of Freedom,' *The Round Table*, Dec. 1918, 1-47
25 Ibid., 21

would have to elaborate certain principles in the hope that they would be recognised. Curtis outlined his:

1  That the maintenance of peace, order, and good government in these territories must be guaranteed.

2  That where their inhabitants are not as yet able to furnish this guarantee, some democratic power shall be made responsible for creating and maintaining peace, order, and good government for their territory, subject to conditions laid down in treaties, for the observance of which the guardian state shall be held responsible to the League of Nations.

3  That such treaties shall include covenants binding the guardian State:

(a) To maintain equality of opportunity to the traders of all nations;

(b) To prohibit forced labour in any shape or form;

(c) To prohibit the liquor traffic;

(d) To abstain from organising native troops except for the purpose of guarding or policing their own territory;

(e) To direct its policy towards fitting the people to govern themselves.[26]

Any trusteeship power that transgressed its privileges would have to answer to the league. Curtis thought that German South-West Africa should become a part of South Africa. As for the rest of the German and Turkish territories, the South Pacific Islands were too primitive to be given independence; it would not be in their own interest. But neither should they be annexed by any power. The only solution to the dilemma was for the peace conference, in the interests of the islanders and of the world at large, to commission a competent power to govern the islands subject to treaties. The power would be responsible to the League of Nations for the observance of the treaties. The only power so qualified, despite its immense burdens, was the British commonwealth. As for West Africa, either the French or the British should be made responsible to the League of Nations for the German colonies there; and the United States should be responsible for Liberia. The latter problem was particularly pressing, and the United States could not avoid her world responsibility by refusing the task. In fact, said Curtis, it was time for America to consider her role in matters such as these:

In tropical Africa, as in the Pacific, the only hope of these races who cannot as yet govern themselves of ever learning to do so is in tutelage by some great democratic civilised nation. Once for all the League of Nations will render obsolete the old pernicious idea of empire, rightly abhorrent to American tradition. The duty of external

26  Ibid., 25-6

government can now once for all be placed on its right footing of trusteeship to society at large, if at this juncture the greatest and wealthiest of all democratic nations will not shrink from assuming her share. Is it too much to ask that in this crisis of human destiny America shall forget to think of herself, and think rather of those infinitely wider interests ... Having put her hand to the plough, can she look back? Can she now shrink from the dignity of her calling? Can she now go back to the plea that American interests are the dominating principle of her policy?[27]

Curtis thought not, and hoped that the United States would make herself answerable to the League of Nations for peace, order, and good government in some or all of the regions of the Middle East. An American assumption of responsibility in the Middle and Near East would have a beneficial effect on Russia as well as on the indigenous peoples; 'for order, no less than anarchy, is infectious.'

Shortly after arriving in London in December 1918, Beer took two of the American delegates, General Bliss[28] and Colonel House,[29] to see Curtis. Both men were impressed by the prophet's arguments, but the final decision had to come from Wilson. In January 1919 Beer and Curtis lunched with Louis Aubert, one of the technical experts in the French delegation, and discussed the problem with him. Finally on 30 January, Wilson stated that he was prepared to have the United States accept mandates. At first glance this appeared to be a remarkable victory for Beer and the movement, but they were soon disillusioned. Wilson made no great effort in following months to obtain a mandate for the United States.[30] Thus the movement failed in its endeavour to prick the American conscience.

On the whole, however, the movement was pleased with the results of the peace conference. A League of Nations was agreed upon and inaugurated on 10 January 1920, and all seemed well for the future until the American Senate virtually sealed the league's fate. Also, a mandates system was established under the supervision of the league. The mandates were given an A, B, or C classification depending upon their political maturity, a system which

27 Ibid., 32-3
28 General Tasker Howard Bliss (1853-1930); American military representative on Supreme War Council, Versailles, 1917-19; member of the American Commission at the Paris Peace Conference 1918-19
29 Edward Mandell House (1858-1938); personal representative of President Wilson to the European governments 1914, 1915, and 1916; special representative of the United States government at the Inter-Allied Conference of Premiers and Foreign Ministers 1917; United States representative at the Armistice 1918; member of the Commission on Mandates 1919
30 For the above account see Louis, 'The United States and the African Peace Settlement of 1919.'

roughly corresponded with the ideas of Curtis and Kerr. The establishment of the trusteeship system, however, was more a division of the spoils among the victors than the noble implementation of an ideal, and most decisions were made for strategic or political reasons. The idealism which pervaded all the Round Table arguments and appeals was missing from the debates and deliberations over the establishment of a mandate system. The text of the mandates was finally published in January 1921 and all were confirmed by late 1924.

The actual effect that the movement or its members had on the peace conference as a whole is difficult to determine, though one can probably safely say it was very little. Kerr usually acted solely in his capacity as secretary to Lloyd George, although he was responsible, after many sessions with Lloyd George and Smuts, for the final draft of the mandates article of the League of Nations. But even this seemingly important task was the shadow not the substance of power.[31] Curtis, whatever he might have wished, rarely had the opportunity for behind-the-scenes intrigue. Shortly after his conversation with Beer and Aubert he suffered a nervous breakdown and departed for Morocco to recuperate. Milner was, of course, at the heart of things and deeply involved. He wrote numerous memoranda, and had many discussions with representatives of the dominions, the United States, and the European powers. As chairman of the commission established by the Principle Allied and Associated Powers in June 1919 to draft the mandates he was in a commanding position. He often met with Lord Robert Cecil, Kerr, and Curtis while in Paris and undoubtedly discussed the progress of the various talks and possibly their relationship to Round Table ideas, but there is no evidence that he carried those ideas with him into conference or expounded them to his government colleagues. If anything, Milner plunged into the murky depths of strategic and geo-political discussions with more enthusiasm than Curtis or Kerr would have wanted.[32]

The movement's part in achieving a League of Nations and a mandates system should not be exaggerated. Neither idea originated with the move-

31 For a general assessment of the Round Table movement's role on the mandates question see Elizabeth Monroe, 'The Round Table and the Middle Eastern Peace Settlement 1917-22,' *The Round Table*, Nov. 1970, 479-90. Stephen Roskill and L.F. Fitzhardinge argue that Smuts, Latham, and Hankey invented the device of the 'Class C' League of Nations mandate at the British Empire Delegation meeting on 29 January 1919. See Roskill, *Hankey*, II, 54; and Fitzhardinge, 'W.M. Hughes.'

32 See in this context Louis, 'Great Britain and the African Peace Settlement.' One can follow Cecil's activities in Paris in his diary. It is unrevealing about the movement. See Lord Cecil's Diary of the British Delegation. Paris. Jan. 6-June 10, 1919; Nov. 22-Dec. 6, 1920, Additional 51131, Cecil Papers

ment, and by the time it took them up early in the war they were already 'in the air,' subjects of wide discussion and speculation. The merit of the movement's activity was that it provided a continuous and serious discussion of the merits of a league and of trusteeship. The idealism underlying the arguments in *The Round Table* was compelling and attracted wide attention wherever the quarterly was read in the English-speaking world. It had certainly influenced Smuts before he drafted his memorable paper *The League of Nations: A Practical Suggestion* in December 1918.[33] But on the few occasions when members of the movement did try to exert some personal influence, it was usually without success.

This whole episode was highly revealing of the movement. Like their involvement in India it laid bare their attitudes toward colonies and dependencies. The members, particularly the London group, openly believed in the inherent worth of 'the white man's burden' and the civilizing mission. They never adequately scrutinised the suggestion that trusteeship and a mandate system might shield another form of 'iniquitous imperialism.' They never associated their ideals with physical or spiritual exploitation. They therefore found it easy to dismiss such ideas. This attitude was yet another example of the underlying paradox of the movement; on the one hand, they were motivated and governed by high ideals; on the other, they were often divorced from everyday reality. The members never fully understood that trusteeship might be a cover for big-power strategy; nor did they appreciate the strength and driving force of local feeling which would not rest content with second or third class status.

Once it was clear that both a League of Nations and a mandates system were going to be created by the peace conference, the members of the movement began to consider the impact of the war and the probable effect of the league on the British commonwealth and on their own organisation.[34] The war, of course, had had a disastrous effect on the movement. This was particularly so in Canada, and Glazebrook was quite frank about the unpopularity of the movement in the northern dominion: 'In its first stage as a more or less esoteric movement appealing to a rather picked lot of young men it was admirable, but nearly all of them were withdrawn to the war and those who took their places were of a far inferior material. The appeal that we made to the general public was useful so far as it went and did something to avert the

33 In this paper Smuts did not recommend the application of the mandates scheme to Africa.
34 At one stage it had been suggested that Curtis run for Parliament in the postwar election; but in the end the London group decided Curtis's services were more valuable outside Parliament. For Curtis's ruminations on this see Curtis to Kerr, 28 Aug. 1918, Curtis Papers.

collapse that threatened us through the publication of Curtis' dogmatic insistence, in the last part of his book, on all the things that happen to be like a red flag to a bull to the average Canadian.'[35] The Canadian organisation, despite valiant efforts in 1917-18, had never really recovered from the death of Edward Kylie. The Executive Committee set up under Walker, although successful in some ways, lacked Kylie's imagination, enthusiasm, and conviction. It was only with great difficulty that the regular article for *The Round Table* was prepared, and group criticism had ceased to exist.[36]

In Australia the Sydney and Melbourne groups had continued to supply a quarterly article of high quality throughout the war, mainly through the adoption of the method of group criticism. Many of the London members, Coupland especially, considered the Australian article one of the best parts of *The Round Table*. But apart from this success, the Australian organisation had suffered from many of the same problems as the Canadian branch. It had lost many of its members to the war and the publication of *The Problem* had aroused some fears in Australia. Despite all their efforts, the original members had found it difficult to establish the 'centres' agreed upon in 1916-17. A general conference of the Australian groups had been held in Sydney in June 1918 at which the overall objectives of the movement and those of the local organisation had been examined and agreement reached on the need for a large-scale Round Table convention after the war to resolve whether the movement should become openly propagandist or attempt to adhere to the principles of study and research. The members, like their counterparts in Great Britain, Canada, and New Zealand, were finding it difficult to draw the fine line between propaganda and education. The Australians had also decided to broaden the purposes of their organisation and to consider Australia's problems and position in an international rather than just a commonwealth setting. These decisions and the searching discussion which preceded them in the three-day meeting had indicated that at the executive level the Australians could muster a commitment and enthusiasm no longer possible in Canada. But this zeal was very difficult to translate into grass-roots activity, and in following months the Australian Round Table situation did not noticeably improve.[37]

By early 1919 the movement's entire organisation was languishing. There was still some activity among the original members in Melbourne and

35 Glazebrook to Milner, 21 May 1918, Glazebrook Papers
36 See Latham to Laby, 20 June 1918, Laby Papers
37 For the Australian meeting see 'Agenda Paper and Minutes of Conference of Groups, 1, 2, 3 June 1918,' Harrison Moore Papers. Also 'Report of the Activities of the Round Table in Australia during 1918,' ibid.

Sydney, but there was no wide-flung group system in Australia and no hope of one being established. In Canada the situation was far worse; there the whole organisation was on the verge of collapse. In South Africa the Round Table position had never been strong, and there was little chance of it becoming so now that the war was over. In India the few groups that had been founded during Curtis's visit soon collapsed when all members of the Indian Civil Service were forbidden to become members. Despite assurances that the ban would be lifted it never was, and the movement did not recover its toe-hold on the subcontinent.

Even in New Zealand, where the movement had flourished in the early years, the war had dealt a damaging blow. In 1919 the extensive programme of operations suggested by Curtis in 1916 remained unfulfilled. Rather than extending their operations and throwing out offshoots, the original groups now met infrequently, had fewer active members, and accomplished little work. Not half a dozen members had been found in the whole of New Zealand to contribute papers for discussion, and there was no great consensus of opinion on the lines of imperial development. The general difficulties facing the movement were best summed up by a member of the Wellington group:

Since Curtis's departure, there has been little demand for the Problem of the Commonwealth or the Commonwealth of Nations and the attitude of the public, like that of many of the members of the groups, has been of apathy. The result is that those who are believers in a federal system are handicapped in their efforts to do propaganda work, as they are scattered, find it difficult to communicate with each other, and in some of the groups are regarded as impractical idealists or else too logical for human nature's daily food. There is too much of a tendency to regard the Round Table member as a politician considering what course or compromise he can induce the House or his constituents to accept rather than as a missionary whose duty it is to discover and point out the truth no matter how unpopular or unpalatable it may be at the moment.[38]

Another problem confronting the movement was that of finance. All the details of Round Table financing may never be known, but for most of its first ten years it had relied primarily on the generosity of Sir Abe Bailey, Lady Wantage, Lord Lovat, Lord Salisbury, Lord Selborne, Lord Anglesey,

---

38 Undated and unsigned memorandum on the state of the Round Table organisation in New Zealand. Written in 1919 by a member of the Wellington group it was kindly shown to the author by Sir John Ilott, a member of the Wellington group for over fifty years.

and the Rhodes Trust which, through Lord Milner, had agreed to match all private donations on a £ to £ basis in the initial years. The contributions had varied in amount and in duration, and there had been a need in 1913 to make an appeal for funds. On occasion friends of the movement or supporters of Round Table ideals had made private donations. But by the end of the war the situation was again pressing, and by early 1919 the London group found it necessary to make a further appeal in order to keep *The Round Table* magazine alive.[39]

Without waiting to hear what response their appeal aroused, the London members pressed ahead with plans for the general Round Table convention rescheduled for London in December. They realised that the war had had an enormous influence on the dominions, arousing them to a greater awareness of foreign affairs than ever before, and making it virtually impossible for them to return to their prewar positions of isolation. The war had also catapulted the dominions into the centres of power, as members of the Imperial War Cabinet and the British Empire Delegation. In Paris they had been recognised as separate entities by the other powers with the right of separate attendance at meetings of the peace conference. When the League of Nations was established the dominions and India were given individual membership. All this was a far cry from their prewar condition. Such rapid and momentous changes posed problems for the movement. They were forced to re-examine the relationship of the dominions with the commonwealth, to analyse the future effect of the league on the commonwealth, and to examine their own aims and purposes in a strange new world. In April 1919 the London members submitted a tentative agenda to the dominion groups. There were two major subjects posed for discussion: first, a reconsideration of the constitutional relations between the various parts of the British commonwealth in light of (a) the circumstances in which war had been declared, (b) the conduct of war, (c) the peace negotiations in Paris, (d) the projected League of Nations, and (e) the various developments in imperial constitutional practice since the outbreak of the war; and second, a re-examination of the future of the movement. The central group invited criticism and further ideas from the dominion organisations.[40]

39 On 30 January 1919 Milner, Hichens, Brand, Coupland, and Holland-Martin met to discuss the finances of the movement. See Milner diary, 30 Jan. 1919, vol. 282, Milner Papers; see also a memorandum circulated to all the dominion groups summarising the movement's precarious position and the merits of *The Round Table*. See undated 'Memorandum,' GD40/17/33, Lothian Papers.

40 Coupland to Laby, 11 April 1919, copy, Harrison Moore Papers. The London group carried its appeal for a constitutional conference into *The Round Table*. See 'The League of Nations and the British Commonwealth,' *The Round Table*, June 1919, 468-94.

By early June there had been some response to the Round Table appeal for funds. Sir Joseph Flavelle, for one, undertook to provide £200 to £300 a year for five years, the exact amount to be decided upon after he had completed his private canvas.[41] But on the whole the movement was finding it difficult to function efficiently, to maintain communications with its members, and to tackle the problems outlined in their memoranda. This, as Brand explained to Flavelle, was especially true of the London group: 'Curtis has been ill in Paris: Kerr has been left in Paris to look after Arthur Balfour, now that Lloyd George has left: Grigg is going to Canada with the Prince of Wales at the beginning of August: Malcolm is just off to South Africa for the Chartered Company: Hichens and I are both absolutely full up with ordinary work: Zimmern has now taken on a job at a Welsh University, and so at the moment we are finding it very difficult either to reformulate our policy in the light of the war or to set about collecting a fund, but we hope that in two or three months our most important members shall be freer to devote time to the work, so that our difficulties should only be temporary.'[42]

But Brand was too optimistic. In late August Coupland complained that 'the Round Table people seem to be even busier now than they were during the war ...'[43] and the following month Grigg, travelling through Canada on the Prince of Wales's tour, painted a gloomy picture of the Round Table organisation in the northern dominion. He was convinced that the organisation in Canada 'should run itself and take its own line.' The London group should just supply information when it was needed. He even suggested that 'the right course here will be for each centre to allow the old Round Table groups to disappear, and to form Commonwealth Clubs on their own lines instead.' He spoke frankly to Glazebrook about the difficulties facing the London group; and as for *The Round Table*, 'I really do not know how London manages to keep the Magazine going. It is a miracle that the Magazine appears at all.'[44]

Obviously the London members thought the same way, and in late October and early November 1919 a number of discussions were held by the moot on the future of the movement and the best method of running *The Round Table*. Although they intended to continue the quarterly in one form or another, Brand could not be very specific when writing to Flavelle in late October.[45] Certainly Brand did not hold any hopes for getting Kerr back as

41 Flavelle to A.F. Park, 4 July 1919, and Flavelle to Brand, 4 July 1919, box 5, Flavelle Papers
42 Brand to Flavelle, 16 July 1919, ibid.
43 Coupland to Willison, 21 Aug. 1919, Willison Papers
44 Grigg to Glazebrook, 27 Sept. 1919, copy, ibid.
45 Brand to Flavelle, 30 Oct. 1919, box 5, Flavelle Papers

editor. 'In any case,' he wrote, 'we shall all of us, including [Kerr], take a part in running it, and we shall no doubt find the right man to do the editing very shortly. We shall have to reconsider our policy also in the light of after the war conditions, and we are engaged now in preparing a Statement.'

In Canada by this time attention was beginning to turn toward League of Nations clubs, although Glazebrook who was much interested in that development still wrote hopefully that the Round Table might be able to begin again on a small scale with some of the good young men returning from the war.[46] In Australia the long-delayed conference of groups was held in Melbourne late in September. The delegates decided that the Australian groups should be composed of people with a variety of views and that the movement should not become committed to any one scheme of imperial organisation or involved in propaganda. Imperial federation was rejected, but their belief in imperial unity was reaffirmed, providing it followed the consultative methods established during the meetings of the Imperial War Cabinet and Imperial War conferences. The Australians planned to use their existing groups as centres for the discussion of imperial and international problems and the preparation of articles for the quarterly. No plans were made to establish further groups.[47]

By November the movement's difficulties over *The Round Table* were partially resolved when Geoffrey Dawson, who had recently resigned as editor of Northcliffe's *Times*, agreed to assume the editorship of the quarterly. Dawson had hopes of devoting much more time to the review than he had in previous years. He also recognised the need for a much stronger organisation than the London group had been able to manage in the past few months. He admitted to Willison that 'all of us hope that Philip Kerr will some day have leisure to return to it.' Despite his good intentions, Dawson was unable to give the time to the quarterly that he had hoped, and in early 1920 John Dove was brought in as assistant editor.[48]

This partial solution to the problems of the quarterly did not lessen the other difficulties confronting the movement, and at the end of the year Li-

46 See Glazebrook to Milner, 7 Oct. 1919, Glazebrook Papers; and Glazebrook to Milner, 24 Nov. 1919, copy, Walker Papers.

47 See 'Order Paper' for the conference 20 and 21 Sept. 1919 and 'Minutes of Conference of Groups,' 20 and 21 Sept. 1919, Harrison Moore Papers. See also notice of meeting of Victorian group, 23 June 1919; 'Memorandum on Conference of Groups' by Laby 24 June 1919; notice of meeting of Victorian group, 7 July 1919; minutes of meeting of Victorian group, 18 Aug. 1919, and notice of meeting of Victorian group, 1 Sept. 1919, ibid.

48 Dawson to Willison, 11 Feb. 1920, Willison Papers. Geoffrey Robinson had changed his name to Dawson in 1917.

onel Curtis wrote at length to the dominion groups outlining the result of the recent deliberations of the London members.[49] He was frank about the pressures on the movement and its members in England during the previous year. He explained that he was only just beginning to get his head above water after suffering a breakdown and being involved in giving evidence to the joint committee appointed to consider the India bill. He admitted that ever since Kerr had gone as private secretary to Lloyd George the Round Table had been 'living simply from hand to mouth' so far as the quarterly was concerned, and it had naturally suffered the consequences. For the past few numbers there had been practically no editor, and the strain of keeping it going was the main factor in his own collapse. The object of his letter was to ask for the patience of the dominion groups to allow the London moot to put things into shape and to permit them to cancel the formal Round Table conference scheduled for the end of the year. Great pressure, travelling difficulties, and the preoccupation of members in other work made a convention impossible. Curtis still believed that the principles he had put forward in 1916 were as true as ever, perhaps more so, but the world was such a new one that the whole problem needed restating, especially in the light of the League of Nations. He did not believe the league would be effective in maintaining the freedom of the world unless the British commonwealth achieved some organic unity, but the problem wanted working out carefully and restating in a book like *The Problem of the Commonwealth*. He had revised his attitude about one thing, however, and that was propaganda. He now believed Round Table action on the imperial question should be confined to research, for there was nothing really to be done in the way of propaganda in Great Britain. If the dominions were prepared to share the burden and control of foreign affairs no party would refuse the offer. But the offer must come from the dominions, and 'any propagandist action on the subject which has its main-spring in London, whatever its immediate effects on the Dominions may be, tends ultimately to produce an even stronger reaction in the Dominions, especially in Canada and Australia. I am convinced that our only sound contribution to the problem will consist in maintaining a supply of information.'[50]

At this time Curtis was deeply involved in establishing the Institute of International Affairs in London, an organisation he had helped to found

49 See Curtis to Dominion Secretaries, 29 Nov. 1919, Harrison Moore Papers.
50 See also a valuable letter Curtis to Witherby, Sept. 1919, copy, ibid. By this time Kerr was becoming despondent about the league in the aftermath of the American withdrawal; he thought the Covenant 'aimed too high and too far.' See [Philip Kerr], 'The British Empire, the League and the United States,' *The Round Table*, March 1920, 221-53.

while in Paris, and when possible he was filling in for Craik at the Commonwealth Trust.[51] Milner and Amery were still at the Colonial Office with little time for Round Table affairs, and Philip Kerr was kept busy as ever as Lloyd George's secretary. Edward Grigg was also occupied on the Prince of Wales's tour. However, he took advantage of a sojourn in Wellington in May 1920 to have a long talk with Von Haast about the movement,[52] and on his return to England he drafted a memorandum on the Round Table and the imperial question, underlining the differences between the problems of 1920 and those of the prewar and early war period. He pointed out that the German menace had disappeared and that closer union no longer commanded much attention or support; instead a looser relationship was being discussed. Before the war the Round Table had said 'The Empire is in danger; we must therefore unite.' This would no longer do. Also the old Round Table method of arguing from the whole to the parts was deeply suspect throughout the dominions as a method of thought which took insufficient account of dominion aspirations. Circumstances demanded a new method of arguing from the parts to the whole. The dominions should think out their positions for themselves and all agitation for constitutional reform, if any, should come from the dominions. *The Round Table* should deal with these new developments in two ways: first, publish the fullest record of the constitutional developments which had taken place during the war so as to make it clear where the nations of the empire stood; and second, the quarterly should endeavour to follow the movement of opinion in the dominions through the dominion articles while the groups of students that still remained should study the new imperial and international conditions.[53]

This memorandum was the spark the London members had long needed and after an intensive discussion during the final months of the year a draft circular was prepared by Grigg in December 1920 which finally outlined the conclusions of the London group. It was a most important document, a major if belated attempt by the original members to redefine the role of the movement and to plan for the future.[54] It revealed that the London members were now fully aware that they had to face the reality of nationalism and

51 Curtis to Flavelle, 29 April 1920, box 6, Flavelle Papers
52 See 'Memorandum for Members of Round Table Groups. A précis of the proceedings of the Conference with Colonel Grigg, 8 May 1920' prepared by Von Haast after the conversation with Grigg, GD40/17/17, Lothian Papers.
53 See also a draft article prepared by Grigg, 26 Oct. 1920 and 'Note by Mr Curtis on Sir Edward Grigg's article,' 28 Oct. 1920, ibid.
54 'Draft circular to the Dominion Groups,' unsigned, 22 Dec. 1920, ibid. See in this context Curtis to Flavelle, 6 Dec. 1920, Box 6, Flavelle Papers.

analyse its implications. But they still believed the movement had a great future provided the dominion groups adopted a fresh approach to central imperial problems 'on their own initiative and from their own distinctive national standpoint.'

Of the four alternatives for the empire postulated in 1913 – *status quo*, co-operation, separation, and organic union – adherence to the *status quo* was obviously not a policy. It was always changing under the pressure of three forces working simultaneously: national feeling in the dominions; imperial sentiment; and the pressure of political, military, and strategic facts which made the dominion governments content to leave the general control of foreign relations to the governments of the United Kingdom. As a result of these conflicting forces co-operation was the policy of the day; a policy of continuous compromise, yielding incessantly to nationalist sentiment while maintaining the actual unity of the empire in world affairs. It was tentative, experimental, and hopelessly illogical, but for the time being it worked and was the only practicable policy. Separation, the third alternative of 1913, was advocated in 1920 by only a minority in Canada and South Africa. It was the product of the narrower form of racial and national sentiment. Its supporters were deeply stirred by national pride and were honestly convinced that the nationalism on which their ideas centred could not reach its full flowering without a break from the mother country and the empire. Separation was in the main an ultimate goal; in the meantime co-operation served. The fourth alternative, organic union, was not advocated by the movement or by anyone else as a policy practicable at present; but the London members were still convinced that it afforded the only permanent alternative to disruption, although they did not pretend to see its ultimate form. Like the separatists the London group believed in co-operation as a policy of the day but, unlike them, they hoped 'to see the sentiment and intelligence of all the British democracies gradually moving towards constitutional forms which will make our common citizenship equal, permanent and complete.' But as much as they believed in its ultimate worth, the central moot were convinced that its achievement would have to depend on the initiative of the dominions.

The London group pointed out that before the war the Round Table studies had been mainly directed to examining what the British commonwealth was and for what principles of civilisation it stood. More especially the movement had tried to formulate a clear-cut conception of the goal or goals toward which it was tending. These studies had been fruitful in revealing and distinguishing differences and in clarifying opinion on the imperial question. But it seemed that the time had now come for the groups to explore the imperial problem from the opposite side by working out the national policy of their own dominions: 'to approach the Imperial problem through national policy seems to us likely to be the means of enlisting much keenness and understanding in Round Table work which would be denied to a purely Imperial line of argument.' But, said the London group, 'it is essential that study on these lines should be carried out with due regard to the actual facts and realities of international life. It is essential for students to realise that the Empire is jealously regarded from many quarters, which may be able, as the German Empire did, to threaten its very life. It is the arch enemy pursued alike by reactionaries and by revolutionary dreamers in all parts of the world: and wreckers of both kinds receive support from honest Nationalist movements, which persuade themselves in their haste that they can reach their goal only by the collapse of British power.'

The issues which the London moot wished the dominion groups to consider were summarized under five heads; first, the character of the state: was it to be monarchical or republican, and if the former how was it to be linked with the British crown; second, national development: trade and commerce, capital, navigation, and tariff laws; third, foreign affairs: such matters as the relation of the dominions to the League of Nations and to the Japanese Alliance, as well as the method of conducting foreign policy and diplomatic relations with foreign powers; fourth, defence: such problems as the maintenance of British sea-power and the security of communications with India and the Middle East; and, fifth, the dependencies and the subject populations: the principle of mandates, the future of India, Egypt, and the other smaller dependencies. The London group believed a thorough study of all these questions from a strongly individual national standpoint would yield valuable results.

To facilitate discussion and the flow of ideas they suggested a number of specific questions that the dominion groups might ponder: 'If the covenant of the League of Nations is revised at the instance of the United States, do the Dominions consider it more important that they should retain their individual votes or that the British Empire should enter the League as a single state? Are the Dominions prepared to see British sea-power inferior to that of Japan and the United States? ... Are they willing to see Egypt withdrawing from the Empire and setting up as a sovereign power? If a similar question arose regarding India, what would be their attitude? ...' The central group emphasized that in any such re-examination of the imperial question two matters were of cardinal importance: the theory of nationality and the distribution of power. 'We would beg the Groups to analyse most faithfully the current phrases on the subject, such as "self-determination," and to arrive, if they can, at some clear concept of what it is that makes a nation. If democratic development really requires that sovereignty should be coterminous with nationality in many of the common acceptations of that term, the world is on the eve of protracted war, disruption and anarchy. On the other hand, the growth of liberty under law has manifestly benefited by the formation of large units of government.' Nothing was 'more necessary in the world than clear thinking on this subject and it is at the root of the constitutional problem of the British Empire.' It was also vain to study national development without taking into account a second factor: the changes in the distribution of material power which were taking place in the world. In the British empire material and financial power was slowly passing to the younger dominions. It was no longer possible for the British Isles alone to sustain the main fabric of the empire. It could be sustained only by the united action of the British peoples. Unless ways could be found to ensure national development while preserving united action, the dominions would have to work out their aspirations as independent sovereign powers amid the ruins of the British commonwealth.

For their part the London group decided to embark on a study of leading questions facing the United Kingdom, such as: 'What is our policy to be if Germany, Russia and Japan were to drift into a combination hostile to the British Commonwealth, supposing the League of Nations should fail to neutralise such combinations? How are we to deal with the situation should the tide of anarchy which flows from Moscow continue to spread over Asia? Can an Egyptian, Arabian or Turkish power be allowed to assume control of the Dardenelles? Should one or more of these situations arise can this country deal with the problem in isolation from the Dominions?' The central moot pointed out that if similar procedures were adopted in all the dominions it would be possible for all the Round Table groups to set to work at once, 'group by group, each in its own way, with the certainty that the completed studies throughout the Empire will supplement each other and lend themselves to effective comparison.' They suggested that for the time being there should be no attempt to arrive at agreement between the several groups in each dominion, but that all groups should send their results to London as soon as possible. It was also hoped that the dominions would conduct their investigations on the same principles as governed the original Round Table studies, that no willing student would be excluded merely by reason of his views on the ultimate goal to which the commonwealth was tending. The value of the work would be greatly impaired if it did not represent the give-and-take of discussion between different and even opposite standpoints. 'It is the essence of our suggestions, not only that the groups should take their own line and work out their conclusions for themselves, but also that they should take into due account all forms of opinion which have any substance in their own democracies, including especially those of Labour.'

Since the main object of the work would be to clarify their own minds and to assist the growth and formation of opinion in each dominion, the London group did not intend to publish the results in any extended form in *The Round Table*. However, each dominion organisation was free to take its own course and to advocate its own policy in its section of the quarterly, and the Londoners hoped that the dominion groups would 'make their work felt in the local press and on local opinion, not so much with a view to advocating policies as to stimulating interest and spreading real information. The greater danger to the Empire at the moment is not anti-Imperial propaganda but popular vagueness and ignorance.'

In concluding their circular, the London group reminded their dominion colleagues that the main causes of international enmity and friction the previous one hundred years had been expanding nationalism and the desire to exploit less civilised peoples and underdeveloped areas in the pursuit of wealth and power. But, said the Londoners, in a statement which revealed both their ideals and the limitations of their approach:

it has been the sovereign and peculiar virtue of the British Empire hitherto to harmonize different forms of national sentiment in free and willing subordination to a common ideal of law and government, and to substitute orderly development for war and exploitation in half the backward areas of the world. If the British Empire fell tomorrow it would leave a mighty memory which the broken world would strive in due time from sheer necessity to revive and restore. The Empire has in fact never been more needed or more powerful than today, but a period of searching trial is already upon it from within and without, and the supreme test will come from the tremendous forces of nationality in the hearts of its own peoples, east and west. Can it reconcile and harmonise those splendid forces in the service of a common ideal of freedom under law, transcending the lesser freedoms to which untutored democracy reaches blindly as the supreme and final good? The future of international peace and order linger upon the test: and if indeed the flowering of the younger British nations be incompatible with their union in a single Commonwealth, the League of Nations must prove as vain and elusive an ideal in this twentieth century of grace as mankind's first glimmering desire for social order in the Age of Stone or Brass.

By early 1921 the process of discussion outlined in the circular had begun in England.[55] But domestic problems were diverting attention in Canada,

55 A.L. Smith to Flavelle, 1 Feb. 1921, box 8, Flavelle Papers

and Flavelle reported that 'no body of men are thinking of imperial relations.'[56] Much the same situation existed in New Zealand. In Australia a conference of Round Table representatives from Victoria and New South Wales was held in Sydney in May to discuss both imperial foreign policy and the future activity of the Australian Round Table. It was a low-key affair, less well attended than usual, and held in the knowledge that the Brisbane branch had just failed. In general, the London group's circular was approved, and the Australians agreed to study the imperial and foreign situations from a national standpoint; but nothing of major significance emerged.[57]

All in all the London circular did not have the rejuvenating effect intended. The dominion organisations in New Zealand and Australia gradually concentrated their attention on imperial and international problems; but, in the main, their activity was reduced to the preparation of quarterly articles. The New Zealanders prepared a statement for the press each year on current problems, but this was never a very stimulating document. In Canada and South Africa the organisations lapsed completely into editorial committees for the preparation of articles, and in May 1921 at a meeting in Toronto it was decided not to revive the local groups.[58] In London it was much the same story. The decision of the dominion and British governments not to hold the long-awaited constitutional conference projected in 1917 was a blow to the central group's plans; and when the Imperial Conference of 1921 also made no provision for one, the enthusiasm of the group waned further. Leo Amery bemoaned the death of the Imperial War Cabinet system,[59] and so apparently did some other members of the moot, including Curtis. Sir Edward Grigg hoped a convention would be summoned later in the year. Amery supported him and dreamed of Round Table men holding prominent positions in the administrative structure of such a convention; possibly Milner as chairman, Grigg as secretary, and himself as a member.[60] But such was not to be. At the end of the year the London group was still

---

56 Flavelle to Curtis, 6 April 1921, box 7, ibid. See also Glazebrook to Milner, 6 April and 5 Nov. 1921, Glazebrook Papers, in which Glazebrook indicated that an education committee had been formed under Hume Wrong and that the old Round Table men were being looked to for information on foreign affairs.

57 Minutes of Round Table Conference, 21 and 22 May 1921, Harrison Moore Papers. For the New Zealand situation see a valuable letter from Curtis to A.S. Malcolm, 17 June 1921, Curtis Papers.

58 This meeting was held on 19 May 1921 and was attended by leading members of the dominion and provincial organisations. Cited in Quigley, 'The Round Table Groups in Canada,' 216.

59 Amery to Grigg, 1 June 1921, reel 1, Grigg Papers

60 Grigg to Curtis, 6 June 1921, copy; and Amery to Grigg, 24 June 1921, ibid.

meeting to discuss *The Round Table* articles in an atmosphere described by Dove as 'religiously earnest,' but their plans for regenerating the movement had failed.[61]

61  See Dove to Brand, 18 Dec. 1921, copy, GD40/17/18, Lothian Papers

# 12
## The twilight years

It becomes increasingly more difficult to speak of the Round Table organisation as a 'movement' after 1920-1. Not that its members had ever completely concurred on the aims and policies of their organisation, but from the early 1920s they disagreed more than ever among themselves. The majority of the original members in London and many of the first adherents in the dominions never abandoned hope for the emergence of a united commonwealth at some distant date, but the degree of unification and the manner in which it should be realised proved contentious issues during the next thirty years. Moreover, many of the leading members of the movement were prominent public or political figures by the twenties, and had less time to devote to either the movement or *The Round Table*. The major concern of all the groups became the preparation of articles, and few policy moots were held in the dominions, although in London the members endeavoured to meet five or six times a year to discuss general commonwealth and international questions. Increasingly after 1921 the commonwealth was viewed in an international setting, and attention was often given to international problems to the exclusion of imperial matters. The Round Table organisation thus ceased to be a movement and *The Round Table* ceased to be a quarterly devoted predominantly to empire-commonwealth concerns; this in itself was a primary cause of much strife and worry. The end of the war also brought a number of new faces into the organisation, especially in New Zealand and Australia and later in England. These men had had no experience of the movement's early more sanguine days and were critical and skeptical of many of the ideals of the older members. There can be little doubt that

Round Table discussions and *The Round Table* quarterly helped widen the horizons of many important and influential men from many walks of life in Great Britain and the dominions during the interwar years, but it is unlikely that many individual actions and pronouncements can be attributed to Round Table influence.

The difficulties facing the central group had already become apparent by 1920 when Lionel Curtis began to devote an increasing amount of time to the newly established Institute of International Affairs. Shortly afterwards Geoffrey Dawson left *The Round Table* to return to the editorial chair of *The Times*, and John Dove became the sole editor of the quarterly. Dove was a deeply religious, highly conscientious man and the movement's affairs were always his first thought; but he was an ailing man who found travel increasingly difficult. Although he journeyed to Europe a number of times during the twenties he never returned to the dominions, to India, or to Africa. As a result he gradually lost touch with developments in the commonwealth, especially in the dependencies. This and his interest in European affairs tended to be reflected in *The Round Table*.

Soon after his appointment as editor of the quarterly Dove left with Curtis for Ireland where they undertook an intensive investigation of the Irish situation. Their trip resulted in an article in the June issue of *The Round Table* which analysed the Irish crisis and ventured some solutions.[1] This led to Curtis's appointment as acting permanent under-secretary for Irish affairs in the Colonial Office, and from 1921-4 he was a civil servant. Curtis's ties with the movement had already become tenuous. In 1918 when many of the central moot had found it impossible to agree with his conclusions, still those of *The Problem of the Commonwealth*, Curtis had stopped drawing a salary from Round Table funds. This had only been reinstituted in 1920 when he had married. His appointment to the Colonial Office once again severed his research relationship with the movement, although he remained a member of the editorial committee.[2]

In March 1921 Lord Milner retired from Lloyd George's government into private life, never again to figure prominently in public affairs. Since 1916 pressure of work had made it difficult for him to remain in close touch with the movement, but he was still the father-figure of the organisation. Any letters he cared to write were eagerly devoured by his ageing kinder-

1 [J. Dove and L. Curtis], 'Ireland,' *The Round Table*, June 1921, 465-535
2 The editorial committee in May 1921 was Kerr, Brand, Curtis, Dawson, Dove, Grigg, Hichens, and Malcolm.

garten, and his ideals still inspired the original founders of the movement. After his retirement he devoted little time to the Round Table, although he attended moots whenever he could. In 1921 he did manage to secure £2500 from the Rhodes Trust to help keep *The Round Table* financially afloat, but he was unable to guarantee any further sums.[3] When he died in 1925 he was deeply mourned by the members of the movement who in the troubled years ahead were to miss his counsel. Two months after Milner's departure from the government, Philip Kerr resigned as Lloyd George's secretary. He was succeeded by Sir Edward Grigg who for some months carried the dual burden of adviser to Lloyd George and general secretary of the Rhodes Trust. After the break-up of the Coalition government in 1922 Grigg was elected to Parliament as an Asquithian Liberal. When he was appointed governor of Kenya in 1925 Philip Kerr succeeded him as secretary of the Rhodes Trust, a position he held until appointed British ambassador to Washington in 1939. Brand and Hichens were both deeply engrossed in financial and business affairs after 1921, and Dougie Malcolm, a director of the British South Africa Company, was frequently out of London. F.S. Oliver drifted away from the movement in the twenties, as Amery and Zimmern had done earlier. Zimmern's departure sharpened his perspective and he admitted to Dafoe, long an arch critic of the movement, that 'we who sat at the Round Table...theorized about a whole without knowing the parts.'[4] By 1921 the hard core of the London group was once again the South African kindergarten, with the sole addition of Grigg, and all of them were severely pressed for time.

These various commitments and pressures account for the central group's inactivity in the twenties. In a decade which witnessed the death of closer union and the enshrinement of the co-operative principle in the Balfour Report and the Statute of Westminster, the Londoners were surprisingly passive. *The Round Table* kept abreast of the various developments and continued to advocate 'the principle of the commonwealth,' but no efforts were made to influence events from behind-the-scenes. If anything, the central group and *The Round Table* gradually accepted the co-operative principle as the most viable base for the evolving commonwealth

To the extent that they could find the time, the Londoners were con-

---

3 Brand to Milner, 19 July 1921; Milner to Holland-Martin, 20 July 1921; and Holland-Martin to Milner, 21 July 1921, box 97, Milner Papers. These letters confirm that the movement received money from the Rhodes Trust before 1914. The details of the transfer of funds from the 'Rhodes-Beit Shares Fund' to the Round Table can be traced in 'Rhodes Sub-Trust 1907-26,' box 97, ibid.
4 Zimmern to Dafoe, 27 Feb. 1923, reel M74, Dafoe Papers

cerned in the twenties with international order, the future of the British commonwealth, and Anglo-American relations. They were increasingly disillusioned with the League of Nations, and Kerr especially felt that Great Britain should not become entangled any more than necessary in the affairs of Europe. He thought that a needless commitment in Europe would only disrupt the commonwealth without doing Europe any good; 'somehow [Great Britain] must be made to look away towards the outer world, as she always has done in the past.'[5] Curtis, of course, still held strongly to his conviction that 'the be-all and end-all of the British Commonwealth is the promotion and extension of responsible government among all races and in all spheres of public life ... To me it represents the possibility of a step which civilisation must sooner or later take from the national commonwealth to the world commonwealth.'[6] In 1922 Curtis and Kerr worked hard to help establish a network of groups in the United States for the study of international affairs, but though they spent some time in North America during the spring and summer of 1922 the venture was unsuccessful.[7]

In the summer of 1923 the whole question of what the movement stood for was raised again for discussion in London, this time by Lord Milner.[8] The Curtis scheme having been definitely abandoned was anything left but the journal? Isbister from South Africa, Witherby of New Zealand, and Harrison Moore of Australia, who were present at this particular discussion, revealed that the usefulness of the Round Table groups was a frequent subject of discussion among the dominion members. Most of them felt they benefited from constant analysis and discussion of commonwealth and international affairs. But new men were needed, particularly young men, since the older ones were finding other matters taking more and more of their time. This was certainly true in England, and to Harrison Moore it seemed that the active roles some of the London members had been called upon to play had driven something of a wedge amongst them. During the discussion Brand and Grigg, two of the busiest, insisted that the movement should restore its 'student and thinking department.' Some one should be delegated to review systematically the imperial and international situation since 1914 and to draft material for circulation. Hopefully this would lead to the re-establishment of the close relationship with dominion groups. Lionel Hichens also suggested that someone from London should visit the dominions as

5 Kerr to Borden, 17 July 1923, OC series, file 627, Borden Papers
6 Curtis to Rowell, 11 Aug. 1921, file 26, Rowell Papers
7 Grigg to Kerr, 6 April 1922, reel 2, Grigg Papers. Dove to Wrong, 11 July and 17 Aug. 1922, Hume Wrong Papers; Kerr to Curtis, 22 April and 28 May 1922, GD40/17/18, Lothian Papers
8 Harrison Moore to Laby, 16 Aug. 1923, Laby Papers

Curtis had done in earlier years. Here the dominion members advised caution; they knew only too well that there was still a grave risk of stirring hostile feelings and arousing mischievous misrepresentation.

This brief flirtation with a reactivation of the movement soon ended, and given the condition of the Round Table organisation in both England and the dominions it was hardly surprising. After the war the Round Table organisations in the dominions had deliberately avoided all propaganda efforts, and had concentrated on the preparation of quarterly articles and quiet attempts at education in imperial and international affairs. It had been decided in May 1921 not to form any more groups in Canada, and that summer the committee method of preparing articles was agreed upon after consultations with the London members. Glazebrook and Willison both asked to be relieved of their responsibilities, and in late 1921 Hume Wrong[9] became chairman of the editorial committee and secretary of the Canadian organisation. Willison found it impossible to work under the committee system, and he retired permanently from the movement at the end of the year.[10] Wrong chaired the editorial committee for the next six years, but found it increasingly difficult to work the system efficiently. By the late twenties he had retired in some despair, and the ever faithful Glazebrook was struggling to keep the Canadian organisation afloat and the articles on time.[11] The Canadian decision not to form a new society or reactivate the old groups was reaffirmed in December 1922 and adhered to throughout the decade. As Wrong pointed out to some enthusiasts who wanted to revive a group in Winnipeg: 'it would be fine if it could be managed but the Round Table has achieved an unfortunate and undeserved reputation in Canada as a propagandist organisation working for imperial federation;' one had to be careful of reviving these antagonisms.[12]

For much of the decade similar organisational difficulties existed in Australia. Finally in the late twenties, through the generosity of E.C. Dyason,[13] a

9 Humphrey Hume Wrong (1894-1954); diplomat; member of the Department of History, University of Toronto, 1921-6; joined the Department of External Affairs 1926; Canadian ambassador at Washington 1946-53
10 See Curtis to Glazebrook, 2 Sept. 1921, Curtis Papers, in which Curtis outlined the method of preparing co-operative articles. This letter was mimeographed and sent to all the dominion secretaries. See also Willison to Dove, 25 Oct. 1921, copy, Willison Papers.
11 Hume Wrong to Dove, Dec. 1922, H. Wrong Papers; also Hume Wrong to Dove, 21 Oct. 1926, and Glazebrook to Dove, 10 May 1927, copies, GD40/17/222, Lothian Papers
12 Wrong to McGhee, 22 April 1923, Hume Wrong Papers
13 Edward Clarence Dyason (1886-    ); economist and company director; practised as a mining engineer 1908-20; president of the Chamber of Mines, Victoria, 1918-22; president, Gold Producers' Association of Australia 1919-25; partner Edward Dyason and Co since 1921; chairman of various economic committees

small office was established in Melbourne which the Round Table shared with three other equally destitute organisations, and a part-time secretary was hired to serve all four. Many new men joined the Sydney and Melbourne groups in these years, and certainly in this regard the Australian organisation did not experience the same problems as the Canadian. But many of these young men had not known the early days of the movement, and their priorities differed from those of the original members. After the war they were anxious to do something constructive, and joined the Round Table in a spirit of enthusiastic idealism in the hope of making the community more aware of imperial and international affairs. But they were not deeply committed to the movement, and tended to be involved in a number of other organisations such as the League of Nations Union and the budding Institute of International Affairs. Like their friends in London they became engrossed in international difficulties and developments to the detriment of imperial and commonwealth affairs.[14]

The attitude of the London group was sharply revealed in 1925 when Grigg made efforts to interest his Round Table fellows in taking up the cause of preference. He felt that the movement had emphasized the political problem almost to the complete exclusion of the economic; this was not only a disproportionate approach but a complete misreading of the signs of the time. He gained support from Hichens and Brand but did not make much progress with the others. As always Curtis was afraid of the tariff question. Grigg, however, thought 'it would be a splendid thing to get *The Round Table* concentrated once again on a definite policy to be secured within a few years, and I shall feel that life is worth living twice over if we can get together on these lines.'[15] Grigg was forced to drop his campaign when he went to Kenya as governor later in the year and no one was sufficiently interested to pursue it.

In Kenya Grigg soon became involved in a scheme for the closer union of East Africa based on previous kindergarten methods in South Africa. He even succeeded in obtaining Feetham for a brief spell to conduct an investigation into East African municipal affairs. Despite his continued efforts Grigg had no success. Although the London members offered to help when they could, they gave him little assistance. Understandably he was annoyed, and he became increasingly critical of the way *The Round Table* quarterly seemed to be avoiding the problems of East Africa, the native question, and

---

14 Sir Keith Officer to J. Kendle, 12 May 1967; T. Buesst to J. Kendle, 17 Nov. 1967; Sir Alfred Stirling to J. Kendle, 23 Oct. 1967; and Patrick Hamilton to J. Kendle, 25 Oct. 1967; and an interview with Sir Leslie Melville, Canberra, Oct. 1967
15 Grigg to Abe Bailey, 19 Feb. 1925 and 20 May 1925, reel 4, Grigg Papers

Sir Edward Grigg

the commonwealth in general. His criticisms foreshadowed those levelled more intensively and across a broader spectrum in the thirties.[16]

By the late 1920s Curtis was once again receiving money from the movement, and was deeply engrossed in a study of recent international and commonwealth developments which were to lead in time to the publication of *Civitas Dei*. The more he studied the question the more he was convinced that his earlier arguments were still relevant, especially those embodied in *The Problem of the Commonwealth*. He talked and wrote more than ever about national and world commonwealths. Many people with whom Curtis spoke thought he generalised far too much and found him difficult to pin down. One Canadian thought him charming, but was a little wary of a man for whom 'politics is a sort of religion.'[17] A further difficulty for the central group was Philip Kerr's preoccupation with Christian Science. Tormented by religious doubts for years, Kerr had finally found solace in the teachings of Mrs Eddy, and in the early twenties he told his Round Table colleagues that Christian Science would in future have the first claim on his time and activities.[18] Although Kerr did not feel his religious beliefs would affect his Round Table work, it certainly affected his standing in the wider community, and his judgment and ideas were soon widely suspect. Sir Robert Borden, long a friend of the movement and a great admirer of their achievements, thought many of the central group so idealistic that he feared 'they might on occasion fall into a ditch or stumble over a low-lying wall through gazing too intently at the stars.'[19]

By 1927 Curtis was becoming interested in the problems of China, and was preparing for the Pacific Conference in Honolulu. Kerr, who was also to attend, was by now a strong advocate of Anglo-American co-operation. In contrast to his earlier opinion, he was now convinced that the Round Table groups, in fact anyone dealing with world politics, should be working to find a positive basis for co-operation between the English-speaking nations.[20] Kerr found it difficult to interest his colleagues in these ideas; and soon Curtis was off to the Far East to study the China question at first hand, and ulti-

16  Dawson to Grigg, 20 Oct. 1925; Feetham to Grigg, 5 Nov. 1925, reel 4, Grigg Papers. Kerr to Dove, 2 Nov. 1925, GD40/17/222, Lothian Papers. Feetham to Grigg, 27 April 1926, reel 4, Grigg Papers. For a perceptive look at the movement's attitude toward Africa see Dame Margery Perham, 'The Round Table and Sub-Saharan Africa,' The Round Table, Nov. 1970, 543-55.
17  Gregory to Bourassa, 9 Oct. 1925, reel M721, Bourassa Papers
18  Kerr to Curtis, 28 May 1922, copy, GD40/17/18, Lothian Papers
19  Borden to Christie, 20 Jan. 1925, copy, post-1921 series, file 58, Borden Papers
20  Curtis to Kerr, 23 May 1927; and Kerr to Curtis, 26 May and 2 Sept. 1927, copies, GD40/17/227, Lothian Papers

mately to make some extraordinary proposals about 'the principle of the commonwealth' being the only possible solution of China's difficulties.

In the late twenties the Round Table organisation was obviously very much in the doldrums. The central group had lost all real contact with the dominion branches, and trips by Amery and Malcolm to Australia and New Zealand at the end of the decade were undertaken for governmental and business reasons. Any Round Table contacts which resulted were incidental. In London *The Round Table* was still managing to pay its way; but in December 1929 a five-year contribution from Sir Abe Bailey came to an end and the movement was faced with £500 less in 1930. The organisation still had investments valued at £13,000 and the interest on them helped to pay running expenses. But contributions in 1929 had amounted to £1300, and with £500 of that gone the prospect of revitalizing the movement would have been difficult even if the incentive had existed. The second decade of the Round Table movement's existence thus ended on a low note.[21]

In 1930 the London members began to consider drawing a number of younger men into the inner sanctums of the moot. The only man who had achieved this during the past ten years had been Percy Horsfall,[22] who had served on the editorial committee, and some thought was being given to asking Sir Arthur Salter[23] and Harry Hodson[24] to come in. This step was long overdue in London. It was finally forced by the severe illness of John Dove and the preoccupation of the original founders with responsibilities other than the movement and its quarterly.[25] In August Curtis suggested that the time had come to reconsider 'the reconstruction of the Round Table Movement.' In order to do this he recommended that 'the five aboriginal and con-

21  'Note on Contributions to the Round Table,' 27 March 1930, GD40/17/23; also Curtis to Sir Arthur Salter, 17 April 1930, copy, GD40/17/247, ibid.
22  Percy Horsfall (1888-1965); private secretary to the governor-general of South Africa 1913-19; returned to London to begin a city career in 1919; managing director of Lazard Bros 1937-63; joined the Round Table movement in 1921; wrote some forty-four articles for the journal
23  Arthur James Salter, 1st baron (1881-    ); director of ship requisitioning 1917; Supreme Economic Council 1919; general secretary, Reparations Commission, 1920-2; Gladstone Professor of Political Theory and Institutions, Oxford, 1934-44; MP (Ind) 1937-50; MP (C) 1951-3; minister of state for economic affairs 1951-2; minister of materials 1952-3
24  Henry Vincent Hodson (1906-    ); fellow of All Souls 1928-35; on the staff of the Economic Advisory Council 1930-1; Ministry of Information 1939-41; assistant editor of *The Round Table* 1931; editor of *The Round Table* 1934-9; reforms commissioner, Government of India 1941-2; assistant editor of the *Sunday Times* 1946-50; provost of Ditchley since 1961
25  Curtis to Salter, 17 April 1930, copy, GD40/17/247, Lothian Papers

tinuous members of the Moot should first come to an agreement as to what should be done.' He therefore wrote in turn to Hichens, Dawson, Brand, and Kerr in identical terms:

We are now considering the evolution of the Round Table to a younger group, reserving to our fast ageing selves a consultative capacity. In taking this step it is vital to be clear in our own minds as to the ultimate object at which the Round Table and its magazine is to aim. Behind our movement is the fundamental belief that the British Commonwealth stands for principles which are vital not merely to itself but to the world at large. It must therefore be preserved and developed not merely for its own sake but for that of the world at large ... With this general aim in view the function of our movement must be to discern the question which at any moment most calls for study and treatment ... our first duty is not to consider what interests people but rather to interest their minds in what really concerns them. The magazine is our chief means to this end. But ... we are in constant danger of losing sight of our real end, and of treating the means as an end ... In preparing to pass our torch to younger hands, we should try to consider the purpose for which it was kindled in 1909 in the light of conditions before us in 1930 and in doing so to recover our sense of proportion.[26]

An indication of the state of Round Table affairs at this time, or perhaps of the attitude toward Curtis's ideas, was that no meeting was held until October.[27] If such a letter had been written and received even ten years earlier, a moot would have been arranged immediately. Nevertheless, one of Curtis's suggestions – that Hodson should become an associate and travelling editor of *The Round Table* – was accepted, and Hodson took up his duties in 1931. Curtis felt rebuffed by his colleagues, and wrote in depressed terms to Kerr who was quick to admonish the self-pitying prophet: 'I won't comment on the picture you have drawn of yourself as the lonely Titan deserted by all your colleagues including myself. Only up to now I have entertained a belief that occasionally I have supported you. I think I shall draw a similar picture of myself as the despised and rejected advocate of Anglo-American relations.'[28] But Curtis was not to be admonished so easily. In the following years, as he became more and more preoccupied with European and world federation, and as the gulf widened between his and Kerr's ideas and those of the other London members, he became highly conscious of himself as an embattled and misunderstood warrior for the cause of international sanity.

26 Curtis to Kerr, 6 Aug. 1930, ibid.
27 Curtis to Lothian, 15 Aug. 1930, ibid.
28 Lothian to Curtis, 27 Aug. 1930, copy, ibid.

The problem was raised again in 1931 by Sir Edward Grigg who for some years had been dissatisfied with the whole Round Table operation. The extensive alteration by Dove of one of his articles on East Africa was the spark which finally set him off. He regretted the departure of *The Round Table* and the movement from their imperial creed and their preoccupation with international affairs. He was especially critical of Curtis: 'Lionel believes in an article of revealed political religion called the Principle of the Commonwealth and thinks that nothing else matters. Before the war he tried to make that principle the basis of a federal constitution for the whole Empire. Having failed magnificently in that, he has washed his hands of circumsicion and is now busy evangelising the Gentiles all over the earth. Of course there is an enormous lot in what he says, but he is a fanatic and a revivalist on this subject and sees only one thing which means the abandonment of faiths which we have held and stood for ever since *The Round Table* came into being. If we do not bring *The Round Table* back to its Imperial mission it will soon be nothing but a subsidiary branch of the Institute of International Affairs.'[29] After threatening to resign from the editorial committee,[30] Grigg wrote sadly to Hichens that *The Round Table*, 'the only relic of a movement into which we all put so much conviction and enthusiam in the years before the war,' was a far cry from a journal supposedly concerned with the affairs of the British commonwealth.[31] There was rarely a special article on the empire-commonwealth and Africa never received the attention it should. He feared that

As a brotherhood we have lost interest in the Empire and are no longer competent to deal with it. I think, therefore, that if *The Round Table* is to go on, it should quite definitely change its character, remove its sub-title, and become, what it is much more fitted to become at the present time, a publication connected with the Royal Institute of International Affairs ... The trouble of course is that of our two whole-timers Lionel has completely gone off the Empire and John is too much of an invalid to do anything but conform to the atmosphere of the moment and trail along. He also has his own special obstinacies. While John carries on in this fashion nothing certainly can be done, but all the heart and soul of *The Round Table* movement is petering out and I really don't know that we stand for anything in particular nowadays. We certainly have no common creed ... We are no longer guides in Imperial policy; we are not even enlightened commentators, because as a rule we are more interested

29 Grigg to Brand, 6 Aug. 1931, copy, reel 5, Grigg Papers
30 Grigg to Dove, 6 Aug. 1931, copy, ibid.
31 Grigg to Hichens, 15 Dec. 1931, copy, ibid.

in other things. This indifference seems to me much worse than mere neutrality. I regard it as the repudiation and betrayal of a great cause to which we once gave our hearts. Is nothing to be done about it?

To this frustrated letter Hichens could only 'confess with great regret that your criticisms are just.'[32] The trouble was to know what to do. As Hichens saw it: 'The root difficulty is that we are no longer a group in the old sense. We hold a meeting, very irregularly attended, once a month or less, and there is never time for a proper discussion of anything. None of us now are primarily concerned with Imperial affairs and the best that can be said of us is that they still find a place in our hearts. But the grinding toil of everyday work and the terrific problems with which we are faced make it impossible for most of us to formulate a constructive Imperial policy. The most we can do is to contribute something – not much perhaps – in respect of the problems with which we are directly connected.'

Because Dove was too ill to travel he could only take from his surroundings while Curtis was no longer a whole-timer; he drew nothing from the funds and was primarily interested in China. Even if Hodson were to make the journeys, Hichens doubted that he would be able to do more than 'pick up the knowledge of a very intelligent globe-trotter': 'The problem [Hichens wrote] is a difficult one and I confess I don't see the solution. But I don't think we ought to give it up. And in fairness two things ought to be said. One is that the Dominion contributions are really valuable and do give a useful picture of the politics of the Empire ... The other thing is that there is nothing at present to take the place of the Round Table and do the work that it set out to do. As a magazine I think it is first class and it has a great reputation. It would be a pity to drop it. What we want is, if possible, to steer it back on to the old lines. And there we get back again to our root difficulty. How can the Round Table Committee be so reconstructed as to carry out this work? I can ask the question, but I can't answer it. I wish I could. We ought to be able to try though.'

In early 1932 these problems finally came to a head when T.H. Laby, the Australian secretary, forwarded to the London group a lengthy letter from Frederic Eggleston which was highly critical of the way *The Round Table* was being produced.[33] Its arrival resulted in the first extensive heart-searching within the London group since the 1920s. Eggleston did not believe that

32 Hichens to Grigg, 22 Dec. 1931, ibid.
33 Laby to Dove, 26 April 1932, copy; enclosed in Eggleston to Laby, 1 April 1932, Harrison Moore Papers

*The Round Table* was serving the purpose for which it had been established – it was not a forum for the discussion of imperial problems. The majority of articles were on British politics and on European problems, and these usually reflected only the opinions of the central moot: 'the Review is a British Review with appendices – it is an organ of British opinion assisted by an outer Empire chronicle.' There was no mutuality, no exchange, and no attempt to discuss fully intra-imperial problems. Eggleston wanted the journal to return to its original purpose.

Eggleston also drew attention to the lack of communication between the dominion groups and London; there had been no emissary from the British group since the war. The visits of Grigg, Amery, and Malcolm had all been in other capacities, and time had only permitted a couple of evenings with each. Eggleston thought the empire was at the crossroads; the organisation had disintegrated and economic dangers were penetrating its defences. 'There never was a time when there was more need for those who believe in the spiritual value of the Empire to formulate means of preserving it.' Australians in the Round Table groups had not been given the chance to suggest alternatives because of the nature of the chronicle articles; as a result the Australian point of view had never been adequately put in the Australian article in *The Round Table*. Similarly *The Round Table* should provide the spiritual leadership so necessary in the empire. Eggleston's practical solution to the difficulty was that Canada and Australia be granted one special article a quarter and South Africa and New Zealand one every second quarter.

The receipt of this criticism caused much concern in London. Shortly after its arrival in early June, the London group held a moot at Hichen's country home. Dove thought the letter an indictment, but acknowledged that it raised vital questions which the central group needed to consider. He did not believe that the adoption of Eggleston's proposals would be in the best interests of the movement or the quarterly, for to adopt them would mean fewer special articles, less appeal, a decline in circulation, and a loss of revenue at a financially difficult time which might jeopardize the existence of the journal.[34] However, the question of the integration of the Commonwealth which Eggleston had referred to was a problem which had been making some of the London members uneasy for some time. 'The equality movement,' as Dove called it, had revolutionised intra-imperial relations since 1914 and had led Great Britain and the dominions away from union. Dove contended that, in the main, the Round Table members had recognised the inevitability of the

34 See 'Memorandum on Mr Eggleston's Letter' prepared by Dove in June 1932 for the Hichen's moot, copy, ibid. Also Dove to Lothian, 16 and 19 June 1932, GD40/17/263, Lothian Papers

process. They had done their best through *The Round Table* to suggest improvements in machinery and to facilitate co-operation. They had not opposed the trend which had ended in the Statute of Westminister. 'Indeed, we welcomed the change, and we have no regrets, for we believe that nothing permanent under the new conditions which arose after the war, could ever have been built upon the old foundations. They had first to be levelled. This, however, has now been done. The question today is, shall we rest content and do nothing – a course ... bound to end in dissolution – or shall we try to build? Mr. Eggleston's letter has reached us at a psychological moment. But for it, the uneasiness ... might have remained in the back of our minds. His letter has brought it to the surface ... What then can we do to promote integration?'[35]

Dove believed the movement might do well to return to its old method of group study. It would re-examine the imperial problem in the light of all that had happened since the movement had printed its first Round Table studies: the war, the peace, the new status of the dominions, the birth of the League of Nations, the growing recognition of the interdependence of all nations, and the danger of a collapse of western civilisation under the strain of a world economic crisis. All these developments had given a new complexion to the imperial problem. Was the British Commonwealth of Nations in 1932 an end in itself or was it a step? It was certainly obvious that all preconceived ideas needed to be set aside and that the movement required a new line of approach in order to grapple with the new difficulties.

Although Dove knew that a study of these matters could put new life into the Round Table organisation, he also recognised that it would involve a great deal of careful thought and work, the main burden of which would fall upon two or three of the London members who already had heavy public engagements. Everything would depend on whether or not they would be able to spare the time; for it was essential that if the new work was taken up it should be completed, otherwise the position of the editorial committee and the Round Table organisation as a whole would be seriously weakened. If the London group did make an affirmative decision it would come at an opportune moment because Hodson, the assistant editor of *The Round Table*, was about to leave for the dominions. If a memorandum could be completed in time Hodson's visits would provide an excellent opportunity for an effective exchange of views with the dominion groups.[36]

---

35  See draft letter Dove to Laby, 16 June 1932, enclosed in Dove to Lothian, 16 June 1932, ibid.
36  See a short note by Dove entitled 'Decision with regard to Imperial Problem,' 18 June 1932, enclosed in Dove to Lothian, 19 June 1932, ibid.

The London members debated Dove's suggestions for almost three weeks, and finally on 4 July decided to postpone an exploration in depth until the autumn when memoranda would be ready for study. But they did decide that most of their number would probably be too busy to undertake anything like the prewar studies. Instead, they recommended that the unofficial conference on commonwealth affairs sponsored by the Canadian Institute of International Affairs and the Royal Institute of International Affairs scheduled for Toronto in 1933 should be used as a means of discussing the imperial problem. Round Table members from all the dominions and from Great Britain would undoubtedly be on the various delegations to the conference and would benefit from the discussions. After the completion of the conference the real work of the movement would begin, and major decisions about Round Table activity should be postponed until that time.[37] For the time being the movement would depend on Hodson to initiate discussions on his travels. This decision, although a good idea and necessary for educational purposes, indicated the difficulties involved in reactivating the movement. Not only were the members of the London group too busy to devote much of their energies to a new phase of Round Table activity, but they were also too divided over the aims of such activity to reach any real agreement.

This division within the central group was reflected in two important memoranda prepared for the autumn moot by Grigg and Curtis. Grigg reminded his colleagues that the movement's prewar contention that the empire would break up unless a more formal imperial union were adopted had not stood the test of events: 'We were wrong ... We overstated the argument for federation of the Empire as an immediate and indispensable necessity. We made much too little of the practical difficulty of working a world-wide federal system under such institutions as we at present possess. We were wrong to assume that organic union of the Empire as a whole is necessarily the first essential step towards a better world-order, based on what Lionel means by "the principle of the Commonwealth."'[38]

It was true that the empire was an epitome of a potential world-state, but its future for decades to come would have to depend on the more advanced white nations. The movement could do more for the empire and the world by working in ever closer affiliation with each other and with nations of kindred aims than by working for organic union between mixed races within the empire itself. Grigg shared Curtis's faith that responsible citizenship must be the ultimate goal of political advance, but the forms in which a world-wide federation of peoples could be workably expressed had not been developed

37 Dove to Laby, 5 July 1932, copy, Harrison Moore Papers
38 'Memorandum' by Grigg, 28 Sept. 1932, copy, GD40/17/264, Lothian Papers

yet. Grigg thought it would take many centuries for the idea of equal responsibility for world order to mature. In the interim he was prepared to follow Cecil Rhodes's main thesis that 'The nations which understand responsible government, and more especially the English-speaking nations, will have to take joint responsibility in some form for the maintenance of those conditions if they are to preserve their present leadership and prevent a long era of political and economic confusion. Believing that, I hold that if we once again made organic union of the Empire our first objective, we should be wrong.'[39] What was necessary was the creation of a British-minded internationalism not a British super-nationalism. Alternatively Curtis saw 'the organisation of human society in one commonwealth as the practical goal of human endeavour ... but I do not believe it will be achieved till one substantial part of human society has succeeded in organising itself as an international commonwealth ... I see the British Empire as marked by its history for that special task. It is not a commonwealth but the project of a commonwealth. Its realisation as a true commonwealth is necessary to show the world how the goal can and will be attained.'[40]

He was convinced that the commonwealth could only become a true commonwealth by uniting into a larger unit. But his earlier experiences had convinced him that the movement would have little impact if it worked for immediate changes and tried to force the issue. Its chances would be much better if it simply left on record some clear conception of what the future development of human society should be, showing the special part which the British commonwealth could and should play in that future development. Curtis elaborated to Brand: '... it is persistence which tells in the long run; that is why I have so much more faith in movements which look to distant than to immediate results. I think that we in the Round Table were somehow misled by the fact that our first efforts in South Africa led to such rapid results. This was in the nature of the situation. I think that we ought to train ourselves to think of and work for results which we ourselves could never hope to see realised.'[41]

These memoranda were discussed at Blickling in early October and Curtis thought the session 'an enormous success,'[42] a view supported by Downie Stewart, a New Zealand guest,[43] but as later developments were to suggest the discussion did not bridge the basic division within the central group.

39 Ibid.
40 Memorandum on 'Is the Empire worth discussing and if so why' prepared by Curtis for discussion at a moot at Blickling on 7 Oct. 1932, copy, GD40/17/263, ibid.
41 Curtis to Brand, 15 Sept. 1932, copy, Curtis Papers
42 Curtis to I. Macadam, 11 Oct. 1932, copy, ibid.
43 D. Stewart to Grigg, 17 Feb. 1933, reel 6, Grigg Papers

In May 1933 a memorandum prepared for the Toronto conference was circulated to the dominion groups for comment.[44] The memorandum, and the discussion of it in Australia, reflected the division within the movement. The majority of the London members and most of those in Melbourne wanted Great Britain and the commonwealth to avoid, if possible, becoming entangled in European affairs. Nevertheless they pledged their support to the Covenant of the league. Sir Edward Grigg and Downie Stewart disagreed with this point of view. Grigg felt support for the league was anti-imperial. He believed efforts should be made to establish a closer relationship with the United States. There needed to be 'a clear understanding between all the English-speaking peoples to keep the peace of the world.' He wished 'the old Round Table groups were younger so that we could campaign again on the old lines. But we are all too preoccupied now, and we cannot form the corporate opinion that was so effective before the war because we no longer live together and swap views day in and day out. My hope, however, is that Macadam will manage to collect a group of younger men who will take this problem in hand.'[45]

The Toronto conference went off as planned and a number of Round Table members from Great Britain and the dominions were present and some took prominent parts in the discussions, but on the whole the conference was not as fruitful as had been hoped. It only served to underline the intense isolationism of the Canadians, and the difficulties to be faced in reactivating the movement.[46] Any chance that Dove might return to the question of the movement's future was lost in April 1934 when the ailing editor of *The Round Table* died. Hodson replaced him, but for the moment the London group were too saddened by their loss to initiate talks on Dove's original proposals.[47] Some thought was given to holding a conference of the New

44 'The Toronto Conference. Memorandum from the London Round Table Group,' 29 May 1933, copy, Harrison Moore Papers; see also 'Summary of Round Table (Melbourne) discussion 21 November 1933 on British Round Table memorandum,' ibid.

45 Grigg to Downie Stewart, 14 Oct. 1933, and Stewart to Grigg, 30 Sept. 1933, reel 6, Grigg Papers. Sir Ivison Macadam (1894–     ); assistant director-general and principal assistant secretary, Ministry of Information, 1939-41; secretary and director-general, Royal Institute of International Affairs, 1929-55; editor of the *Annual Register of World Events*

46 Toynbee, *British Commonwealth Relations*. The following men, known to be Round Table members or associates, were present in Toronto. Australia: Ernest Scott, Alfred Stirling, W.J.V. Windeyer, R. Latham; Canada: Sir Robert Falconer, Sir Joseph Flavelle, Vincent Massey, J.M. Macdonnell, G. Glazebrook; New Zealand: Downie Stewart, H.F. Von Haast; South Africa: Eric Walker; United Kingdom: H.V. Hodson, Sir Robert Cecil, A. Zimmern. Hodson to Harrison Moore, 28 Feb. 1934, Harrison Moore Papers

47 Douglas Malcolm was of the opinion that Dove 'came as near to real saintliness as is given to our frail humanity ...' Malcolm to Grigg, 21 April 1934, reel 6, Grigg Papers

Zealand and Australian groups in Melbourne in early 1934 at which Von Haast, the New Zealander, hoped to 'cut out all Golden Rule discussion, platitudes and generalities and to get right down to bed-rock practical matters in which there is something to be *done*, and not talked about, that we should not beat the air but should take votes and pass resolutions.'[48] Nothing, however, appears to have resulted from this enthusiasm. The situation was much the same in Canada where George Glazebrook,[49] Arthur's son, believed there was 'no possibility of reviving anything in the nature of the old study groups.'[50] Despite the amount of discussion which had taken place in the inner circle of the movement in both Great Britain and the dominions, none of the suggestions made by either the London or dominion members had been implemented or even considered very seriously. Certainly Grigg's and Eggleston's criticisms and suggestions had had little effect. *The Round Table* followed the same format even after Dove's death. Relatively little attention was given to Africa or the dependencies, although India, on the eve of yet another constitutional reform, commanded attention. Curtis later revealed that 'a split had gradually developed which varied at each meeting according to the particular members who happened to attend. Philip headed a party that wanted the Round Table to appoint the policy of organic union for the British Commonwealth ... The endorsement of this policy in *The Round Table* was opposed by those who shared the outlook of Bob [Brand]. As the moot was divided *The Round Table* gave no lead on the subject.'[51]

Matters were brought to a head with the approach of the twenty-fifth anniversary of the quarterly. A week-end meeting was held at Blickling in the early summer of 1935 at which Lothian[52] argued the case for a commitment to the policy of organic union. Although he had made clear in his Burge lecture of May that he did not believe the world was yet ready for federation, he did believe it could be organised within the next decade or so 'into four or five great units.'[53] After a long discussion Lothian's view was approved by a narrow margin. In a lead article written by Hodson entitled 'Twenty-Five Years' and published in the 100th issue of *The Round Table* the main aim of the quarterly was stated to be the organic union of the British common-

48 Von Haast to Laby, 24 Jan. 1934, copy, Harrison Moore Papers
49 George Glazebrook (1900-    ); member of staff of the Department of History, University of Toronto, 1925-41, 1946-8; special wartime assistant, Department of External Affairs, 1942-6; member of the Department of External Affairs 1949-53; Canadian minister to the United States 1953-6; special lecturer in history, University of Toronto, 1963-7
50 George Glazebrook to Curtis, 15 Aug. 1934, copy, GD40/17/282, Lothian Papers
51 Curtis to Macadam, 26 April 1945, copy, Curtis Papers
52 Philip Kerr inherited the title Lord Lothian in 1930.
53 Lothian to Buell, 30 April 1935, GD40/17/289, Lothian Papers

wealth. After twenty-five years 'the spirit and purpose of the review and of the groups of men responsible for it remain the same. The organic commonwealth of free peoples, as the only permanent foundation for liberty and peace, is still a vision, but it is a vision that has inspired twenty-five years of effort, and that will continue to inspire the renewal of that effort in the years to come.'[54]

The decision to stand by their early policy of organic union was not a popular one with many of the members. The vote in committee had been very close and if the usual practice of group unanimity had been adhered to the affirmation would never have been published. The decision to publish the article widened rather than narrowed the split in the London group. In the late thirties it hardened into two camps: one, led and increasingly solely occupied by Curtis, although Lothian did tend to support him; and another, containing Brand, Grigg, and Horsfall. Grigg had been especially annoyed, and wrote a book *The Faith of an Englishman* which was 'a statement of Round Table policy as one member at least of the brotherhood understands it and would wish it to be.'[55] By late 1936 Grigg had become an infrequent attender at editorial moots, and in late October Hichens wrote: 'I am very glad you are coming to the Moot on Tuesday – in fact I had intended to urge you to return and help us. As a matter of fact Bob and I have had rather an uphill battle to fight, but things are coming round our way now and with your help we shall I believe be able to put forward a constructive program in the Round Table ... We have had no policy for years – although the articles have been interesting and have reached a high standard.'[56]

In the late thirties Lothian and Curtis continued to argue the federal, organic position. Lothian claimed at one point that the central lesson of all history was that nothing could be done by any system of co-operation between sovereign states; if mankind was to be saved the member states of the commonwealth should pool their sovereignty and federate.[57] Lothian talked increasingly of Anglo-American alliances and Curtis of world commonwealths. In 1938 Curtis published the last volume of *Civitas Dei*, in progress since the mid-twenties. In it he simply reaffirmed at greater length, in more detail, and with equally loose generalisations, his pre-1914 argu-

---

54  See [H.V. Hodson], 'Twenty-Five Years,' *The Round Table*, Sept. 1935, 653-9. Also Curtis to Macadam, 26 April 1945, copy, Curtis Papers; and Hodson to Laby, [nd] 1935, Harrison Moore Papers; Lothian to Hodson, 6 Aug. 1935, copy, GD40/17/301, Lothian Papers; Hodson to Laby, 1 Oct. 1935, Laby Papers
55  Grigg to Hodson, 2 Nov. 1936, reel 7, Grigg Papers
56  Hichens to Grigg, 12 Oct. 1936, ibid.
57  Lothian to Lord Davies, 10 Dec. 1936; and Lothian to [unclear], 27 July 1937, GD40/17/326, Lothian Papers

ments published in *The Commonwealth of Nations*. In 1939 both men were greatly influenced by *Union Now*, a book written by a former American Rhodes Scholar, Clarence Streit,[58] which recommended the 'union *now* of the United States of America with other Democracies, under one Federal Union Government, as a practical first step toward World Federal Union, and a realistic way to prevent war, establish prosperity, and maintain our individual liberties.'[59] Lothian was especially enthusiastic, and vigorously supported the establishment in July 1939 of an organisation known as World Federal Union designed to implement Streit's proposals. By this time Lothian had already been appointed British ambassador to Washington. The whole situation greatly distressed Lord Milner's widow, and she gave vent to her feelings in a letter to Grigg:

... the most serious effort that is being made to weaken [the British] purpose takes the form of internationalism. We must fight for 'something higher' than our country, and all she stands for, 'to preserve our homes and liberties is not enough'. This sort of stuff is easily picked up and repeated by highbrow noodles, of whom there are always a lot. They have a slogan, why not a new League of Nations, the old one having broken down? They have a new Bible, a book called *Union Now*, by one Streit, which advocates this new League as a 'Federation' ... We need hardly say that the Round Table has fallen for this. Mr. Lionel Curtis can hardly think of anything else, and Lord Lothian is going to America to tell the Americans that they have another Washington (with a German name) among them. It will be too foolish if we listen to people who have always been wrong, in a matter of such importance.[60]

In Grigg, Lady Milner had a sympathetic confidant. He had been critical of Curtis's and Lothian's aims and ideals for some years. Leo Amery, still a friend of the movement although no longer an intimate associate, tended to agree with Grigg. He found Streit's conclusions crude and regretted Lothian's and Curtis's attachment to them. Amery supported the idea of eventual European union, but he thought it foolish to think that anything approaching a federal scheme on American lines could be created in the near future. To him, 'the British approach of voluntary cooperation between na-

---

58  Clarence Kirshman Streit (1896-    ); newspaper correspondent; Rhodes Scholar 1920-1; with the *Philadelphia Public Ledger* 1920-4; Paris Bureau 1920 and 1924; with the *New York Times* since 1925; attached to the American delegation at the Paris Peace Conference 1918-19
59  Streit, *Union Now*
60  Lady Milner to Grigg, 28 July 1939, reel 7, Grigg Papers; for Curtis's enthusiasm see Curtis to F.W. Preston, 26 Oct. 1939, copy, Curtis Papers.

tions retaining their sovereignty but animated by a common ideal' was far more feasible as well as more flexible.[61] Grigg would have heartily agreed.

In addition to the split which had emerged in the ranks of the central group in the late thirties, the movement was also facing a severe financial crisis. Their endowment was almost exhausted, and although Bailey had given *The Round Table* £500 in 1934 this had not been continued on a regular basis after 1937.[62] The need was partially met by a donation secured by Lothian from Sir Ernest Oppenheimer,[63] the South African financier; and then on Bailey's death in August 1940 *The Round Table* received an annual bequest of £1000. According to Curtis the payment of the bequest was to depend upon the quarterly continuing to fulfil its original object, as outlined in 1910 and reaffirmed in 1935.[64]

The outbreak of the Second World War caused an upheaval in the moot, and much to the consternation of Curtis led to a reversal of the 1935 policy. Lothian went to America, Hodson became director of the Empire Division in the Ministry of Information, and Coupland came back as editor of *The Round Table*. The majority in the editorial committee, including Coupland, were now opposed to the promotion of organic union of the empire, of Europe, and of the world. In October 1940 Curtis lamented to Lothian: 'Since your departure the moot has been growing more and more negative and unconstructive, especially under the influence of Horsfall. I have got a meeting convened here in All Souls for Saturday afternoon in order to have a showdown. Horsfall and I have both circulated our views. My own are that it is time that the Round Table should put forward some constructive ideas as to what is to be done about external relations when hostilities cease.'[65]

At the meeting in Oxford on 5 October Curtis pleaded with Hichens, Horsfall, Hailey,[66] Coupland, and Ivison Macadam that *The Round Table* continue on the lines set out in 1935. He was strongly opposed. In order to

---

61 Amery to John Buchan, 20 Nov. 1939, Buchan Papers
62 Lothian to Dove, 14 Dec. 1933 and 1 Feb. 1934, copies; and Bailey to Lothian, 12 Nov. 1937, GD40/17/273 and 344, Lothian Papers
63 Sir Ernest Oppenheimer (1880-1957); knighted 1921; mayor of Kimberley 1912-15; MP in the South African Parliament 1924-38; formed the Anglo-American Corporation of South Africa Ltd 1917
64 Curtis to Hailey, 23 Dec. 1941, copy, Curtis Papers. Curtis to Macadam, 2 May 1946, copy, ibid.
65 Curtis to Lothian, 3 Oct. 1940, copy, ibid.
66 William Malcolm Hailey, 1st baron (1872-1969); joined the Indian Civil Service 1895; chief commissioner of Delhi 1912-18; governor of the Punjab 1924-8; governor of the United Provinces 1928-30 and 1931-4; director of the African Research Survey 1935-8

effect a compromise, Hichens succeeded in carrying a proposal that a composite article on the postwar international settlement should be undertaken by Coupland based on the memoranda prepared by Curtis and Horsfall.[67] A week later Horsfall refused to have anything to do with a composite article. He did not believe that the majority opinion should be set down in such a way that Curtis's views would appear to have equal support within the moot. Horsfall was supported by Brand.[68]

In November Lothian, back on leave, spoke to the moot at Cliveden on the policy of *The Round Table*. He suggested that the quarterly should look ahead to the postwar international situation. Lothian believed there should be some kind of 'Amphictionic Council for the British Commonwealth and the United States' which would agree on purposes and deliberate on their execution. Since the position of the dominions was inseparable from that of the United States, no separate plea should be made for imperial federation. What was needed was a 'Pan-American-British Empire Conference' for political and economic co-operation in war and peace. *The Round Table* should consider how to maintain the basis of this democratic world-security. It should not dogmatise but invite discussion.[69] The Cliveden moot took Lothian's advice and decided that since *The Round Table* could not run a foreign policy of its own distinct from that of the government it should concentrate on examining the various problems which would emerge after the war.[70] Four weeks later Lothian died in Washington, shortly after the untimely death of Hichens in an air-raid. Suddenly, in the space of a few weeks, two of the stalwarts of the movement, two of its original members, had been lost. It was a blow to them all, particularly to Curtis who lost the friendship and understanding of the one man in the group who was willing to sympathise with his point of view.

Curtis spent the early months of 1941 preparing a pamphlet entitled *Decision*, designed to show the practical steps that should be taken to implement the policy of organic union as the only preventative of war. It was based to a great extent on the ideas about international order expounded by Lothian since his Burge lecture of 1935. While working on *Decision* Curtis suggested to Hailey that something should be done to implement Hichen's idea for a composite article. But when the suggestion was considered by the moot, they unanimously decided that *The Round Table* should confine its treatment of international postwar settlement to the publication of articles

67  Hailey to Curtis, 3 Oct. 1941, and Curtis to Macadam, 26 April 1945, Curtis Papers
68  Hailey to Curtis, 3 Oct. 1941, ibid.
69  Memorandum entitled 'Lord Lothian's Last Talk at Cliveden,' reel 7, Grigg Papers; for the date of the moot see Hailey to Curtis, 3 Oct. 1941, Curtis Papers.
70  Hailey to Curtis, 3 Oct. 1941, ibid.

dealing with separate postwar problems. The London members did not see any advantage at that stage in publishing either an analysis of the overall problem or a statement of the various possible solutions.[71] This decision greatly distressed Curtis who believed *The Round Table* had been founded 'in the hope of providing some leadership to the British democracies,' instead it offered no practical guidance and engendered 'a sense of doubt, hesitation and pain in the mind of the reader.' He believed that the quarterly was now the negation of the attitude it had been 'conceived, founded and endowed to promote.' He could no longer remain associated with the quarterly, and he informed the committee of his intention to resign.[72] For Curtis the Round Table movement and the quarterly had been his whole life for over thirty years, and he was greatly distressed at the prospect of exile from the moot. Only the pleading of Macadam and the assurance from the committee that they would never think of accepting his resignation compelled Curtis to return. But he did so a saddened man.[73] In March 1942 Herbert Baker informed Grigg that 'Lionel Curtis writes mournfully of his loneliness; even his own creation the Round Table won't recognise his pamphlets; but a prophet must not be surprised that he has no honour in his own generation.'[74] Grigg regretted Curtis's loneliness, but reminded Baker that 'he is rather apt to demand 100 percent submission to his point of view about turning *The Round Table* into a propaganda organ for World Federation.'[75]

During the remainder of the war Curtis devoted his energies to the preparation of a number of pamphlets and books in which he urged that the British commonwealth should take the initiative in world affairs by forming an organic union for common defence, 'in the faith that ultimately the union might be joined, first by our Allies in Western Europe and ultimately by the U.S.A.' *Action* appeared in 1942, *Faith and Works* in 1943, *The Way to Peace* towards the end of the war, and *World War; its Cause and Cure* in 1945. *Faith and Works* and *The Way to Peace* cost Curtis nearly £400 out of his own pocket, and the £600 printing bill for *World War; its Cause and Cure* was raised by friends.[76] Curtis's ideas were considered impossible by most members of the moot, and when he suggested that his opinions be jux-

---

71 Curtis to Hailey, 8 Sept. 1941, copy, and Hailey to Curtis, 3 Oct. 1941, ibid.
72 Curtis to Hailey, 23 Dec. 1941, copy, ibid.
73 Macadam to Curtis, 6 Jan. 1942; and Curtis to Macadam, 8 Jan. 1942, copies, reel 7; and 26 April 1945, copy, reel 8, Grigg Papers
74 H. Baker to Grigg, 10 March 1942, reel 7, ibid.
75 Grigg to Baker, 11 March 1942, copy, ibid.
76 Curtis to Macadam, 26 April 1945, Curtis Papers. In 1947 Curtis published *The Master-Key to Peace* which restated the basic doctrine, unaltered since the days of *The Commonwealth of Nations* and *The Problem of the Commonwealth*.

taposed with those of the majority in the pages of *The Round Table*, Geoffrey Dawson, again the interim editor, advised him that the quarterly could not become 'a forum for the rival exponents in a quarrel which seems largely imaginery and likely to be solved by events.' He was opposed to *The Round Table* declaring itself for organic union or for any particular policy, and he believed Curtis's contention that the issue was between either an international government or compacts between individual governments a false reading of events.[77]

This situation continued until early 1945 when a request from the Melbourne group for a definite statement of policy brought the whole question to the fore once again. Curtis was as adamant as ever, and told Macadam that

It is hard to see how the Round Table can now get out of the mess into which it has drifted. Nothing can now alter the contrast between the policy of its founders as reaffirmed after 25 years in No.100 with the numbers printed during the years of the war ... The issue raised [by Melbourne] cannot be evaded ... I think each member of the moot, old and new, must now face the question whether, in the light of the policy declared in Round Table No.100, he is justified in administering the endowments, especially the Abe endowment, on continuing the policy, or rather the negation of policy, followed during the war. If a majority think they are, then ... the minority must decline to share this responsibility and resign. I certainly must ... If ... a majority feel that they are now morally bound to conduct the Round Table on the lines enunciated in No.100, then obviously those who cannot support that policy must retire. In either case the places vacated can quickly be filled. This at least is clear, that the Round Table can no longer halt between two opinions.[78]

Faced with this challenge, the moot reverted to its 1935 statement. In late 1945 it circulated a memorandum reaffirming its basic adherence to the pre-war policies of the quarterly, but indicating that all solutions of the imperial problem, of which the federal idea was still one, would now be considered. Greatly heartened, Curtis plunged anew into his task of expounding the ideas that he and Lothian had promoted for much of their association with the movement. Despite his advancing years, he was now seventy-three, Curtis claimed he would carry on his work 'because the cause for which Milner, Selborne, Philip and Abe founded and endowed the Round Table must not go by default in the crisis of the commonwealth they greatly served.'[79] But as

77 Curtis to Irvine, Oct. 1942; Dawson to Curtis, 14 Oct. 1942; and Curtis to Dawson, 19 Oct. 1942, Curtis Papers
78 Curtis to Macadam, 26 April 1945, copy, ibid.

usual Curtis was too hopeful. The London memorandum was greeted with skepticism by all the dominion groups. The difficulties in the way of achieving a world federation, even a commonwealth federation, seemed insuperable to the Newfoundland members.[80] In Wellington the majority could not even agree that 'the *ultimate ideal* of the Group or the movement should be an organic union,'[81] while the Melbourne group, still the strongest of all the dominion branches, felt that 'the cooperative method on the administrative level should be tried to the utmost as the most hopeful line of advance towards such closer integration as may emerge.'[82]

By the autumn of 1947 Grigg, now Lord Altrincham, was growing increasingly restless at *The Round Table*'s handling of commonwealth problems. He was convinced that insistence upon federal union as the goal of British policy both in Europe and the commonwealth was wrong and dangerous. He believed that the commonwealth's role should be to stand between the two great federal blocs, the American and the Russian, and to restore its strength by the many practical forms of co-operation and reciprocal aid open to sovereign states. He claimed that the moot was continuing to ignore the methods of closer co-operation between sovereign parliaments which he had advocated in his book *The British Commonwealth* published in 1945, and which he believed offered the only practical road to closer commonwealth and European association. Altrincham was in fundamental disagreement with the moot's policy. He planned to write another book and possibly secure the control of a monthly magazine so he could put his case: 'This, I am afraid, leaves no time for writing in the Round Table ... I am deeply miserable to be thus at odds with the brotherhood which has done so much over a generation and meant so much to me personally ... I feel (like Lionel and quite as intensely) that one must be either for federal union or against it. Attempting to differentiate between immediate aims and ultimate ideals only befogs the issue and makes effective argument either way impossible; and as the life of the greatest political association in the world is at stake, I think blurring and glossing indefensible.'[83]

Dermot Morrah,[84] now the editor of *The Round Table*, found himself in

79 Curtis to Macadam, 2 May 1946; and D. Morrah to Curtis, 16 Jan. 1946, ibid.
80 'Observations of the Newfoundland Group on the Memorandum submitted by the Editorial Committee in November 1945,' 26 March 1946, copy, ibid.
81 Von Haast to Curtis, 29 Aug. 1946, ibid.
82 'The reply of the Melbourne Group to the London memorandum of November 1945 on Round Table Aims and Policy,' 20 Dec. 1946, copy, ibid.
83 Altrincham to Morrah, 7 Oct. 1947, copy, ibid. On a copy of this letter Curtis scrawled against the last phrase: 'Here Ned and I agree.'
84 Dermot Michael Macgregor Morrah (1896-    ); fellow of All Souls 1921-8; Home Civil

a difficult position. He could not afford to have 'an opinion about the big question at issue between Altrincham and Curtis' if he was to go on editing 'on behalf of a body that is so acutely divided.' He pointed out that the blurring of the vital issue was implicit in the compromise statement agreed upon in 1945. But until the moot agreed to a change, Morrah as editor could only attempt to abide by the policy memorandum which all members had agreed upon in 1945: 'It seems to me the first function of The Round Table to go on discussing all doctrines of imperial cooperation, of which the federal idea is still one. But how impossible it is to put forward any clear-cut argument on behalf of a group of men who differ so strongly upon methods, even though they are agreed on the one goal of imperial unity.'[85]

When this correspondence was circulated to the editorial committee, Dougie Malcolm and Brand found it distressing. Malcolm admitted that to accept the doctrine of 'organic union as the ultimate ideal' with the emphasis on 'ultimate' did have a blurring effect, but there seemed little else the quarterly could do. Although Malcolm was opposed to Curtis's current schemes of federal and organic union, he did believe, or at least hope for, the eventual union of nation states. Brand was more emphatic, and referred to Curtis as an impractical idealist. He believed the prophet's advocacy of specific solutions for the union of the commonwealth and Western Europe was a bar to a careful discussion and examination of all practicable steps of closer co-operation between not only the states of the commonwealth but also the states of Western Europe.[86]

The result of this clash of opinion was the decision to publish in March 1948, on the anniversary of the 150th issue of The Round Table, an article by Curtis entitled 'Untempered Mortar: The Case for Organic Union,' and one by Altrincham entitled 'Britain's Role in the World Today: A Criticism of the Federal Case.' An introductory article by Morrah dissociated The Round Table from either view, but indicated that since it was no longer possible for the quarterly to try and hold the balance between conflicting opinions it would in future allow the matter to be debated in its pages. In this way the members of the Round Table organisation in Great Britain and the dominions hoped to clarify thinking on one of the great issues before the commonwealth, while at the same time confirming their belief in the need for a free but united commonwealth as one of the buttresses of peace and a guar-

Service 1922-8; leader-writer *Daily Mail* 1928-31; *The Times* 1932-61; *The Daily Telegraph* 1961-6; editor of *The Round Table* 1944-65
85  Morrah to Altrincham, 8 Oct. 1947, copy, Curtis Papers
86  Malcolm to Morrah, 10 Oct. 1947, copy; Curtis to Brand, 15 Oct. 1947, copy; and Brand to Curtis, 17 Oct. 1947, ibid.

antee of the survival and spread of free institutions.[87] The debate continued in the next two numbers with the publication of an article on 'British Commonwealth and Western Union' in June, and in September a rebuttal by Curtis and a counter-rebuttal by the author of the June article.[88] With the publication of these articles Curtis could no longer complain of the refusal of *The Round Table* to publish his ideas. But it did little to alter either his colleague's views or the relations within the commonwealth and between national governments. To within a year or so of his death in 1955 Curtis continued to battle for his beliefs with much of his old flair and sparkle. But it was all in vain. The European Economic Community which emerged was not at all what he had hoped for, and he would have been saddened by the extreme nationalism of many commonwealth governments in the fifties and sixties. Perhaps mercifully he did not live to witness Suez.

By the time of Curtis's death *The Round Table* was following a standard format of surveying international and commonwealth problems in special articles, publishing chronicle articles from the dominions, and keeping abreast of the nuances of commonwealth development. It never pledged itself to any specific belief apart from underlining the role that the commonwealth could and should play in the world. By the late fifties and early sixties few of the original members were left. Malcolm, Grigg, Kerr, Hichens, Marris, Feetham, Duncan, Oliver, Milner, Selborne, Dawson, Coupland, Zimmern were all gone; and in 1963 Lord Brand, the last of the kindergarten, passed away. Those who remained in London had never known the early days when the movement was at its height and had been a worthy and recognised adversary in intellectual and political circles. By the time of Brand's death funds were running low and drastic decisions had to be made. In 1966, after fifty-six years, *The Round Table* abandoned its policy of anonymity and all the special articles were henceforth signed. Morrah retired as editor and was succeeded, first by a young Canadian journalist, Leonard Beaton, subsequently by joint editors Michael Howard and Robert Jackson and then by Jackson alone. For the first time there was a concerted effort to make the quarterly commercially viable. This appears to have succeeded without really jeopardising the comprehensive, if conservative, treatment of international and commonwealth affairs for which *The Round Table* has long been known.

87　[D. Morrah], 'Two Views of Empire, An Introduction to Debate'; [L. Curtis], 'Untempered Mortar: The Case for Organic Union'; [Lord Altrincham], 'Britain's Role in the World Today: A Criticism of the Federal Case,' *The Round Table*, March 1948, 519-23, 524-34, 535-44
88　'British Commonwealth and Western Union,' ibid., June 1948, 633-42; and [L. Curtis and anon.], 'A Debate Continued,' ibid., Sept. 1948, 749-61

# Conclusion

For any one at all interested in the twentieth-century empire common-wealth, in the changes in anglo-dominion and anglo-Indian relations, and particularly in the assumptions and attitudes which determined the actions of imperial idealists, some knowledge of the Round Table movement is essential. It was a highly active organisation for about a decade after its for-mation, and it had some measure of influence at the level of public debate and, on occasion, behind-the-governmental scenes. Many of its major goals, especially imperial federation, were never realised and were probably hope-less aspirations from the beginning. But some of its ideas such as self-government for India, the gradual extension of self-government to all com-monwealth countries, and certain suggested reforms in imperial organisa-tion were valuable, eventually were realised, and when initially suggested were in advance of their time. Moreover, of all the groups, societies, and organisations founded in the late nineteenth and early twentieth centuries to promote imperial union, the Round Table movement was the only one which succeeded in putting down firm roots in all the dominions.

For much of its existence the movement was hampered by trying to shape everything to its precommitment to an organic union of the empire. Its ideol-ogy was an impediment to constructive political action. The London mem-bers certainly tried to be realistic, but their difficulties were always the same. They consistently underestimated the nature and extent of the forces with which they were dealing. In Ireland they failed to grasp that the nationalists had no interest in the British commonwealth as the embodiment of a moral idea, and in India they did not realise that the Congress party and the Muslim League were reasoning from different assumptions about the nature and purpose of empire.[1] Above all they never really understood dominion feelings. Its members in the dominions were not usually reliable indicators of changing dominion attitudes, and even when criticisms were levelled at the central group's assumptions the London members paid them little heed. Viewed logically their case for imperial union was virtually unassailable, but logic was not enough. As they later realised they had been discussing the whole without knowing the parts.

Dominion nationalism[2] at the turn of the century and its coherence and importance at given moments can be over-emphasized, but a new self-consciousness did exist after the Boer War and the London group never really came to grips with it. Curtis was the worst offender. He recognised it, wrote about it, and claimed his schemes would satisfy it, but he was so zealous in his pursuit of imperial unity that he brushed dominion feelings aside in a spate of remorseless logic. This lack of real understanding doomed any chance the movement may have had of being truly effective. Professor F.L. Wood, a New Zealand member of the movement since the thirties, recently referred to this shortcoming: 'In my day I have been a good deal impressed by the attitude of the surviving London members and their immediate descendants who have always been very nice and well informed but somehow unable to conceive that London could ever cease to be the centre of the world.'[3] Curtis, of course, was often criticised for his arguments and conclusions, supposedly based on a reading of the past. He did not deliberately deceive, but his history could be very bad. Even his colleagues winced at his generalisations and his manipulation of evidence.

Throughout these years all the members of the movement were liberal imperialists. They had no use for the tory-jingoism and expansionist fever of the late nineteenth century. They simply held the anglo-dominion relationship up for examination and found it sadly wanting. They also helped demolish the prejudice against granting self-government to India, and were in the vanguard of those arguing for everyman's right to self-rule. They were concerned about the relations of East and West, and argued that the superior position of the European in the world involved not a privilege but 'a special obligation to serve.'

But having acknowledged the movement's sincerity and genuine concern

1 Allison, 'Imperialism and Appeasement,' 289-90
2 Perhaps patriotism is a better term; see Cole, 'The Problem of "Nationalism" and "Imperialism.
3 F.L. Wood to Professor Keith Sinclair, May 1966, enclosed in Sinclair to Kendle, 11 June 1966

for the development and protection of the so-called 'backward peoples,' it is necessary to consider their basic assumption that British civilisation and British rule were inherently superior to any other. The members were un-ashamedly pan-anglo-saxon nationalists with a deep faith in the con-tribution that the commonwealth could make to humanity and to the sta-bility of the world. The London members' belief in the qualities of the British race rarely descended into blatant bigotry, but if they were not racists in quite the way the term is understood today their discussions of policy toward non-Europeans in Africa and India were often couched in terms reminiscent of Karl Pearson and Houston Stewart Chamberlain. They believed in Rhodes's maxim 'equal rights for every civilised man,' and argued that there was a civilisation line above which men were capable of self-government but below which they still needed education and training. This has a curiously old-fashioned ring to it. Certainly it reveals the blinkered perspective with which the movement viewed non-whites. The members of the movement, particularly the London group, gave little consideration to the institutions and ways-of-life being disrupted or replaced by the British in Africa and In-dia, and they were too uncritical of governmental policy in the interwar years. Admittedly many of the crucial developments in Africa, India, and the rest of the empire were taking place at a time when the majority of the mem-bers, particularly in London, were engrossed in other matters and unable to devote much time or attention to these problems. Nevertheless, *The Round Table* quarterly and its supporters were always too easily satisfied with su-perficial and partial solutions to the problems of alien rule and the transfer of power.

This forces the question: Did the Round Table members really believe in, have faith in, the African's and the Indian's capacity for self-rule? The evi-dence is certainly not clear-cut, but it would suggest that doubts may well have lingered in the subconscious if not the conscious mind of many mem-bers.[4] By 1914 the majority of the London group seem to have accepted that Indians were capable of self-government, providing the proper education had been obtained. Their attitude toward the other 'backward peoples' was not as clear. In the main they believed the lack of political development was due to environmental and sociological reasons, not to biological differences, and they did argue that self-government would eventually be given to all the 'backward peoples.' However, there remained a lingering doubt that 'the lower races' could ever rise very high in the scale of civilisation. This is appar-ent from their correspondence, from Curtis's writings on India, and from the activities of men like Grigg and Malcolm in Africa. A good example is a con-

4 See Perham, '*The Round Table* and Sub-Saharan Africa.'

fession made by John Dove to Brand in 1919 during a visit to India: 'Do you remember your nursery ideas of a savage? Can a man who is nearly stark naked and brown and painted and whose long black hair calls up "Man Friday" running across the sands from the cannibal bonfires, ever be really fit for a vote? I have changed since I came here, but I still, I confess, feel old prejudices pulling at me. This is especially so when from time to time one of those strange outbursts of inconceivable brutality occurs.'[5]

The movement was unequivocal on the problem of emigration. They did not want to see Indians or Africans flooding into the white dominions. They, in fact, would have preferred to see the world divided between white and black areas, one in the temperate and the other in the tropical zone. This attitude was one the kindergarten had carried with them to South Africa; and it was one they never really eradicated despite their wealth of experience and their moderated stance toward India. As late as 1952 Curtis was still advocating the creation of a black dominion to the north of South Africa to which all the South African 'natives' could be moved.

The Round Table movement has often been credited with an influence and a group cohesiveness which it really lacked. The original members, especially those in London, were often at odds over basic issues and, at times, in fundamental disagreement over the methods to be adopted. The unwillingness of the majority of members to come to grips with the economic problems of the anglo-dominion, and later the anglo-african, relationship was a cause of great concern to men like Amery, Cecil, and Grigg. An additional source of disagreement was Curtis's dogmatic assertion that the alternative facing the empire-commonwealth was union or disruption. Both Brand and Grigg were never sympathetic to this viewpoint while Amery gradually drifted away from the central group, primarily because he and Curtis were so fundamentally at odds on this issue. Much the same point can be made about the dominion members. They were often skeptical of the London group's assumptions and contentions, and they also had differences of opinion among themselves. Thus it would be misleading to think of the movement as a cohesive unit providing a solid front to the world. However, there was one matter they did all agree on – the need to preserve the empire-commonwealth in some form; to both the British and dominion members it represented a positive step in man's search for peace and understanding.[6]

5 Dove to Brand, 9 Sept. 1919, printed in Brand, *The Letters of John Dove*, 103
6 As recently as 1968 the editorial committee claimed rather defiantly that '*The Round Table* is the journal of those who believe the Commonwealth is a force for good in the world and refuse to see it destroyed.' Taken from an advertisement enclosed with the October 1968 issue of *The Round Table*.

As for the influence of the movement this has often been exaggerated both by contemporaries and by later writers. On occasion, of course, especially before 1914, the movement, particularly the London group, did have some influence in governmental circles in Great Britain and the dominions; and obviously *The Round Table* was a most important vehicle for the circulation of ideas and information about empire-commonwealth and international affairs, although it will never be possible to ascertain the full nature and extent of its influence. Even so it must be realised that very few of the Round Table members were really influential – in positions of power or with long-time access to powerful men.[7] Despite the prominent roles many of them played in British and dominion public life, most were on the periphery of power. Even when they did gain momentary access to the centre of affairs, it is doubtful that Round Table aims and ideals were their primary concern.

The British and dominion groups were also hampered by the nature of their membership and the mystery and anonymity surrounding their activities. Most of the movement's members were representative of the affluent, the well-placed, the intellectual, and generally the most acceptable members of society. Businessmen, lawyers, academics, journalists, politicians, they were hardly a representative cross-section of the population of Great Britain and the dominions. There were very few members of Labour leanings, hardly any French-Canadians or Akrikaners, no Africans, and only a handful of Indians. It was essentially a white, anglo-saxon, protestant organisation of the upper middle class with aristocratic underpinnings. At a time of great economic, social, and political change the Round Table members, particularly those in London, were far removed from tragedy with too little experience of everyday life. They were too prosperous or too well-placed to be able to identify with issues and problems that intellectually they knew to be sensitive. They possessed too much 'effortless superiority'; perhaps this partially explains their difficulties with the dominions, and it is evident in their attitude toward India and the dependencies.

The members of the movement had ability, money, or access to money, and the fervour and conviction necessary to sacrifice time and energy in the pursuit of their ideals, but unfortunately their aims and methods aroused suspicion. Almost from the moment of its founding critics have accused the movement of being a conspiracy. Laurier believed this and in recent years one historian has suggested that the movement was only one link in a vast

7 I should again make it clear that I make this statement only in the context of imperial affairs. A somewhat different assessment might be required if foreign affairs and the problem of appeasement were being examined.

nexus of influence controlled by Milner.[8] This argument collapses under close examination. It was always the movement's intention to place its findings and conclusions before the public. The members realised there was little to be gained by prolonged secrecy and anonymity except suspicion. Nevertheless, their methods were often disingenuous; and their desire for temporary anonymity and the manner in which some groups became centres of propaganda rather than of study laid them open to criticism. By the time the movement awakened to the problem it was too late to erase the widespread skepticism in the dominions.

8   Quigley, 'The Round Table Groups in Canada.' See also Quigley, *Tragedy and Hope.*

# Bibliography

MANUSCRIPT SOURCES

*Official*
Cabinet Records, Public Record Office, Cab. 4/5/1, Cab. 17/101, Cab 37/105

*Private Papers*
Balfour Papers, British Museum
Robert Borden Papers, Public Archives of Canada
Henri Bourassa Papers, Public Archives of Canada
John Buchan Papers [Lord Tweedsmuir], Queen's University Archives
Lord Robert Cecil Papers, British Museum
Chelmsford Papers, India Office Library
Loring Christie Papers, Public Archives of Canada
Curtis Papers, Round Table Offices, London
Curzon Papers, India Office Library
Dafoe Papers, Public Archives of Canada
Deakin Papers, Australian National Library
Denison Papers, Public Archives of Canada
Sanford Evans Papers, Manitoba Provincial Archives, Winnipeg
J.S. Ewart Papers, Manitoba Provincial Archives, Winnipeg
Fortnightly Club Papers, Library of the University of Cape Town
Joseph Flavelle Papers, Public Archives of Canada

Arthur Glazebrook Papers, Public Archives of Canada
Earl Grey Papers, Prior's Kitchen, Durham, England and Public
    Archives of Canada
Grigg Papers [Lord Altrincham], Queen's University Archives, Kingston
Harrison Moore Papers, University of Melbourne Archives
Jebb Papers, Institute of Commonwealth Studies, London
Arthur Jose Papers, Mitchell Library, Sydney, New South Wales
Mackenzie King Papers, Public Archives of Canada
T.H. Laby Papers, held by Dr Jean Laby, Melbourne
Lloyd George Papers, Beaverbrook Library, London
Lothian Papers, Scottish Record Office, Edinburgh
Meston Papers, India Office Library
Milner Papers, Bodleian Library
Montagu Papers, India Office Library
W.B. Matheson diary, Alexander Turnbull Library, Wellington
Parkin Papers, Public Archives of Canada
Rowell Papers, Public Archives of Canada
Adam Shortt Papers, Queen's University Archives
Clifford Sifton Papers, Public Archives of Canada
Malcolm Lindsay Shephard 'Memoirs'. Commonwealth
    Archives, Canberra
Arthur Steel-Maitland Papers, Scottish Record Office
Walker Papers, University of Toronto Library
Willison Papers, Public Archives of Canada
George Wrong Papers, University of Toronto Library
Hume Wrong Papers, Public Archives of Canada

PRINTED PRIMARY SOURCES

*Parliamentary Debates*
Great Britain

*Publications by members and associates of the movement*
Amery, L.S. *The Case Against Home Rule.* London 1912
– *The Fundamental Fallacies of Free Trade.* London 1908
Amery, L.S.,ed. *'The Times' History of the War in South Africa 1899-1902,*
    7 vols. London 1900-9
– *My Political Life,* 3 vols. London 1953
– *Thoughts on the Constitution,* 2nd ed. London 1953
– *Union and Strength.* London 1912

Atkinson, Meredith. *The New Social Order: A study of Post-War Reconstruction.* Melbourne 1920

Beer, George Louis. *The English-Speaking Peoples: Their Future and Joint International Obligations.* New York 1917

Brand, R.H.,ed. *The Letters of John Dove.* London 1938
- *The Union of South Africa.* Oxford 1909

Buchan, John. *The African Colony: Studies in the Reconstruction.* Edinburgh 1903
- *Memory Hold-the-Door.* London 1940

Cecil, Lord Robert [Viscount Cecil of Chelwood]. *All the Way.* London 1949
- *A Great Experiment: An Autobiography.* New York 1941

Chirol, V. *India Old and New.* London 1921
- *Indian Unrest.* London 1910

Curtis, L. *Action.* London 1942
- *The Annotated Memorandum.* London 1911 (unsigned)
- *A Practical Inquiry into the Nature of Citizenship in the British Empire and into the Relation of Its Several Communities to Each Other.* London 1914 (unsigned)
- *Australian Notes.* London 1911 (unsigned)
- *Civitas Dei: The Commonwealth of God.* London 1938

Curtis, L., ed. *The Commonwealth of Nations.* Part I London 1916
- *Decision.* London 1942
- *Dyarchy.* Oxford 1920
- *Faith and Works, or a World Safe for Small Nations.* London 1943
- *The Government of South Africa,* 2 vols. Cape Town 1908 (unsigned)
- *The Green Memorandum.* London 1910 (unsigned)
- *The Master-Key to Peace.* London 1947
- *New Zealand Notes.* London 1912 (unsigned)
- *Notes on the Progress of the Movement in Australia.* Bombay 1916
- *The Open Road to Freedom.* Oxford 1950
- *The Problem of the Commonwealth.* London 1916
- *The Project of a Commonwealth.* London 1915 (unsigned)
- *The Round Table Movement: Its Past and Future.* Toronto 1913
- *The Strawberry Memorandum.* London, May 1914 (unsigned)
- *With Milner in South Africa.* Oxford 1951
- *World Revolution in the Cause of Peace.* London 1949
- *World War: Its Cause and Cure.* London 1945

Egerton, H.E. *An Analysis of the System of Government throughout the British Empire.* London 1912 (unsigned)
- *Federations and Unions within the British Empire.* Oxford 1911

Eggleston, F.W. *Reflections on Australian Foreign Policy.* Melbourne 1957

Garran, Sir Robert R. *Prosper the Commonwealth.* Sydney 1958

Grigg, Sir Edward (Lord Altrincham). *Britain Looks at Germany.* London 1938

– *The British Commonwealth.* London 1943

– *The Faith of an Englishman.* London 1936

– *The Greatest Experiment in History.* London 1924

– *Kenya's Opportunities: Memories, Hopes and Ideas.* London 1955

Gwynn, Stephen, ed. *The Anvil of War: Letters between F.S. Oliver and His Brother 1914-18.* London 1936

Hancock, W.K. and J.Van Der Poel, eds. *Selections from the Smuts Papers,* 4 vols. Cambridge 1966

Headlam, Cecil, ed. *The Milner Papers,* 2 vols. London 1931, 1933

Hearnshaw, F.J.C., ed. *King's College Lectures on Colonial Problems.* London 1913

Hodson, H.V., ed *The British Commonwealth and the Future, Proceedings of the Second Unofficial Conference on British Commonwealth Relations, Sydney, 3-17th September 1938.* Oxford 1939

– *The British Empire.* London 1939

– *The Twentieth Century Empire.* London 1948

Kerr, Philip (Lord Lothian). *The American Speeches of Lord Lothian, July 1939 to December 1940.* London 1941

– *Liberalism in the Modern World.* London 1933

– *Pacifism is not Enough, nor Patriotism Either.* Oxford 1933

– 'The Political Relations of Advanced and Backward Peoples,' in *Introduction to the Study of International Relations* ed. by A.J. Grant et al. London 1916

Kerr, Philip and L. Curtis. *The Prevention of War.* New Haven 1923

Laby, T.H. *New Zealand's Naval Policy.* Wellington 1913

Lash, Z.A. *A Canadian Criticism on "The Problem of the Commonwealth" and the author's reply thereto.* London 1916 (unsigned)

– *Defence and Foreign Affairs: A Suggestion for the Empire.* Toronto 1917

Long, B.K. *The Framework of Union.* Cape Town 1908 (unsigned)

Massey, V. *What's Past is Prologue.* Toronto 1963

Milner, Alfred (Lord Milner) *Arnold Toynbee: A Reminiscence.* London 1895

– *The British Commonwealth.* London 1919

– *Constructive Imperialism.* London 1908

– *England in Egypt.* London 1892

- *Imperial Unity: Speeches delivered in Canada in the Autumn of 1908.* London 1909
- 'The Key to My Position,' *The Times,* 27 July 1925
- *The Nation and the Empire.* London 1913
- *Questions of the Hour.* London 1923
Muir, Ramsey. *National Self-Government.* London 1918
- *Nationalism and Internationalism.* London 1916
- *A Short History of the British Commonwealth,* 2 vols. London 1920-2
Oliver, F.S. *The Alternative to Civil War.* London 1913
- *Alexander Hamilton: An Essay on American Union.* London 1906
- *Federalism and Home Rule.* London 1910 (signed Pacificus)
- *Ordeal by Battle.* London 1915
- *What Federalism is Not.* London 1914
Peterson, Sir William. *Canadian Essays and Addresses.* London 1915
Selborne, Lord. *The State and the Citizen.* London 1913
Seton-Watson, R.W., ed. *The War and Democracy.* London 1914
Streit, Clarence K. *Union Now.* London 1939
Williams, Basil, ed. *The Selborne Memorandum.* Oxford 1925
Willison, Sir John Stephen. *Reminiscences, Political and Personal.* Toronto 1919
Zimmern, Alfred.*The Greek Commonwealth.* London 1911
- *The League of Nations and the Rule of Law 1918-1935.* London 1936
- *Nationality and Government.* London 1918
- *The Third British Empire.* London 1926


CONTEMPORARY BOOKS

Allen, J.H. *A Naval Policy for New Zealand.* Dunedin 1912
Borden, Sir Robert. *The War and the Future.* London 1917
Borden, Henry, ed. *Robert Laird Borden: His Memoirs,* 2 vols. Toronto 1938
Bourassa, Henri. *Independence or Imperial Partnership? A Study of the Problem of the Commonwealth by Mr. Lionel Curtis.* Montreal 1916
Chamberlain, Austen. *Politics from Inside: An Epistolary Chronicle, 1906-1914.* London 1936
Cole, M.I., ed *Beatrice Webb's Diaries 1912-1924.* London 1952
Croft, H.P. *The Path of Empire.* London 1912
Dilke, Sir Charles. *Greater Britain.* London 1868
- *Problems of Greater Britain,* 2 vols. London 1890

Eastwood, R.A. *The Organization of a Britannic Partnership.* Manchester 1922
Ewart, J.S. *The Kingdom of Canada.* Toronto 1908
– *The Kingdom Papers,* 2 vols. Ottawa 1912
Findlay, Sir J.G. *The Imperial Conference of 1911 from Within.* London 1912
Fletcher-Vane, F.P. *Pax Britannica.* London 1905
Goldman, R. *A South African Remembers.* Cape Town nd
Hordern, L.H. *The Beginnings of an Imperial Partnership.* London 1907
Hurd, P. and A. Hurd. *The New Empire Partnership.* London 1915
Jebb, Richard. *The Britannic Question: A Survey of Alternatives.* London 1913
– *Empire in Eclipse.* London 1926
– *The Imperial Conference,* 2 vols. London 1911
– *Studies in Colonial Nationalism.* London 1905
Miller, J.O., ed. *The New Era in Canada.* Toronto 1917
Montagu, E.S. *An Indian Diary.* London 1930
Parkin, G.P. *Imperial Federation.* London 1892
Riddell, Lord. *Intimate Diary of the Peace Conference and After, 1918-23.* London 1933
Seeley, Sir J.R. *The Expansion of England.* London 1883
Shotwell, J.T. *At the Paris Peace Coference.* New York 1937
Worsfold, W.Basil. *The Empire on the Anvil.* London 1916
– *Lord Milner's Work in South Africa from its Commencement in 1897 to the Peace of Vereeniging in 1902.* London 1906
– *The Reconstruction of the New Colonies under Lord Milner,* 2 vols. London 1913

PERIODICALS AND NEWSPAPERS

*The National Review*
*The Quarterly Review*
*The Round Table*
*The State*
*University Magazine*
*The Advertiser* (Adelaide)
*The Argus* (Melbourne)
*The Auckland Star*
*The Brisbane Courier*
*The Daily Telegraph* (Sydney)
*The Dominion* (New Zealand)

*The Lyttelton Times*
*The New Zealand Times*
*Otago Daily News*
*The Press* (Christchurch)
*The Register* (Adelaide)
*Sydney Morning Herald*
*The Telegraph* (Brisbane)
*The Times* (London)
*The Toronto Star*
*The Wanganui Herald*

SECONDARY SOURCES

*Books*

Amery, Julian. *The Life of Joseph Chamberlain,* vols. III, IV., & V. London 1951, 1969

Astor, Michael. *Tribal Feeling.* London 1963

Barker, Sir Ernest. *The Ideas and Ideals of the British Empire.* Cambridge 1941

Beloff, Max. *Imperial Sunset.* I: *Britain's Liberal Empire 1897-1921.* London 1969

Benians, E.A., J.R.M. Butler, C.E. Carrington, eds. *The Cambridge History of the British Empire.* III: *The Empire-Commonwealth 1870-1919.* London 1959

Berger, Carl. *The Sense of Power: Studies in the Ideas of Canadian Imperialism, 1867-1914.* Toronto 1970

Blake, R. *The Unknown Prime Minister: The Life and Times of Andrew Bonar Law, 1858-1923.* London 1955

Butler, J.R.M. *Lord Lothian (Philip Kerr), 1882-1940.* London 1960

Colquhoun, A.H.V. *Press, Politics and People: The Life and Letters of Sir John Willison, Journalist and Correspondent of The Times.* Toronto 1935

Colvin, Ian. *The Life of Jameson,* 2 vols. London 1922

– *The Life of Lord Carson.* Toronto 1935

Cook, R. *The Politics of John W. Dafoe and the Free Press.* Toronto 1963

Cowen, Z. *Sir John Latham and Other Papers.* Melbourne 1965

Crankshaw, Edward. *The Forsaken Idea: A Study of Viscount Milner.* London 1952

Cross, J.A. *Whitehall and the Commonwealth.* London 1967

Dafoe, J.W. *Laurier.* Toronto 1922

Davenport, T.R.H. *The Afrikaner Bond: The History of a South African Political Party, 1880-1911.* London 1966

Davies, Joseph. *The Prime Minister's Secretariat, 1916-1920.* Newport, Mon. 1951

Dawson, R.M. *The Development of Dominion Status, 1900-1936.* London 1937

Denoon, Donald. *A Grand Illusion: The failure of imperial policy in the Transvaal Colony during the period of reconstruction 1900-1905.* London 1973

Elton, G.E., ed. *The First Fifty Years of the Rhodes Trust and the Rhodes Scholarships 1903-1953.* Oxford 1956

Fitzpatrick, Sir Percy. *Lord Milner and His Work.* Cape Town 1925

– *South African Memoirs.* London 1932

Fry, Michael. *Illusions of Security: North Atlantic Diplomacy 1918-22.* Toronto 1972

Gelfand, L.E. *The Inquiry: American Preparations for Peace 1917-19.* New Haven 1963

Glazebrook, G.P. de T. *Sir Edmund Walker.* London 1933

Gollin, A.M. *The Observer and J.L. Garvin 1908-14.* London 1960
- *Proconsul in Politics: A Study of Lord Milner in Opposition and In Power.* London 1964

Gordon, D.C. *The Dominion Partnership in Imperial Defense, 1870-1914.* Baltimore 1965

Grant, W.L. and F. Hamilton. *George Monro Grant.* Toronto 1905

Guinn, Paul. *British Strategy and Politics 1914 to 1918.* Oxford 1965

Hall, H.D. *The British Commonwealth of Nations.* London 1920
- *Commonwealth: A History of the British Commonwealth of Nations.* Toronto 1971

Halpérin, V. *Lord Milner and the Empire: The Evolution of British Imperialism.* London 1952

Hancock, W.K. *Australia.* London 1931
- *Smuts,* 2 vols. Cambridge 1962, 1968
- *Survey of British Commonwealth Affairs* I: *Problems of Nationality 1918-1936.* London 1937

Hyde, H. Montgomery. *Carson.* London 1953

Kendle, John E. *The Colonial and Imperial Conferences 1887-1911: a study in imperial organisation.* London 1967

King-Hall, Stephen. *Chatham House: A Brief Account of the Origins, Purposes and Methods of the Royal Institute of International Affairs.* London 1937

La Nauze, J.A. *Alfred Deakin,* 2 vols. Melbourne 1965

LeMay, G.H.L. *British Supremacy in South Africa 1899-1907.* Oxford 1965

Lindley, Sir Francis. *Lord Lovat.* London 1935

Mehrotra, S.R. *India and the Commonwealth 1885-1929.* London 1965

Miller, J.D.B. *Richard Jebb and the Problem of Empire.* London 1956

Milner, Viscountess. *My Picture Gallery 1886-1901.* London 1951

Nimocks, Walter. *Milner's Young Men: The "Kindergarten" in Edwardian Imperial Affairs.* Durham, NC 1968

Preston, R.A. *Canada and "Imperial Defense."* Toronto 1967

Pyrah, G.B. *Imperial Policy and South Africa 1902-10.* Oxford 1955

Quigley, C. *Tragedy and Hope: A History of the World in our Time.* New York 1966

Richter, M. *Politics of Conscience: T.H. Green and his Age.* London 1964

Roskill, Stephen. *Hankey: Man of Secrets,* 2 vols. London 1970, 1972

Rowse, A.L. *Appeasement: A Study in Political Decline 1933-1939.* New York 1961

Schull, J. *Laurier.* Toronto 1965

Semmel, B. *Imperialism and Social Reform: English Social-Imperial Thought 1895-1914.* London 1960

Sinclair, K. *Imperial Federation, A Study of New Zealand Policy and Opinion 1880-1914.* London 1955

Skelton, O.D. *Life and Letters of Sir Wilfrid Laurier,* 2 vols. London 1922

Smith, Janet Adam. *John Buchan.* London 1965

Smith, V.A. *The Oxford History of India,* 3rd ed. Oxford 1961

*The History of "The Times."* III: *The Twentieth Century Test 1884-1912;* IV: *The 150th Anniversary and Beyond 1912-1948.* London 1947, 1952

Thompson, L.M. *The Unification of South Africa, 1902-1910.* Oxford 1960

Thornton, A.P. *The Imperial Idea and Its Enemies.* London 1959

Toynbee, A.J. *Acquaintances.* London 1967

Toynbee, A.J., ed. *British Commonwealth Relations: Proceedings of the First Unofficial Conference at Toronto, 11-21 September 1933.* Oxford 1934

Van Heerden, J. *Closer Union Movement 1902-10: Bibliography.* Cape Town 1952

Waley, S.D. *Edwin Montagu: A Memoir and an Account of his Visits to India.* Bombay 1964

Wallis, J.P.R. *Fitz: The Story of Sir Percy Fitzpatrick.* London 1955

Willison, Sir John. *Sir George Parkin.* London 1929

Wilson, M. and L.M. Thompson, eds. *The Oxford History of South Africa,* 2 vols. Oxford 1969, 1971

Winkler, H.R. *The League of Nations Movement in Great Britain 1914-19.* New Brunswick, NJ 1952

Woolf, L. *Beginning Again: An Autobiography of the Years 1911-1918.* London 1964

Wrench, J.E. *Alfred Lord Milner: the Man of No Illusions, 1854-1925.* London 1958

– *Geoffrey Dawson and Our Times.* London 1955

Articles

Beer, G.L. 'Lord Milner and British Imperialism,' *Political Science Quarterly,* June 1915, 301-8

Bennett, Neville. 'Consultation or Information? Britain, the Dominions and the Renewal of the Anglo-Japanese Alliance, 1911', *New Zealand Journal of History,* Oct. 1970, 178-94

Brown, R.C. and R. Bothwell. 'The "Canadian Resolution"' in M. Cross, and R. Bothwell, eds., *Policy by Other Means: Essays in Honour of C.P. Stacey,* Toronto 1972, 163-178

Cole, Douglas. 'Canada's Nationalistic Imperialists,' *Journal of Canadian Studies,* Aug. 1970, 44-9

- '"The crimson thread of kinship": ethnic ideas in Australia, 1870-1914,' *Historical Studies,* April 1971, 511-25

- 'The Problem of "Nationalism" and "Imperialism" in British Settlement Colonies,' *Journal of British Studies,* May 1971, 160-82

Conway, J.S. 'Anti-Imperialism before 1914,' Canadian Historical Association, *Report,* 1961, 86-95

Cook, George L. 'Sir Robert Borden, Lloyd George and British Military Policy, 1917-18,' *Historical Journal,* June 1971, 371-95

Cooke, A.C. 'Empire Unity and Colonial Nationalism, 1884-1911,' Canadian Historical Association, *Report,* 1939, 77-86

Cross, J.A. 'Whitehall and the Commonwealth,' *Journal of Commonwealth Political Studies,* Nov. 1964, 189-206

- 'The Colonial Office and the Dominions before 1914,' *Journal of Commonwealth Political Studies,* July 1966, 138-48

Danzig, Richard. 'The Announcement of August 20th, 1917,' *Journal of Asian Studies,* Nov. 1968, 19-37

Donnelly, M.S. 'J.W. Dafoe and Lionel Curtis-Two Concepts of the Commonwealth,' *Political Studies,* VIII, 1960, 170-82

Eayrs, J. 'The Round Table Movement in Canada, 1909-1920,' *Canadian Historical Review,* March 1957, 1-20

Egerton, George W. 'The Lloyd George Government and the Creation of the League of Nations,' *American Historical Review,* April 1974, 419-44

Ellindwood, DeWitt C. 'The Future of India in the British Empire: The Round Table Group Discussions, 1912,' *Nanyang University Journal,* III, 1969, 196-204

- 'The Round Table Movement and India, 1909-1920,' *Journal of Commonwealth Political Studies,* Nov. 1971, 183-209

Fitzhardinge, L.F. 'W.M. Hughes and the Treaty of Versailles, 1919,' *Journal of Commonwealth Political Studies,* July 1967, 130-42

Gordon, D.C. 'The Admiralty and the Dominion Navies, 1902-1914,' *Journal of Modern History,* Dec. 1961, 407-22

Grimshaw, C. 'Australian Nationalism and the Imperial Connection, 1900-1914,' *Australian Journal of Politics and History,* May 1958, 161-82

Hall, Duncan. 'The British Commonwealth and the Founding of the League Mandate System,' in Bourne, K. and D.C. Watt, eds., *Studies in International History,* London 1967, 345-68

Hancock, I.R. 'The 1911 Imperial Conference,' *Historical Studies: Australia and New Zealand,* Oct 1966, 356-72

Hancock, W.K. 'Boers and Britons in South African History, 1900-1914,' *Australian Journal of Politics and History,* May 1963, 15-26

Howard, M. and R. Jackson. 'Empire to Commonwealth, 1910-1970,' *The Round Table: Diamond Jubilee Number,* Nov. 1970

Kendle, John. 'The Round Table Movement, New Zealand and the Conference of 1911,' *Journal of Commonwealth Political Studies,* July 1965, 104-17

– 'The Round Table Movement: Lionel Curtis and the Formation of the New Zealand Groups in 1910,' *New Zealand Journal of History,* April 1967, 33-50

– 'The Round Table Movement and "Home Rule All Round,"' *Historical Journal,* July 1968, 332-53

Louis, W.R. 'The United States and the African Peace Settlement of 1919: The Pilgrimage of George Louis Beer,' *Journal of African History,* IV, 3, 1963, 413-33

– 'Great Britain and the African Peace Settlement of 1919,' *American Historical Review,* April 1966, 875-92

MacKintosh, J.P. 'The Role of the Committee of Imperial Defence before 1914,' *English Historical Review,* July 1962, 490-503

Mansergh, N. '*The Round Table,* The Records and the Pattern of Commonwealth History,' *The Round Table,* Nov. 1970, 473-78

Mehrotra, S.R. 'Imperial Federation and India, 1868-1917,' *Journal of Commonwealth Political Studies,* Nov. 1961, 29-40

– 'On the Use of the Term "Commonwealth,"' *Journal of Commonwealth Political Studies,* Nov. 1963, 1-16

Miller, J.D.B. 'The Utopia of Imperial Federation,' *Political Studies,* IV, 195-7

Monroe, E. '*The Round Table* and the Middle East Peace Settlement, 1917-22,' *The Round Table,* Nov. 1970, 479-90

Naylor, John F. 'The Establishment of the Cabinet Secretariat,' *Historical Journal,* Dec. 1971, 783-803

Neatby, H.B. 'Laurier and Imperialism,' Canadian Historical Association, *Report,* 1955, 24-32

Nimocks, W.B. 'Lord Milner's "Kindergarten" and the Origins of the Round Table Movement,' *South Atlantic Quarterly,* autumn 1964, 507-20

Page, R.J.D. 'The Canadian Response to the "Imperial" Idea during the Boer War Years,' *Journal of Canadian Studies,* Feb. 1970, 33-49

– 'Carl Berger and the Intellectual Origins of Canadian Imperialist

Thought, 1867-1914,' *Journal of Canadian Studies,* Aug. 1970, 39-43

Penny, Barbara. 'Australia's Reaction to the Boer War: a Study in Colonial Imperialism,' *Journal of British Studies,* Nov. 1967, 97-130

– 'The Australian Debate on the Boer War,' *Historical Studies,* April 1971, 526-45

Perham, Dame Margery. *'The Round Table* and Sub-Saharan Africa,' *The Round Table,* Nov. 1970, 543-55

Quigley, C. 'The Round Table Groups in Canada, 1908-38,' *Canadian Historical Review,* Sept. 1962, 204-24

Randall, J.H. jr. 'T.H. Green: The Development of English Thought from J.S. Mill to F.H. Bradley,' *Journal of the History of Ideas,* April-June 1966, 217-44

Soward, F.H. 'Sir Robert Borden and Canada's External Policy, 1911-1920,' Canadian Historical Association, *Report,* 1941, 65-82

Stokes, E. 'Milnerism,' *Historical Journal,* v, 1, 1962, 47-60

Tucker, G.N. 'The Naval Policy of Sir Robert Borden, 1912-14,' *Canadian Historical Review,* March 1947, 1-30

Watt, David. 'The Men of the Round Table: An American View of the Kindergarten,' *The Round Table,* July 1969, 327-36

– 'The Foundations of *The Round Table,' The Round Table,* Nov. 1970, 425-33

Weinstein, W.L. 'The Concept of Liberty in Nineteenth Century English Political Thought,' *Political Studies,* June 1965, 145-62

Yarwood, A.T. 'The Overseas Indians: A Problem in Indian and Imperial Politics at the end of World War I,' *Australian Journal of Politics and History,* Aug. 1968, 204-18

UNPUBLISHED THESES

Allison, George Richard. 'Imperialism and Appeasement: A Study of the Ideas of the Round Table Group,' PH D, Harvard University, 1964

Conway, John. 'The Round Table: A Study in Liberal Imperialism.' PH D, Harvard University, 1951

Egerton, George William. 'The British Government and the Evolution of the League of Nations: A Study in Official Attitudes and Policies with Regard to the Creation of an International Organization for Peace, Cooperation and Security 1914-1919.' PH D, University of Toronto, 1970

Ellinwood, DeWitt C., jr. 'Lord Milner's "Kindergarten", The British Round Table Group, and the Movement for Imperial Reform, 1910-1918.' PH D, Washington University, 1962

Shepardson, J.W. 'Lionel Curtis.' BA honours thesis, Harvard University, 1949

# Index

Abrahams, Sir Lionel 230, 234n

Afrikaner Bond 23, 29, 35, 38, 43

*Alexander Hamilton* 30, 50; impact on the kindergarten 24

Allen, James 128

All Souls: and the kindergarten 21; and Curtis 160

Altrincham, Lord. *See* Edward Grigg

Amery, Leo 11, 12, 56, 57, 59n, 73, 121, 267, 282, 286; and the formation of the movement 46-72 *passim*; and the Compatriots 46, 50-51; and imperial organisation 48-52; differences with Curtis 71, 162, 175, 184, 293, 304; and the 1911 Imperial Conference 89-93 *passim*, 112-13; and *The Times,* 125; and home rule all round 133-55 *passim*; and the London group 159, 162, 163n, 276; and imperial preference 159, 166-7, 170; and party politics 165; and the Ginger Group 183-4; and the War Cabinet Secretariat 184, 215; and the Imperial War Cabinet 215, 272

Anglesey, Lord 163n, 262; and the formation of the movement 61, 63

Anglo-Japanese Alliance 109-10, 126

Anson, Sir William 14

Asquith, H.H. 113, 121, 150, 183; and Government of Ireland Bill 145-6; and home rule negotiations 153-4

Astor, Nancy 120; and the London group 159; and Curtis 162

Astor, Waldorf 120, 162, 163n, 183; and home rule all round, 145, 151-3; and the London group 159; and the 'Garden Suburb' 184, 215

Atkinson, Arthur Richmond 83, 84-5, 157

Atkinson, S.A. 83, 98, 158

Aubert, Louis 258, 259

Auckland 81, 90, 156

*Auckland Star, The,* and criticism of Curtis's ideas 200-1

Australia: formation of groups in 94-9; Curtis's 1916 trip 198-9, 201-3, 234; re-organisation of groups in, 213-14, 222, 261-2

*Australian Notes* 156, *170*

Bailey, Abe: and closer union of South
Africa 31, 33-4; and *The State,* 44;
and movement finances, 59, 65, 262,
282, 294; and the London group 159,
297
Baker, Herbert 21, 43, 296
Balfour, Arthur 139, 140n, 264; and
home rule all round 141-2
Barton, Sir Edmund 202
Basu, Bhupendra Nath 237-8
Beaton, Leonard 300
Beauchamp, Sir Harold 82
Beer, George Frank 122; and imperial
convention memorandum 208-9
Beer, George Louis 248, 252; and a
mandate system 254-5, 258
Bikanir, Maharajah of 216
Blackmoor 162, 231n; and home rule
all round 142-4
Blickling 162, 289
Bliss, General T.H. 258
Blunt, Thomas 82
Borden, Sir Robert 107, 184, 204, 213n;
and Curtis 102, 112, 116-21; and
Canadian naval policy 115-24, 128;
attitude to imperial problems 115-16;
and the CID 119-21, 124, 128; and *The
Problem of the Commonwealth* 187;
and the Imperial War Cabinet and
the Imperial War Conference (1917)
217-19; and the London group 281
Botha, Louis 43; and closer union of
South Africa 33; and Het Volk 35-6;
and the 1907 Colonial Conference 48;
and the 1911 Imperial Conference 113
Bourassa, Henri 116, 204
Bowles, Walter 208
Braddon, Sir Henry 96, 222n

Brand, Robert 11, 20, 44, 59, 101, 120,
142n, 157, 183, 209, 219, 222, 263n,
276, 300, 304; and the Inter-Colonial
Council 14-15; advisor to Smuts 14,
41-2; and the kindergarten 15-16; education of 17; and the closer union of
South Africa 27-45 *passim;* and the
Compatriots 51; and the formation of
the movement 63, 68-71; differences
with Curtis 71, 161-2, 175, 219-20,
291-300 *passim,* 304; and *The Round
Table*115, 163-4, 169, 264-5, 295; and
home rule all round 136, 143, 145,
151, 153-4; and the London group
162-3; and imperial munitions 184;
and *The Problem of the Commonwealth* 189-90; and the Imperial War
Cabinet and the Imperial War Conference (1917) 215-16; and the future
of the movement 277, 283-300 *passim;*
and imperial preference 279
Bridges, Jack 96
Brisbane, Round Table group in 95-7,
156
*Britannic Question, The,* and the Round
Table movement 125, 128
Bryce, James 152
Buchan, John 12
Buchan, W.H. 228n-9n
Burrell, Martin 103
Burt, A.L. 160

Canada: the visit of Kerr, Curtis, and
Marris 65-8; Curtis's 1911 trip, 99-
106; and imperial defence and foreign
policy 107-29 *passim;* and the naval
question 115-24; Curtis's 1916 trip
195-8, 234; re-organisation of groups
in 206-23 *passim*
Canadian Bank of Commerce 188; and

Milner 53

Canadian Club 31n, 53, 197

Canadian Institute of International Affairs 288

Cape Colony 11, 23, 33; and the 1908 election 36, 40

Carson, Sir Edward 145, 153-4, 183

Cecil, Lord Robert 142n, 304; and home rule all round 132-3, 136, 145; and the London group 159, 163n; and imperial preference 167; and the Paris Peace Conference 248-9, 252n, 259

Cecil, Violet (Lady Milner): and Curtis 162, 293

Chamberlain, Austen 139, 153, 168, 21n, 236

Chamberlain, Joseph 4

Chamberlain, Neville 244

Chaytor, Sir Edward 84

Chelmsford, Lord: and the Australian groups 95-7; and Asian immigration 204, 234; and India 232-4, 236n, 239-47 *passim*

Chinese labour 14, 35

Chirol, Valentine 120; and *The Problem of the Commonwealth* 187; and India 227-9, 234-5, 237

Christchurch: and Round Table group in 81, 84, 156-7

Churchill, Winston: and the CID 117, 121, 123n, 125; and home rule all round 149-50, 151, 153

*Civitas Dei* 281, 292

Clifford, Sir George 83

Cliveden 120, 123n, 162, 295; crucial 1914 meeting at 179

Closer Union Societies 22, 31-3, 42-4, 58

Coefficients 46

Colonial Conference of 1907 47-8

Colonial Office: and the 1907 Conference 48; and Amery 50-2; and the 1911 Conference 111-13; and the CID 128

Committee of Imperial Defence (CID) 113-14; dominion representation on 79, 117-29 *passim*; and Borden 119-21, 124, 128; and Edward Grigg 125-9

*Commonwealth of Nations, The* 157n, 171, 198, 204, 293; Curtis's speech about 200; effect of publication on the movement 208

'Commonwealth Society' 211

Compatriots 46-8; in South Africa 50-1

Congress-League scheme 236-7, 240

Constitutional Conference of 1910 130, 133, 142

Constitutional Party 35

Cooper, John A. 122

Coupland, Reginald 263n, 300; and the London group 159-60, 264; differences with Curtis 162, 175, 294; and the principle of the commonwealth 171-2; and *The Round Table* 215, 252, 294-5; and the Imperial War Cabinet and the Imperial War Conference (1917) 219-20; and post-war convention 223; and India 230

Craik, George 21, 63, 68, 142n, 163n, 267; and *The Round Table* 164, 169; and India 227-9

Crew, C.P. 33n

Curtis, Lionel 12, 209, 219; responsibilities in the Transvaal 13, 36-7; idealism of 16, 281; and the kindergarten 16; education of 17-18; influence of T.H. Green 18; and social reform 18; annoying air of authority 20, 57; and closer union of

South Africa 22-45 *passim*; and *Alexander Hamilton* 24; and the Rhodes Trust 25; and Smuts 31-4, 37, 40; and *The Government of South Africa* 39; and the Closer Union Societies 42-4; impact of South African sojourn 45; and the formation of the movement 56-72 *passim*; 1909-10 trip to Canada 64-8; differences with colleagues 66-8, 71, 85-8, 92-3, 160-2, 186-7, 275, 283-300 *passim*, 304-5; and the Green Memorandum 71, 73-80; and *The Round Table* 71, 85-8; and formation of first dominion groups 80-5, 94-106; and the 1911 Conference 89-95 *passim*, 112-14; his 'guiding principles' 86-8, 166, 187, 204-5, 225, 266, 277, 283-300 *passim*; attitude to India 99-100, 204-5, 224-47 *passim*, 303-5; and imperial defence and foreign policy 107-29 *passim*; and home rule all round 131-55 *passim*; with Churchill on the *Enchantress* 149; and *Australian* and *New Zealand Notes* 156, 170; and Beit lectureship 160; and position in London group 160-2, 182-3, 283-300 *passim*; and imperial preference 166-7, 279, and the 'Egg' 170-80 *passim*; illness of 170; and the principle of the commonwealth 171-5, 282; and the future of the movement 175-80, 192-4, 196, 203-5, 223, 274-300 *passim*; and *The Problem of the Commonwealth* 179-80, 185-205 *passim*, 206, 266, 281; and South African group 181-2; and 1916 trip to the dominions 195-203, 234; and post-war convention 221-3; and 'backward peoples' 224-5, 253-60,

302-5; impact of Marris upon 225; and Montagu 238-47 *passim*; and the Paris Peace Conference 248-9; and the mandate system 249, 253-60; and a League of Nations 251-2; and trusteeship 253-60; and 'Windows of Freedom' 249, 256-8; and nervous breakdown 259, 264, 266; and Parliament 260n; and post-war problems 266, 272, 277, 281; and Ireland 275; and Grigg 284-300 *passim*; death of 300

Curzon, Lord 43, 242

Dafoe, John W. 196, 208, 276; and Canadian naval policy 122-4; and the movement 209-10
David, Tannatt William Edgeworth 97
Dawson, Geoffrey. *See* Geoffrey Robinson
Deakin, Alfred 165; and Milner 47-8; and the Compatriots 48; and Leo Amery 48, 50, 121; and Curtis 95, 98, 112
Denison, George 50
Devolution. *See* Home rule all round
Dominion nationalism, and the movement 302
Donaldson, Archbishop 96
Dove, John 15, 21, 60, 273, 304; arrival in South Africa 14; education of 17-18; and the Australian groups 95-8; and London 'moots' 163n; and *The Round Table* 265, 275, 284, 286-8; and Ireland 275; illness of 282, 285; and the future of the movement 286-8; death of 290
Duff, Major Adrian Grant 120
Duke Memorandum 232-4, 236, 240
Duke, Sir William 230; and the Duke

Memorandum 232-4, 236, 240, 242-3
Duncan, Patrick 12, 13, 15, 20, 44, 48,
  73, 157, 300; responsibilities in the
  Transvaal 14; advisor to Smuts 14,
  41-42; and the kindergarten 16; education of 17-18; and closer union of
  South Africa 27-45 passim; and home
  rule all round 132-3; and the London
  group 157, 163n; and South African
  groups 181-2
Du Vernet, Ernest 117; and formation
  of Toronto club 54
Dyarchy 232
Dyarchy 231-4, 237-47 passim
Dyason, E.C. 278

'Egg' the: preparation of 170-80
Eggleston, Frederic William 97-9, 157,
  248; and Smuts 219-20; and criticism
  of The Round Table 285-7, 291
Empson, Walter 84
Evans, William Sanford 100
Ewart, J.S. 104-5

Fairfax, John 96
Falconer, Sir Robert 103
Farrar, Sir George 33n, 43
Federalism. See Home rule all round
Feetham, Richard 20, 73, 157, 279, 300;
  responsibilities in the Transvaal 13,
  37; education of 17-18; and 'Moot
  House' 21; and closer union of South
  Africa 26-45 passim; and federation
  of South Africa 26-7; and the
  formation of the movement 68; and
  home rule all round 132-3, 154; and
  the London group 158, 163n; and the
  South African groups 181-2; and
  India 244
Feiling, Sir Keith 54

Fischer, Abraham 43
Fisher, Andrew 91, 93, 135
Fisher, H.A.L. 18, 43
Fitzpatrick, Sir Percy 10n, 23, 24n
Flavelle, Sir Joseph 103, 209, 213, 272;
  attitude to empire 104; and the
  Imperial Munitions Board 184; and
  Round Table finances 264
Fortnightly Club 37, 182; formation
  and early meetings 26-7
Foster, Sir George 119

'Garden Suburb' 184, 215
Garran, R.R. 248
Garvin, J.L.: and home rule all
  round 139n, 141, 142, 152, 155
George, Lloyd 141, 142, 152-3, 183,
  214, 242, 264, 275; and a League of
  Nations 252n, 259
Ginger Group 183-4, 216
Glazebrook, Arthur 158, 198, 208, 215,
  272n; and Milner 51-4; Canadian
  convenor 71, 103, 105, 278; and the
  Green Memorandum 101-2; and the
  CID 117-19; and The Round Table
  164, 261, 278; and the future of the
  movement 175-80, 207, 209, 211, 214,
  260-1, 264; and The Problem of the
  Commonwealth 188-96 passim, 207,
  260-1; and 'study or propaganda' 207,
  209; and League of Nations Clubs
  265
Glazebrook, George 291
Goschen, George 7
Government of Ireland Bill 145-9; and
  F.S. Oliver 146
Government of South Africa, The 39,
  41, 42
Green Memorandum 71, 73, 81, 84-5,
  94, 96, 156, 170; contents of 74-80;

and the Canadians 100-2; and Joseph Ward 113; and Borden 117; and Churchill 121, 149; and imperial preference 166-7

Green, T.H.: influence on the kindergarten 18, 172

Grey, Earl 50, 103, 157; and Stephen Leacock 47; and Lord Milner 47, 54; and home rule all round 131-2, 136, 138

Grey, Sir Edward 113, 121

Grigg, Edward 65, 131, 158, 159, 182-4, 264, 276, 286, 300; and the CID 125-8, 168; and Richard Jebb 125-8; and *The Times* 125, 164-5; co-editor of *The Round Table* 145, 163-5; and home rule all round 145-55 *passim*; with Churchill on the *Enchantress* 149, 151; and London group 162, 179; and imperial preference 168-9, 279; and 1915 Imperial Conference 184; and the future of the movement 267-73, 277, 284-300 *passim*; and Kenya 276, 279; and differences with Curtis, 284-300 *passim*, 304

Hailey, William 294; and India 237

Haldane, R.B. 113

Hankey, Maurice 120, 184, 215

Harcourt, Lewis 121

Harmsworth, Harold 139n

Haslam, Francis 82

Hawkesley, B.F. 65

Headlam, Cecil 60

Het Volk 34-6, 38, 43

Hichens, Lionel 13, 15, 20, 52, 88, 120, 142n, 157, 209, 263n, 276, 300; colonial treasurer of the Transvaal 14; and closer union of South Africa 27-36 *passim*; and the formation of the

movement 68; and home rule all round 133-55 *passim*; and Curtis 160-1, 182-3, 294-5; and London group 162-3, 264; and imperial munitions 184; and the future of the movement 277-8, 283-95 *passim*; and imperial preference 279; death of 295

Hight, James 82

Hill, Sir Claude 235

Hodson, Henry Vincent 282-3, 287-8, 290-2, 294

Holland-Martin, R.M. 63 and 63n, 142n, 163n, 227, 263n

Home rule all round 130-55 *passim*

Horsfall, Percy 292; differences with Curtis 294-5

Hosking, Hon. Mr Justice 202

House, Colonel E.M. 258

Howard, Michael 300

Howick, Lord 59, 63, 142n, 159

Hughes, Colonel Sam 103

Hughes, William Morris 91, 135, 204

Hunt, Atlee 113-14

Hurd, Percy 206

Ilott, Sir John 262n

Imperial Conference of 1911 111-14, 135; and New Zealand 89-93

Imperial Conference of 1921 272

Imperial defence: and the kindergarten 45, 62, 107; and the movement 62, 66, 68-71, 74-5, 94, 107-29 *passim*, 210-11; and imperial preference 166-7; and *The Problem of the Commonwealth* 185-6

Imperial Defence Conference of 1909 109

Imperial federation: and Parkin 6; and Milner 6-9; and the movement 68-71, 74-80, 107-14; and Richard Jebb 125-

8, 131n; and home rule all round 130-55 *passim*

Imperial foreign policy: and the movement 62, 68-71, 74-5, 94, 107-29 *passim*, 210-11; and imperial preference 166-7; and *The Problem of the Commonwealth* 185-6

Imperial organisation 47-8, 50-2, 77-9, 111-13, 160; and Richard Jebb 125-8; and Edward Grigg 125-8

Imperial preference 166-7

Imperial secretariat 48; and Amery 50; and the movement 89

Imperial War Cabinet (1917): and the movement 206-7, 214-23 *passim*, 239

Imperial War Conference (1917): and the movement 206-7, 214-23 *passim*; 239

India 195, 260, 291; Curtis's attitude toward 99-100, 204-5, 224-47 *passim*, and the Imperial War Conference (1917) 214-19, 221, 239; and the movement 224-47 *passim*

Indian National Congress 236-7, 247, 301-2

'Indian Studies' 238, 239

Indigency Commission 36-7, 39

Innes, Sir James Rose 31, 32n

Institute of International Affairs 266-7, 275, 279, 288

Inter-Colonial Council 23, 36; Milner's plans for 14; and Robert Brand 14-15; and Philip Kerr 15

Ireland 130-55 *passim*, 275

Irish question 130-55 *passim*

Irvine, Robert 96

Islington, Lord; and the 1911 Imperial Conference 89-93 *passim*, 112

Jackson, Robert 300

Jameson, Dr Starr 43, 46, 58n, 63-4, 120-1, 133, 183; and the Raid 4; and the Selborne Memorandum 29; and the Cape Colony Progressive (Unionist) government 36; and the Compatriots 47-8; and the 1907 Colonial Conference 48; Rhodes Trustee 65; and the London group 159

Jebb, Richard 31n, 41, 56, 58n, 84, 96, 175; and Milner 51; and Round Table assumptions 125-8, 166-70; and home rule all round 131n; and imperial preference 166-70; and Lionel Curtis 166-7

Johannesburg 23, 42; and Lionel Curtis 13; and Lionel Hichens 13; and Round Table group 73, 156

*Johannesburg Star, The* 23

Jose, Arthur 55, 128; and Leo Amery 50-1

Kerr, Philip 20, 52, 58, 157, 182-3, 187, 219, 264, 297, 300; arrival in South Africa 15; character and personality of 16; education of 17-18; influence of T.H. Green on 18; and closer union of South Africa 22-45 *passim*; and *Alexander Hamilton* 24; and the Indigency Commission 36-7; and nervous strain 37, 115, 163-4; and *The State* 43; and the formation of the movement 59-72 *passim*; and *The Round Table* 64, 71-2, 88, 115, 144, 163-5, 264-5; and 1909 trip to Canada 64-8; disagreement with Curtis 66-8, 161-2, 219-20; and the 1911 Imperial Conference 89-93 *passim*, 111-14; and Curtis's 1911 trip to Canada 101-2; and imperial defence and foreign policy 107-29 *passim*; and Germany 108-

10; and Canadian naval policy 122-4; and home rule all round 131-55 *passim*; and the London group 162-3, 179; and imperial preference 168-70; and the principle of the commonwealth 171-5, 250-1; and the Ginger Group 183; and the 'Garden Suburb' 184, 215; and *The Problem of the Commonwealth* 189, 196; and the future of the movement 209-23 *passim*, 283-300 *passim*; and the Imperial War Cabinet and the Imperial War Conference (1917) 215-23 *passim*; and post-war convention 221-3; and India 225-47 *passim*; private secretary to Lloyd George 248, 251, 259, 266-7, 276; and a League of Nations 250-2; and trusteeship 253-60; and a mandate system 253-60; and the Rhodes Trust 276; Ambassador to Washington 276, 294; and Anglo-American relations 277, 281, 283, 295; and Christian Science 281; and the split within the movement 291-5; death of 295

Kindergarten 6; influence of Milner 10, 18-21, 23; recruitment of 11-15; composition of 15; characteristics of 15-16, 20; and Kerr and Curtis 16; education of 17-18; ideas and attitudes of 17-18, 224-5; camaraderie of 20-1; and closer union of South Africa 22-45 *passim*; and F.S. Oliver 24; and the Rhodes Trust 25, 33-4; and the Selborne Memorandum 27-30; and Smuts 34, 40, 41-2; and Abe Bailey 31; and the Transvaal Progressive Association 35-6; and the Closer Union Societies 42-4; impact of South Africa sojourn 45; and the formation of the movement 46-72;

hard core of the movement 276

King, William Lyon Mackenzie 31n, 188

Kisch, C.H. 230

Knibbs, Sir George 97, 201n, 202

Kruger, Paul 3-4

Kylie, Edward Joseph 54, 103, 117, 119n, 157-8, 181, 184, 192, 196; and Canadian naval policy 122-4; and *The Round Table* 164; and the future of the movement 175-80; death of 197, 261

Laby, T.H. 82, 85, 158, 181, 201n, 219, 222n, 285

*Land and Water* 194

Lansdowne, Lord 153

Lash, Zebulon Aiton 217; and *The Problem of the Commonwealth* 188-9

Latham, J.G. 201n, 222n, 248, 259n

Laurier, Sir Wilfrid 128, 213n, 305; and the 1907 Colonial Conference 48; and the 1911 Imperial Conference 113; and Canadian naval policy 115-16, 124

Law, Andrew Bonar 150, 151, 153-4

Leacock, Stephen 55; imperial missionary 47; and the CID 117-19

League of Nations 265; and the movement 249-52, 257-60, 277

League of Nations Union 279

Ledbury: meeting at 68-70, 132

Lemieux, Rodolphe: impression of the movement 165-6

'Letter to the People of India' 236

'Letters to the People of India on Responsible Government' 240

Lewis, John 189, 196

Leys, Thomas Wilson; criticism of Curtis's ideas 200-1

Long, B.K., associate of the kinder-
garten 39; and *The State* 43
Long, Walter 218n
Loreburn, Lord 152
Lothian, Lord. *See* Philip Kerr
Lovat, Lord 59, 63-4, 70, 262; and
home rule all round 145, 154n; and
the London group 159

Macadam, Sir Ivison 290, 294, 296
Macalpine, C.N.H. 158
MacCallum, Mungo 96-7
Mackinder, Halford 55; and imperial
organisation 51
Malan, Francis S. 43; and the Selborne
Memorandum 29
Malcolm, Dougie 28, 105-6, 157, 163n,
264, 276, 282, 286, 300, 304; arrival in
South Africa 15; and the 1911
Imperial Conference 89-90; Earl
Grey's secretary 103; and India 227-9;
and the future of the movement 299
Mandate system 249, 253-60
Marris, William 82, 86, 100, 163n, 300;
and South Africa 39; and the
formation of the movement 61, 63,
68; and 1909 trip to Canada 64-8,
225; and the Irish question 131;
impact on Curtis 225; and India 226-
47 *passim*; relations with Montagu
241-7
Marshall, Patrick 82
Massey, Alice 195
Massey, Vincent 158, 160; and the
future of the movement 176-80, 222-
3; and Newfoundland groups 181;
and *The Problem of the Commonwealth* 190-7 *passim*; and reorganisation of Canadian groups 208-9, 222-3
Massey, William F. 216

Matheson, W.B. 199
Melbourne: and Round Table
group 97-9, 156-7, 184-5, 213, 255,
261-2, 279, 297-8; and 1916 meetings
201-3; and *The Round Table* 261;
post-war meetings 265, 291
Merriman, J.X. 43; and closer union of
South Africa 22-3, 33, 40-1; and the
South Africa party 36, 40
Meston, Sir James 120; and the
Imperial War Cabinet and the
Imperial War Conference (1917) 216-
16; and India 226-47 *passim*
Milner, Lord 18, 24, 58n, 101, 142n,
157-8, 165, 219, 267, 297, 300, 306;
appointment to South Africa 4-6;
character of 4; political ideas of 4, 7-
10, 38; his 'Credo' 7-8; and imperial
union 8-9, 53, 55; influence on the
kindergarten 10, 18, 21, 23, 38; and
recruitment of the kindergarten 11-
15; and the closer union of South Africa 22-45 *passim*; and the Rhodes
Trust 25, 33-4, 46-7, 263, 276; and the
formation of the movement 46-72
*passim*; and the Compatriots 46; and
the Coefficients 46; and the Pollock
Committee 46; and Stephen Leacock
47; and imperial organisation 47-8,
52, 54; and Leo Amery 50-2; 1908 trip
to Canada 51-5; and Lionel Curtis 56-
7; 'father figure' of the movement 60-
1, 68, 159, 160, 184, 275-6; and movement finances 65, 263; and the 1911
Imperial Conference 114; and Borden
120; and home rule all round 143-55
*passim*; and the London group 162,
165-6, 179; and imperial preference
167; and World War I 183-4; and *The
Problem of the Commonwealth* 186-

7, 194-5; and the Imperial War
Conference (1917), 214-16; and India
226n, 229, 241, 242; and the Paris
Peace Conference 248, 259; and the
post-war movement 275-8
Molony, E. 228n
Monk, F.D. 116
Montagu-Chelmsford Report 240-7
Montagu, Edwin 154; and India 232,
238-47 *passim*; and Curtis 238-47
*passim*; relations with Marris 241-7
Montgomery, William 84, 85
Montreal: and Round Table group
in 106, 156
Moor, Sir Frederick Robert 43
Moore, Sir William Harrison 97, 157,
201n, 222n, 277
'Moots': nature of 162-3
Morley, John 6-7
Morley-Minto reforms 225, 233, 236-7
Morrah, Dermot 298-300
Muir, Ramsey: and the principle of the
commonwealth 171; and *The
Problem of the Commonwealth* 187
Murray, Gideon (Master of
Elibank) 139n
Muslim League 236-7, 247, 301-2
Myers, Sir Arthur 82, 84, 85
Myers, Sir Michael 83

Nair, Sir Sankahan 235, 241
Nathan, Cecil 97
National Convention 40, 44
Naval Service Act of 1910 116
New College; and the kindergarten 11-
15, 17, 21
New Zealand: and Round Table groups
in 80-5 *passim*, 262, 272; and resolu-
tions to 1911 Conference 89-94;
Curtis's 1916 trip 198-201, 234

New Zealand Notes 156, 170

Oliver, F.S. 88, 99, 159, 183, 187, 219,
300; and the kindergarten 24; and the
formation of the movement 63-4, 70;
and *The Round Table* 115, 164, 167-
8; and home rule all round 136-55
*passim*; as 'Pacificus' 138, 142, 144n,
146; and London group 163, 276; and
imperial preference 167-9; and the
principle of the commonwealth 171-2
Oppenheimer, Sir Ernest 294
Orange River Colony 23, 26, 33; Milner's plans for 10; political
organisation in 34-5; 1907 election in
36, 40; and responsible government
38
Orangie Unie 35-6, 40

'Pacificus.' *See* F.S. Oliver
Parkin, George 6, 8
Paterson, Graeme 159-60, 162, 164
Peacock, Edward Robert 163n, 209;
and the Green Memorandum 101-2;
and Curtis 105
Pearce, George 128
Percy, Lord Eustace 255
Perry, J.F. (Peter) 11-13, 20-1, 37, 52,
120, 163n; and Chinese labour 14;
and home rule all round 132; and
Imperial Munitions Board 184
Plas Newydd 65; meeting at 61-4
Pollock Committee 46
'Principle of the Commonwealth' 171-5,
200, 250-1
*Problem of the Commonwealth, The*
157n, 171, 198-9, 204, 230, 275, 281;
genesis of 179-80; contents of 185-6;
reaction of London group to 186-7,
189-90; Canadian reaction to 187-91,

197; publication of 189-95, 197, 214; Curtis's speech about 200; New Zealand and Australian reaction to 199-203; Australasian edition of 202; effect of publication on the movement 206-23 *passim*, 260-1

*Project of a Commonwealth, The* 157n, 171, 185

'Prophet.' *See* Lionel Curtis

Prussianism 108-9, 250

Reece, William 83

Reed, Sir Stanley 234

Rhodes, Cecil 4, 10, 31, 65, 289, 303

Rhodes Trust 71, 162; and kindergarten finances 25, 33-4, 41n; and Amery 51; and movement finances 59, 263, 276; and Grigg 276; and Kerr 276

Roberts, Lord 152-3, 183, 244

Robinson, Geoffrey 13, 16, 21, 52, 54, 73, 126, 127, 159, 182, 300; relationship with Milner 14; education of 17; and *The Johannesburg Star* 23, 36, 37; and closer union of South Africa 28-45 *passim*; and kindergarten finances 34; and the Transvaal Progressive Association 36; and *The Times* 37, 125-6, 164-5, 168-9, 265; and the Compatriots 51; and the formation of the movement 60-1; and London 'moots' 163n; and the Ginger Group 183; and *The Round Table* 265, 275, 297; and the future of the movement 283

Roe, Reginald 96

Rolleston, Hector 83, 84

Rosebery, Lord 65

*Round Table, The* 82, 108, 112, 114-15, 156, 171, 221, 263-4, 271, 276, 303, 305; origins of 64, 66, 70-2; and misunderstandings about 85-8; and the CID 125-8; and home rule all round 136, 144, 146-7, 150-2; preparation of articles for 157, 163-4, 278; format of 163, 274, 278, 291; editors of 163-5, 183, 215, 265, 275, 283, 287, 290, 294, 297, 299-300; non-political stance of 165-70; and imperial preference 168-70, 279; and the future of the movement 210-11, 276, 291-2; and a League of Nations 250-2, 260; and a mandate system 254, 256-8, 260; criticisms of 279-81, 284-7, 291; policy of 291-2, 295-300, 304n

Round Table movement 24; formed 46-72 *passim*; assumptions of 53, 57, 68-71, 74-80, 110, 155, 165-6, 171-5, 247, 253-4, 260, 301-6; finances of 59-60, 63, 65, 262-4, 282, 294; Milner as 'father figure' 60-1; identification with political parties 63, 159, 165-70; the nucleus of 68; formation of dominion groups 80-106 *passim*; and the 1911 Imperial Conference 89-93, 111-14; attitude to defence and foreign policy 107-12; and 'backward peoples' 110, 224-9; and Canadian naval policy 115-24; and Richard Jebb 125-8; 166-70; and home rule all round 130-55 *passim*; and importance of Canadian groups 157-8, 199; and the London group 158-80 *passim*, 276, 281-306 *passim*; influence of Curtis on 160-1, 203, 283-300 *passim*; and 'moots' 162-3; and imperial preference 166-70, 279; and the 'Egg' 170, 175-80 *passim*; and the principle of the commonwealth 171-5, 250-1; and its future 175-80, 196, 203-5, 207-23 *passim*, 249, 263, 267-72, 274-300

*passim*; and the Ginger Group, 183-4; and *The Problem of the Commonwealth* 186-223 *passim*; impact of the war on 206-7, 214, 248-73 *passim*; and Canadian 'Memorandum' 208-9, 212-13; and the Imperial War Cabinet and the Imperial War Conference (1917) 214-23 *passim*; and post-war convention 221, 263, 266; and India 224-47 *passim*, 262, 301-5; and trusteeship 247, 249, 253-60; and mandate system 249, 253-60; and League of Nations 249-52; and post-war problems 260-7; 274-82; and Grigg's circular 267-73; and new members 274-5, 282; and the differences within it 284-300 *passim*, 304-5; significance of 301; failures of 301-6; its influence 304-6
Round Table Studies 177-80, 182-3, 185. *See also* the 'Egg'
Rowell, Newton 213

Salisbury, Lord 262; and the kindergarten 44, 59
Salter, Sir Arthur 282
Sargant, E.B. 51
Schreiner, W.P. 42
Scott, Ernest 97, 157
Seely, Sir John Edward Bernard 121
Selborne, Lady Beatrix Maud 142n, 159, 187; and home rule all round 132; and Churchill 149; and London 'moots' 162-3
Selborne, Lord 15, 183, 297, 300; and the closer union of South Africa 25-45 *passim*; and the Selborne memorandum 28-30; and kindergarten finances 34; and *The State* 43-4; and the formation of the move-

ment 59; and home rule all round 135-55 *passim*; and the London group 159; and India 238n, 245; and Round Table finances 262
Selborne Memorandum 22, 39, 50, 73; and Curtis 27-30, 41; and Selborne 28-30; and Jameson 29; and Francis S. Malan 29; contents of 29-30
Seton, M.C. 230
Sinha, Sir S.P. (Lord) 216, 239
Shand, Judge A.B. 96
Shortt, Adam 103, 105
Shuckburgh, J.E. 230-1, 234n
Smuts, Jan 14, 16, 41, 43; and closer union of South Africa 22-45 *passim*; and Curtis 31-4, 37, 40; and Het Volk 35; and a National Convention 40; and Brand and Duncan 41-2; and the Imperial War Cabinet and the Imperial War Conference (1917) 216-20; and a mandate system 254, 259-60; and a League of Nations 260
South Africa Act 22, 44
Southborough, Lord 244
*State, The* 22, 43-4, 45, 58n, 62
Stead, W.T. 7
Steel-Maitland, Arthur 55, 65, 142n; and Milner 51-2, 54; and formation of the movement 59-72 *passim*; and home rule all round 136, 145, 147; and the London group 162, 163n; and *The Problem of the Commonwealth* 189, 194n
Stevenson, John A. 157
Stewart, Downie 83, 85, 289-90
Story, J.W. 96
Streit, Clarence 293
*Studies in Colonial Nationalism* 96
'Sunnyside' 12, 21
Sydney; and Round Table group 96-7,

156-7, 261-2; and 1921 Round Table conference 272

*Times, The* 120, 244, 265; and the Round Table movement 114-15, 125-8; and the CID 125-8; and Edward Grigg 125-8; and Richard Jebb 125-8; and 'Pacificus' 138, 142, 144n, 146

Toronto: and Canadian naval policy 122-4

*Toronto Star, The* 189

Toynbee, Arnold 18

Transvaal 3, 23, 26, 33; and imperial federation 9; Milner's plans for 10; and the kindergarten 18-20; political organisation in 34-5; 1907 election in 34-6, 40; and responsible government 38

Transvaal National Association. *See* Transvaal Responsible Government Association.

Transvaal Progressive Association 35-6, 38

Transvaal Responsible Government Association (Transvaal National Association) 35-6

Tregear, Edward 84

Trusteeship 247, 249

Uitlanders 3, 4

Ulster 141, 150

*Union Now* 293

Union of South Africa 22, 44; and the kindergarten 22-45 *passim*; contribution of Smuts 22-3; contribution of Merriman 22-33

University Magazine 194

Villiers, Chief Justice de 31, 32n

Vincent, Sir William 241

von Haast, Heinrich 83, 85, 267, 291

Walker, Sir Edmund 53, 103, 158, 184, 188, 261; attitude to empire 104-5; and the CID 117-19; and Canadian naval policy 122; and the 'Imperial Convention Memorandum' 213; and the future of the movement 220

Wantage, Lady 65, 81, 94, 262

Warburton, G.A. 207

Ward, Sir Joseph 216; and the 1907 Colonial Conference 48; and the Round Table movement 89-93 *passim*; and the 1911 Imperial Conference 112-14

Ware, Fabian 51, 55, 84, 126; and disagreement with the movement 175

Webb, Beatrice 46

Webb, Sydney 46

Wellington: and its Round Table group 82-5, 156-7, 199-200, 298

White, Sir Thomas 102

Wigram, Sir Henry 82

Williams, Basil 12, 13, 20

Williams, Rushbrook 238

Willison, Sir John 54, 85, 86, 103-4, 131, 157, 184, 265; and the formation of the movement 65-6; and the Green Memorandum 100-2; and the CID 117; and *The Round Table* 164, 278; and *The Problem of the Commonwealth* 191, 195-6

Wilson, Sir Henry 183

Wilson, Woodrow 249, 252, 255, 256, 258

Winnipeg: and Canadian naval policy 122-4

Wolmer, Lord 59, 63, 159

Wood, F.L. 302

Wood, George Arnold 97

Woolcock, John 96
Woolf, Leonard 249n
Workers' Educational Association 182
Worsfold, Basil 206
Wrong, George 103, 157-8, 209; and the
  Canadian groups 106; and the CID
  117-19; and Canadian naval policy
  122; and Curtis's 1916 trip to Canada
  197-8, 207
Wrong, Hume 272n, 278

Wyndham, Hugh 12-13, 21, 37, 73, 157,
  181; and the Transvaal Progressive
  Association 35-6; and the London
  group 158

Zimmern, Alfred 187, 219, 300; and the
  London group 159-60, 264, 276; and
  the principle of the commonwealth
  171-2, 251